U0587547

中泰职教联盟国际化在线精品开放课程配套教材
"中文+职业技能"旅游管理类专业教材

前厅服务与管理

Hotel Front Office Service and Management

主　编◎陈　萍
副主编◎李晓琳　刘媛媛　周　蕊
　　　　李　颖　胡文权　田力羽

重庆大学出版社

图书在版编目（CIP）数据

前厅服务与管理 / 陈萍主编 . -- 重庆 : 重庆大学
出版社 , 2025.3
ISBN 978-7-5689-3218-9

Ⅰ . ①前… Ⅱ . ①陈… Ⅲ . ①饭店—商业服务—高等
职业教育—教材②饭店—商业管理—高等职业教育—教材
Ⅳ . ① F719.2

中国版本图书馆 CIP 数据核字（2022）第 072843 号

前厅服务与管理
QIANTING FUWU YU GUANLI

主 编 陈 萍
副主编 李晓琳 刘媛媛 周 蕊
李 颖 胡文权 田力羽
策划编辑：龙沛瑶

责任编辑：杨育彪 版式设计：龙沛瑶
责任校对：谢 芳 责任印制：张 策

*

重庆大学出版社出版发行
出版人：陈晓阳
社址：重庆市沙坪坝区大学城西路21号
邮编：401331
电话：（023）88617190 88617185（中小学）
传真：（023）88617186 88617166
网址：http://www.cqup.com.cn
邮箱：fxk@cqup.com.cn（营销中心）
全国新华书店经销
重庆正文印务有限公司印刷

*

开本：787mm×1092mm 1/16 印张：24 字数：588千
2025年3月第1版 2025年3月第1次印刷
ISBN 978-7-5689-3218-9 定价：69.00元

本书如有印刷、装订等质量问题，本社负责调换
版权所有，请勿擅自翻印和用本书
制作各类出版物及配套用书，违者必究

随着中国对外开放和国际影响力的不断提高，越来越多国家的人开始了解中国，前往中国旅游、生活、就业等。酒店接待业作为旅游业重要的支柱产业之一，前厅部是酒店的门面和神经中枢，是现代酒店运行与管理的重要组成部分，是酒店对客服务开始和最终完成的场所，也是客人对酒店形成第一印象和最后印象之处。在此背景下，校企合作开发编写一本新型活页式教材，主要针对来华的国际留学生和有双语教学需求的酒店管理、旅游管理专业的学生，也适用于普通高职学院旅游管理与酒店管理专业学生及广大旅游和酒店人员自学或参考。

本书设计遵循"以职业岗位能力标准为教学目标，以职业能力培养和职业素养养成为教学核心，以工学结合的真实项目为课程载体，以行动导向的做学教为教学方法，以职业资格标准进行认证鉴定，以实战创业推进学生职业生涯发展"原则，按照"专业的职业岗位选择→工作过程分析→提炼典型工作任务→转化学习领域（课程）→设计教学项目→构建教学性工作任务→配置相应的教学资源"课程设计流程，设计基于工作过程、行动导向的课程，以适应现代酒店业前厅人才培养的需求。本书围绕完成前厅各工作任务所需要的基础知识、基本素养、操作技能来选择和组织课程内容。本书内容主要包括前厅认知、客房预订服务、礼宾服务、总台服务、前厅服务质量管理、销售管理、客史档案管理、宾客关系管理等。

本书由重庆电子工程职业学院陈萍担任主编，李晓琳、刘媛媛、周蕊、李颖、胡文权、田力羽担任副主编。其中，陈萍负责统稿和全书审校，并编写工作领域二的项目二、项目三；李晓琳编写工作领域三的项目二、项目三；刘媛媛编写工作领域一的项目一、项目二；周蕊编写工作领域一的项目三；李颖编写工作领域二的项目一；胡文权编写工作领域三的项目一、项目四；田力羽编写工作领域二的项目四、项目五。洲际酒店集团旗下重庆保利花园皇冠假日酒店黄妍总监、张浩铭主管，唐风国际教育集团庄雷参与本书的审核与指导。

由于编者水平有限，书中难免有疏漏和错误之处，敬请读者批评指正，以便进一步修订完善。

编　者

2024 年 12 月 1 日

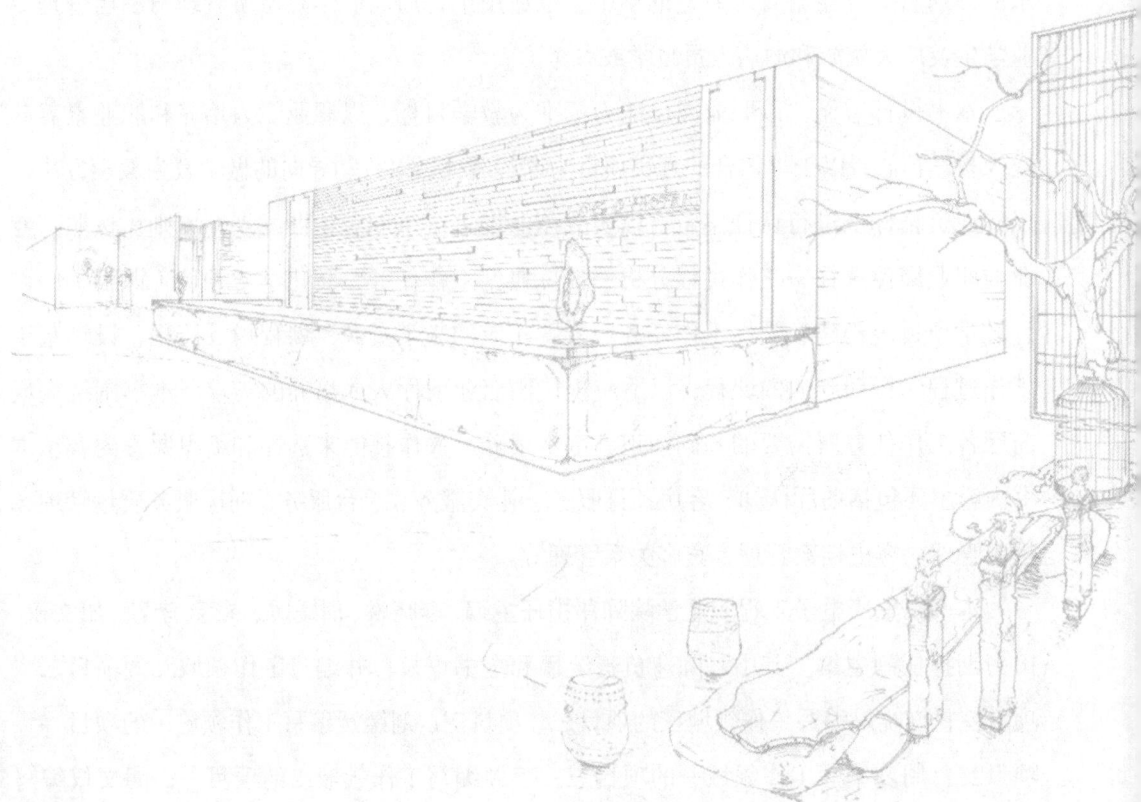

工作领域一　前厅认知

》 学习目标

正确认识前厅部在酒店中的重要地位以及前厅部的主要工作任务，理解并掌握前厅部的服务及管理发展趋势。

Work Area I　To Know the
Front Office Department

》 Learning Objectives

To understand the important position of the front office department in the hotel and its main tasks. To understand and grasp the service and management trends of the front office department.

项目一
前厅部岗位工作认知

【案例导入】

某日早晨，有两位年近 50 岁的日本客人，来到前台咨询高尔夫球场在哪里，并告知接待员他们想去打高尔夫球。由于客人中英文讲得不是很好，如果你是接待员的话，你会怎么办？

Project 1
Job Knowledge of the Front Office Department

【Case Introduction】

One morning, two Japanese guests who were almost 50 years old came to the front desk to inquire where the golf course was and told the receptionist that they wanted to go golfing. Since the guests can neither speak Chinese nor English very well, what would you do if you were the receptionist?

【任务布置】

①如果你是前台接待，遇到这两位客人，你会如何处理？

②谈谈前厅部在酒店的重要地位。

③请列举前厅部的主要工作任务。

④只有顾客满意我们才高兴，这是每个酒店服务员在踏入这一行时就必须明确的。回忆一件你最难忘的让顾客满意的事情与我们分享。

【Assignments】

① If you were the receptionist and met these two guests, how would you handle this?

② Talk about the important position of the front office department in the hotel.

③ Please list the main tasks of the front office department.

④ We are happy only when customers are satisfied. This is what every hotel attendant must be clear when entering the business. Please recall an unforgettable thing that makes your customers satisfied and share it with us.

【案例分析】

经了解，日本客人此次旅途并未带任何球具，他们只是想了解台达高尔夫球场在哪里，怎么去。考虑到两位客人语言沟通上的障碍，为了不让客人对此次异国的旅途及娱乐产生失落感，陈×接待员做了以下服务。

①联系高尔夫球场前台，了解打球所需物品租用的各项收费标准、付款方式、路线、联系电话等，并一一记录。

②帮助客人先预订好球场，并将两位住店客人的特征告之球场，以便球场更好地识别客人的身份特征，做好酒店客人的接待。

③一切都安排妥当后，接待员才将所有信息转达给日本客人，并嘱咐客人带上酒店名片。日本客人感到很惊喜，并乐意接受酒店为其所做的安排。

④考虑到日本客人去的球场较远，语言沟通不便，我们的接待员还向客人介绍酒店的车队，客人欣然接受并租用了酒店的车往返球场。此外，还与车队负责人交代好，指定司机为客人进行接送服务。

作为前台来讲，如有客人询问球场在哪里，怎么去，服务意识不强的员工，只是简单地告诉客人球场在哪个地方，坐什么车去就行了。但是，服务意识强的员工，始终想在客人前面，妥当地安排客人，安全地接送客人，不仅让客人感到高兴、满意，还让客人感受到幸福。

同时，案例也告诉我们前厅工作的重要性，前厅工作人员应熟悉岗位职责，做好组织、销售、沟通、协调等工作。

【Case Analysis】

It is known that the Japanese guests did not bring any golf equipment on this trip. They just wanted to know where the Taida Golf Club was and how to get there. At that time, considering the language barriers of the two guests, the receptionist Chen offered the following services.

① The receptionist contacted the front desk of the golf course to learn about the charges, payment methods, routes, contact numbers of the rental items required for golf playing, and record them all.

② The receptionist helped guests to book the golf course first, and informed the golf club of the characteristics of the two guests, so they can be identified easier with good reception by the club.

③ Only when everything was arranged, did the receptionist convey all the information to the Japanese guests and ask the guests to bring the hotel business card. The Japanese guests were surprised and happy to accept the arrangements made by the hotel.

④ Considering the golf course was far away and the Japanese guests had difficulty in language, the receptionist also introduced the hotel's fleet to the guests. They gladly accepted and rented the hotel's car to the course. In addition, the receptionist also connected with the fleet leader and designated driver for the pick-up service.

Receptionists with a low sense of service simply tell the guests the address of the course and the car to take when a guest asks where the course is and how to get there. However, receptionists with a strong sense of service always think more. They arrange all things properly and pick up guests safely. In this way, guests not only feel happy and satisfied, but also experience a sense of well-being.

At the same time, the case also teaches us the significance of the front office work. The front office staff should be familiar with job responsibilities and do a good job in organization, sales, communication and coordination.

任务一　前厅部岗位工作职责

前厅部也称客务部、前台部、大堂部，是酒店以客房住宿服务为中心，组织客源、销售客房商品、沟通和协调各部门的对客服务，并为宾客提供前厅系列服务的综合性部门。

Task 1
Job Responsibilities of the Front Office Department

The front office department, also known as guest service department, front desk department, lobby department, which offers guests a series of the front office services, is a comprehensive department of hotel. Taking accommodation services as the center, it is responsible for the organization of guest sources, sales of room commodities, communications and coordination with other departments for guest services.

一、前厅部的地位

前厅部是酒店具有计划、组织、指挥、协调职能的首席管理部门。它是执行酒店经营计划和信息反馈及管理的中枢，是酒店为宾客提供接待和服务，以及协助酒店建立与宾客之间良好关系的窗口与桥梁。同时，前厅部也是为酒店高层领导和营业部门提供经营决策的参谋机构，其工作与管理质量的优劣，不仅会影响酒店的经济效益，而且会影响酒店的社会效益。

I　The Status of the Front Office Department

The front office department is the chief management department of the hotel with planning, organizing, directing and coordinating functions. It is not only the hub for the implementation of the hotel's business plan and information feedback and management, but also the bridge for the hotel to provide guests with reception and services and to establish a good relationship with the guests. At the same time, it is also the advisory body for the hotel's senior leaders and business departments to make decisions. The quality of its work and management not only affects the economic benefits but also the social benefits of the hotel.

（一）业务活动中心

客房是酒店销售最主要的产品。前厅部通过客房的销售带动酒店其他各部门的经营活动。为此，前厅部积极开展客房预订业务，为抵店的客人办理登记入住手续及安排住房，积极宣传和推销酒店的各种产品。同时，前厅部还要及时地将客源、客情、客人需求及投诉等各种信息通报有关部门，共同协调全酒店的对客服务工作，确保服务工作的效率和质量。同时，前厅部自始至终是为客人服务的中心，是客人与酒店联络的纽带。前厅部工作人员为客人服务从客人抵店前的预订、入住，到客人结账，建立客史档案，贯穿于客人与酒店交易往来的全过程。

（1）Business Activity Center

Guest rooms are the main product of the hotel sales. The front office department promotes the business activities of other departments in the hotel through the sale of guest rooms. The front office department is responsible for room reservation business, such as check-in, housing arrangements and promotion of the hotel. At the same time, the front office department should also promptly inform the relevant departments the information of guests, such as their needs and complaints, and coordinate all to ensure the efficiency and quality of service work. Furthermore, the front office department is the center of the guest service from the beginning to end as well as the link between the guests and the hotel. The front office staff serves the guests from the reservation and check-in to the checkout, and establishes the guest history file, which runs through the whole process of the transaction between the guest and the hotel.

（二）机构代表

前厅部是酒店的神经中枢，在客人心目中它是酒店管理机构的代表。客人入住登记在前厅，离店结算在前厅，遇到困难寻求帮助找前厅，感到不满时投诉也找前厅。

前厅工作人员的言行举止将会给客人留下深刻的第一印象，最初的印象极为重要。如果前厅工作人员能以彬彬有礼的态度待客，以娴熟的技巧为客人提供服务，或妥善处理客人投诉，认真有效地帮助客人解决疑难问题，那么客人对酒店的其他服务也会感到放心和满意。反之，则客人对一切都会感到不满。前厅部的工作直接反映了酒店的工作效率、服务质量和管理水平，直接影响酒店的总体形象。

（2）Representative of Hotel

As the front office department is the nerve centre of the hotel, guests consider it as the representative of the hotel. Since guests check in and check out at the front office, seek the front office for help when encounter difficulties and make complaints when feel unsatisfied, the front office staff's behavior will give guests a deep first impression, which is extremely important. If the front office staff can treat guests with a courteous attitude, provide services for guests with skills, handle guest complaints properly, help guests solve difficult problems seriously and effectively, guests will feel relieved and satisfied with other services in the hotel. On the contrary, the guest will feel dissatisfied with everything. The work of the front office department reflects the efficiency, service quality and management of the hotel, and affects the overall image of the hotel directly.

（三）参谋和助手

作为酒店业务活动的中心，前厅部能收集到有关整个酒店经营管理的各种信息，并对这些信息进行认真整理和分析，每日或定期向酒店管理机构提供真实反映酒店经营管理情况的数据和报表。前厅部还定期向酒店管理机构提供咨询意见，作为制订和调整酒店计划和经营策略的参考依据。综上所述，前厅部是酒店的重要组成部分，是加强酒店经营的第一个重要环节。

（3）Adviser and Assistant

As the center of hotel business activities, the front office department can collect various information about the operation and management of the whole hotel, and carefully organize and analyze the information. Moreover, it provides the hotel's management organization with data and reports that truly reflect the operation and management of the hotel on a daily or regular basis. The front office department also provides advice to the hotel management group regularly as a reference for plans and business strategies of hotel. To sum up, the front office deparment is an important part of the hotel and the first important link to strengthen the hotel operation.

（四）建立良好宾客关系的重要环节

前厅部是宾客接触最多的部门，其员工与宾客接触频繁，最易获知宾客的需求。因此，应尽可能地提高宾客对酒店的满意度，建立良好的宾客关系。

（4）An Important Part of Establishing Relationships with Guests

As the front office department maintains frequent contacts with guests, its employees have frequent contact with guests and are most likely to be informed of their needs. so they should try to improve their satisfaction with the hotel as much as possible in order to establish good relations with guests.

二、前厅部主要工作职责

前厅部是客人与酒店接触的主要场所，是协调酒店所有对客服务并为客人提供各种综合服务的部门。前台部所有的功能、活动及组成都是为了支持、促进对客销售和对客服务。

II　Main Responsibilities of the Front Office Department

The front office department is the main place for guests to contact with the hotel. It coordinates all guest services in the hotel and provides guests with various services. All the functions, activities of the front office department are to support and promote sales and services to guests.

（一）销售客房

前厅部的首要任务是推销客房，客房是酒店销售的主要产品。酒店每日客房出租率的高低在很大程度上取决于前厅部的销售工作。

（1）Selling Rooms

The primary task of the front office department is to sell rooms which are the main product of hotel sales. The daily room occupancy percentage of the hotel depends largely on the sales of the front office department.

（二）提供信息

前厅部是酒店经营活动的主要信息源，包括酒店经营的外部市场信息（如旅游业发展状况、国内外最新经济信息、宾客的消费需要与心理、人均消费水平、年龄结构等）和内部管理信息（如出租率、营业收入、宾客投诉、客情预测、宾客住店离店以及在各营业点的消费情况等）。

（2）Providing Information

The front office department is the main source of information for hotel business activities, which include external market information（such as tourism development, the latest economic information at home and abroad, guests' consumption needs and psychology, per capita consumption level, age structure, etc.）and internal management information（such as occupancy percentage, business income, guest complaints, guest forecast, guest arrival and departure, and consumption in other business departments, etc）.

（三）协调对客服务

酒店服务质量的好坏取决于宾客的满意程度，而宾客的满意程度是对酒店每一次具体服务所形成的一系列感受和印象的总和。前厅部作为酒店的"神经中枢"，承担着对酒店业务安排的调度工作和对客服务的协调工作。

（3）Coordinating Guest Services

The quality of hotel service depends on guest satisfaction, which is the result of feelings and impressions about each service offered by the hotel. As the "nerve center" of the hotel, the front office department is responsible for the arrangement of hotel businesses and the coordination of the guest service.

（四）房态控制

房态是指酒店客房的使用情况，通常分为长期和短期两类。及时、准确地显示客房状况的目的是使酒店最大限度地利用客房这一酒店最大的获利产品。

（4）Controlling Room Status

Room status refers to the use of hotel rooms, which is usually divided into two types: long-term and short-term. With the room status displayed timely and accurately, the hotel maximizes the use of guest rooms, the hotel's most profitable product.

（五）账务管理

前厅部要为住客制作账单，接受各营业点转来的经宾客签字的客账资料，并及时记录、累计及审核宾客的各项欠款，确保客账账目的准确无误。同时，为离店宾客办理结账、收款或转账等服务事宜。

（5）Accounting Management

As the front office department should make bills for the guests, it receives the signed guest account information from other business departments. Then, it should record, accumulate and audit the guest's arrears to ensure the accuracy of the guest accounts promptly. At the same time, it handles checkout, collection and transfer services as well.

（六）提供各类前厅服务

前厅服务范围涉及机场和车站接送服务、门童行李服务、入住登记服务、离店结账服务，还涉及换房服务、退房服务、问询服务、票务代办服务、邮件报刊（函件）服务、电话通信服务、商务文秘服务等。

（6）Providing All Kinds of the Front Office Services

The front office services not only include pick-up service at airport and station, porter luggage service, check-in service, but also include charging service, room change service, check-out service, inquiry service, ticket agency service, mail and newspaper (letter) service, telephone communication service, business secretarial service, etc.

（七）建立宾客档案

前厅部为更好地发挥信息集散和协调服务的作用，一般都要为住店一次以上的客人建立客史档案。

总的来说，酒店前厅部的工作任务十分繁杂。根据其销售客房商品的不同阶段，可以将前厅部的工作任务划分为售前服务、售中服务、售后服务 3 个主要阶段，每个阶段的工作任务见表 1.1。

（7）Establishing Files of Guests

In order to play the role of information gathering and coordination services better, the front office department generally needs to establish files for guests who stay in the hotel more than once.

In general, the hotel front office department has complicated tasks. According to the different stages of its sales of rooms, the tasks of the front office department can be divided into three main stages: pre-sales service, sales service, and after-sales service. The tasks of each stage are shown in the table 1.1.

表 1.1　前厅运行三阶段及其主要任务

售前服务	远程询问服务，如电话、传真、电传、信函、网络咨询等
	各种预订服务，如散客预订客房、团队客人预订客房等
售中服务	抵店时，迎接客人、应接行李、登记入住等
	逗留期间，问询、邮件、委托代办、客账管理、总机话务服务等
	离店时，退房结账、行李服务、相关离店服务等
售后服务	建立客史档案
	与宾客保持联系，如节假日信函问候等

Table 1.1　The Three Phases of the Front Office Operation and Its Main Tasks

Pre-sales Service	Remote inquiry service, such as telephone, fax, telex, letter, Internet inquiry, etc.
	All kinds of reservation services, such as room reservation for individual guests and group guests, etc.
Sales Service	Upon arrival, greeting guests, picking up luggage, checking in, etc.
	During the stay, inquiry, mail, commissioning, guest account management, switchboard service, etc.
	Upon departure, check-out, luggage service and other related departure services, etc.
After-sales Service	Establishing files of guests
	Keeping in touch with guests, such as sending holiday letters, etc.

三、前厅部岗位职责和工作内容

（一）前厅部经理岗位职责

［直接上级］总经理

［直接下级］前厅部主管、领班、收银、接待、保安

［岗位职责］负责制订本部门的服务标准及工作程序，保证本部门员工保持高标准的服务质量和各业务环节的正常运转，保证高质量、高效率的服务，最大程度地提高房间出租率、房间收入及平均房价。参加酒店组织的各项会议。

Ⅲ Duties and Responsibilities of the Front Office Department

（1）Responsibilities of the Front Office Manager

［Direct Superior］general manager

［Direct Subordinates］the front office supervisor, foreman, cashier, receptionist, security

［Job Responsibilities］being responsible for the development of the department's service standards and work procedures; ensuring the staff to offer a high-quality service and the normal operations of various businesses; ensuring high-quality and high-efficiency services; maximizing room occupancy percentage, room income and average price; participating in various meetings organized by the hotel.

［工作内容］

①直接对总经理负责，贯彻执行总经理下达的经营管理指令及行政命令，严格按照酒店的政策制度和规定办事，以身作则。

②制订前厅部工作计划，并指导、落实、检查、协调计划的执行。

③组织主持每周例会，听取汇报，布置工作，解决工作难题。

④对主管和领班下达工作任务，并组织督导检查落实情况。

⑤为适应发展，不断完善前厅部的组织机构及各项规章制度。

⑥了解房间的预订情况，密切注意客情，督导本部员工提供优质高效的接待服务，并控制成本消耗。

⑦向总经理提出有利于客房销售的各项建议，并提供信息反馈，供总经理等参考决策。

⑧加强与有关部门的横向联系，加强沟通与合作。

⑨督查各岗位的工作进度，纠正偏差。定期对员工进行绩效评估，按照奖惩制度实行奖惩。

⑩负责本部门的安全及消防工作。协调与客人的关系，处理客人的投诉。

⑪定期审阅工作日记和每周办公会总结汇报，并将办公会会议精神传达给本部门员工。

⑫做好酒店重要客人的接待工作。

［Job Description］

① Reporting to the general manager directly; implementing the business management instructions and administrative orders issued by the general manager; acting in accordance with the hotel's policies and regulations, and leading by example.

② Making work plans of the front office department, and guiding, implementing, inspecting and coordinating the staff to implement the plan.

③ Organizing and hosting weekly meetings, listening to reports, assigning tasks, and solving work problems.

④ Being responsible for assigning tasks to supervisors and foremen, and supervising the implementation.

⑤ In order to adapt to development, the front office manager should improve the organization of the front office department and its rules and regulations constantly.

⑥ Grasping the information about the room reservation, paying close attention to the guest situation, supervising the staff to offer efficient hospitality services with high quality, and controlling the cost consumption.

⑦ Proposing various suggestions to the general manager in favor of room sales, and providing feedbacks for the general manager as references.

⑧ Keeping contact with relevant departments and enhancing communication and cooperation.

⑨ Supervising the work progress of each task and correct the faults; conducting performance evaluation on employees regularly and implementing rewards and punishments according to the system.

⑩ Being responsible for the department's safety and fire prevention; coordinating with guests and handling their complaints.

⑪ Reviewing the work diaries and weekly meeting reports; conveying the key points of the meetings to the staff.

⑫ Performing well in the reception of important guests.

（二）前厅部主管岗位职责

［直接上级］前厅部经理

［直接下级］领班、收银、接待、礼宾

［岗位职责］协助前厅经理管理前厅的各项日常工作，确保工作的顺利进行，提供高质量的服务，以及保证各环节的正常运转，准确、迅速地处理各种问题。

（2）Responsibilities of the Front Office Supervisor

［Direct Superior］the front office manager

［Direct Subordinates］foreman, cashier, receptionist, concierge

［Job Responsibilities］assisting the front office manager to manage the daily work of the front office; ensuring the staff to offer high-quality service and the normal operations of various businesses; handling various issues accurately and rapidly.

［工作内容］

①全面负责前厅的接待和问询等工作，督导员工为客人提供高效优质的服务。直接对前厅部经理负责。

②主持前厅工作例会，上传下达，做好本部门与其他部门的协调工作。

③安排员工班次，根据酒店业务特点合理安排各班次的岗位分工及人力配备。

④负责客人投诉的处理。

⑤负责每天检查员工外表及工作情况。

⑥负责员工的培训，协助经理督导实施部门培训的工作计划。

⑦负责掌握当日及次日的客房状态，在下班之前与客房部核对好。

⑧每天定时、认真检查收银账目及现金和信用卡情况。

⑨检查有特殊要求的客人的房间，并保证这些特殊要求得到关照。

⑩及时申领、申购物品，保证前台有足够的办公用品。

⑪检查大厅卫生，陈列酒店介绍等宣传品，并在用餐时间，临时接替前厅其他岗位的工作。

⑫努力完成前厅部经理或其他管理部门交给的任务。

［Job Description］

① Being responsible for the reception and inquiry of the front office; supervising the staff to provide efficient and high-quality services to guests; reporting to the front office manager directly.

② Hosting the regular meetings of the front office work, sharing information, and coordinating with other departments.

③ Arranging staff shifts, clearing job duties and allocating manpower for each shift reasonably according to the hotel's business.

④ Handling complaints from guests.

⑤ Being responsible for daily inspection of staff appearance and working performance.

⑥ Being responsible for training employees and assisting the manager to supervise and implement the training.

⑦ Mastering the status of the guest rooms of the day and the next day, and checking with the housekeeping department before the end of the day.

⑧ Checking the cashier accounts, cash and credit card carefully every day.

⑨ Checking the rooms of guests with special requirements and ensuring that these special requirements are met.

⑩ Promptly applying for and purchasing necessary items to ensure the front desk has enough office supplies.

⑪ Checking the hygiene of the hall, displaying the hotel introduction, and taking over the work of other positions in the front office temporarily during meal time.

⑫ Completing the tasks assigned by the front office manager or other management departments

（三）前厅部领班岗位职责和工作内容

［直接上级］前厅主管

［直接下级］接待、收银

［岗位职责］负责前厅日常工作，督导员工顺利开展各项工作，处理岗位发生的一切问题并及时向上级领导汇报，提高服务质量。

（3）Tasks and Responsibilities of the Front Office Foreman

［Direct Superior］the front office supervisor

［Direct Subordinates］cashier, receptionist

［Job Responsibilities］managing the daily work of the front office; ensuring operations of various businesses; handling various issues and reporting to the superior timely; improving the quality of service.

［工作内容］

①每天对租住客人的房间报表进行检查。

②检查、督导员工履行对客服务标准，确保员工为客人提供规范化、标准化的服务。

③与客房部、营业部保持联系，协调合作。

④检查员工仪容仪表、行为规范和出勤情况。

⑤准确掌握有关客房、客人可能问询的信息。

⑥保持工作区域的干净整洁。

［Job Description］

① Checking the room statements every day.

② Checking and supervising the staff to fulfil the services to ensure that the staff provides standardized services for the guests.

③ Maintaining contact with the housekeeping department, the sales department for coordination and cooperation.

④ Checking the staff's appearance, behavior and attendance.

⑤ Grasping the information about the rooms and those guests may ask for.

⑥ Keeping the work area clean and tidy.

（四）前台收银员岗位职责和工作内容

［直接上级］前厅领班

［岗位职责］严格遵守财务制度和服务操作规程，快速、准确地清算客人在酒店内的一切消费，正确、工整地填写各种有价票证（如信用卡、支票、发票等），熟知长住客的资料，严格按合同规定条款执行。

（4）Tasks and Responsibilities of the Front Office Cashier

［Direct Superior］the front office foreman

［Job Responsibilities］abide by the financial system and service operation procedures strictly; figuring out all the guests' consumption in the hotel quickly and accurately; filling out all kinds of valuable tickets（such as credit cards, checks, invoices, etc.）correctly; being familiar with the information of the long-stay guests and implementing them in strict accordance with the provisions of the contract.

［工作内容］

①负责办理客人离店结账手续，确保客人结账时准确无误、及时迅速。

②做好账目、现金交接及备用金的管理。

③按规定程序核对客人资料和房账，发现差异及时更正。

④预付金的收取，单据接收入账。

⑤延期离店账务的处理。

⑥按照规定处理应收账款。

⑦客人拒付费用的处理。

⑧负责前台内的清洁卫生工作及设备设施的维护。

⑨负责制作酒店的营业日报。

⑩积极参加酒店和公司组织的各类培训活动。

⑪做好客人损坏酒店物品赔偿的处理工作并报告上级主管。

⑫熟悉酒店相关的安全规范，做好可疑客人的监控，发现问题及时通知行李员。

⑬服从上级的工作安排，准确、按时地完成工作。

⑭做好员工间的协调工作，完成上级交办的其他工作。

⑮监督商品部、客房部上报的账目无误。

⑯审核当班次所有客人账目，核对收银报表。

［Job Description］

① Handling the guests' checkout issues to ensure that the guests check out accurately and promptly.

② Managing accounts, cash handover and petty cash.

③ Checking the guest information and bills according to the prescribed procedures, and correcting faults in time.

④ Collecting the prepayment and ensuring the receipt of documents into the accounts.

⑤ Handling accounts of postponed check-out.

⑥ Handling accounts receivable in accordance with regulations.

⑦ Handling accounts guests refuse srefuse to pay.

⑧ Being responsible for cleaning work in the front desk and the maintenance of equipment and facilities.

⑨ Making the hotel's daily business report.

⑩ Participating in various training activities organized by hotels and companies.

⑪ Dealing with the compensation for guests' damage to hotel and reporting to the supervisor.

⑫ Be familiar with hotel safety regulations, monitoring suspicious guests, and reporting to the bellman in time when problems are encountered.

⑬ Obeying the work arrangement of superior and completing it accurately and on time.

⑭ Coordinating among employees and completing other tasks assigned by supervisor.

⑮ Supervising the accounts reported by the commodity department and housekeeping department.

⑯ Auditing all guest accounts of the current shift and checking the cashier's report.

（五）前厅接待岗位职责及工作内容

［直接上级］前厅领班

［岗位职责］负责为住店客人办理登记手续，做好对客人的接待、问询、预订，确保为住店客人提供高效、优质的服务。

（5）Tasks and Responsibilities of the Front Office Receptionist

［Direct Superior］the front office foreman

［Job Responsibilities］being responsible for registration, reception, inquiries and reservations for the guests with efficient and high-quality services.

［工作内容］

①为散客、团队、会务客人办理入住登记手续，发放、回收房卡钥匙。

②随时准确掌握和了解客房状态、价格等信息，积极有效地推销客房及服务项目。

③负责办理客房的换房手续。

④保存好住店客人的资料。

⑤按规定程序提供客人留言服务。

⑥向客人介绍协议、会员制度，协助客人办理协议及会员卡。

⑦随时熟知当班预订情况，负责散客（电话、上门、网络、协议）的预订服务。

⑧负责酒店电话业务和促销房价的解释工作。

⑨正确、有效地接待客人问询。

⑩负责前台卫生区域内的卫生清洁工作及设备设施的维护。

⑪为住店客人提供叫醒服务。

⑫耐心接受客人投诉，并及时向上级反馈客人的意见和诉求。

⑬负责提供客人电话和访客查询，办理访客登记手续，不得把住店客人的资料泄露。

⑭积极参加酒店和公司组织的各类培训活动。

⑮负责按规定程序提供开房门服务。

⑯做好各种资料的整理工作。

⑰协助客房部安排房间的清理。

⑱按标准及时准确地将入住客人信息输入电脑，并做好户籍传输。

⑲做好员工间的协调工作，完成上级交办的其他工作。

[Job Description]

① Checking in for individual guests, groups, and business guests; issuing and collecting room cards.

② Grasping the information about status and prices of rooms accurately at all times, and marketing rooms and service items actively and effectively.

③ Changing rooms for guests.

④ Keeping the information of the guests.

⑤ Offering message service to guests in accordance with prescribed procedures.

⑥ Introducing the agreement and membership system to the guests and assisting them to apply for the agreement and membership card.

⑦ Grasping information of reservation when on duty, and being responsible for reservation service of individual guests（telephone, door-to-door, network, agreement）.

⑧ Being responsible for the hotel telephone business and the explanation of the promotional rates.

⑨ Receiving guests inquiries correctly and effectively.

⑩ Being responsible for cleaning work in the front desk and the maintenance of equipment and facilities.

⑪ Providing wake-up call service for the guests.

⑫ Accepting guests complaints, and making feedbacks to superviors.

⑬ After checking phone numbers of guests, receptionist can make registration and cannot disclose the information of guests.

⑭ Participating in various training activities organized by hotels and companies.

⑮ Offering room opening service to guests in accordance with prescribed procedures.

⑯ Organizing various information well.

⑰ Assisting the housekeeping department to arrange room cleaning.

⑱ Imputing the guests' information into the computer timely and accurately transferring room registration.

⑲ Coordinating among employees and completing other tasks assigned by superviors.

（六）前厅部行李员岗位职责及工作内容

[直接上级] 前厅经理

[岗位职责] 热情地为客人提供信息服务，收送行李服务，确保为客人提供高效优质服务，推销酒店各项服务设施及小商品的销售保管。

（6）Tasks and Responsibilities of the Front Office Bellman

[Direct Superior] the front office manager

[Job Responsibilities] providing information for guests enthusiastically; collecting and delivering luggage with efficient and high-quality services; promoting the sales of various facilities and small commodities in the hotel.

[工作内容]

①负责客人行李运送和寄存，确保行李安全。

②负责酒店各处安全巡视，保证酒店安全。

③保证酒店大堂及酒店门厅的卫生。

④负责大堂休息区客人的茶水服务。

⑤在门厅迎送客人。

⑥引领客人参观或进入房间，并向客人介绍酒店设施设备和服务项目。

⑦负责酒店内部各种文件及报纸、书刊的派发。

⑧客人调房时，协助客人搬运行李。

⑨积极参加酒店和公司组织的各类培训活动。

⑩负责行李房、监控室的卫生清洁工作及设备设施的维护。

⑪负责酒店各处绿色植物的浇水及修剪。

⑫完成上级布置的其他任务。

[Job Description]

① Delivering and depositing luggage to ensure the safety of luggage.

② Patrolling in all parts of the hotel to ensure the safety of the hotel.

③ Maintaining the hotel lobby and hotel foyer clean.

④ Providing tea service for guests in the lobby lounge.

⑤ Greeting and seeing off guests in the foyer.

⑥ Leading the guests to visit the room and introducing the hotel facilities and equipment as well as service items to them.

⑦ Being responsible for the destribution of various internal documents, newspapers, books and magazines.

⑧ Helping guests with luggage when they change rooms.

⑨ Participating in various training activities organized by hotels and companies.

⑩ Being responsible for cleaning work of luggage room and monitoring room and the maintenance of equipment and facilities.

⑪ Watering and pruning green plants in all parts of the hotel.

⑫ Completing other tasks assigned by supervisors.

任务二　前厅部岗位工作流程

【案例导入】

老顾客刘军先生为7月24日入住2709房的许应学客人在前台订了一间双标房间，电脑系统中已做了预订，也收取了客人的信用卡预授权。老顾客刘军交代前台接待员待他的客人到前台后报"刘军"名字就给其房卡即可。住客许映雪到前台后称"军哥"订的房间，接待员就把"朱军"的预订给了其入住，所有费用也挂在了"朱军"的账上，导致最后"刘军"的预订变成了取消未到，并且将之前刷的信用卡预授权也取消了，直到客人朱军来结账时才发现，是接待员弄错了，朱军先生根本就不认识许映雪。

Task 2
Work Flow of the Front Office Department

【Case Introduction】

Mr. Liu Jun, a regular guest, booked a double standard room at the front desk for Xu Yingxue, who would stay in room 2709 on July 2. The reservation was made in the computer system, and pre-authorization of credit card from the guest was charged. Liu Jun, a regular guest, told the receptionist when his guest informed the name of "Liu Jun" at the front desk, he/

she can give her his room card. Xu Yingxue went to the front desk and said "Jun" booked the room, checked in under the name of "Zhu Jun" and all the expenses were put on Zhu Jun's bill, resulting Liu Jun's reservation and credit card pre-authorization being cancelled. It was only when the guest Zhu Jun came to check out that he found the receptionist had made a mistake and he did not know Xu Yingxue at all.

【任务布置】

①如果你是前厅工作人员，你应该如何处理这个问题？

②本次案例的问题出在哪里？

③入住登记的标准流程是什么？

【案例分析】

接待员出现这样的错误是非常严重可怕的，把根本不认识、不相关的客人账务搅和在一起，如果朱军客人一直未来结账，而刘军也不是酒店老顾客，或者接待员没有客人的联系方式，最严重的后果将是混淆的账务客人不认账，那所有费用将由出错的接待员自己支付。

如果接待员能按标准流程和取房客人核对清楚全名就可避免错误产生。出现这样的事情，客人不仅会觉得员工职业素养差，还会认为酒店管理混乱。

【启示】

①前厅部是与客人接触最多的部门，任何工作一定要仔细谨慎。

②各岗位对工作流程的熟悉尤为重要，是前厅部工作质量的保证。

【Assignments】

① If you are the front office staff, how should you handle this problem?

② What is the problem of this case?

③ What is the standard procedure of check-in?

【Case Analysis】

This mistake made by the receptionist is very terrible. It mixes up the accounts of unrelated guests who do not know each other at all. If Zhu Jun postpones check-out, Liu Jun is not a regular guest, or the receptionist does not have the guest's contact information, the most serious consequence will be that the guest does not accept the bill, and all expenses will be paid by the receptionist who made the mistake.

If the receptionist can check the full name of the guest in accordance with the standard process, then mistakes can be avoided. When such things happen, the guests not only feel that the staff professionalism is poor, but also think that the hotel management is in chaos.

【Enlightenment】

① The front office department contacts with guests most. Any work must be done carefully.

② Being familiar with the work process of each position is particularly important, which is the assurance of the front office department work quality.

前厅部是酒店与客人建立良好关系的重要环节，处于酒店与客人的中介桥梁位置上，也是与客人接触最多的部门。根据希尔顿酒店手册，在与客人的关系中每一位员工都是"希尔顿"，在客人面前都是希尔顿大使，必须与客人建立良好的关系。保证酒店服务质量从各岗位工作流程标准化着手，以"客人满意程度"作为重要的评价指标，从而建立良好的宾客关系。

The front office department which contacts with guests most is an important part of the hotel to establish a good relationship with guests, and is an intermediary bridge between the hotel and guests. According to the Hilton hotel manual, in the relationship with guests, each employee is a Hilton ambassador in front of guests and must establish a good relationship with guests. To ensure the quality of hotel services, we must standardize the workflow of each post and use "guest satisfaction" as an important evaluation index, so as to establish good guest relations.

一、预订

● 电话预订

（一）散客电话预订操作步骤

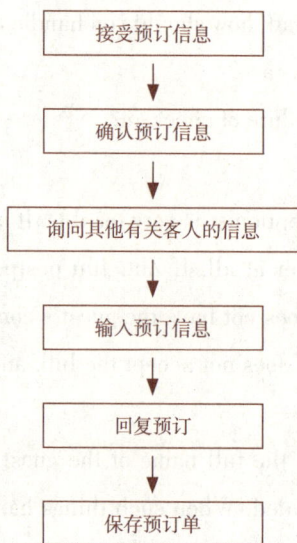

```
接受预订信息
   ↓
确认预订信息
   ↓
询问其他有关客人的信息
   ↓
输入预订信息
   ↓
回复预订
   ↓
保存预订单
```

（二）操作标准

操作步骤	操作标准
接受预订信息	铃响 3 声之内接电话。 使用标准敬语问候客人。"您好！海福特商务酒店。" 问清客人的姓名，在随后的整个接待过程中，必须称呼客人的姓氏。 问清客人预订入住的日期、数量、天数、房型。 查看电脑中客房的预订情况，判断是否有房间。 如有房间： 介绍房间的种类和房价，尽量从高到低，与客人确认房价。 询问客人是否为会员或公司协议。 查询电脑，确认是否属实，便于确定优惠价。 确定客人的联系电话。 询问客人的抵达时间、支付方式等，告诉客人预订房间保留的最后时限
确认预订信息	及时准确地填写"散客订房单"。 复述预订内容：日期、房间种类、房价、数量、姓名、住宿天数、电话号码、付款方式等
询问其他有关客人的信息	询问客人有无特殊的服务需求并记录。 确定结账方式。 感谢客人选择本酒店，向客人道别： "感谢您的来电，× 先生 / 小姐，再见。"
输入预订信息	填写预订单并输入电脑。 在已输入电脑的预订单上注明预订号，并签名
回复预订	如有必要，发书面的传真与客人进行确认
保存预定单	将预订单按日期分类保存

I Room Reservation

- Reservation by Telephone

（1）The Process of Individual Guests Room Reservation

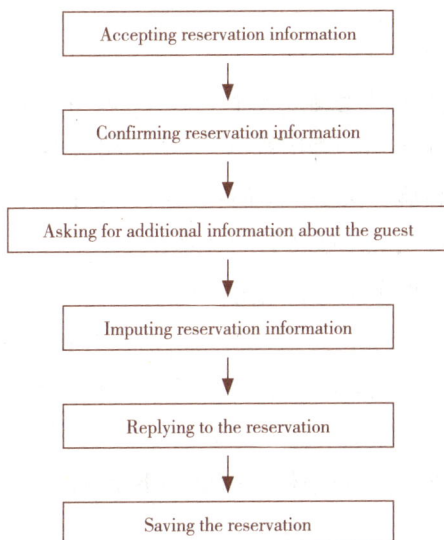

```
┌─────────────────────────────────────────┐
│     Accepting reservation information     │
└─────────────────────────────────────────┘
                    │
                    ▼
┌─────────────────────────────────────────┐
│    Confirming reservation information     │
└─────────────────────────────────────────┘
                    │
                    ▼
┌─────────────────────────────────────────┐
│  Asking for additional information about the guest  │
└─────────────────────────────────────────┘
                    │
                    ▼
┌─────────────────────────────────────────┐
│     Imputing reservation information      │
└─────────────────────────────────────────┘
                    │
                    ▼
┌─────────────────────────────────────────┐
│        Replying to the reservation        │
└─────────────────────────────────────────┘
                    │
                    ▼
┌─────────────────────────────────────────┐
│          Saving the reservation           │
└─────────────────────────────────────────┘
```

（2）Standards

Process	Standards
Accepting reservation information	Answer the phone within three rings. Greet the guest using the salutation: "Hello! Haifute Business Hotel." Ask for the guest's name and address his or her last name throughout the reception. Check the date, number, days and room type of hir/her reservation Check the reservation status of the rooms to know whether there are rooms available. If a room is available: Introduce the room type and rate from high to low, and confirm the room rate with the guest. Ask the guest if he/she is a member or has company agreement. Confirm the identities and give discounted rate. Determine the guest's telephone numbers. Ask the guest's arrival time, payment method, etc. Tell the guest the deadline for reserving the room
Confirming reservation information	Fill out the "Reservation Form for Individual" timely and accurately. Repeat the information about reservation: date, room type, rate, number of rooms, name, number of days, phone number, payment method, etc.
Asking for additional information about the guest	Ask the guest if he/she has any special needs and record them. Confirm payment method. Thank the guest for choosing the hotel and say goodbye to the guest. "Thank you for your call, Mr. or Ms. ×. Goodbye."
Imputing reservation information	Fill out the reservation form and impute it into the computer. Indicate the reservation number on the form and sign on it
Replying to the reservation	If necessary, send a fax to confirm with the guest
Saving the reservation	Sort and save the reservation orders by date

（三）注意事项

● 客人预订时经常会有意无意地对房价产生不满，作为前台服务员要善于将客人对房价的注意力尽量转移至本店的客房特色上，表达房价与客房的实际价值是相符的。

● 在接受预订时，前台服务员要主动向客人询问和介绍推荐。

● 确定结账方式后，要按照结账所需的程序办理。

● 要明确告知所有预订服务员房价的处理权限。

● 对传真预订客人（公司），必须及时用电话核对和传真确认（10 分钟以内）。对能确认的传真预订，应在传真来函上盖"确认"章，并签名后回传，预订信息及时（回传后 12 分钟内）录入电脑。

● 预订房间要有保留时间，旺季保留时间为下午 6:00，淡季根据实际情况请示当值管理人员保留时间，如提供担保预订，则所预订的客房一般可不设保留时间，遇特殊情况需及时请示当值管理人员。如客人预订时要超出保留时间，应立即请示当值管理人员，并做交接。在预计出租率达到90%以上时，需提前4个小时联系确认预订客人到达与否，联系预退客人续住与否，在下午4：00前掌握准确的出租状况，以采取进一步措施。避免客房空置或者超订无法安排住宿的情况发生。

预订取消：问清客人取消预订的原因，在预订单上备注，在电脑中操作预订取消，取消单必须由当班管理人员签字确认，并集中保留。

● 如有需要，客人入住前一个小时，通知客房部将空调打开，客人入住时，由行李员将取电卡取出（视情况而定）。

（3）Notes

● When guests make reservations, they are often dissatisfied with the room price intentionally or unintentionally. As receptionist, we must be good at diverting guests' attention from prices to the hotel's features, expressing that the room price is consistent with the actual value of the room.

● When accepting reservations, receptionist should take the initiative to ask and introduce rooms to guests.

● After confirming the payment method, follow the procedures required for payment.

● It is necessary to clearly inform guests their authority of the room rate.

● For fax reservation, it must be confirmed by phone and fax in a timely manner（within 10 minutes）. For fax reservations that can be confirmed, the fax letter should be stamped with "confirmation" and signed then sent back, and the reservation information should be imputed into the computer in a timely manner（within 12 minutes of fax）.

● Make sure there are enough time for reservation. In the peak season, the time is 18:00 p.m, while in the off-season, the reservation time is determined according to the actual situation to ask the on-duty manager, such as the guaranteed reservations which are not limited to reservation time. In case of special circumstances, it is necessary to inform the on-duty manager in time. When a guest's reservation exceeds the time, asking the on-duty manager immediately and make a handover. When the occupancy rate is expected to reach 90% or more, it is necessary to contact in 4 hours earlier to confirm the reservation. Contact guests who are ready to check out to see if they want to continue to stay and get the accurate occupancy status before 4:00 pm to take further measures. Avoid the situation when the room is vacant or overbooked which cannot be arranged for accommodation.

Reservation cancellation: ask the reason why the guest cancels the reservation, make a note on the reservation form, and cancel the reservation on the computer. Cancellation documents must be signed and confirmed by the on-duty management staff and must be kept the files.

● If necessary, one hour before the guest checks-in, inform the housekeeping department to turn on the air conditioner. When the guest checks in, the bellman may take out the electricity card（It depends）.

● 接待上门散客

（一）散客预订操作步骤

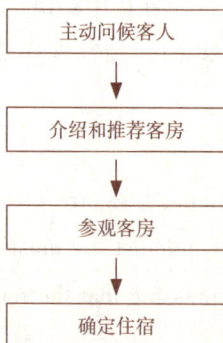

```
┌─────────────┐
│  主动问候客人  │
└─────────────┘
        ↓
┌─────────────┐
│ 介绍和推荐客房  │
└─────────────┘
        ↓
┌─────────────┐
│   参观客房    │
└─────────────┘
        ↓
┌─────────────┐
│   确定住宿    │
└─────────────┘
```

（二）操作标准

操作步骤	操作标准
主动问候客人	对步入大堂的上门散客主动上前问候客人，面带微笑，表现真诚。 "您好！先生／女士／小姐，请问有什么可以帮您？" 如此时正在接待其他客人，应对至前台 1～2 m 处的来客微笑并点头示意说："您好！请稍等。"
介绍和推荐客房	如客人提出住店，应询问客人是否有预订。"请问您有预订吗？"如有预订，按"入住登记"的服务流程操作。 如客人无预订，询问客人需要的房型："请问您需要标准间还是大床房？" 介绍房间设备和房价，如有两种以上房价，尽量从高到低报。 如客人表示犹豫，说明客人有住宿需求，应尽量突出客房的优点，如："酒店现在正好有 1 间……的客房""酒店能提供宽带上网""酒店免费早餐品种丰富"等。或者尽量引导客人参观客房，打消客人顾虑，争取客人入住。"先生／女士／小姐，先带您看一看客房，您再作决定，好吗？"
参观客房	一般由礼宾员带客人参观客房。 参观的客房应是同房型中朝向较好、面积较大、设施较好的房间。而且是已打扫好的空房。 对房型不确定的客人，应带客人参观不同房型的客房。 如酒店有不同等级和价格的客房，应注意先带客人参观高价格的客房
确定住宿	如客人确认住宿，应立即与客人确定房型、房间数量、房价、住宿天数，并为客人办理入住登记手续。 对客人提出的折扣要求，一般应礼貌地回答："对不起，酒店的房价已经打过折了。"并告知客人此房间的挂牌价。如客人坚持要给予折扣或表露出如不优惠就不入住的想法，前台服务员应注意不要固执己见（即使在高出租率的情况下），应回答客人："先生／女士／小姐，请稍等，让我请示主管，好吗？" 如客人预订以后房间，应根据客人的情况做好预订登记

- Walk-in Room Reservation

（1）The Steps of Walk-in Room Reservation

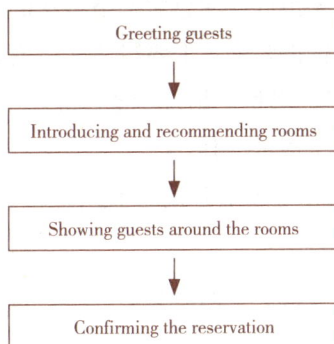

```
┌─────────────────────────────────┐
│         Greeting guests          │
└─────────────────────────────────┘
                 │
                 ▼
┌─────────────────────────────────┐
│ Introducing and recommending rooms │
└─────────────────────────────────┘
                 │
                 ▼
┌─────────────────────────────────┐
│   Showing guests around the rooms │
└─────────────────────────────────┘
                 │
                 ▼
┌─────────────────────────────────┐
│    Confirming the reservation    │
└─────────────────────────────────┘
```

（2）Standards

Process	Standards
Greeting guests	Greet walk-in guests in a courteous and friendly manner. "Hello! Sir/Madam/Miss, how can I help you?" When you are receiving other guests, smile and nod to the guest who is 1~2 meters away from the front desk and say, "Hello! Please wait a moment."
Introducing and recommending rooms	If guest wants to stay in hotel, ask he or she about reservation. "Do you have a reservation?" If there is, follow the "check-in" service procedure. If the guest has no reservation, ask the guest what type of room he/she needs: "Do you need a standard room or a large bed room?" Introduce the facilities in rooms and room rates from high to low. When the guest hesitates about it, it means that he/ she wants to stay. In this case, the advantages of rooms should be heightened. For instance, "the hotel now has a special room"; "the hotel can provide Internet access"; "the hotel has a rich variety of free breakfasts", ect. In addition, try to show the guest rooms, dispel the guest's worries, and persuade the guest to stay. "Sir/Madam/Miss, please allow me to show you the guest rooms first, and then you can make a decision, okay?"
Showing guests around the rooms	The concierge will show the guest rooms. The room to be visited should be the one with better orientation, larger size and better facilities among the same room type. Also, the rooms should be cleaned and available. For guest who is not sure of the room type, he/she should be shown to rooms of different types. If the hotel has various room rates, the concierge should pay attention to show the guest to the rooms with higher price first
Confirming the reservation	If the guest shows his or her desire to stay, confirm the room type, number of rooms, room rate, and number of days of stay with the guest immediately. And check in for the guest. To the guest's request for a discount, politely reply to the guest: "Sorry, the hotel room rate has already been discounted." And inform the guest of the listed price of this room. If the guest insists on discount or expresses the idea that he/she won't check in unless there is discount. The receptionist should not be stubborn (even in the case of high occupancy) and should reply to the guest: "Sir/Madam/Miss, please wait a moment and let me ask the supervisor, okay?" If a guest books a room, the reservation should be registered well according to the guest's information

（三）注意事项

● 接待上门散客时要特别注意切忌冷淡客人，因为漠视客人而流失客源。

● 上门散客要问清客人有无预订，注意对网络订房的客人报价。

● 对上门散客提出的房价打折要求，不要轻易允诺或拒绝，应请示当值管理人员；在了解情况后，一般应根据当日出租率情况给予 5% ~ 10% 的优惠（尽量不要低于订房中心和公司协议价），争取客人的入住。

● 带客人参观房间前，要先了解清楚所参观房间的房态。杜绝参观住客房间，尽量不要参观未打扫房间。

● 如客人对房间不满意，可留下客人的联系方式，将酒店宣传材料赠予客人。

（3）Notes

● Pay special attention to extend courtesy when receiving walk-in guests. You may lose guests because of indifference to guests.

● Ask the walk-in guests whether they have reservations, and pay attention to quotation for the guest who booked rooms on the Internet.

● To the request for discounts, do not accept or refuse immediately. You should ask the on-duty manager and give 5% ~ 10% discount according to the occupancy rate of the day（the price should not be lower than the agreement price of booking center and the company）, striving for the guest's stay.

● You must know the state of the room before taking guests to visit. Avoid visiting occupied rooms and try not to visit uncleaned rooms.

● If the guest is not satisfied with the room, you can leave his/her contact information and give the hotel promotional materials to the guest.

二、入住登记

（一）操作步骤

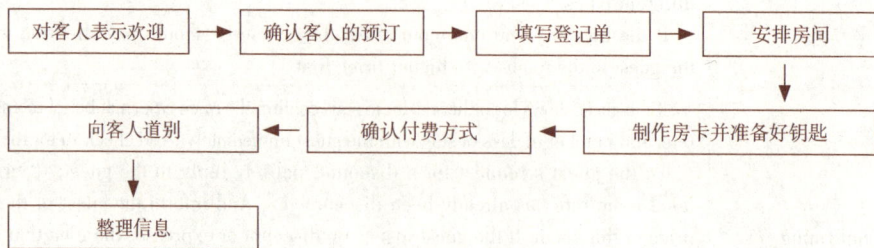

（二）操作标准

操作步骤	操作标准
对客人表示欢迎	主动上前欢迎客人的到来，面带微笑，目光正视客人。 "先生/女士/小姐，欢迎光临。……请问您有预订吗？"如果有预订，"请稍等，我帮您查一下。" 注意：①若事先知道客人的姓名应称呼客人姓名。 ②若正在为其他客人服务时，要示意其稍等。"对不起，请稍等。" ③确认客人是否需要办理入住手续或其他服务。 ④如查不到预订，不要简单地回答客人没有预订，注意查找传真机上是否有刚来的预订；或耐心询问客人："请问是您本人预订的吗？""请问您是否以其他姓名预订？" 如客人没有预订，重复"散客上门预订程序"，然后按此程序操作
确认客人预订	根据客人的姓名调出客人登记单和预订资料。 简要复述客人的订房种类、住店期限、付费标准及方式等。"×× 先生/女士/小姐，您预订了 × 间 × 客房，住 × 晚，房价是 × 元，对吗？"
填写登记单	"×× 先生/女士/小姐，请您出示证件。"收到证件要致谢："谢谢。"按照"临时入住登记单"的要求详细完整填写，查验证件并与所登记的项目核对，交由客人确认签字。注意笔应是质量完好，笔头向自己。客人签名后应致谢。 客人签字确认的同时完成房卡填写手续。交还证件时说："这是您的证件，请收好。"
分配房间	确保房间为可售房并符合客人的要求，30 秒内完成。 操作电脑，调整房态为入住。 注意：若客人所订房间尚未整理好。可调整相应预订，如没有相应房型可安排，应向客人致歉并提供适当礼遇。"对不起，房间还未整理好，我会通知服务员尽快打扫，请您稍等。" 请客房部安排客房服务人员尽快整理。 将预计能够进房时间向客人说清楚。 如客人询问原因，可回答："由于昨天客满，房间刚退，还没来得及整理。"
确认付费方式	费用自理的，除了符合免收预付款范围的客人外，均按预计住店天数收取定金，一般为房价 × 入住天数 +200 元向上取整百数，并对客人作说明。 "×× 先生/女士/小姐，请您预付 ×× 元。"收到定金要复点和唱收，并致谢："收您 ×× 元，谢谢，请稍等。" 由公司付费的客人，根据接待文件所列付费项目决定是否收取定金。 开具"预收款收据"，请客人签字，将客人联交给客人，并说："请您收好。"
制作房卡并准备好钥匙	具体写明称呼、房号、抵离日期及经办人签名。 若房费中包括其他费用（如餐费、交通费等），应向客人具体说明。 制作钥匙和房卡
向客人道别	将房卡递给客人，并作说明。 "×× 先生/女士/小姐，这是您的房卡，您的房间含两份免费早餐，早餐时间是早上 7：00—9：00，拿房卡在一楼餐厅用餐。" 告诉客人房间所在楼层及房号。"您的房间是 × 层、××。"指示电梯位置，必要时亲自送客人进房间。"×× 先生/小姐/女士，电梯在这边，您这边请。" 语言亲切自然，祝客人住店愉快。"祝您入住愉快。"
整理信息	及时准确地将登记单、预收款收据、现款放入指定位置。 根据登记资料将客人具体信息通过电脑补齐并建立客史档案。 进行公安上传

Ⅱ Check-in Service

（1）Check-in Process

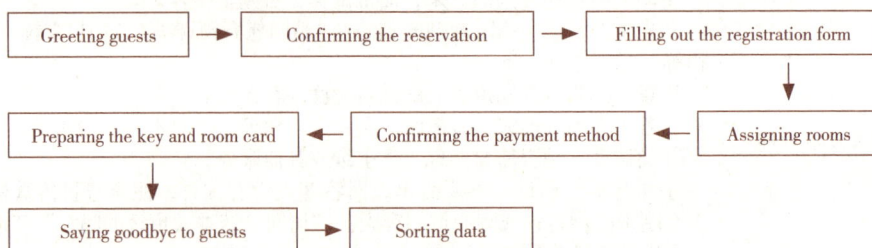

| Greeting guests | → | Confirming the reservation | → | Filling out the registration form |

| Preparing the key and room card | ← | Confirming the payment method | ← | Assigning rooms |

| Saying goodbye to guests | → | Sorting data |

（2）Standards

Process	Standards
Greeting guests	Greet walk-in guests in a courteous and friendly manner. "Hello, sir/madam/miss. Do you have a reservation?" If there is a reservation, "Please wait a moment and I will check for you." Note: ① If you know the guest's name in advance, you should address the guest by name. ② If you are serving another guest, gesture to him/her to wait. "Excuse me, please wait." ③ Confirm whether the guest needs check-in or other services. ④ If you can't find the reservation, don't simply answer the guest that he/she has no reservation. To find out if there is a new reservation on the fax machine; or ask the guest patiently, "Did you make the reservation yourself?" "May I ask if you booked under another name?" If the guest does not have a reservation, repeat the "Process for Walk-in Reservations" and follow it
Confirming the reservation	Find the guest registration form and reservation information according to the guest's name. Briefly repeat the guest's room type, days of stay, payment rate and method, etc. "Mr./Ms./Miss × ×, you have booked × room（s）for × night（s）, the price is ×, right?"
Filling out the registration form	"Mr./Ms./Miss × ×, May I see your ID, please." When receiving the ID, you should say "Thank you." Fill out the "Temporary Check-in Registration Form" in detail, check the verification document with the registered items, and hand it to the guest for confirmation and signature. Note that the pen is good, and the nib is towards yourself. Express thanks after signing. At the same time, fill out the room card. When returning the document, say: "Here you are, please keep it."
Assigning rooms	Ensure rooms are available and meet the guest requirements within 30 seconds. Adjust the room status for check-in on the computer. Note: If the room booked by the guest is not yet ready. The reservation can be adjusted accordingly. If there is no other room type to be arranged, apologize to the guest and provide appropriate courtesy. "Sorry, the room has not prepared well. I will inform the attendant to clean it as soon as possible, please wait." Ask the housekeeping department to make it up as soon as possible. Make it clear to the guest the expected time he/she can enter the room. If the guest asks reason, you should reply, "Since the room was full yesterday and the room has just been checked out, it is too late to make it up.

Continued

Process	Standards
Confirming the payment method	Except for guests who meet the scope of exemption from advance payment, guests should be charged deposit according to the expected number of days of stay, which is generally the room rate × the number of days of stay + 200 yuan up to the whole number of hundred. Explain to the guests. "Mr./Ms./Miss × ×, please pay × × yuan in advance" When you receive the deposit, you have to count and thank the guest: "Receive you × × yuan, thank you, please wait a minute." Guests paid by the company, should be charged a deposit or not according to the payment items listed in the reception document. Issue a "receipt for deposit", ask the guest to sign, and hand the copy to the guest and say "Please keep it."
Preparing the key and room card	Specify the name, room number, date of arrival and departure and the signature of the person in charge. If other expenses (such as meals, transportation, etc) are included in the room rate, explain to the guest. Make the key and room card.
Saying goodbye to guests	Hand the room card to the guest with an explanation. "Mr./Ms./Miss × ×, this is your room card. Your room includes two free breakfasts and the breakfast time is 7:00—9:00 a.m. Take your room card to dine at the restaurant on the first floor." Tell the guest the floor where the room is located and the room number. "Your room is on··· floor." Indicate the elevator location and usher the guest into the room if necessary. "Mr./Miss/Ms./ × ×, the elevator is in here, this way please." Use friendly and natural language and wish the guest a pleasant stay. "Wish you a pleasant stay."
Sorting data	Put registration forms, deposit receipts and cash away immediately. Complete guest specific information via computer based on registration data and make guest files. Upload information in public security.

（三）注意事项

● 客人在入住登记时经常会有意无意地对房价产生不满，作为前台工作人员要善于将宾客对房价的注意力尽量转移至本酒店的客房特色上，表达房价与客房的实际价值是相符的。过分地对价格进行争辩是不可取的。

● 在接待客人时，前台工作人员面对客人时要事事主动，问候主动，介绍主动，服务主动。

● 入住登记时，客人对时间是十分敏感的。尽可能缩短登记的时间，并与客人亲切自然的交流，让客人感到满意。

● 客人预付房金时，如果使用有效的信用卡，可根据本卡银行规定予以确认。

● 为吸烟客人主动递上烟灰缸。注意烟灰缸应保持洁净。

● 在预订信息中没有找到客人预订资料时，应耐心询问客人的相关信息，如客人报出协议公司名称，可安排客人以协议价入住。如还没有，若是现付，和客人暂确定门市价并安排入住，请客人稍候再联系确认房价。尽量满足客人要求，安排住宿。

● 房卡制作的天数要按照客人的预订天数及预付押金的金额确定，如客人有任何异议，前台工作人员需向客人介绍原因。

前台办理临时入住登记管理制度

● 前台严格按照公安机关颁布的《关于临时住宿登记管理制度》操作。

● 在酒店入住的客人，一律凭护照、身份证、旅行证等有效证件登记入住。无证件或持过期证件的人员，一律不允许办理入住手续。

● 前台工作人员在为客人办理登记入住时，必须在项目上做到如实登记，字迹清晰，不漏登错登；在服务上做到文明、礼貌、主动、热情、周到。

● 客人要在"临时入住登记单"上签名，前台工作人员按规定收取房费押金，并将入住房间的房卡转交给客人。

● 客人入住后，前台工作人员必须根据当地公安机关的要求，1小时内将客人信息录入电传网，上传客人资料。

● 前台工作人员必须做到住客名单，电传网记录在案客人数量、信息等完全一致，不允许出现漏登、错登，更不可不传。

● 前台工作人员发现形迹可疑的人员和被公安机关通缉的罪犯时，应立即向当值管理人员报告，不得知情不报或隐瞒包庇。

（3）Notes

● Guests are often dissatisfied with the room rate intentionally or unintentionally during check-in. The front desk staff must be good at diverting guests' attention from prices to the hotel's features, expressing that the room price is consistent with the actual value of the room. Excessive argument about the price is undesirable.

● When receiving guests, the front desk staff should take the initiative in everything, such as greeting, introduction, services.

● When checking in, guests are very sensitive to time. To make guests feel satisfied, shorten the time of registration as much as possible and communicate with guests cordially and naturally.

● If the guest uses a valid credit card, it can be confirmed according to the card's bank regulations.

● Offer ashtrays to guests who smoke. Ashtrays should be clean.

● If the reservation is not found, the front desk staff should patiently ask the guest for relevant information. If the guest gives the name of the agreement company, you can arrange the guest to check in at the agreement rate. If not, tell guests the rack rate and contact the guest later to confirm the price. Try to meet the requirements of guests and arrange accommodation.

• The number of days in room card should be in accordance with the number of days of the guest's reservation and the amount of deposit. If the guest has any questions, the front desk staff needs to explain it.

Management system for temporary check-in registration at the front desk

• The front desk operates in strict accordance with the *Management System on Registration of Temporary Accommodation* announced by the public security authorities.

• All guests staying at the hotel will be registered with valid documents such as passports, ID cards and travel certificates. Those without documents or with expired documents will not be allowed to check in.

• When checking in for guests, the front desk staff must register the items truthfully, with clear handwriting; do not miss any information or make it wrong; be polite, proactive, enthusiastic and thoughtful in service.

• The guest's should sign on the "Temporary Check-in Registration Form". The front desk staff charges deposit according to the provisions, and hand over the room card to the guest.

• After the guest check-in, the front desk staff should upload the guest information into the telex network according to the requirements of the local public security authorities within one hour.

• The front desk staff must make sure the number and information of guests in guest list are the same with the records in the telex network. Do not miss any information or make it wrong. Do not forget to upload it which is even more important.

• The front desk staff finds the guest with suspicious behavior and criminals who have been tracked by the public security authorities, he/she should report to the on-duty manager immediately. Do not fail to report or conceal.

三、入住开门
（一）操作步骤

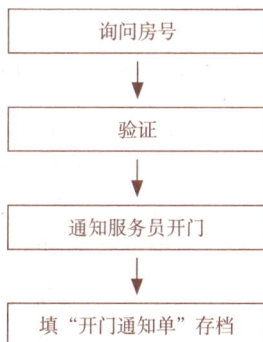

（二）操作标准

操作步骤	操作标准
询问房号	用礼貌的态度问清客人的姓名和房号。 "先生 / 小姐 / 女士，请问您的房号……请告诉我登记的客人姓名。"
验证	请客人出示证件或房卡。"×× 先生 / 小姐 / 女士，请出示您的证件或房卡。" 核对证件或房卡上的客人姓名、身份证号码或生日。 若不符，在电脑所有住宿客人中查询，如属客人报错房号，提醒客人正确的房号并得到确认
通知服务员开门	立即通知客房服务员开门。 "请为 ×× 房间的 ×× 先生 / 小姐 / 女士开门。"
填写"开门通知单"存档	填写"开门通知单"存档附在入住登记单后

III Check-in and Opening the Door

（1）Process

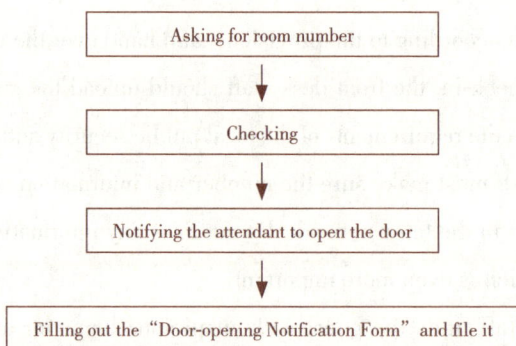

（2）Standards

Process	Standards
Asking for room number	Ask for the guest's name and room number in a polite manner. "Sir/Miss/Madam, may I have your room number. ... Please tell me the name of the registered guest."
Checking	Ask the guest to show the ID or room card. "Mr./Miss/Ms. × ×, please show your ID or room card." Check the guest's name ID number or birthday on the ID or room card. If it does not match, check on the computer about all the guests information. If it is the guest who reported the wrong room number, remind the guest of the correct room number and confirm it.
Notifying the attendant to open the door	Inform the attendant to open the door immediately. "Please open the door for Mr./Miss/Ms. × ×"
Filling out the "Door-opening Notification Form" and file it	Fill out the "Door-opening Notification Form" and attach it to the check-in form.

（三）注意事项

● 身份经验证和电脑记录不符的客人，并且没有住店客人留言关照为其开门的，应婉言谢绝客人："非常抱歉，电脑中没有您的住宿登记记录，请您联系该房登记的客人过来为您开门。"并请客人在大堂等候。

● 如住宿客人外线来电，要为在前台的客人开门。首先应电话核对房号、住客姓名、身份证号码或生日、同住人姓名，若全部相符，则基本能确定来电人的身份，然后电话问清前台客人的姓名，核对证件相符，为来客开具"开门通知单"，并将证件号码抄在"开门通知单"上。

（3）Notes

● For the guests who have been verified that their identities do not match computer records, and there is no stay guest leaving message to open the door for them, decline the guest politely: "Sorry, there is no registration record of your accommodation, please contact the guest registered to come over to open the door." And ask the guest to wait in the lobby.

● If the resisted guest calls from an outside line, ask for opening the door for the guest at the front desk. First, check the room number, the name of the guest, ID card number or birthday, the name of the person living with him/her. If all match, the front desk staff can ensure identity of the caller, and then ask for the name of the guest at front desk, check the documents, issue the "Door-opening Notification Form" for the visitor, and copy the ID number on the "Door-opening Notification Form".

四、延住

（一）操作步骤

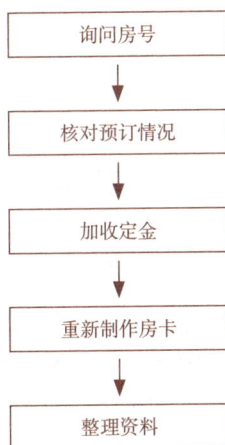

（二）操作标准

操作步骤	操作标准
询问房号	用礼貌的态度问清客人的房号。"先生 / 小姐 / 女士，请问您的房号是多少？"

续表

操作步骤	操作标准
核对预订情况	核对这间客房的预订情况。若没有预订可直接延住。 如已有预订，首先查询是否可以调节预订，如无法调节，应征询客人为其换房："××先生／小姐／女士，您住的房间今天已被预订，能否帮您换一间同样的客房？……谢谢您的配合和支持。"
加收定金	问清客人需续住几天，根据客人续住天数、房费标准及酒店预收金标准，请客人加付定金："请您预付×××元……谢谢。" 填写"延住登记单"，为客人开具押金收据，递给客人并请客人签字
重新制作房卡	请客人出示房卡，并致谢："请出示您的房卡……谢谢。" 问清客人需续住几天："请问您续住到几号？"并复述。 检验房卡中记录的房号是否与客人所报一致。 修改电脑中离店日期并重新制作房卡。"这是您的房卡和收据，谢谢，再见。"
整理资料	将收取的押金录入酒店管理系统的相应房间。 将"延住登记单"与"原始入住登记单"并存。 通知客房部房间延住

IV Asking for Extension

（1）Process

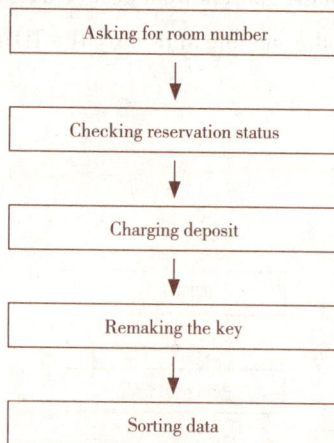

```
┌──────────────────────────────┐
│    Asking for room number    │
└──────────────────────────────┘
              ↓
┌──────────────────────────────┐
│  Checking reservation status │
└──────────────────────────────┘
              ↓
┌──────────────────────────────┐
│       Charging deposit       │
└──────────────────────────────┘
              ↓
┌──────────────────────────────┐
│       Remaking the key       │
└──────────────────────────────┘
              ↓
┌──────────────────────────────┐
│        Sorting data          │
└──────────────────────────────┘
```

（2）Standards

Process	Standards
Asking for room number	Ask for the guest's name and room number in a polite manner. "Sir/Miss/Madam, may I have your room number?"
Checking reservation status	Check the reservation status of this room. If there is no reservation, it can be extended directly. If there is a reservation, try to adjust the reservation. If you cannot adjust, ask the guest to change the room: "Mr. / Miss / Ms. ××, the room you are staying in today has been booked, can I help you change a room of the same type? ... Thank you for your cooperation and support."

Continued

Process	Standards
Charging deposit	Ask the guest about days they need to stay, and ask the guest to pay deposit according to the days they renew, the room rate and the hotel charge standard, "Please pay deposit in advance, ... thank you." Fill out the "Extended Stay Registration Form", issue the deposit receipt for the guest, hand it to the guest and ask the guest to sign.
Remaking the key	Ask the guests to show the room card and thank them. "Please show your room card, ... thank you." Ask the guest how many days he/she needs to stay. "May I ask you how many days do you continue to live?" and repeat it. Verify that the room number recorded in the room card is the same as the one told by the guest. Change the departure date on the computer and recreate the room card. "Here is your room card and receipt, thank you. Goodbye!"
Sorting data	Record the deposit into the hotel management system. Keep the "Extended Stay Registration Form" together with the "Original Check-in Registration Form". Notify the housekeeping department of the room extension.

（三）注意事项

● 有的客人为公司付费或挂账单位，在询问客人意见后需与单位负责订房人核实，如与客人不符，应及时与客人沟通。

（3）Notes

● For costs are paid by guests' companies, contact their company to verify their identities. Inform the guests immediately if the information cannot match.

五、换房

（一）操作步骤

（二）操作标准

操作步骤	操作标准
问清换房的原因	接到客人换房的要求时，需问清原因，必要时表示道歉。"对不起，我尽快为您安排解决。"
尽量满足客人的要求	根据客人的合理要求，选择适当的房间。 必要时可以提供几种方案供客人选择。"您看这样可以吗？"

续表

操作步骤	操作标准
更换房卡和钥匙	填写新的房卡，并填写换房单，制作新房卡，收回先前的房卡。将换房单交客人签字认可，为客人更换新房卡。 及时通知有关部门
客人签字认可	
帮助客人搬运行李	通知相关人员协助客人搬运行李。"需要帮您搬行李吗？"
通知有关人员对要更换的房间进行查验	要求客房部员工对房间进行检查。 如是设备问题，通知维修人员进行维护
更改电脑资料	及时对房内消费品入账，更改电脑内的相关资料

V Changing the Room

（1）Process

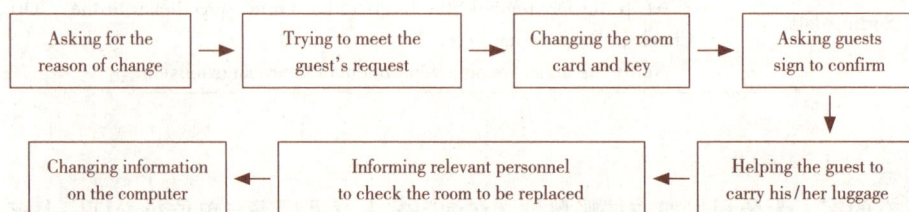

（2）Standards

Process	Standards
Asking for the reason of change	When receiving a request from a guest to change rooms, ask the reason and apologize if necessary. "Sorry, I will arrange a solution for you as soon as possible."
Trying to meet the guest's request	Select the appropriate room according to the guest's request. If necessary, offer several options for the guest to choose. "Do you think this is okay?"
Changing the room card and key	Fill in the new room card and room change form, create the new room card and take back the previous one. Give the room change form to the guest for signature, and replace the new room card for the guest. Notify relevant departments in time
Asking guests sign to confirm	
Helping the guest to carry his / her luggage	Inform relevant personnel to assist guests with luggage. "Do you need to help with your luggage?"
Informing relevant personnel to check the room to be replaced	Ask the housekeeping staff to check the room. If there is problem of equipment, notify the staff for maintenance
Changing information on the computer	Account consumer goods in the room and change the relevant information on the computer

（三）注意事项

● 通常情况下，客人提出换房要求时，总会带有不满的情绪，要注意避免让客人的不满升级。

● 在换房过程中，要时刻考虑客人的需求，主动帮助客人。

● 如果是酒店方的错误，要注意向客人表示歉意。

（3）Notes

● Usually, when a guest requests a room change, he/she is unsatisfied. Avoid escalating the guest's dissatisfaction.

● In the process of changing rooms, the front desk staff must always consider the needs of the guest and help him/her.

● If it is the hotel's fault, apologize to the guest.

六、结账

（一）操作步骤

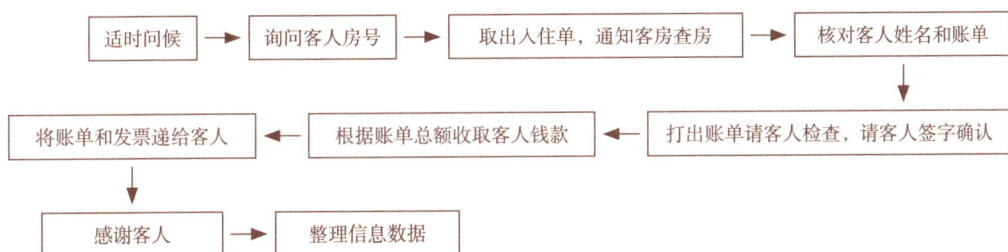

（二）操作标准

操作步骤	操作标准
适时问候	主动、热情、礼貌、微笑。"您好，先生 / 女士 / 小姐，您要结账 / 退房吗？"
询问客人房号	"先生 / 女士 / 小姐，请问您的房号是……" 请客人出示房卡钥匙和预收款收据并双手接过。"请出示您的房卡和预付收据。""谢谢，请稍等。"读取房卡核对信息，在公安系统中退房
取出入住单，通知客房查房	准确、快速、口齿清楚。 取出客人入住单并核对。 通知客房服务员检查客人房间的使用情况，核对物品、商品等。"客房，×× 房间退房，请查房。"同时关闭房间电话并做好记录
核对客人姓名和账单	与电脑记录核对相符。 "请问是 ×× 先生 / 女士 / 小姐吗？" 核对客人其他消费。"房间消费了一个 ×× 元，总共消费是 ×× 元，对吗？请问需要开发票吗？"
打出账单请客人检查，请客人签字确认	双手呈送。 "×× 先生 / 女士 / 小姐，这是您的账单，请核对并在账单上签字，谢谢。"

续表

操作步骤	操作标准
根据账单总额收取客人钱款	双手接过客人所付钱款，唱收唱付。"谢谢。" "××先生/女士/小姐，这是××元，账单总额是××元，找零××元，谢谢。" 如果客人使用信用卡、支票付账，要严格参照银行规定操作程序执行。"请您签字确认，谢谢。"
将账单和发票递给客人	双手呈送。 "××先生/女士/小姐，这是您的账单和发票，请收好。" 退还客人余款或补收差额款
感谢客人	热情而礼貌，面带微笑。"欢迎您再次光临，祝您旅途愉快，再见。"
整理信息数据	在电脑系统中完成离店结账信息的更新。装订、整理账单

VI Checking out

（1）Process

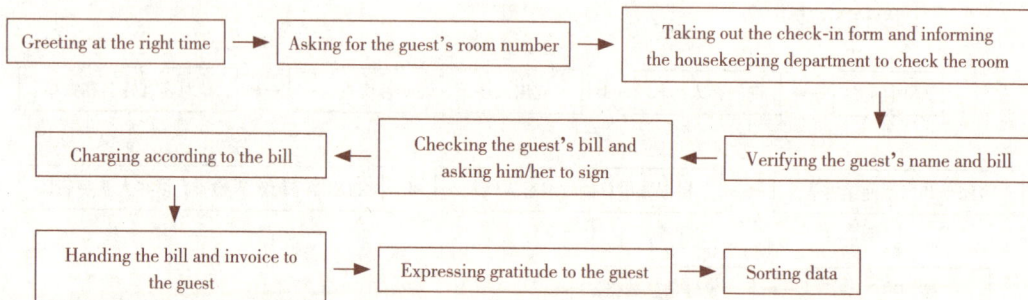

（2）Standars

Process	Standards
Greeting at the right time	Greet guests in a courteous and friendly manner. "Hello, Mr./Ms./Miss, do you want to check out?"
Asking for the guest's room number	"Mr./Ms./Miss, may I ask your room number ......" Ask the guest to show the room card and the receipt of deposit and take it with both hands. "Please show your room card and prepaid receipt." "Thank you, please wait a moment." Check the room card to verify the information and check out in the public security system.
Taking out the check-in form and informing the housekeeping department to check the room	Be accurate, fast and articulate. Take out the guest's check-in form and check it. Inform the room attendant to check the status of the guest's room and verify the equipment and goods. "Housekeeping, guests from ××× room is checking out, please check the room." Turn off the room phone and make a record.
Verifying the guest's name and bill	Check records on the computer. "Excuse me, is this Mr./Ms./Miss ××?" Verify the guest's consumption. "You consume ×× yuan, the total consumption is ×× yuan, right? Do you need an invoice?"

Continued

Process	Standards
Checking the guest's bill and asking him/her to sign	Present it with both hands. "Mr./Ms./Miss × ×, here is your bill, please check and sign it, thank you."
Charging according to the bill	Take the money paid by the customer with both hands. "Thank you." "Mr./Ms./Miss ×, this is × × yuan, the total bill is × × yuan, change × × yuan, thank you." If the guest uses credit card or check to pay, strictly follow the regulations by bank. "Please sign to confirm. Thank you."
Handing the bill and invoice to the guest	Present it with both hands. "Mr./Ms./Miss × ×, here is your bill and invoice, please keep it." Refund the balance of the guest or make up the difference
Expressing gratitude to the guest	Be warm and polite, with a smile on face. "Welcome to our hotel again. Have a nice trip. Goodbye."
Sorting data	Update the check-out information in the computer system. Bind and sort the bill

（三）注意事项

● 结账人员最基本的要求是结账准确、快速。

● 客人在其他部门消费挂账的账单，必须由客人本人签字和部门经手人的签字确认。

● 客人离店结账时，如果需要挂账，需由挂账单位及部门经理同意并签字。

● 客人用信用卡付账时，一定要对信用卡进行核对，并请客人在账单上签字。

● 客人支票付账时，有担保结账的可以离店时结账，无担保结账的，需提前押支票并由财务确认支票。

● 与客人发生纠纷时，要及时请示上级主管处理。

● 尽可能地了解客人对酒店产品与服务质量的意见，帮助酒店提高服务质量。

● 对客人递交酒店"宾客意见反馈表"时，要双手呈送和接下，表示感谢，并存入制订档案内。

（3）Notes

● The most basic requirement of the checkout is accurate and quick.

● A guest's bill for consumption in other departments must be confirmed by the guest's signature and the signature of the department manager.

● When a guest checks out, if he/she pays on credit, the account holder and the department manager must agree and sign.

● When a guest pays by credit card, the credit card must be checked and the guest must sign the card slip.

● When a guest pays by check, some with guarantee can check out when he/she leaves the hotel, while others without guarantee need to deposit the check in advance and have the check confirmed by the finance.

● When there is dispute with guest, ask the supervisor to deal with it promptly.

● Know the guest's views on the quality of products and services as much as possible and help the hotel to improve the quality of service.

● When the guest submits the hotel "Guest Feedback Form", accept it with both hands, express gratitude, and save it in files.

七、电话转接操作流程

（一）操作步骤

```
┌──────┐   ┌──────┐   ┌────────┐
│ 外线 │   │ 内线 │   │ 需求服务 │
└──────┘   └──────┘   └────────┘
              │
         ┌────────┐
         │ 问候语 │
         └────────┘
              │
         ┌──────────┐
         │ 核对客人信息 │
         └──────────┘
       ┌──────┼──────────────┐
   ┌──────┐        ┌────────┐   ┌────────┐
   │ 保密房 │        │ 非保密房 │   │ 转接电话 │
   └──────┘        └────────┘   └────────┘
       │          ┌────┴────┐        │
 ┌──────────┐  ┌──────┐ ┌──────┐ ┌────────┐
 │ 礼貌回绝客人 │  │ 同意 │ │ 不同意 │ │ 无人接听 │
 └──────────┘  └──────┘ └──────┘ └────────┘
                  │        │        │
              ┌──────┐ ┌──────────┐ ┌────────┐
              │ 转接 │ │ 礼貌回绝客人 │ │ 礼貌道别 │
              └──────┘ └──────────┘ └────────┘
```

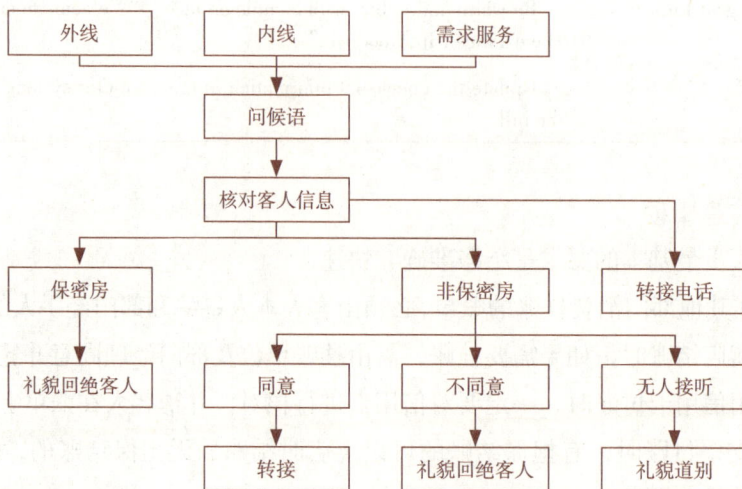

Ⅶ Telephone Transfer Operation Process

（1）Operation Process

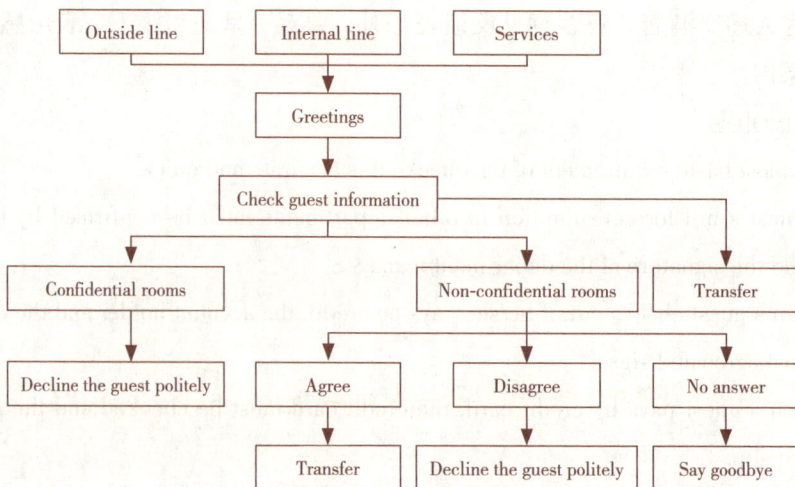

```
┌────────────┐  ┌─────────────┐  ┌──────────┐
│ Outside line│  │ Internal line│  │ Services │
└────────────┘  └─────────────┘  └──────────┘
                      │
                ┌──────────┐
                │ Greetings │
                └──────────┘
                      │
            ┌────────────────────┐
            │ Check guest information │
            └────────────────────┘
         ┌──────────┼────────────────────┐
  ┌──────────────┐      ┌──────────────────┐  ┌──────────┐
  │ Confidential rooms│      │ Non-confidential rooms│  │ Transfer │
  └──────────────┘      └──────────────────┘  └──────────┘
         │            ┌──────────┴──────────┐        │
┌────────────────────┐ ┌───────┐ ┌──────────┐ ┌──────────┐
│ Decline the guest politely│ │ Agree │ │ Disagree │ │ No answer │
└────────────────────┘ └───────┘ └──────────┘ └──────────┘
                          │          │            │
                      ┌────────┐ ┌────────────────────┐ ┌────────────┐
                      │ Transfer │ │ Decline the guest politely│ │ Say goodbye │
                      └────────┘ └────────────────────┘ └────────────┘
```

（二）电话转接操作标准

程序	电脑操作程序	服务要求
外线	0+ 手机号 / 手机号 / 座机号	您好，×××时尚商务酒店
内线	8077+××××	您好，前台
需求服务		按客人要求转接到相关部门
核对客人信息		
保密房		
礼貌回绝客人		礼貌告知客人："对不起，先生 / 小姐，我们没查到您要找的客人"
非保密房		询问来电客人信息，与住店客人联系
同意		规范用语："请稍等"
不同意		礼貌告知客人："对不起，先生 / 小姐，我们没查到您要找的客人"
转接电话		
无人接听		询问客人是否需要留言
礼貌道别		先生 / 小姐，感谢您的来电，再见

（2）Standards

Process	Computer operating procedures	Demand for services
Outside line	0+phone number	Hello! × × × Fashion Business Hotel
Internal line	8077+× × × ×	Hello! Front desk
Services		Transfer to the relevant department as requested by the guest
Check guest information		
Confidential rooms		
Decline the guest politely		Tell the guest politely: "Sorry, sir/madam, we didn't find the guest you are looking for"
Non-confidential rooms		Ask for information about the guest and contact with the guest
Agree		Standard phrase: "Please wait"
Disagree		Tell the guest politely: "Sorry, sir/madam, we didn't find the guest you are looking for"
Transfer		
No answer		Ask the guest if he/she needs to leave a message
Say goodbye		Sir/Madam, thank you for your call. Goodbye!

八、普通物品寄存

（一）操作步骤

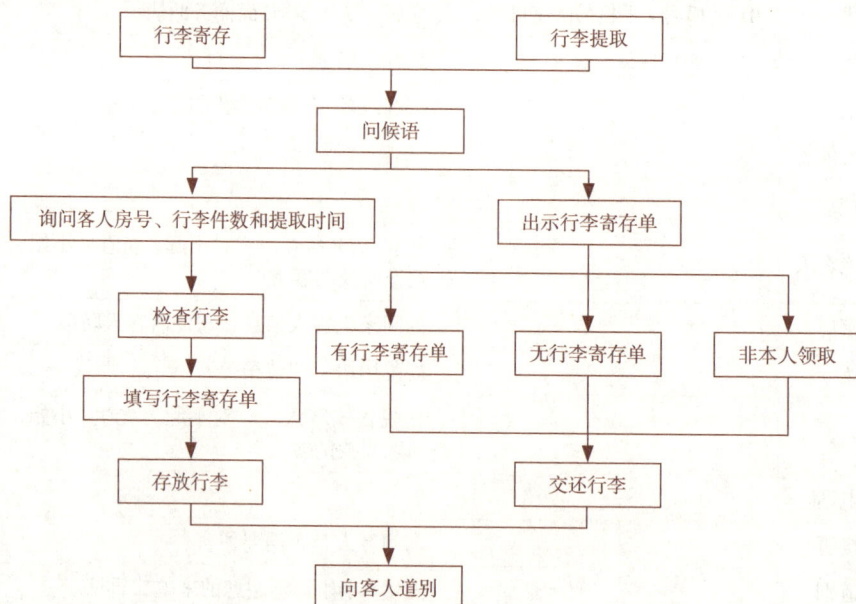

Ⅷ Common Goods Deposit

（1）Process

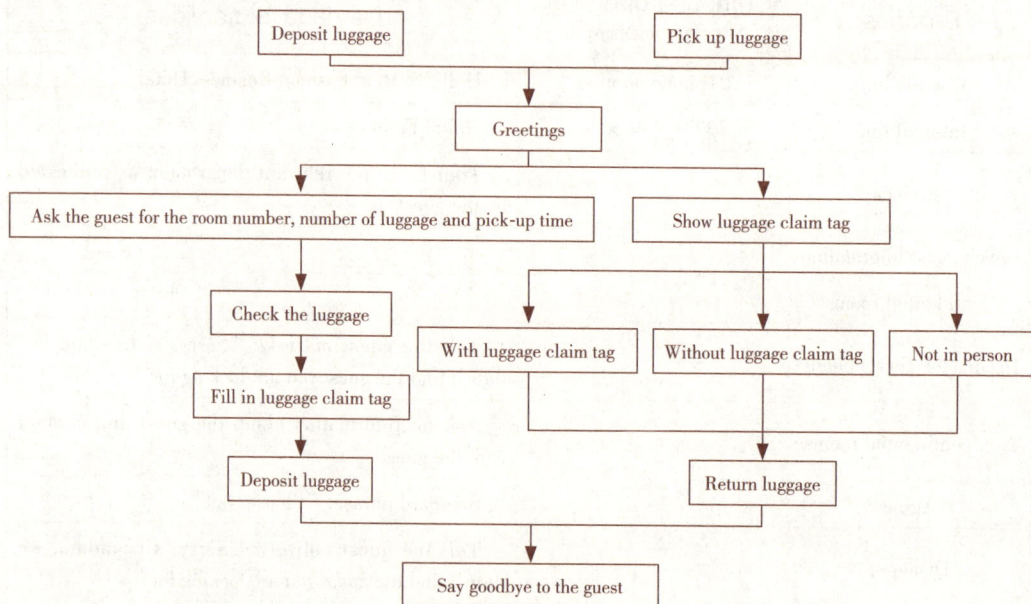

（二）操作标准

	程序	电脑操作程序	服务要求
寄存	问候语		您好，先生／小姐，请问有什么可以帮您的吗？

	程序	电脑操作程序	服务要求
寄存	询问客人房号、行李件数和提取时间		礼貌告知客人禁止存放违禁品、易燃易爆危险品
	检查行李		是否符合寄存规定，是否完好，上锁
	填写行李寄存卡		填写相关内容并请客人在行李寄存卡上签名并留下联系电话，将下联交与客人，上联挂在行李上
	存放行李		放在酒店指定地点
	向客人道别		先生 / 小姐，再见
提取	问候语		您好，先生 / 小姐，请问有什么可以帮您的吗
	出示行李寄存单		
	有行李寄存单		核对上下联信息是否一致
	无行李寄存单		如客人遗失行李寄存单下联，请客人详细描述行李的寄存时间、特征、件数等，并请客人出示有效证件，填写遗失证明单，复印客人证件，请客人在遗失证明单上签字并留下联系电话
	非本人领取		致电寄存人核对领取人身份，出示领取人证件，复印领取人证件，请领取人在领取单上签字并留下联系电话
	交还行李		
	向客人道别		先生 / 小姐，欢迎下次光临！再见

（2）Standards

	Process	Computer operating procedures	Demand for services
Deposit luggage	Greetings		Hello, sir/madam, how can I help you?
	Ask the guest for the room number, number of luggage and pick-up time		Inform the customer in a polite manner that prohibited goods, flammable and explosive dangerous goods are not allowed to be stored
	Check the luggage		Ensure it meets the deposit regulations and is intact, then lock it
	Fill in luggage claim tag		Fill in luggage claim tag and ask the guest to sign and leave the contact number. Hand the bottom part of the tag to the guest and attach the top part with the luggage
	Deposit the luggage		Put it in the designated place in the hotel
	Say goodbye to the guest		Goodbye, sir/madam

Continued

	Process	Computer operating procedures	Demand for services
Pick up luggage	Greetings		Hello, sir/madam, how can I help you
	Show luggage claim tag		
	With luggage claim tag		Check the information on the bottom part of the tag and top part
	Without luggage claim tag		If the guest loses the bottom part of the tag, ask the guest to describe in detail about the time, characteristics, number of items, etc. And ask the guest to show the valid ID and fill in the lost certificate form, then copy the customer's ID, ask the guest to sign on the lost certificate and leave the contact number
	Not in person		Call the guest to check the identity of the recipient, show the card of the recipient. Copy the recipient's ID, ask the recipient to sign the luggage claim form and leave the contact number
	Return luggage		
	Say goodbye to the guest		Sir/Madam, welcome to come back next time! Bye

九、转交物品流程

（一）操作步骤

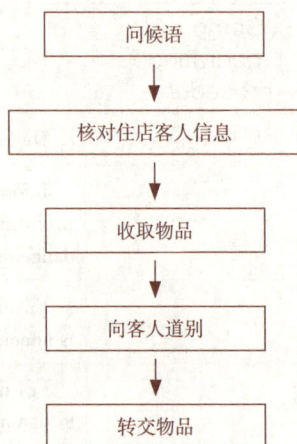

问候语

↓

核对住店客人信息

↓

收取物品

↓

向客人道别

↓

转交物品

IX Process of Transferring Goods

（1）Process

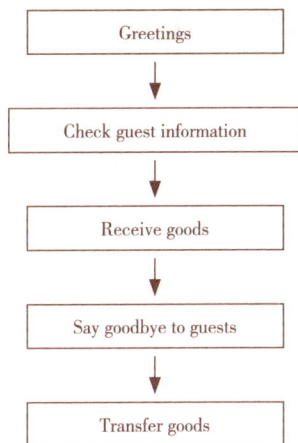

（二）操作标准

程序	电脑操作程序	服务要求
问候语		您好，先生 / 小姐，请问有什么可以帮您的吗
核对住店客人信息		核对房号、客人姓名
收取物品		留下转交人的姓名和手机号码；贵重物品不得转交
向客人道别		将转交单的一联随物品送到客房，另一联存档
转交物品		若客人不在房内，填写留言单

（2）Standards

Process	Computer operating procedures	Demand for services
Greetings		Hello, sir/madam, how can I help you
Check guest information		Check room number and guest's name
Receive goods		Leave the name and cell phone number of the person; valuable goods are not allowed to be transferred
Say goodbye to guest		Send one copy of the transfer form to the guest room with the items, and keep the other copy for records
Transfer goods		If the guest is not in the room, fill in the message form

十、租借物品流程

（一）操作步骤

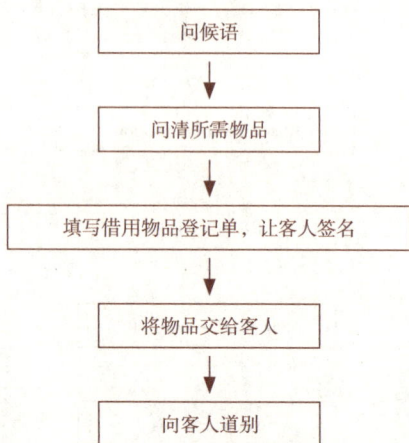

X The Process of Renting Goods

（1）Process

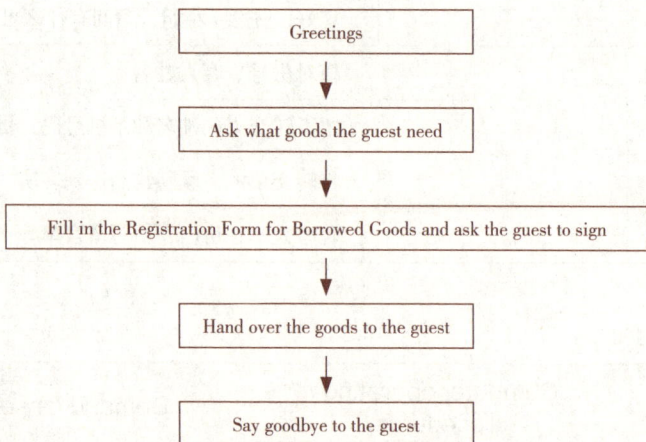

（二）操作标准

程序	电脑操作程序	服务要求
问候语		您好，先生／小姐，请问有什么可以帮您的吗
问清所需物品		
填写借用物品登记单，让客人签名		一联给客人，一联存档，退房的客人租借雨伞，需支付相应的押金，并开具收据，请客人签名并提醒客人保管好收据
将物品交给客人	在退房提醒栏内输入备注	
向客人道别		先生／小姐，再见

（2）Standards

Process	Computer operating procedures	Demand for services
Greetings		Hello, sir/madam, how can I help you
Ask what goods the guest need		
Fill in the Registration Form for Borrowed Goods and ask the guest to sign		One copy to the guest, the other copy for the file. When the check-out guest wants to rent an umbrella, charge the deposit and issue a receipt. Ask the guest to sign and remind the guest to keep the receipt
Hand over the goods to the guest	Write a note in the check-out reminder	
Say goodbye to the guest		Goodbye, sir/madam

十一、留言服务流程

（一）操作步骤

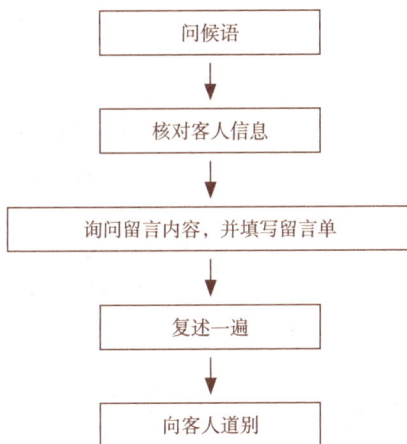

XI The Process of Leaving Messages

（1）Process

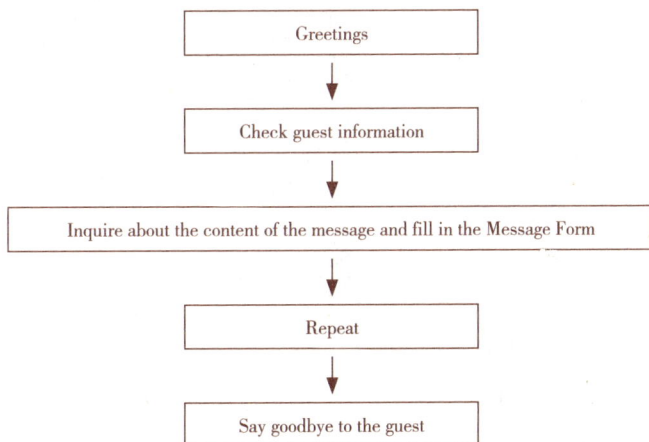

（二）操作标准

程序	电脑操作程序	服务要求
问候语		您好，先生／小姐，请问有什么可以帮您的吗
核对客人信息		核对房号、客人姓名
询问留言内容，并填写留言单		问清来电人姓名、手机号码、留言内容，并记录在案，留言单一式两联
复述一遍		再次确认来电人姓名、手机号码、留言内容
向客人道别		先生／小姐，感谢您的来电，再见！将留言单的一联送到客房，另一联存档

（2）Standards

Process	Computer operating procedures	Demand for services
Greetings		Hello, sir/madam, how can I help you
Check guest information		Check room number and guest's name
Inquire about the content of the message and fill in the Message Form		Ask the caller's name, phone number and message content, and record it with the Message Form in duplicate.
Repeat		Confirm the caller's name, cell phone number and message content
Say goodbye to the guest		Mr./Madam, thank you for calling, goodbye! Send one copy of the Message Form to the guest room, and save the other copy

十二、自助早餐服务流程

（一）操作步骤

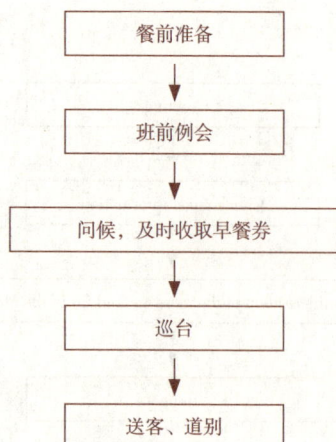

餐前准备 → 班前例会 → 问候，及时收取早餐券 → 巡台 → 送客、道别

XII　Buffet Breakfast Service Process

（1）Process

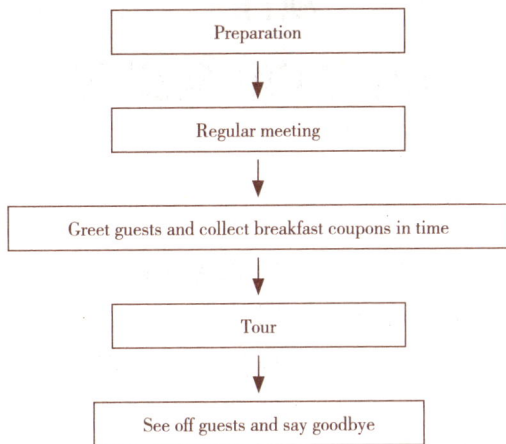

（二）操作标准

程序	电脑操作程序	服务要求
餐前准备		检查餐具、摆台的标准、备料，做好开档前的准备工作
班前例会		工作安排，检查仪表仪容
问候，及时收取早餐券		礼貌用语：早上好，欢迎光临
巡台		及时清洁餐桌，整理自助餐台；及时添加菜肴、餐具、酒精；及时为客人添加咖啡、茶等
送客、道别		谢谢，欢迎下次光临

（2）Standards

Process	Computer operating procedures	Demand for services
Preparation		Check the tableware and table setting and prepare materials
Regular meeting		Work arrangement, check the appearance
Greet guests and collect breakfast coupons in time		Polite language: good morning, welcome to the restaurant
Tour		Clean the table in time; add dishes, tableware and alcohol in time; add coffee and tea for guests in time
See off guests and say goodbye		Thank you! See you next time

项目二
前厅部工作环境认知

【案例导入】

多伦多希尔顿酒店的改造

多伦多希尔顿酒店建于 1970 年，位于市中心边缘的一条比较清冷的街道上。由于酒店陈设古板、简单，大堂装饰摆设没有吸引力，缺少现代感，酒店生意冷清。后来，酒店业主用了两年的时间，对 27 层 600 间客房、大堂和酒店其他部位进行了全面改造。承担改造任务的 KPMB 建筑设计公司首先从大堂着手，以几何技术作为总规划的主导手法，再注入明亮柔和的色彩和一种波浪形的分点灯光创作，彻底改变了原有的布局和基调，将大堂设计成新欧陆式的公众空间，并融入了大量的现代元素。

入口处地面铺设浅色大理石，休息区地面抬高并改铺深色实木地板，局部却铺入白色鹅卵石。

总台由原来的死角位置改在电梯厅附近。

合成竹片加钢管编制成的屏风隔开大堂休息区与电梯入口，既充分利用了空间，也明确了交通导向。同时，与天花透明玻璃窗垂下的布幔形成呼应，形式鲜明而独特。

与第二层回廊连接的楼梯护栏以透明石材配合钢制材料，处理手法简洁、大方、精巧。

只对原有空间进行务实的利用，但取消了所有古旧的设计与装饰物。

整个大堂的改造设计充分利用了自然光线的折射，大堂空间布局中丰富而简练的层次都在折射光温和的点拨中显得动人。

此设计集辉煌、自然、现代于一体，三者简洁巧妙的结合使大堂舒适明朗，焕然一新。

【任务布置】

①你认为酒店前厅环境由哪些方面构成？

②说一说让你印象深刻的酒店前厅环境。

【启示】

酒店的内装饰设计作为室内环境艺术，始终处在探索和发展中，其核心思路可以概括为功能和美感的统一，即科学性和艺术性的统一。这个案例涉及酒店前厅在设施设备布局、空间、色彩、氛围等设计方面的知识，这也是本章内容的重点。

（资料来源：徐文苑，严金明.酒店前厅管理与服务［M］.北京：清华大学出版社，2004：32.）

Project 2
To know the Working Environment of the Front Office

【Case Introduction】
Renovation of Hilton Toronto

The Hilton Toronto was built in 1970 on a relatively quiet street on the edge of downtown. The hotel's business declined due to its antiquated, simple furnishings and unattractive lobby decor. The owners spent two years renovating 600 rooms on 27 floors, the lobby and other parts of the hotel. KPMB undertook the renovation. It started with the lobby, using geometric techniques as the dominant method, and then injected bright and soft colors and a wave-shaped point lighting creation, which completely changed the original layout and style. The lobby was designed into a neo-European public space with a lot of modern elements.

The entrance floor was paved with light-colored marble, and the floor of the lounge area was raised and paved with dark-colored solid wood, but partially paved with white pebbles.

The main desk was changed from the original corner position to near the elevator hall.

The screen made of synthetic bamboo and steel pipe separated the lobby lounge area from the elevator entrance, which not only made full use of the space but also clarified the direction. At the same time, it echoed the draping of the transparent glass window from the ceiling, which was distinctive and unique.

The staircase guardrail connecting with the second-floor corridor was made of transparent stone with steel material, which was simple, generous and delicate.

Original space was used thoroughly while all antique designs and decorations were eliminated.

After renovation, the whole lobby made full use of the refraction of natural light. The rich and concise layers in the layout of the lobby space were moving in the gentle pointing of the refracted light.

The simple and clever combination of the brilliance, nature and modernity made the lobby comfortable, bright and new.

【Assignment】
① What do you think makes up the hotel lobby environment?

② Tell us about the hotel front lobby environment that impressed you.

【Enlightenment】

As indoor environmental art, hotel interior design is always in the process of exploration and development. Its core ideas can be summarized as harmony between function and aesthetic, that is, the unity of science and artistry. This case involves the design knowledge of hotel lobby in the layout of facilities and equipment, space, color, atmosphere, etc. which is also the key point of this chapter.

（Source: Xu Wenyuan, Yan Jinming. Hotel front office management and service［M］. Beijing: Tsinghua University Press, 2004: 32）

任务一　前厅工作环境评估

从酒店建筑角度来看，前厅是指酒店的正门、大厅、楼梯、电梯和公共卫生间等，属于前厅部管辖范围。前厅是酒店建筑的重要部分，每一位客人抵达和离开酒店都必须经过这里，是客人对酒店产生第一印象和留下最后回忆的重要空间，是集交通、服务、休息等多种功能为一体的共享空间。

一、酒店大堂的设计基本原则及设计类型

（一）前厅设置的基本原则

尽管前厅的设置随着酒店业的发展在不断更新，各类酒店在前厅设计上都突出自己的特点，但是前厅的设计都要遵循如下基本原则，以利于前厅的运转。

①经济性。

前厅一般设在酒店的大堂，而大堂是酒店的寸金之地。酒店可以充分利用这一客流量最大的地方，设置营利设施。因此，前厅的设置要尽量少占用大堂空间。

②安全性。

前厅的设置遵循安全性原则。其含义一方面是指前厅的设置必须确保"收银处"的安全，防止有害酒店现金和账务活动的事情发生；另一方面，前厅的设计要能够为客人保密，不能让客人轻易得知其他客人的情况。因此，酒店的前厅以直线形、半圆形为多，而圆形较少。

③明显性。

前厅的位置应该是明显的，也就是前厅的可见度比较强。客人一进入酒店就能发现前厅，同时前厅的员工也能够看清酒店大堂出入的来往客人。如果一家酒店的前厅

不易让客人找到，那么其设置是不合理的。此外，前厅的明显性原则还包括前台各业务处明确的中英文标示。

④效益性。

前厅的设置还应该注意各工作环节的衔接，确保前台接待人员工作效率的提高和节省客人的时间与体力，绝大多数酒店的前厅都是以"客房控制架"为中心进行设计的。这种方法最利于提高前厅接待工作效率。"时间与动作研究"是设计前厅必须进行的工作。

⑤美观性。

前厅不仅要高效、准确地完成客人的入住登记手续，而且要能够给客人留下深刻的良好形象。因此，前厅的布局、灯光、色彩以及气氛都是不容忽视的内容。

Task 1
Assessment of the Working Environment of the Front Office

From the perspective of the hotel building, the front lobby refers to the main entrance and lobby of the hotel, as well as the stairs, elevators and public restrooms, etc, which belong to the jurisdiction of the front lobby department. The front lobby is an important part of the hotel building, since every guest must pass through here when arriving and leaving the hotel. It is an important space for guests to leave the first impression and the last memory of the hotel. In addition, it is a shared space integrating transportation, service, rest and other functions.

I　The Basic Principles and Types of Hotel Lobby Design
（1）The Basic Principles of Hotel Lobby Design

With the development of the hotel industry, design of the front lobby is constantly updated and hotels desire to highlight their own specialty. However, the design of the front lobby should follow the following basic principles in order to facilitate the operation.

① Economic Efficiency.

The front office is generally located in the lobby of the hotel, which is scarce and expensive. The hotel can make full use of this place with the largest passenger flow to layout facilities to make a profit. Therefore, the front office should take up as little space as possible in the lobby.

② Security.

The design of front lobby should follow the principle of security. On the one hand, it means that the front lobby must ensure the safety of the "cashier's office" and prevent the loss of cash and account; on the other hand, the design of the front lobby should keep the guests confidential, so that guests cannot know other guests easily. Therefore, the front desk of the hotel is mostly in a straight line, semi-circular, but less circular.

③ Obviousness.

The location of the front desk should be obvious, that is, the visibility of the front lobby is relatively strong. Guests can find the front desk as soon as they enter the hotel, while the staff in the front desk can also see the passing guests in and out of the hotel. If a hotel's front desk is not easy to find, then its layout is unreasonable. In addition, the principle of obviousness of the front lobby also includes a clear sign in English and Chinese at the front desk.

④ Effectiveness.

The layout of the front office should also pay attention to the connection of various work links to ensure reception staff's efficiency and save guests' time and energy. The vast majority of hotel front desks are designed with "room rack" as the center. This method improves the efficiency of front office reception most. "Time and motion research" is the work that must be done to design the front desk.

⑤ Aesthetics.

The front lobby should not only be efficient and accurate at completing the guest check-in procedures, but also be able to leave a deep and good image on the guest. Therefore, the layout, lighting, color and atmosphere of the front lobby cannot be ignored.

（二）酒店大堂设计装饰的类型

①古典式。

这是一种具有浓厚传统色彩的设计装饰类型，大堂内古董般的吊灯、精美的古典绘画以及造型独特的楼梯杆栏，让客人感受到大堂空间的古朴典雅。随着各种新材料如亚光漆、彩色金属板和亚纹定型板等的应用,酒店大堂古典式设计装饰有了新的生机。

②庭园式。

庭园式设计装饰引入山水景点与花木盆景，犹如"庭中花园"，如在大堂内利用假山、叠石让水自高处泻下，其落差和水声使大堂变得有声有色；或者在大堂的一角，种植大量的热带植物，设置小巧的凉亭与瀑布，使大堂空间更富自然山水的意境。在设计装饰庭园式大堂时，应注意确保整体空间的协调，花木搭配应与季节、植物习性等自然规律相符，假山体量、溪涧宽窄应与空间大小相称等。

③重技式。

重技式设计装饰显露出严谨的结构、粗实的支柱。如美国的希尔顿酒店的大堂，设置了用几十根金属管组成的高达雕塑，并以金黄色喷漆涂于表面，使整个大堂空间充满了生机和活力，营造出迎候八方来客的浓郁氛围。

④现代式。

这类大堂设计装饰追求整洁、敞亮、线条流畅。如大堂顶面球面型和地面圆形图案互相呼应，再配以曲面形墙壁与淡雅的色彩，大堂顶面设计有犹如星星闪烁的灯光，让客人如身临太空，情趣无穷；若再辅以玻璃、不锈钢和磨光花岗岩等反光性强的材料装饰的通道，则大堂更显得玲珑剔透，充满了现代感。

（2）The Type of Hotel Lobby Design and Decoration

① Classical style.

This kind of design and decoration is featured with strong traditional colors, antique chandeliers in the lobby, exquisite classical paintings and unique staircase rails, so that guests can feel the antique and elegance of the lobby. With the application of various new materials such as matte paint, colored metal plates and sub-patterned plates, the classical design and decoration gained a new vitality.

② Garden style.

The design and decoration use landscape attractions and bonsai, like a "garden in the courtyard". For example, the use of rockery, stacked stones in the lobby makes the water to flow from high. The drop and the sound of the water make the lobby vivid. Or in a corner of the lobby, planting a large number of tropical plants, setting up small pavilions and waterfalls, can make the lobby space richer in the natural landscape. In the design of a garden-style lobby, attention should be paid to ensure the overall coordination of space. The arrangement of flowers and trees conforms to the natural laws of the season and plant habits. The volume of the rockery, the width of the stream should be proportional to the size of the space, etc.

③ Heavy technique type.

Its design reveals a rigorous structure, thick and solid pillars. For example, the lobby of the Hilton Hotel in the United States is equipped with a Gundam sculpture composed of dozens of metal pipes, and the surface is painted with golden yellow spray paint, which makes the entire lobby full of vitality, creating a strong atmosphere for welcoming guests from all directions.

④ Modern style.

This type of lobby design and decoration pursues neatness, brightness and smooth lines. The lobby's spherical roof and round pattern on the ground echo each other combined with curved walls and light colors. The lobby roof is designed with lights as if the stars flash, so that guests feel like being in space with endless fun. If supplemented by glass, stainless steel and polished granite and other reflective materials decorating the channel, the lobby looks more exquisite and modern.

二、前厅的功能布局

前厅规模的大小受酒店性质、规模、位置等因素影响，不过，按功能布局来划分，可将前厅分为正门入口处及人流线路、服务区、休息区和公共卫生间等主要区域。

（一）正门入口处及人流线路

正门入口处是酒店之窗口，具有招徕客人、引导人流的作用。大门作为内外空间交界处，设计日趋多样、完善。酒店大门的类型分为手推门、旋转门、自动感应门等，一般多为组合设置，即设手推门加自动感应门或手推门加旋转门等，以满足多方面的需求。

大门在设计上不仅要考虑一般客人的进出，还要考虑团体客人、轮椅客人的进出，也要方便行李的进出。一般正门分为两扇，便于客人进出及提供拉门服务，但一般会在正门两侧各开一两扇边门，以方便客流量大时使用以及行李进出。大门外应备有遮雨棚和宽敞的车道，门的规格大小应考虑客流进出量、服务水准、规格等。大门要求有隔音、隔尘、防风、恒温的功能，以保证大厅内空气清新、温度适宜。因此，酒店大门一般都设置双重门，以保持大厅内空调温度的稳定及节约能源，在二门之间的隔厅里，应放置地脚垫和雨伞架，以减少带进的尘土和污渍。另外，旋转门能有效地解决内外温度的空气阻隔问题，降低暖气或空调的成本。

目前，酒店前厅入口常见的设计类型有如下三种。

*花园式。这类酒店前厅入口占地面积较大，通常有流畅的回车线环绕其间，有由绿树与花草组成的各种颇具创意的图案、标志，再辅以雕塑、园林灯柱、精致栏杆的适当点缀，并与门旁的花草盆景相呼应，整个酒店门前洋溢着浓郁的自然气息。

*支架式。支架式亦称棚架式入口，一般采用玻璃钢、金属材料与透明塑料等构成斜坡式、半球式、帐篷式和尖顶式等形态各异的棚架造型，并采用富有立体感、光亮度强与特殊质地的新材料和新工艺，再配上流动感强的现代灯光，足以引起宾客的浓厚兴趣。这类酒店前厅入口处造型新颖、美观且富有现代特色。但设计时，应考虑到与酒店主体建筑相协调，棚架须安全可靠。

*门面式。门面式前厅入口的特点是将门面设计装饰与广告促销进行有效组合，以吸引更多的客人。如有些酒店利用玻璃门与落地窗张贴巨大的广告艺术画，安装立面霓虹灯，以展示酒店的特色风貌。

从前厅入口到酒店各个目的地，便形成了人流线路。各条人流线路要经过装修或铺设条形地毯，加上适当的装点，以形成明确的人流方向，使具有动感的走线与相对平静的休息区和服务区互不影响。酒店正门入口处及人流线路如图2.1所示。

团队入口　团队休息室　主入口　大厅　宴会厅入口　宴会厅过厅

鲜花店
精品店
商务中心
书店
美容美发店
小商店

咖啡厅
酒吧
西餐厅
各式餐厅
⋮

宴会厅
多功能厅
大型会议厅
⋮

健身中心
健身浴
游泳池
乒乓球室
保龄球场
棋牌室
桌球室
舞厅、卡拉OK厅
⋮

客房

—————　住宿客人、团队客人流线
- - - - - - -　宴会客人流线
◄◄◄　流动方向

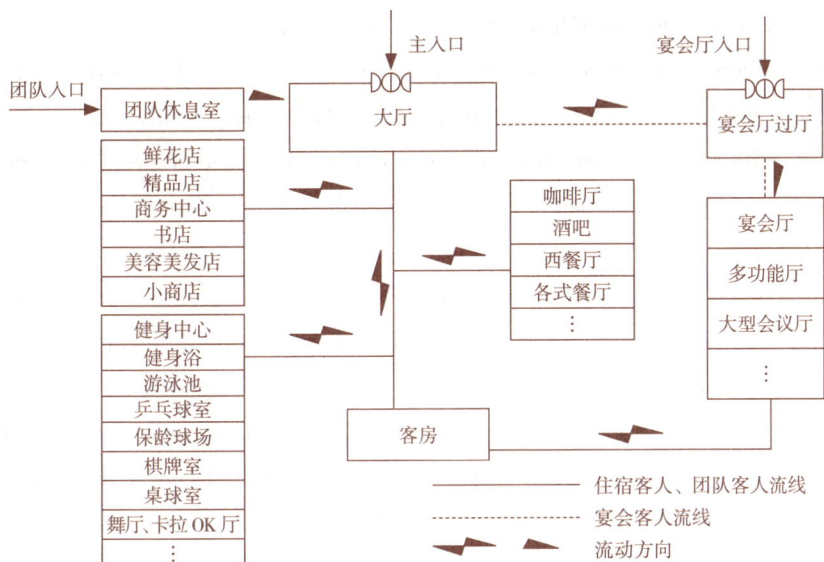

图 2.1　酒店正门入口处及人流线路

II　The Functional Layout of the Front Lobby

The size of the lobby is affected by the nature, scale, location and other factors of the hotel. However, according to the functional layout, the lobby can be divided into main areas such as the main entrance and pedestrian lines, service areas, rest areas and public restrooms.

（1）The Main Entrance and Pedestrian Lines

The main entrance is the window of the hotel, with the role of attracting guests and guiding the people. As the junction of internal and external space, the design of gate is increasingly diverse and perfect. The types of hotel doors are divided into hand push doors, revolving doors, automatic induction doors, etc. Generally, to meet various needs, they are set up in combination, such as hand push doors plus automatic induction doors or hand push doors plus revolving doors.

When design the main door, not only the access of general guests should be considered, but also the access of group guests, wheelchair guests and luggage. Generally, the main door is divided into two, which is convenient for guests to enter and exit and provide sliding door service. However, one or two side doors are generally opened on both sides of the main entrance to facilitate the large passenger flow and luggage. There should be equipped with a canopy and a spacious driveway outside the door. When determine the size of the gate, the volume of passenger flow, service level, and specifications should be taken into account. The gate should have the function of sound insulation, dust barrier, windproof and constant temperature to ensure fresh air and suitable temperature in the hall. Therefore, the door is generally set double doors to maintain the stability of the air temperature in the hall and save energy. In the partition hall between the two doors, foot mats and umbrella stands should be placed to reduce the dust and stains. In addition, the revolving door can effectively solve the air barrier of internal and external temperature and reduce the cost of heating or air conditioning.

At present, there are three common design types for hotel front lobby entrance as follows.

*Garden Style. This type of hotel entrance covers a large area, usually with a smooth return line around it. With a variety of creative patterns and signs composed of green trees and flowers, supplemented by sculptures, garden lamp posts, exquisite railings, echoed with flower and plant bonsai near the door, the entire hotel front is full of strong natural atmosphere.

*Stand Style. It is also known as scaffolding type, which generally adopts glass fiber reinforced plastics, metal materials and transparent plastics to create different forms of scaffolds such as slope, hemisphere, tent and spire. The use of new materials and technology with rich three-dimensional effect, strong brightness and special texture, coupled with modern lighting with strong sense of flow, is enough to arouse the strong interest of guests. This kind of lobby entrance shape is new, beautiful and modern. However, the design should take into account the coordination with the main building of the hotel and the scaffolding must be safe and reliable.

* Facade Style. It is characterized by the effective combination of facade design and advertising promotion to attract more guests. For example, some hotels use glass and floor windows to post huge advertising art paintings and install neon lights on the facade to show the characteristics of the hotel.

From the lobby entrance to each destination of the hotel, it forms a line of pedestrian flow. Each line of pedestrian flow should be decorated or paved by strip carpet, plus appropriate decoration, to form a clear direction of pedestrian flow, so that the dynamic route and the quiet rest area and service area do not affect each other. The main entrance and flow line of the hotel are shown in the figure 2.1.

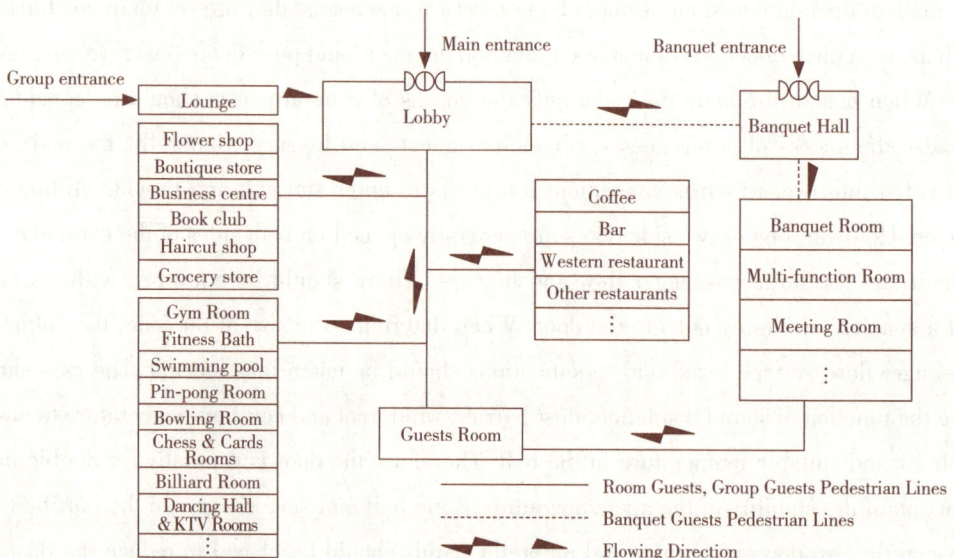

Fig 2.1　The main entrance and flow line of the hotel

（二）服务区

前厅的对客服务区主要包括总服务台、大堂副理处和行李处等。

①总服务台。

总服务台应设在前厅醒目的位置，主体包括接待、问询、收银三部分。

根据前厅设计布局，总服务台最好能正对前厅入口处，这样，不仅使总服务台工作人员能观察到整个前厅、出入口、电梯等活动场所的情况，而且也使总服务台工作人员能清楚地观察到正门外客人车辆的到达情况，从而做好接待准备工作。同时，也有利于及时发现各种可疑情况，以消除隐患，确保安全。另外，以团队客为主要客源的酒店，在总服务台外另设团队接待处。

（2）Service Area

The service area of the front office mainly includes the general service desk, assistant manager's office and luggage office, etc.

① General Service Desk.

The general service desk should be located in a conspicuous position in the lobby, and the main body includes reception, inquiries, cashier.

According to the layout of the lobby, the general service desk should preferably face the entrance of the lobby. In this way, the receptionist can observe not only the whole front hall, entrances and exits, elevators and other places, but also the arrival of the guest vehicles outside the front door, so as to prepare for reception. At the same time, it is convenient to detect suspicious situations in order to eliminate dangers unhappened and ensure safety. In addition, for the hotel whose guests are groups, besides the front desk, the team reception should be set.

【知识拓展】

前厅的设置是前厅业务运转的基础，而且，前厅一旦落成就很难改变，因此在设置前一定要进行可行性研究。总服务台的高度应以方便客人住宿登记和总服务台工作人员的接待服务工作为原则，其理想高度为 110 ~ 125 cm。柜台内侧设有工作台，供总服务台工作人员使用，其台高为 85 cm，宽为 30 cm。工作台面最好设计成倾斜式，有一定的坡度，以方便员工使用，且不影响其服务仪态（站姿等）。

总服务台的大小是由酒店接待人数、总服务台服务项目和计算的应用水平等因素决定的。酒店的规模越大，接待人数和服务项目越多，则总服务台设计的面积越大；反之，则越小。如国际喜来登集团的总服务台指标是：满 200 间客房，柜台长 8 m，台内面积 23 m²；满 400 间客房，柜台长 10 m，台内面积 31 m²；满 600 间客房，柜台长 15 m，台内面积 45 m²。

【To Know More】

The setting of the front desk is the basis for the operation of the front office business. Once the front office is completed, it is difficult to change it. Therefore, the feasibility study must be conducted before setting. The height of the general service desk should be based on the convenience for guest accommodation registration and reception service. The ideal height is 110 to 125 cm. The desk is equipped with a worktable on the inside for general office staff, whose height is 85 cm and the width is 30 cm. The worktable should be inclined, with a certain slope for the convenience for staff's and won't affect their service（standing posture, etc）.

The size of the general service desk is determined by the number of people received by the hotel, the service items of the general service desk and the calculation application. The larger the scale of the hotel, the more the number of receptions and service items, the larger the area of the general service desk should cover conversely, smaller hotels requireless space. For example, according to the general service desk indicators of the International Sheraton Group: When it reaches 200 rooms, the length of desk should be 8 meters, and the area should be 23 square meters; When it reaches 400 rooms, the length should be 10 meters, and the area should be 31 square meters; When it reaches 600 rooms, the length should be 15 meters, and the area should be 45 square meters.

②大堂副理处。

大堂副理处一般设在距离总服务台和大门不远的、视野开阔的安静地方。通常放置一个办公桌、两三张座椅，供办公和接待客人。

大堂副理，或叫大堂经理、客务经理，一般在大厅的一角或某处设置大堂副理处，为大堂副理值班处，一般是大堂副理在此接待客人，处理客人投诉，维持大堂的正常工作秩序，处理前厅出现的各类问题、突发事件等。因为他的工作涉及对客服务的其他部门，因此，为了能更好地协调各部门的对客服务，其职位比部门经理低，比主管高，不直接服从前厅部经理的指挥，而直接服从房务总监或总经理的指挥。

② Assistant Manager's Office.

The assistant manager's office is usually located in a quiet place with a wide view, not far from the general service desk and the entrance. A desk and two or three chairs are placed for office and guest reception.

Assistant manager, also known as lobby manager or guest service manager, receives guests, handles guest complaints, maintains the normal working order of the lobby, and handles various problems and emergencies in his/her office which lies in a corner of the lobby. Because his/her work involves other departments of the guest service, in order to better coordinate the various departments of the guest service, its position is lower than the department manager, higher than the supervisor. He/she does not report to general manager of the front office directly, but the director of housekeeping or general manager.

③行李处。

行李处一般在大门内侧，目的是让行李员尽早看到车辆驶进通道。

大厅内侧设大厅服务处（也有的在大门外），一般由服务处领班在其值班台接待客人，安排调度行李进出等。值班台后应设有行李房，以放置寄存的行李和集中或疏散团队行李。

另外，前厅部办公室、总机室、账务室等机构，与前厅接待工作密切相关，但又不必直接与客人打交道，一般应设在总服务台后面联络方便但较为隐秘之处。

③ Luggage Office.

The Luggage office is generally on the inside of the main door, in order to make the bell staff see the vehicle driving into the channel as early as possible.

The lobby service office is set up on the inside of the lobby（some of them are outside the gate）. The foreman of the service office generally receives the guests at his/her duty desk and arranges luggage in and out. Behind the duty desk, there should be a luggage room to place and store luggage of individuals or groups.

In addition, the front office, switchboard, accounting room and other institutions are closely related to the reception work in the front office, but do not have to deal with guests directly. Generally, they should be located behind the general service desk in a convenient but relatively secret place.

（三）休息区

大厅休息区是客人来往酒店等候、休息或约见亲友的场所，它要求相对安静和不受干扰。休息区的主要家具是供客人休息的沙发座椅和配套茶几。沙发可根据需要围成几组方形，也可围着柱子设置，在人流进出频繁、充满动感的大厅空间中，构筑一个宁静舒适的小环境。

（3）Rest Area

The lounge rest area in the lobby is a place where guests wait, rest or meet relatives and friends. It requires quiet and undisturbed circumstance. The main furniture in the lounge area is sofa and coffee table. The sofa can be arranged in groups of squares as needed, or set up around pillars to construct a quiet and comfortable environment in the dynamic hall with frequent people in and out.

（四）公共卫生间

酒店大厅或附近通常设有供男女客人使用的公共卫生间。公共卫生间的设施主要有便器和洗脸盆，还有烘手器、手纸、面巾纸、小毛巾、香皂等器具和用品。公共卫生间要宽敞干净，设施要完好，用品要齐全。

从一定意义上讲,公共卫生间可以反映出酒店的档次和服务水准,是酒店的"名片"。所以，公共卫生间的装饰材料选择与大堂其他部分在规格和质地上要相一致,如现代酒店的大堂一般选用大理石装修,其公共卫生间也应选用同样的材料装修。大堂有进出的人流众多,要考虑公共卫生间的位置,既方便客人又能避开外人的直视,且标志要明显。

（4）Public Restrooms

There are usually equipped with public restrooms for male and female guests in the hotel lobby. The facilities in public restrooms mainly include toilets and washbasins, as well as hand dryers, toilet paper, facial tissues, small towels, soap and other utensils and supplies. Public restrooms must be spacious and clean, with good facilities and complete supplies.

In a certain sense, the public restroom can reflect the grade and service standard of the hotel, and it is the "business card" of the hotel. Therefore, the choice of decorative materials for public restrooms should be consistent with other parts of the lobby in terms of specifications and textures. For example, the lobby of a modern hotel is generally decorated with marble, and the public restroom should also be decorated with the same materials. Since there are a lot of people coming and going in the lobby, the location of the public restroom should be taken into consideration. It should be convenient for guests and avoid the direct sight and its sign should be obvious.

三、前厅环境氛围的营造

前厅的装饰、灯光、布置,必须有特色,必须体现酒店的级别、服务特点及管理风格,必须对客人有较强的吸引力,并具备宁静的气氛。更重要的是,前厅的布局要考虑到酒店经营与管理的需要。

III The Creation of the Atmosphere of the Lobby

The decoration, lighting and layout of the lobby must be distinctive and can reflect the hotel's level, service characteristics and management style. It must have a strong attraction to guests, and a peaceful atmosphere. Moreover, the layout of the lobby should take into account the needs of hotel operation and management.

①光线。

前厅内要有适宜的光线,要能使客人在良好的光线下活动,员工在适当的光照下工作。前厅内最好通入一定的自然光线,同时配备层次、类型各不相同的灯光,以保证良好的光照效果。客人从大门外进入大厅,是从光线明亮处进入到光线昏暗处,如果这个转折过快,客人会很不适应,睁不开眼睛,所以,灯光的强弱变化应逐步进行。要使每位客人都能逐步适应光线明暗的变化,可采用不同种类、不同亮度、不同层次、不同照明方式的灯光，配合自然光线达到上述要求。

① Light.

There should be suitable light in the lobby, to enable guests to move and employees to work. It is best to have a certain amount of natural light into the lobby and equip with different levels and types of lights to ensure good lighting effects. When guests enter the lobby from outside, they are from the place with bright light to the dim light. If this turn is too fast, guests will be very uncomfortable and cannot open their eyes, so the change of light intensity should be carried out gradually. To make each guest's eyes can gradually adapt to the changes of light, different types, different brightness, different levels, different lighting methods can be used to meet the above requirements with natural light.

②色彩。

前厅环境的好坏，还受前厅内色彩的影响。前厅客人主要活动区域的地面、墙面、吊灯等，应以暖色调为主，以烘托出豪华热烈的气氛。而前厅的服务环境及客人休息的沙发附近，色彩应略冷些，让人有一种宁静、平和的心境，适应服务员工作和客人休息对环境的要求，创造出前厅特有的安静、轻松的气氛。

② Color.

The environment of lobby is also affected by the color in the front hall. of The main activity area including floor, wall and chandeliers in the lobby should mainly be in warm colors to bring out the luxurious and warm atmosphere. And in the service area and rest area near the sofa, the color should be slightly colder, so that people can have a quiet, calm state of mind. To meet requirements of the staff's work and guest rest, a quiet, relaxed atmosphere should be created.

③温度、湿度与通风。

前厅要有适当的温度，酒店通过单个空调机或中央空调，一般都可以把大厅温度维持在人体所需要的最佳温度，一般是 22 ~ 24 ℃，再配合以适当的温度（40 ~ 60 ℃），整个环境就比较适宜了。

前厅内人员集中，密度大，人员来往活动频繁，耗氧量大，如果通风不畅，会使人觉得闷，有一种压抑感，应使用性能良好的通风设备及空气清新剂等，改善大厅内的空气质量，使之适合人体的要求。通常高星级酒店大厅内风速应保持在 0.1 ~ 0.3 m/s，大厅内新风量一般不低于 160 $m^3/$（人·h）。大厅内的废气和污染物的控制标准是：一氧化碳含量不超过 5 mg/m^3；二氧化碳含量不超过 0.1 %；可吸纳颗粒物不超过 0.1 mg/m^3；细菌总数不超过 3 000 个 $/m^3$。

③ Temperature, Humidity and Ventilation.

Lobby must have a appropriate temperature. The hotel can maintain the hall temperature in the best temperature suitable for the human body through a single air conditioning or central air conditioning. Generally, the temperature is 22 – 24 ℃. Coupled with the appropriate temperature（40 – 60 ℃）, the whole environment is more appropriate.

As many people gather together in the lobby with frequent movements, the oxygen consumption is high. If the ventilation is not good, people will feel stuffy and have a sense of depression. Good ventilation equipment and air freshener should be used to improve the air quality in the hall to make it suitable for human requirements. Generally, the wind speed in the lobby of high-star hotels should be maintained at 0.1 ~ 0.3 m/s, and the fresh air volume in the lobby is generally not less than 160 cubic meters/person-hour. According to the control standard of exhaust gas and pollutants in the hall: carbon monoxide content should be no more than 5 mg/m^3; carbon dioxide content should be no more than 0.1%; absorbable particulate matter should be no more than 0.1 mg/m^3; total number of bacteria should be no more than 3 000 pcs/m^3

④声音。

如果声音过于集中，就会超过人体感觉舒适的限度，使人烦燥不安，容易出错，易于激动和争吵，降低效率。因而在建造前厅时，应考虑使用隔音板等材料，降低噪音。酒店员工工作交谈时，声音应尽量轻些，有时甚至可以使用一些体态语言，代替说话进行沟通（如用手势招呼远处的同事）。要尽量提高工作效率，使客人在高峰时间不致长久滞留于大厅，破坏大厅安静的气氛。酒店应尽可能播放轻松动听的背景音乐，以减少噪声对客人的危害。一般而言，大厅内的噪声一般不得超过 50 dB，大厅背景音乐以 5 ~ 7 dB 为宜。

④ Sound.

If the noise is too much, it will exceed the comfort limit of the human body, making people irritable, easy to make mistakes, easy to be excite and quarrel, and lower efficiency. Therefore, when building the lobby, the use of sound insulation panels and other materials should be considered to reduce the noise. When hotel employees work and talk, their voices should be as low as possible, and sometimes they can even use some body language to communicate instead of speaking（such as hailing colleagues in the distance with hand gestures）. Work efficiency should be improved as much as possible, so that guests do not stay in the lobby for a long time during peak hours and destroy the quiet atmosphere of the lobby. The hotel should play relaxing music as much as possible to reduce the harm of noise to guests. Generally speaking, the noise in the lobby should not exceed 50 decibels, and the background music in the lobby should be 5 to 7 decibels.

［典型案例］

"开元香氛"是开元酒店的嗅觉标识，属开元酒店品牌嗅觉识别系统。"开元香氛"为开元与 air-aroma 公司于 2010 年联合研发，目前有"祺香"和"水天之吻"两种。"祺香"香氛由"海洋清风"精油调制而成，为开元旗下"开元名都"品牌酒店所采用；"水天之吻"香氛由"姜花"精油调制而成，为"开元度假村"品牌酒店所采用。"开元香氛"主要用于酒店大厅、走廊等区域，营造芳香的空气氛围，让客人体验高贵舒适，感到愉悦。

开元《和·雅音》即开元酒店原创音乐，是开元酒店听觉标识之一，属于开元酒店品牌听觉识别系统。开元《和·雅音》于 2011 年研发创立，也是国内首创的酒店原创背景音乐 12 支乐曲，由著名音乐家李志辉先生担纲主创。开元《和·雅音》很好地体现了"将东方文化与国际标准完美融合"的服务追求，也是"听"得到的开元企业文化。

[Classic Case]

The "New Century Perfume" is the olfactory identity of New Century Hotel, which is part of the brand olfactory identity system of New Century Hotel. The "New Century Perfume" was jointly developed by New Century Hotel Group and air-aroma in 2010, and there are two types of scents: "QiXiang" and "Kiss of Water and Sky" now. The "QiXiang" perfume is made from "Ocean Breeze" essential oil, which is used by Grand New Century hotels; The "Kiss of Water and Sky" perfume is made from "Ginger Flower" essential oil and is used by the "New Century Resort" hotels. The "New Century Perfume" is mainly used in the hotel lobby, corridors and other areas to create an aromatic air atmosphere, so that guests can experience noble comfort and feel happy.

New Century *Harmonious-Elegant Sound*, the original music of New Century Hotel, is one of the aural logos of New Century Hotel and belongs to the aural identification system of New Century Hotel brand. It is also the first hotel that has original background music of 12 pieces in China, which was created by the famous musician Li Zhihui. The *Harmonious-Elegant Sound* of New Century reflects the pursuit of "perfect integration of oriental culture and international standards", and is also the "audible" New Century corporate culture.

任务二　前厅工作环境优化

【案例引入】

2020 年 12 月 18 日，阿里巴巴旗下未来酒店"菲住布渴"（FlyZoo Hotel）官宣，是全球第一家支持全场景身份识别、大面积使用 AI 智能的酒店。

以往酒店办理入住的流程相对较多，不仅要签名，还要刷卡付押金。在未来酒店，客人可以通过大厅的自动入住机进行办理，要是赶时间，客人可以提前通过菲住 App

掌上办理，在线选择房间楼层、位置和朝向，关联支付宝、身份证后，对着手机镜头"眨眨眼"即可。到了退房时间，打开 App，确定好预计退房的时间，一键解决所有问题，简化了烦琐的入住和退房流程。

穿过时空通道，来到了电梯间。电梯通过无感体控系统，识别客人身份，自动开启并调至即将入住的楼层。如果想邀请朋友来访，可以通过 App 发送邀请码作为凭证。

到达房间门口，刷脸后房门自动开启。无须插卡取电，步入房间，灯光会自动进入欢迎模式，电视机自动开启，并进入欢迎界面。房间内的空调、电视、灯光、窗帘等设备全部不用手工操作，只要对着天猫精灵下达指令即可。

在未来酒店，"脸"是通行证，乘电梯、开房门、去餐厅、去健身中心，统统可以刷脸。

【任务布置】

①你对阿里未来酒店的创新有何看法？你认为满足了顾客对前厅服务的哪些要求？

②谈谈前厅服务与管理的未来发展趋势。

Task 2
Optimization of Working Environment in the Front Office

【Case Introduction】

On December 18, 2020, Alibaba's future hotel "FlyZoo Hotel" officially announced that it is the first hotel in the world that supports full-scenario identification and uses AI intelligence in a large scale.

In the past, the check-in process in a hotel was relatively long, requiring a signature and paying a deposit by card. In future hotels, guests can check in through the automatic check-in machine in the lobby. If the guest is in a hurry, he/she can check in advance through the FlyZoo App. Guests can select the floor, location and orientation of the room online. After linking Alipay and ID card, guests can "wink" at the camera of their mobile phones. When it's time to check out, guests open the App, determine the expected check-out time, and solve all the problems with one click. The tedious check-in and check-out process are simplified.

Passing through the space-time channel, guests come to the elevator room. The elevator identifies guests through a no-touch body control system, automatically opens and transfers to the floor where they will be staying. If guests want to invite friends to visit, they can send the invitation code as a voucher through the App.

When guests arrive at the door of the room, the door opens automatically after the face is scanned. There is no need to plug in the card to get electricity. When guests step into the room, the lights will automatically enter the welcome mode and the TV will automatically turn on and enter the welcome mode. The air conditioning, TV, lighting, curtains and other equipment in the room all do not need to be manually operated and the instructions can be given to the Tmall Genie.

In the future hotel, "face" is the pass. When people take the elevator, open the room door, and go to the restaurant and go to the fitness center, they can have their faces scanned.

【Assignment】

① What do you think about the innovation of Ali Future Hotel? What do you think the customer's requirements for front office services have been met?

② Talk about the future development trend of front office service and management.

随着时代的发展，以人为本、共建和谐社会已成为各国的普世观念，在这一大体的趋势下，酒店的服务和管理理念也必然与这一趋势共融，前厅部的服务与管理也将会发生一些变化。本节将从前厅部的服务方式和管理方式两个方面探讨前厅部的发展趋势。

一、前厅服务方式的发展趋势

（一）"快捷服务"成为前厅对客服务的追求目标

在各种信息变化更新、更快的时代，客人希望有更多的私人空间，入住的快捷服务和离店的快捷服务将成为大部分客人的期盼，这也对前厅员工的服务技能提出更高、更快的要求。"三分钟开房"入住和"两分钟结账"离店将会在各酒店中逐渐形成工作规程。对于顾客而言，既可以获得高效率的服务，又可以欣赏酒店员工的高素质和勤勉工作状态。

（二）入住体验由"站式"转变为"坐式"

传统酒店的总台接待是客人站立办理入住登记，员工也站立服务客人。在21世纪将有越来越多的酒店改变传统接待模式，将站式接待服务改为坐式服务。这样的转变会使长途旅行劳累的客人得到彻底放松，增加酒店的亲和力，拉近酒店与客人距离，且将商务楼层的客人待遇延展到普通客人，增加客人的满足感，而员工同样坐着为客人办理入住或结账服务，也体现和谐社会对员工的关爱。

（三）个性化服务向"共性规则"制度转变

随着"个性化"服务的普及和成熟，前厅部在未来的发展中可以将个性化服务进行规范和固化。可以将经典的个性化服务案例分类别地进行专业梳理，逐步形成规范型的各类"个性化"服务手册，如《前厅温馨服务手册》《前厅金钥匙服务手册》《前厅快捷服务手册》。将各类个性化服务的要素进一步总结，将个性化服务的案例变为系统性的"个性服务操作手册"，也就完成了"个性化"服务向"共性规则"制度化建设的转变过程，这一系统工作的产生和完成，将为酒店个性化服务的普及及实施提供可持续运作的范本。

（四）"一键通"和"一站式"的普及

总机接线员会承担多项服务职能，客人按下房间电话机上客房服务中心功能键，总机话务员接听后传递接听信息，然后交相关部门跟办，"一键通"已在很多酒店实行。随着前厅部员工素质和技能的提高，前厅部的任何一位员工都是"一站式"服务员，都可以为有需要的客人提供服务和帮助，不会由于岗位的不同而怠慢客人，客人只需要将问题向一位员工提出就可得到解决，不会遭遇搪塞、推诿现象。酒店"一条龙"服务将变成规范程序。如酒店代表在机场接客后会致电相关部门，接待处会准备客人入住资料、钥匙，在车上还有香巾、茶水服侍，在去酒店的途中酒店代表会对本地和酒店作简单介绍，金钥匙和礼宾员会在门口迎候，客人一下车会称呼其姓名并带客人登记取匙，员工会带领客人进入客房，整个过程顺畅、自然、体贴。

With the development of the times, building a people-oriented and harmonious society has become the universal concept of all countries. Under this general trend, the service and management concepts of the hotel will inevitably be in harmony with this trend. The service and management of the front office will change. This section will discuss the development trend of the front office from two aspects: the service and the management of the front office.

I The Development Trend of the Front Office Service

（1）"Quick service" has become the front office's pursuit of customer service

In an era where various information changes and updates fast, guests want more private space. Quick check-in service and quick check-out service will become the expectation of most guests, which also affect the service skills of the front office staff with higher and faster requirements. "Three minutes to check in" and "two minutes to check out" will gradually become working procedures in each hotel. For customers, they can not only get high-efficiency service but also appreciate the high quality and diligence of hotel staff.

（2）The check-in experience has changed from a "stand-style" to a "sitting-style"

In the reception of traditional hotels, guests stand to check in, while employees stand to serve guests. In the new century, more and more hotels will change the traditional reception mode, from the standing reception service to sitting service. Such a change will completely relax guests who are tired from long-distance travel, increase the affinity of the hotel, and narrow the distance between the hotel and the guests, which extends the treatment of business guests to ordinary guests, increasing the satisfaction of the guests. In addition, the employees also sit for check-in or check-out service which reflects the care of the harmonious society to its employees.

（3）Change from "personalized" services to "common rules" system

With the popularization and maturity of "personalized" services, the front office can standardize personalized services in the future. The classic personalized service cases can be sorted into categories and professionally sorted out, and gradually form a variety of standardized "personalized" service manuals, such as *Front Office Warm Service Manual*, *Front Office Golden Key Service Manual* and *Front Office Quick Service Manual*. The elements of various types of personalized services are further summarized, and individualized service cases are turned into a systematic "Personal Service Operation Manual", which completes the transformation from "personalized" services to "common rules" institutionalization. The generation and completion of a system will provide a model of sustainable operation for the popularization and implementation of personalized services in hotels.

（4）Popularization of "One-click" and "One-Stop"

The switchboard operator will take on a number of service functions. The guest presses the room service center function key on the room telephone. After the switchboard operator answers the call, the switchboard operator will pass the answering information to the relevant department for follow-up. "One-click" has been implemented in many hotels. With the improvement of the quality and skills of the front office staff, any employee in the front office department is a "one-stop" waiter, and can provide services and assistance to the guests in need, and will not neglect the guests due to different positions. Guests only need to raise their problems to an employee and they can be resolved without prevarication. The hotel's "one-stop" service will become a standardized procedure. For example, the hotel representative will call the relevant department after picking up the guests at the airport. The receptionist will prepare the guest check-in information and keys. There are scented towels and tea in the car. On the way, the hotel representative will give a brief introduction to the local area and the hotel. The bellman and the concierge will greet guests at the door. The guest will be addressed by his/her name when gets off the car. The staff will lead the guest to register and get the key, then usher guest into the room. The whole process is smooth, natural and considerate.

二、前厅管理方式的发展趋势

（一）精简机构，合理定编

前厅部的组织机构将化繁为简。人力上力求最大限度的节约，不雇用一个多余的人。酒店会根据来年预计的营业情况，重新定编。同时，充分利用社会上的专业公司为酒店服务，如将酒店外围的保安工作（正门、停车场等）交由专业的保安公司承包，将商务中心出租等，使酒店的组织机构更加精简。

（二）酒店的定价策略将更加灵活

酒店的灵活定价策略主要体现在以下两个方面：

第一，前台接待人员将得到更大的授权，根据客人及酒店的实际情况，灵活定价。为了提高前台销售人员工作的积极性，最大程度地提高酒店的经济效益，酒店会将接待人员的奖金与其每月的销售效果挂钩。

第二，越来越多的酒店将没有固定的房价，而是根据当天的开房率来定价，以创造最大的利润。但也有些酒店为了维持其档次及其在消费者中的信誉，会保持其相对固定的价格水平，不会轻易降低或提高价格。

（三）酒店预订方式网络化

未来酒店为了提高客房利用率和市场占有率，将利用包括价格在内的各种手段鼓励客人提前预订客房，客人将根据其提前预订期的长短，在房价上得到不同程度的优惠（提前期越长，优惠程度越大），而且，信息技术的发展也极大地方便了客人的预订，绝大部分客人在来酒店前将通过电话和互联网预订客房，没有预订而住店的"散客"将越来越少。其中通过电脑、手机等各种网络终端来实现客房预订已具有一定规模并必将会有更大的发展趋势。

（四）越来越多的酒店将实施"收益管理"

收益管理能够使酒店的客房等资料得到最有效的利用，使酒店管理从经验管理上升为科学管理，从而较大程度地提高酒店的经济效益。因此，越来越多的酒店前厅部将日益重视并实施收益管理。

II The Development Trend of the Front Office Management

（1）Streamline and rationalize the organization

The organization of the front office will be simplified. In terms of human resources, hotels strive for maximum savings and will not hire a redundant person. The hotel will restructure according to the expected business situation in the coming year. At the same time, they make full use of professional companies in the society to serve the hotel. For example, the security work outside the hotel（main entrance, parking lot, etc.）is contracted by a professional security company, and the business center is rented out, so that the hotel organization is more streamlined.

（2）The pricing strategy of the hotel will be more flexible

The pricing strategy of the hotel is mainly reflected in the following two aspects:

First, the receptionists will be authorized for flexible pricing based on the actual situation of the guests and the hotel. In order to increase the enthusiasm of sales in front office and maximize the economic benefits of the hotel, the hotel will link the bonus of the receptionists to their monthly performance in sales.

Second, more and more hotels will not have a fixed room rate. Hotels set prices based on the opening rate of the day in order to create the greatest profit. However, some hotels will maintain their relatively fixed price level in order to maintain their quality and reputation among consumers, and will not lower the price or raise it easily.

（3）Networking of hotel reservations

In the future, the hotel will use various methods including price to encourage guests to book rooms in advance in order to increase the room utilization rate and market share. Guests will receive different discounts on the room rate according to the length of their advance reservation period（the longer the advance period, the greater the degree of discount）. In addition, the development of information technology has greatly facilitated the reservation of guests. The vast majority of guests will book rooms through the telephone and the Internet before coming to the hotel. The walk-in guests will be less and less. Among them, room reservation through various network terminals such as computers and mobile phones has a certain scale and is bound to have a greater development trend.

（4）More and more hotels will implement "revenue management"

Revenue management can use the hotel's guest room and other information in an effective way. The hotel management can be upgraded from experience management to scientific management, improving the hotel's economic benefits to a greater extent. Therefore, more and more front offices will pay more attention and implement revenue management.

项目三

前厅部员工素质认知

【案例导入】

一位常住酒店的外国客人从外面回来，当他走到服务台，还没等他开口，接待员就主动微笑着把钥匙递上，并轻声称呼他的名字，使这位客人大为吃惊，产生了一种强烈的亲切感。

一位周姓客人在服务台高峰时进店，服务员准确地叫出："周先生，服务台有您一个电话。"这位客人又惊又喜，感到自己受到了重视，受到了特殊接待，不禁增添了一份自豪感。

此外，一位 VIP 客人随陪同人员来到前台登记，服务人员通过接机人员的暗示，得知其身份，马上称呼客人的名字，并递上打印好的登记卡请他签字，使客人感到自己的地位不同，由于受到额外尊重而感到格外开心。

Project 3

To Know the Working Requirements of the Front Office Staff

【Case Introduction】

A foreign guest who always stays in the hotel came back from outside. When he came to the service desk, before he could say anything, the receptionist handed over the key with a smile and called him by his name gently, which surprised the guest. This created a strong sense of cordiality in him.

A guest whose surname is Zhou entered the hotel at the peak hour and the receptionist called out accurately, "Mr. Zhou, there was a phone call for you at service desk." The guest was surprised and delighted, feeling that he was valued and received in a special way. He could not help but felt proud.

In addition, a VIP guest came to the front desk to register with the escort. The receptionist learned his identity through the hint of the pick-up staff, immediately called the guest's name, and handed him a printed registration card to sign, so that the guest felt himself has a different status and felt happy because of the respect.

【思考】

请分析案例中让客人产生亲切感、自豪感、格外开心的原因是什么？

【解析】

根据马斯洛需求层次理论，人们具有得到社会尊重的需求。当自己的姓名为他人所知晓，是对这种需求的一种很好的满足。在酒店及其他服务行业中，主动热情地称呼客人的名字是一种服务艺术，也是一种艺术的服务。

这也对前厅服务人员的知识、能力与素质提出了较高的要求。不管是前厅部的管理人员还是普通服务员都应努力提高自身素质，以便更好地为客人提供高质量、有针对性的服务。

【Reflection】

Please analyze what made the guest feel a sense of affection, pride and happiness in the case.

【Analysis】

According to Maslow's hierarchy of needs theory, people have the need to be respected by society. When one's name is known to others, it is a good satisfaction for this need. In hotels and other service industries, calling guests' names actively and enthusiastically is an art of service, as well as an artistic service.

This also puts forward high requirements for the knowledge, ability and quality of the front office service personnel. Whether it is the management staff of the front office department or ordinary waiters, they should strive to improve their own quality in order to better provide customers with high-quality and targeted services.

任何一家酒店前厅部员工都是该酒店形象的代表，可以说前厅服务人员的形象影响着整个酒店的服务质量和服务效果。同时，前厅人员也身兼酒店的推销员、公关员、调解员、信息资料员以及业务监督员等数职。酒店的成功经营与否，客人对酒店的第一印象、口碑，甚至是否在本店住宿往往取决于酒店前厅服务员的素质和服务态度。

因此，作为一名合格的前厅部员工，应不断地提高自己的综合素质和业务能力，酒店也应选拔素质较高且业务能力较强的员工在前厅部工作。

The front office staff is the representative of the hotel. The image of the front office staff affects the service quality and service effect of the entire hotel. At the same time, the front office staff also serve as salespersons, public relations officers, mediators, information clerks, and business supervisors in the hotel. The success of hotel, the guest's first impression of the hotel, and their willing to stay in the hotel are often determined by the performance and service attitude of the staff in the front office of the hotel.

Therefore, a qualified front office employee should continuously improve professional ability. The hotel also should select highly qualified staff with strong business skills to work in the front office department.

知识链接

目前，国内著名的酒店规定：在为客人办理入住登记时至少要称呼客人名字 3 次。前台服务人员要熟记 VIP 客人的姓名，尽可能多地了解他们的资料，同时，还可以使用电脑系统，为所有下榻的客人做好历史档案记录，把每一位客人都看成 VIP，使客人从心底感受到酒店永远不会忘记他们。

Knowledge links

At present, the famous domestic hotel stipulates that the guest's name must be called at least three times when checking in for the guest. The front desk staff should memorize the names of VIP guests and learn as much their information as possible. At the same time, they can also use the computer system to make historical records for all the guests staying, and treat each guest as a VIP, so that guests feel that the hotel will never forget them sincerely.

一、仪容仪表要求

优秀的前厅服务员，必须着装整洁、大方、面带微笑、主动热情，讲究礼仪礼貌，彬彬有礼地接待客人，而且头脑反应灵敏、记忆准确、表情自然、观察细致，注意客人动作，掌握客人心理。前厅部员工的仪表、仪容、礼仪、礼貌直接影响酒店的形象，关系服务质量、客人的心理活动，甚至影响酒店的经济效益。酒店前厅服务员首先应在仪表、仪态上给客人留下一个管理有素、经营有方的印象，从而觉得受到尊重并且感到能在这样的酒店里住宿有种自豪感，从而愿意再次光临或成为酒店的 VIP 客户。

（一）仪容要求

①员工进入公司时，发型、服装、鞋饰等应统一。

②女员工应化淡妆，朴素雅致；头发前不遮掩，后不过肩，长发后束，须用暗色发网将头发盘起；不能佩戴饰品（除婚戒外），不使用有颜色的指甲油及浓味香水等。

③男员工头发前不遮眉，后不盖领，侧不过耳，发型朴素大方，梳理整齐；无胡须。

④不得染发，定期清洗头发，每周至少两次；一般情况下，男员工应每月修剪 1～2 次头发。

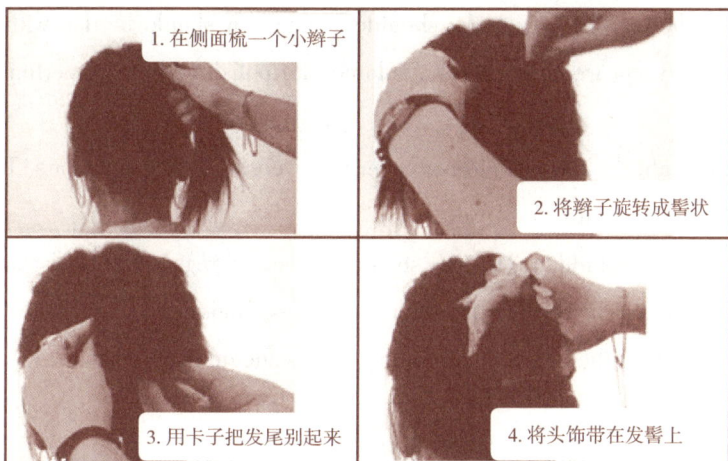

1. 在侧面梳一个小辫子
2. 将辫子旋转成髻状
3. 用卡子把发尾别起来
4. 将头饰带在发髻上

⑤注意以下情况应梳理自己的头发：

a. 上班（岗）前；

b. 进入工作区域前；

c. 摘下帽子时；

d. 参加会议或集会前；

e. 其他重要场合。

⑥梳理头发时应注意：

a. 不宜当众或当着客人的面进行；

b. 不宜徒手进行；

c. 断发、头屑不宜随手乱扔。

I　Appearance and Dress Requirements

An excellent front office staff must be neat, generous and enthusiastic, and pay attention to courtesy, receive guests politely. They should be smart, good at memory and have natural expressions and careful observation. Pay attention to guests' behavior, mastering the psychology of the guests. The appearance, etiquette, and courtesy of the front office staff directly affect the image of the hotel, the quality of service, the psychological activities of the guests, and even the economic benefits of the hotel. The staff in the front office of the hotel should leave an impression of good management in appearance and manners to guests, so that they feel respected and proud to stay in such a hotel and are willing to consume again or become hotel VIP customers.

（1）Appearance Requirements

① Employees enter the company with uniform hairstyle, clothing and shoe ornaments.

② Female employees should wear light makeup which is simple and elegant. The hair should not cover the face and reach the shoulder. Long hair should be tied with the dark hair net. Accessories（except wedding rings）, colored nail polish and strong perfume, etc. are not allowed.

③ For male staff, the hair should not cover the eyebrows, collar and ears. The hairstyle is simple and neat without beard.

④ Dyeing hair is forbidden. The hair should be cleaned regularly, at least twice a week. In general, male employees should trim their hair $1 \sim 2$ times a month.

⑤ When encounter the following cases, employees should comb the hair:

a. Before going to work;

b. Before entering the work area;

c. After taking off the hat;

d. Before attending meetings or gatherings;

e. Other important occasions.

⑥ Pay attention when combing your hair:

a. It is not suitable to comb your hair in public or in front of guests;

b. Do not comb your hair with your hands barely;

c. Broken hair and dandruff should not be thrown away casually.

1. comb your plaits

2. coil it up around your head

3. use hairpins to control hair tail

4. wear the headdress

（二）仪表要求

前厅部人员要有得体的举止，因为他们的一言一行都关系到客人对员工及酒店的印象。如在站立服务时，不得踱步、转圈、把手插入口袋或抱在胸前，以免给客人留下急促、忙乱、坐立不安的印象等。

①基本要求。

● 要面带微笑、和颜悦色，给客人以亲切感；不能面容冷漠、表情呆板，给客人以不受欢迎感。

● 要聚精会神、注意倾听，给客人以尊重之感；不要没精打采或漫不经心，给客人以不受重视之感。

● 要坦诚待客，不卑不亢，给人以真诚，不要给人以虚伪感。

● 要沉着稳重，给人以镇定感，不要慌手慌脚，给客人以毛躁感。

● 要神色坦然、轻松、自信，给人以宽慰感；不要双眉紧锁，满面愁云，给客人以负重感。

● 不要带有厌烦、僵硬、愤怒的表情，也不要扭捏作态，做鬼脸、吐舌、眨眼，给客人以不受敬重感。

②目光。

● 对初次见面的客人，应头部微微一点，行注目礼，表示尊重的礼貌。

● 在与客人交谈时，应不断通过各种目光与客人交流，调整交谈的气氛。

● 交谈中，应始终保持目光的接触。

（2）Behavior Requirements

The front office staff should have a decent behavior, because their words and actions are related to the guest's impression of the staff and the hotel. For example, when they stand for service, they are not allowed to walk, turn in circles, put hands in their pockets or hold chests, so as not to leave the impression of haste, disorder, restlessness, etc.

① Basic requirements.

● Smile and be with kind and pleasant countenance, giving guests a sense of cordiality; do not show indifferent face, dull expression, to give guests a sense of unwelcome.

● Be concentrate, listen carefully, to give guests a sense of respect; do not be listless or careless, to give guests a sense of inattention.

● Be honest rather than too humble or condescending, giving guests a sense of sincerity rather than hypocrisy.

● Be calm and steady, giving guests a sense of calm; do not be panic, giving guests a sense of fidgety.

● Be frank, relaxed, confident, giving guests a sense of relief; do not frown with bad emotions, giving guests stress.

● Do not show boredom, stiffness, or anger in your expressions, and do not squeeze, make a face, stick out the tongue or wink, giving guests a sense of disrespect.

② Eyes.

● You should nod at the guest whom you meet for the first and make a salute to show respectful courtesy.

● When talking with guests, you should constantly communicate with them through various glances to adjust the atmosphere of the conversation.

● Always maintain eye contact during conversation.

二、卫生要求

（一）面部卫生

①男员工面部保持洁净清爽，胡须剃净，鼻毛不得露出鼻孔。

②女员工需对眉毛、嘴唇做适当修饰，宜淡妆。

（二）口腔卫生

①进餐后要刷牙或漱口，如要剔牙则不能当着别人的面。

②上班前不吃葱、蒜、芥末等刺激性味道的食物。

③每天坚持刷牙 1 ~ 2 次。

（三）手部卫生

①指甲须常修剪，保持整齐、美观，不留长指甲，不涂有色指甲油。

②上班时不戴首饰（可戴婚戒）。

③手部须保持干净。

（四）个人卫生

①常洗澡，保持身体无异味。

②剧烈运动后，应洗澡后再上岗。

③不使用味道过浓的香水。

④使用香水时，应注意用量不宜过多。

（五）着装卫生

①工作时一律穿统一工作服。

②工作服要求配套完整、干净整洁、大小得体、熨烫平整，纽扣全扣好。

③男员工穿黑色或深色袜子，女员工穿肉色袜子，无破痕、抽丝。

④男女员工均穿规定的工作鞋或黑色皮鞋，并保持光亮、洁净。

⑤工号牌佩戴于左胸处，并保持洁净。

Ⅱ Hygiene Requirements

（1）Facial Hygiene

① Male employees should keep their faces clean and fresh, shave their beards, and should not let their nessal hair show outside their nostrils.

② For female employees, the eyebrows and lips should be properly groomed, and light makeup is recommended.

（2）Oral Hygiene

① Brush your teeth or rinse your mouth after eating. If you want to floss your teeth, you can't do it in front of others.

② Do not eat green onions, garlic, mustard and other pungent foods before going to work.

③ Brush your teeth 1~2 times a day.

（3）Hand Hygiene

① Nails are often trimmed to keep them neat and beautiful; do not keep long nails; do not apply colored nail polish.

② Do not wear jewelry when going to work（except wedding rings）.

③ The hands must be kept clean.

（4）Personal Hygiene

① Take a bath often to keep your body free of odor.

② After strenuous exercise, you should take a bath before going to work.

③ Do not use perfume with strong smell.

④ When using perfume, pay attention to the amount and do not to use too much.

（5）Dress Hygiene

① Wear uniforms at work.

② Work clothes are required to be complete, clean and tidy, decent in size, flat ironed, and required to be fully buckled.

③ Male employees wear black or dark socks, and female employees wear flesh-colored socks with no broken marks.

④ Male and female employees wear work shoes or black leather shoes, and keep them bright and clean.

⑤ Wear the employee's card on the left chest and keep it clean.

三、礼貌品德

（一）礼貌修养

礼貌修养是以人的德才学识为基础，是内在美的自然流露。前厅部人员应具有的礼貌修养具体表现在以下几个方面。

①言谈方面：应做到用语规范、声调柔和、语言亲切、表达得体。

②举止方面：应做到站立挺直自然，不倚不靠，行走轻快，不奔跑。

③工作作风方面：应做到朴实、谦虚、谨慎。

④服务态度方面：应做到一视同仁、不卑不亢、待人热情、分寸适度。

⑤表情方面：应做到自然诚恳，微笑服务。

（二）品行道德

前厅部员工首先必须品行端正、诚实且具有较高的修养及职业道德水平。前厅部的工作会涉及价格、现金及酒店营业机密，如果员工品行不正，就很容易利用酒店管理中的漏洞为个人谋取私利；如果员工没有良好的修养，很难提供高水平、高质量的服务。

Ⅲ　Politeness

（1）Cultivation of Politeness

The cultivation of politeness is based on a person's moral and academic knowledge, and it is a natural expression of inner beauty. The courtesies that the front office staff should have are specifically manifested in the following aspects.

① Speaking: speak standardized language with soft tones and appropriate expression.

② Behavior: stand upright and natural rather than lean; walk briskly rather than run.

③ Work style: be simple, humble and cautious.

④ Service attitude: treat guests equally, neither too humble or condescending, treating guests with enthusiasm and proportionality.

⑤ Expression: be natural and sincere with smile.

（2）Ethics

First of all, the front office staff must first be of good character, honesty, cultivation and professional ethics. The work of the front office will involve prices, cash and hotel business secrets. If the staff is not good, it is easy to use loopholes in the hotel management for personal benifit; if the staff is not well-trained, it is difficult to provide high-level and high-quality services.

【拓展知识 1】

前厅人员的礼貌用语

①欢迎语。

适用于客人刚进入酒店或营业点时；使用时语言要热情，语速稍快；语调上扬，声音清脆或轻柔。

"早上／下午／晚上好，欢迎光临！"

"欢迎入住城际快捷酒店××店！"

对于熟悉的宾客："见到您很高兴！"

对于很熟悉的宾客："非常高兴再次见到您！"

②称谓语。

语气诚恳，辅以真挚的眼神；清楚亲切、灵活恰当；不使用具有侮辱、歧视意味的称呼，如老外；在正式场合使用尊称称呼宾客。

泛尊称：男士称先生，未婚女士称小姐，已婚女士称太太或夫人，难以判断婚否时可称女士。

荣誉性称呼：以客人拥有的学位、学术头衔、专业技术头衔、军衔、爵位等称谓。如博士、教授、医生、律师、法官、将军等。

公务性称呼：以客人职务相称，如局长、部长、董事长等。

已知客人姓氏：以姓氏连同尊称一同称呼宾客，并较为频繁地使用。

特别熟的常客：以客人乐于接受的昵称、尊称称呼客人。

【To Know More 1】
Politeness Formulae for the Front Office Staff

① Welcome.

It is suitable for guests when they just enter the hotel or place of business; be enthusiastic and speak it a little faster; the intonation should be up, and the voice should be soft.

"Good morning/afternoon/evening, welcome to the hotel."

"Welcome to Intercity Express Hotel ××."

For familiar guests: "Nice to meet you!"

For very familiar guests: "I am very glad to see you again!"

② Appellation.

Use a sincere tone with sincere look; be clear, kind, flexible and appropriate; do not use insulting and discriminatory terms, such as foreigners; use honorific titles to address guests in formal occasions.

General title: Men are called Mr., unmarried women are called Miss and married women are called Mrs.. When it is difficult to judge whether they are married, they can be called Ms..

Honorary title: use the guest's degree, academic title, professional technical title, military title, knight title, etc. such as doctor, professor, physician, lawyer, judge, general, etc.

Official title: use the guest's position, such as director, minister, chairman, etc.

Known guest surnames: Address guests by their surnames and honorifics, and use them more frequently.

Particularly familiar regular guests: address guests with nicknames and honorifics that they are willing to accept.

③问候语。

使用时，表情自然、和蔼、亲切，语调平和，加上温和的微笑，并配合点头或鞠躬；与礼貌用语连用，常常根据问候时间、场地、客人状况、与客人的熟悉程度来选择；注意时间与地点的差异，若只有"先生，您好！"一句话，客人听起来会感到单调、乏味，新年到来可向客人说声"先生，新年好！"更能突出节日气氛。

对于初次见面的客人，常用标准式："您好！"

对于比较熟悉的客人，常用轻松式："近来好吗？"

对于很熟悉的客人，常用个性式或客人所喜欢的方式："××先生，您来了！"

问候多位宾客："大家好！"

根据问候的时间与地点差异："早上好！"（00:00—12:00）、"下午好！"（12:00—18:00）、"晚上好！"（18:00—24:00）。

根据客人的状况：客人身体欠安时，"您今天感觉好些了吗？"；客人比较疲惫时，"您休息得还好吗？"

④征询语。

注意客人的形体语言；用协商的口吻；应把征询当作服务的一个程序，先征询意见，得到客人同意后再行动，不可自作主张。

"请问您贵姓？"

"请问怎么称呼您？"

"请问有什么可以帮您？"

"请问我能为您做点什么？"

"请问有什么可以为您效劳的吗？"

"请问您还有其他吩咐吗？"

"请问您还满意吗？"

⑤答应语。

客人有事呼叫时：

"好的，马上就到！"

"请稍等，我马上就来。"

"好的，现在就为您办理。"

"好的，我让服务员马上给您送过去可以吗？"

客人致谢时：

"不客气，这是我们应该做的！

"很高兴为您服务！"

客人致歉时：

"不，一点都不麻烦。"

"没关系！"

③ Greeting.

Greeting guests with a natural, amiable, cordial expression, calm tone and gentle smile, and nod or bow at the same time; choose polite words according to the time, venue, guest condition, and familiarity with the guests; pay attention to the difference between time and place. If say "Sir, hello!" only, guests will feel monotonous and boring. When the New Year comes, you can say "Happy New Year, sir!", which can highlight the festive atmosphere.

For guests whom meet for the first time, the standard form is often used: "Hello!"

For well-acquainted guests, a relaxed style is often used: "How are you doing?"

For guests who are very familiar with you, you should greet them in a personalized way or in the way they prefer: "Mr. × ×, you're here!"

Greeting many guests: "Hello, everyone!"

Depending on the time and place: "Good morning!" （00:00-12:00）, "Good afternoon!" （12:00-18:00）, "Good evening!" （18:00-24:00）.

According to the condition of the guests: when the guest is not feeling well, "Do you feel better today?" When the guest is tired, "Did you have a good rest?"

④ Inquiry.

Pay attention to the body language of the guest; use the tone of negotiation; regard consultation as a procedure of service, ask for opinions first and get the guest's consent before acting.

"May I have your last name?"

"How should I call you?"

"What can I help you?"

"What can I do for you?"

"Is there anything I can do for you?"

"Is there anything else you want?"

"Are you satisfied?"

⑤ Promise.

When a guest calls for something:

"Okay, I'll be there soon!"

"Please wait a moment, I'll be right there."

"Okay, I will handle it for you now."

"Okay, I'll have the waiter bring it to you right now?"

When guests thank you:

"You're welcome. It is what we should do!"

"It's a pleasure to serve you!"

When guests apologize:

"No, it's no trouble at all."

"That's ok!"

⑥道歉语。

不能满足客人需求时应使用商量的语气。

"对不起，这个问题我暂时无法解决，我请示一下稍后给您回复好吗？"

"对不起，请稍等，我尽力帮您联系。"

"对不起，由于现在网络无法连接暂时不能打印发票，请留下您的地址和联系电话，我打印好后给您寄过去好吗？"

"实在是对不起！"

"实在抱歉！"

引发客人不满时语气必须非常诚恳。

"对不起，让您久等了！"

"很抱歉，给您添麻烦了！"

"请您原谅……"

打扰或即将打扰客人时必须轻声说。

"对不起，能否打扰一下……"

"很抱歉，打扰了！"

⑦答谢语和婉拒语。

答谢语：

客人表扬、帮忙或者提意见时，均需要使用答谢语；使用时，语气要清楚、爽快、诚恳。

"谢谢您的宝贵建议，我会转告给我们的管理层，改进我们的工作。"

"谢谢您的理解！"

"谢谢您的夸奖！"

婉拒语：

语气应客气委婉，不简单拒绝；以抱歉的口吻或感谢的语言为题头；以充足的理由为内容；以拒绝为目的。

"非常抱歉，酒店规定员工工作时不得……"

"实在对不起，我已经尽了最大的努力了，但是……"

"对不起，今晚我有一个约会，不能久陪了！"

"承蒙您的好意，但我真的……"

⑧祝福语和告别语。

祝福语：

使用时，声调上扬，语速稍快，语音清脆，表现出愉悦之情，利于缩短双方的心理距离。

祝贺时："恭喜、恭喜！""祝您生日快乐！"

节日祝贺时："新年好！""圣诞快乐！""小朋友，节日快乐！"

祝愿语："祝您住店愉快！""祝您心想事成！""祝您万事如意！"

告别语：

与客人告别时，应行注目礼，直至电梯关闭或不在客人视线内。

客人离店或送梯时："祝您一路平安！""欢迎您再次光临！"

客人起身离开时："再见！""您走好！"

⑥ Apology.

When you can't meet the needs of the guests, you should use a negotiating tone.

"I'm sorry. I can't solve this problem at the moment. May I reply to you later?"

"I'm sorry, please wait. I'll try my best to help you get in touch."

"Sorry, the invoice cannot be printed temporarily because the network is unable to connect. Please leave your address and contact number. Will I send it to you later?"

"I'm really sorry!"

The tone must be very sincere when arousing guest dissatisfaction.

"Sorry to keep you waiting!"

"I am very sorry to trouble you!"

"I beg your pardon..."

Speak softly when disturbing or being about to disturb the guests.

"I'm sorry if I can bother you..."

"Sorry to bother you!"

⑦ Acknowledgement and Decline.

Acknowledgement:

When the guests praise, help, or make comments, you need to use thank-you words; when using them, be clear and be sincere in tone of voice.

"Thank you for your valuable advice. I will pass it on to our management to improve our work."

"Thank you for your understanding!"

"Thank you for your compliments!"

Decline:

Be polite and euphemistic, do not refuse directly; use an apologetic tone or thankful language as the beginning, with sufficient reasons as the content and with rejection as the purpose.

"I'm very sorry. the hotel rules prohibit employees from... while working."

"I'm really sorry. I have tried my best, but..."

"Sorry, I have an appointment tonight. I can't stay long!"

"Thanks for your kindness, but I really..."

⑧ Blessing and Farewell.

Blessing:

When used, the tone is raised, the speaking speed is slightly faster, the voice is clear, and it shows pleasure, which is beneficial to shorten the distance between the hearts of both parties.

When congratulating: "Congratulations, congratulations!", "Happy birthday to you!"

Holiday congratulations: "Happy New Year!" "Merry Christmas!" "Boy/girl, happy holidays!"

Wish words: "Enjoy your stay!" "I wish you all the best!"

Farewell:

When saying goodbye to the guests, salute until the elevator is closed or out of sight of the guests.

When the guests leave the hotel or take off the elevator: "Wish you a safe trip!" "Welcome back!"

When the guests get up and leave: "Goodbye!" "Good luck!"

四、语言要求

优秀的前厅服务员不仅应有良好的仪容、仪表，而且还应具备优秀的语言能力、令人愉快的声调、恰当的内容和灵活策略的语言技巧。女士说话的声音要温柔、甜美，男士说话要富有磁性，这样更容易得到客人的欣赏，此外还应具备良好的语言基础。

①良好的汉语表达能力及理解能力，普通话发言应标准，音质纯美，圆润动听。

②熟练掌握一门以上的外语，并在听、说、读、写几个方面，特别是口语方面达到较好水平。

③掌握一些常用的当地方言，如广东话、闽南语等，以便更好地接待来自全国各地的客人。

Ⅳ Language Requirements

An excellent front office staff should not only have good appearance, but also a good language skill, a pleasant tone of voice, appropriate words and flexible strategy of language skills. Women's voice should be gentle and sweet, while men's voice should be magnetic, which will be more appreciated by guests. In addition, the front office staff should have a good language foundation.

① Good Chinese expression and comprehension ability. Mandarin should be standard with pure and beautiful sound.

② Master more than one foreign language, and reach a high level in several aspects of listening, speaking, reading and writing, especially in speaking.

③ Master some common local dialects, such as Cantonese, Hokkien, in order to better receive guests from all over the country.

五、能力素养

（一）应变能力

酒店在经营中也会出现各种特殊的情况，在任何情况下，前厅服务员都应沉着冷静，采用灵活多变的方法处理好每个特殊的事件。因此，优秀的前厅服务员还需具备应变能力，具有特殊服务技能与素质。因为客人来自全国各地或异国他乡，不同的生活习惯、不同的知识与修养都会有不同的表现。酒店在经营中会出现各种特殊的情况，如发生火灾、失窃、与宾客的账目纠纷等，因此只有具备较强的应变能力，才能妥善处理好这些特殊问题。

（二）业务操作技能

前厅服务员必须能够熟练、准确地按程序完成本职工作。工作的快速敏捷、准确无误也反映了酒店的管理水平。任何业务操作失误，不仅会给酒店造成经济损失，还会破坏客人对酒店的总体印象。

①人际关系能力。与同事、宾客及上级领导都应搞好关系，互相理解，互相合作，以便顺利完成工作。

②业务操作技能。动手能力强，反应敏捷，能够熟练、准确地按照操作程序完成本职工作。

（三）知识面

优秀的前厅服务员还需具备较广的知识面和丰富的专业知识，才能为客人提供旅游、风俗、文化以及相关的准确信息。这些问题通常会涉及政治、经济、旅游、风俗、文化以及有关酒店情况，前厅服务员必须对历史、地理、气候、金融、风景名胜、交通状况、异国风俗、宗教等方面的知识有较全面的了解。

V Abilities and Qualities

（1）Ability to Adapt

Various special situations may also occur in the hotel's operation. In any case, the front office staff should be calm, and use flexible and versatile methods to deal with each special event. Therefore, an excellent front office staff also need to have the ability to adapt, with special service skills and qualities. Because guests from all over the country or foreign countries, different habits, different knowledge and cultivation will develop different performance. A variety of special circumstances may occur, such as fire, theft, and guest account disputes, so only with strong ability can staff properly deal with these special issues.

（2）Business Operation Skills

The front office staff must be able to complete their jobs well in accordance with the procedures. The speed, agility and accuracy of the work also marks the hotel management level. Any business operation error will not only cause economic losses to the hotel but also destroy the overall impression of the guests to the hotel.

① Interpersonal ability. Build good relationships with colleagues, guests and supervisors, understand and cooperate with each other in order to complete the work smoothly.

② Business operation skills. Have a strong hands-on ability, quick response, be able to complete the job according to the operating procedures proficiently and accurately.

（3）Knowledge

An excellent front office staff also need to prepare a wide range of knowledge and rich professional knowledge in order to provide guests with accurate information about travel, customs, culture and related matters. These issues often involve politics, economy, tourism, customs, culture, and related hotel conditions. The front office staff must have a better knowledge of history, geography, climate, finance, scenic spots, traffic conditions, foreign customs, religions, etc.

课堂练习

推荐重庆市及周边景点。

In-class exercises

Recommend scenic spots in and around Chongqing.

（四）团队合作精神

前厅的每一位员工都应该意识到，前厅就是酒店的一个"舞台"，每个人都在扮演一个特定的角色，要想演好这场戏，需要员工的集体合作。当某一个员工忙于其他事情或因特殊情况需要离开工作岗位时，其他员工必须能够替代其工作，共同使客人满意，个人的意见或恩怨决不能表现到工作中来，否则会破坏整个酒店的形象。

（4）Teamwork Spirit

Every employee in the front office should realize that the front office is a "stage" of the hotel. Everyone is playing a specific role. To play a good show, the collective cooperation of employees is needed. When an employee is busy with other things or needs to leave the job due to special circumstances, other employees must be able to replace his/her work and satisfy the guests jointly. Personal opinions or grievances must not be expressed in the work, otherwise it will destroy the image of the entire hotel.

六、服务意识

服务意识是指酒店全体员工在与一切酒店利益相关的人或组织的交往中所体现的为其提供热情、周到、主动的服务的欲望和意识。

前厅部员工应具有良好的服务意识，随时为客人服务，并通过自己的细心观察，及时发现客人尚未提出的服务要求，并予以满足，以达到优质服务的水准。

VI　Service Consciousness

Service consciousness refers to the desire and consciousness of all hotel employees to provide warm, thoughtful and active service to all hotel-related people or organizations.

The front office staff should have good service consciousness, ready to serve the guests at any time. Through their careful observation, they should find out the service requirements that guests have not yet proposed, and meet them to achieve the standard of quality service.

知识链接

一、前厅部经理的素质要求

（1）知识要求

①掌握现代酒店经营管理知识，熟悉旅游经济、旅游地理、公共关系、经济合同等知识。

②掌握前厅部各项业务标准化操作、客房知识，了解客人心理和推销技巧。

③掌握酒店财务管理知识，懂得经营统计分析。

④熟悉涉外纪律，了解我国主要客源国的旅游法规。

⑤能熟练地掌握一门外语，阅读翻译专业文献，并能流利、准确地与外宾交流。

⑥具有一定的电脑管理知识。

⑦了解宗教常识和国内外民族习惯及礼仪要求，了解国际时事。

（2）能力要求

①能根据客源市场信息和历史资料预判用房情况，决定房价，果断接受订房协议。

②能够合理安排前厅部人员有条不紊地工作，能处理好与部门的横向联系。

③善于在各种场合与各阶层人士打交道，并能够积极与外界建立业务联系。

④能独立起草前厅部工作报告和发展规划，能撰写与酒店管理有关的研究报告。

⑤遇事沉着冷静，有自我控制能力。

⑥善于听取他人的意见，能正确评估他人的能力，能妥善处理客人的投诉。

Knowledge Link

1. Quality requirements of the front office manager

（1）Knowledge requirements

① Master the modern hotel management knowledge; be familiar with the tourism economy, tourism geography, public relations, economic contracts and other knowledge.

② Master the standardized operation of various business in the front office department and housekeeping knowledge; understand the guest psychological and sales techniques.

③ Master the knowledge of hotel property management and know the operation statistics analysis.

④ Be familiar with foreign-related discipline; understand the main source countries of China's tourism regulations.

⑤ Master a foreign language, can read and translate professional literature, and can communicate with foreign guests fluently and accurately.

⑥ Have some knowledge of computer management.

⑦ Understand general knowledge of religion, national customs and etiquette requirements at home and abroad, and international current affairs.

（2）Ability requirements

① Be able to anticipate occupancy situation based on market information and historical data, decide room rate and accept booking agreement decisively.

② Be able to arrange the front office department personnel to work in an orderly manner and be able to handle the connection with other departments.

③ Be good at dealing with people from all walks of life on various occasions and be able to establish business contacts with the outside world actively.

④ Be able to draft work reports and development plans independently for the front office department, and be able to write research reports related to hotel management.

⑤ Be calm when encounter problems, and have self-control ability.

⑥ Be good at listening to others' opinions, be able to assess others' abilities correctly, and be able to handle guest complaints properly.

二、大堂副理的素质要求

①掌握现代酒店的管理知识，特别是营业运转部门的管理知识，熟悉旅游学、旅游地理、公共关系、旅游心理学以及宗教、民俗、礼仪等方面的知识。

②熟悉酒店的运转体系，熟悉酒店的各项政策及管理规定，了解酒店安全和消防方面的规章制度、处理程序及应急措施。

③具有高度的责任心和服务意识，为人正派，热情大方，办事稳重。

④有较强的应变能力、组织指挥能力和是非判断能力，能独立处理较复杂的紧急问题。

⑤能处理好人际关系，善于与人交往。

⑥有较好的外语口语表达能力和文字表达能力，能流利准确地使用外语与客人交流。

⑦具有从事酒店工作5年以上的经验，有在一两个前台运转部门（特别是前厅部）基层管理工作的经历。

⑧仪表端庄，风度、气质良好。

2. Quality requirements of the lobby assistant manager

① Master modern hotel management knowledge, especially business operation department management knowledge；be familiar with tourism, tourism geography, public relations, tourism psychology, religion, folklore, etiquette, etc.

② Be familiar with the hotel's operating system, the hotel's various policies and management regulations, and understand the hotel's safety and fire protection regulations, handling procedures and emergency measures.

③ Have a high sense of responsibility and service consciousness; be decent, enthusiastic and generous, and act steadily.

④ Have a strong ability to respond, organize and command, and judge right from wrong; be able to deal with more complex emergency issues independently.

⑤ Be able to handle interpersonal relationships well and be good at interacting with others.

⑥ Have good oral and written expression skills in foreign languages, and be able to communicate with guests in foreign languages fluently and accurately.

⑦ Have more than five years of experience in hotel work, and have one or two management experience in front office operations（especially the front desk）.

⑧ Have good appearance and good manners.

三、主管（或领班）的素质要求

①比较系统地掌握旅游经济、旅游地理和主要客源国的民俗礼仪及现代酒店管理知识。

②能坚持原则，敢于负责，作风正派，办事公道，在工作中的各个方面都能起表率作用。

③受过严格的操作训练，精通业务，熟练掌握服务技能和技巧，并能带领全体员工共同完成客房销售和对客服务任务。

④有较好的外语口头表达能力和文字表达能力，能流利、准确地使用外语与宾客对话。

⑤善于处理人际关系，会做思想工作，关心本班组员工的合理要求和切身利益。

⑥有处理各种突发事件的应变能力。

⑦仪表端正，气质好。

3. Quality requirements of the supervisor（foreman）

① Master the tourism economy, tourism geography, folk customs and etiquette of the main source countries and modern hotel management knowledge more systematically.

② Adhere to principles, dare to be responsible, decent and fair, and can play an exemplary role in all aspects of work.

③ Receive strict operation training, be proficient in business, service skills and techniques, and can lead all employees to complete room sales and customer service tasks.

④ Have good oral and written expression skills in foreign languages, and be able to use foreign languages fluently and accurately to talk to guests.

⑤ Be good at handling interpersonal relationships, be able to do ideological work, and care about the reasonable requirements and vital interests of the employees in the team.

⑥ Have the ability to deal with various emergencies.

⑦ Have presentable appearance and good temperament.

【拓展知识2】

酒店人员应注意的礼节

一、握手礼

行握手礼时，与客人距离一步远，上身稍向前倾，两足立正，伸出右手，四指并齐，拇指张开朝上，轻微一握，礼毕，松开。

➤握手时讲究先后秩序，应由主人、年长者、身份高者、女士先伸手，同客人握手时，必须由客人主动伸出手后，我们才伸手与之相握。

➤与女士握手时，不要满手掌相触，轻握手指部位即可。

➤一般情况下，行握手礼时，双方应脱下手套，男士还应摘下帽子。

➤行握手礼时，要双目注视对方的眼、鼻、口，微笑致意并说些问候及祝贺语，握手时切忌看着第三者。

➤在迎送客人时，不要因客人多、熟人多就图省事，做交叉式握手。

➤和初次见面的女士、小姐，通常不握手，而行鞠躬礼。

➢ 如手上有疾病、有污渍或刚从洗手间出来，可向客人说明，请他原谅，不行握手礼。

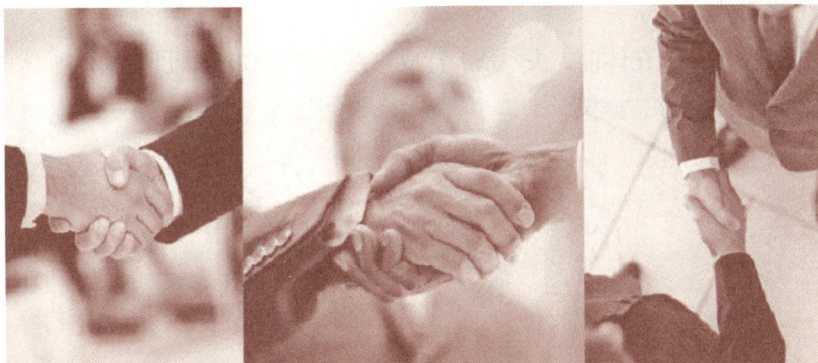

【To Know More 2】
Etiquette for Hotel Staff

I   Handshake

When handshaking hands, be a step away from the guest, lean forward slightly, stand upright with both feet, stretch out your right hand with four fingers together and thumbs up, shake slightly, and release.

➢ Pay attention to the order of handshake. The host, the elderly, the high-status, and the lady should stretch out the hands first. When shaking hands with the guests, the guests must actively stretch out their hands before we reach out and shake them.

➢ When shake hands with the lady, don't touch the palms all over, just lightly shake the fingers.

➢ In general, when shaking hands, both sides should take off their gloves, and men should also take off their hats.

➢ When shaking hands, look at each other's eyes, nose, and mouth, smile and say greetings and congratulations, and avoid looking at the third party when shaking hands.

➢ When welcoming and setting off guests, don't cross handshake just because there are too many guests and acquaintances.

➢ When meeting the lady or girl for the first time, usually bow instead of shaking hands.

➢ If you have a disease or a stain on your hands, or you just come out of the restroom, you can explain to the guest and ask him to forgive you for not shaking hands.

二、鞠躬礼

● 15°鞠躬礼

站立，双手交叉放在体前，头、颈、背成直线，前倾15°，目光约落于体前

1.5 m 处，再慢慢抬起，注视对方，微笑。

● 30° 鞠躬礼

站立，双手交叉放在体前，头、颈、背成直线，前倾 30°，目光约落于体前 1 m 处，再慢慢抬起，注视对方，微笑。

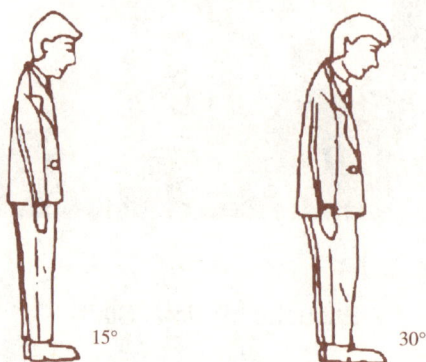

Ⅱ Bowing

● 15-degree bowing

Stand with arms folded in front of the body, head and neck in a straight line, leaning forward 15 degrees, and gaze about 15 meters in front of the body, then slowly lift up, look at the other person, and smile.

● 30-degree bowing

Stand with arms folded in front of the body, head and neck in a straight line, leaning forward 30 degrees, and gaze about 1 meters in front of the body, then slowly lift up, look at the other person, and smile.

三、人际交往的距离

亲密区：0.15 ～ 0.46 m

个人区：0.46 ～ 1.2 m

交往区：1.2 ～ 3.6 m

公众区：3.6 m 之外

前厅部员工与客人交流的有效距离：0.8 ～ 1 m

Ⅲ The Social Distance

Intimate zone: 0.15 – 0.46 meters

Personal zone: 0.46 – 1.2 meters

Interaction zone: 1.2 – 3.6 meters

Public area: 3.6 meters away

Effective distance of communication between the front office staff and guests: 0.8~1 meters.

实训任务

前厅部人员素质要求对表自查。请填写以下表格，确认是否达到前厅部人员的素质能力标准。

课堂小结

员工的素质是酒店的核心软实力，关系到酒店的服务水平和声誉。前厅部员工与客人的接触最为频繁，所以前厅部员工的素质更是酒店的窗口与招牌。作为未来的酒店人，同学们需要从各个方面提升自身的素质，以便更好地服务客人和酒店，为自身的职业生涯打下坚实的基础。

前厅部人员素质要求对标自查表

班级		姓名		学号

序号	素质要求	自查达标程度（100%）	自查不足问题（3～5点）	改进措施（对应不足）
1	仪容仪表要求		1	1
			2	2
			3	3
			4	4
			5	5
2	卫生要求		1	1
			2	2
			3	3
			4	4
			5	5

续表

序号	素质要求	自查达标程度（100%）	自查不足问题（3～5点）	改进措施（对应不足）
3	语言要求		1	1
			2	2
			3	3
			4	4
			5	5
4	礼貌品德要求		1	1
			2	2
			3	3
			4	4
			5	5
5	能力素养要求		1	1
			2	2
			3	3
			4	4
			5	5
6	服务意识要求		1	1
			2	2
			3	3
			4	4
			5	5

课后思考

你认为前厅部的工作人员应该具备怎样的基本素质？

参考解析

业务熟练；热情待客；语言能力；协调能力；沟通能力；理解能力；把握自己的能力；时刻保持精力充沛和微笑。

Tasks

Self-check the quality requirements of the front office personnel against the table. Please fill in the following form to confirm whether you meet the quality and ability standards of front office personnel.

In-class Summary

The quality of hotel staff is the core soft power of the hotel, which is related to the service level of the hotel and the reputation of the hotel. The front office staff has the most frequent contact with the guests, so the quality of the front office staff is the window and signature of the hotel. As future hotel professionals, students need to improve their own quality from all aspects, in order to better serve the guests and hotel, and lay a solid foundation for their career.

Form of Requirements on the Front Office

Class			Name	Student ID
No.	Requirements	Standards（100%）	Problems (At least 3-5)	Improvements
1	Appearance Requirement		1	1
			2	2
			3	3
			4	4
			5	5
2	Cleaning Requirement		1	1
			2	2
			3	3
			4	4
			5	5
3	Language Requirement		1	1
			2	2
			3	3
			4	4
			5	5
4	Politeness Requirement		1	1
			2	2
			3	3
			4	4
			5	5
5	Ability Requirement		1	1
			2	2
			3	3
			4	4
			5	5
6	Service Requirement		1	1
			2	2
			3	3
			4	4
			5	5

Thinking after Class

What kind of basic qualities do you think the front office staff should possess?

Reference Analysis

Business proficiency; hospitality; language skills; coordination skills; communication skills; understanding ability; ability to grasp oneself; always keeping energetic and smiling.

工作领域二　前厅客人服务工作

Work Area Ⅱ　The Front Office Guest Service Work

》 Learning Objectives

项目一
前厅客人服务工作

【思政目标】

培养学生热爱祖国的家国情怀，培养学生爱岗敬业的职业道德，树立"顾客为本、服务至诚"的核心价值观。

【能力目标】

①能够为客人提供标准化、高效的客房预订服务。

②能够设计客房预订单、客房预订确认函等表单。

③能够控制好超额预订数。

④能够有效处理预订失约。

⑤能够运用一定的方法和技巧正确处理订房纠纷。

Project 1
The Front Office Guest Service Work

【Political Objectives】

To cultivate students' awareness of their love for the motherland, their professional ethics and the core values of "customer-oriented and sincere service".

【Ability Goals】

① Be able to provide standardized and efficient room reservation service for guests.

② Be able to design room reservation forms, room reservation confirmation letters, etc.

③ Be able to control overbooking.

④ Be able to deal with reservation failure effectively.

⑤ Be able to use certain methods and skills to handle reservation disputes correctly.

【案例导入】

5月15日23:55，M公司的预订客人钟先生到前台要求办理入住手续，因客房已满，未能安排客人入住。客人对此非常不满，并称他的飞机21:00才从上海飞往广州，故到店时间肯定已过23:00，而他是酒店的常客，未有预订不到的不良记录，对于晚到而不为他保留房间，钟先生很失望，并表示回到公司会投诉。

当值大堂经理向当值接待员了解情况时，据当值接待员讲，客人的订单确认最晚到达时间为23:00，在最后到达时间过后，钟先生仍未到店。而当晚亦有相当多的未预订客人要求入住，且在23:00—23:53在多次联系钟先生未果的情况下，直至23:53，在客人的一再要求下，决定将剩余的一间客房出售给客人，所以未能满足钟先生的预订服务。

【问题】

①如何解决此投诉?

②今后如何避免类似的事情发生?

在经营管理与服务的过程中，经常会碰到公司利益之间出现冲突的情况。在此案例中，客人是M公司的员工，他事先有非保证性预订，但由于他到店时间比房间预留时间晚了近一个小时，在此期间，多次有散客要求入住，但考虑到钟先生未有预订未到的记录，接待员一直为其保留房间，直到近一个小时后，才将房间出售给强烈要求入住的散客，对于这种情况我们一定要慎重处理，稍有不慎，可能会影响与M公司的合作关系。

【处理】

①诚恳地向客人道歉，并向客人解释清楚整件事情的经过及情况。

②站在客人的角度理解客人，并积极为客人寻找解决办法，尽量在酒店内想办法安排客人入住。如果酒店内实在安排不了，在征得客人同意的前提下，就近安排同星级的酒店。

③再次向客人致歉，并提出今后避免此类事件发生的措施。如让客人留下能方便联系的通信方式，及时与客人沟通。

④做好客人档案记录，以便能为客人提供更优质的服务。

【Case Introduction】

At 23:55 pm on May 15, Mr. Zhong whose room was booked by Company M, asked to check in at the front desk, but the guest could not be accommodated because the room was full. The guest was very dissatisfied, and said his flight from Shanghai to Guangzhou at 21:00 pm, so the arrival time must have been after 23:00. He is a regular guest of the hotel with no bad record. For hotel's not keeping a room for him because of late arrival, Mr. Zhong expressed disappointment, and said he would make a complaint when he went back to the company.

When the lobby manager on duty asked the on-duty receptionist to understand the situation. According to the receptionist on duty, the latest confirmed arrival time of the guest's order was 23:00 p.m. After the last arrival time, Mr. Zhong still had not arrived at the hotel. There were many unreserved guests requesting to stay that night, and after several unsuccessful connections with Mr. Zhong during 23:00-23:53 that night. The receptionist decided to sell the remaining room to another guest at 23:53 after repeated requests from other guests. It failed to meet Mr. Zhong's reservation service.

【Questions】

① How to resolve this complaint?

② How to avoid similar things in the future?

In the process of business management and service, we often encounter situations where the interests of the company conflict with each other. In this case, the guest was an employee of IBM, and he had a non-guaranteed reservation in advance. Because he arrived almost an hour later than the reserved time for the room, during this period, there were several requests from walk-in guests to stay. Considering that Mr. Zhong did not have a record of not arriving for the reservation, the receptionist kept the room for him until almost an hour later, and then sold the room to the walk-in guests who strongly requested to stay. We must handle this carefully, because a slight mistake may affect the partnership with Company M.

【Handling】

① Sincerely apologize to the guest, and explain clearly to the guest the whole thing and the situation.

② Understand the guest from his perspective and actively look for solutions for the guest. Try to find ways to arrange for the guest to stay in the hotel. If it cannot be arranged, with the consent of the guest, arrange the nearest hotel with the same star.

③ Apologize to the guest again and propose measures to avoid such incidents in the future. For example, ask for guest's contact details and communicate with the guest in a timely manner.

④ Make a good record of the guest file so that we can provide better service for our guests.

知识链接 1

客房预订认知

前厅部是酒店组织客源、销售客房商品、组织接待和对客服务，并对客人提供各种综合服务的部门，是整个酒店业务活动的中心，是酒店销售部门及总经理做出经营决策的最高参谋机构。前厅部又称客务部、前台部、大堂部，是酒店对外的窗口，是酒店的大脑和神经中枢，是联系客人的桥梁和纽带，是酒店管理的关键部门，其直接影响酒店的整体服务质量和管理水平、经济效益和市场形象。前厅部的管理体系、工作程序，前厅部及其员工的服务质量、职业道德、知识结构、操作技能、应变能力、语言能力和言谈举止等，无一不影响酒店的形象和声誉。

前厅部的首要功能是销售客房，销售客房的数量和达成的平均房价，是衡量其工作绩效的一项重要的客观标准。

客房预订（Room Reservation）就是客人在抵店前对酒店客房的预先订约，酒店则根据客房的可供状况，为其在某一段时间内保留客房所履行的手续，也叫订房。客房预订是客房商品销售的中心环节。这种预订一经酒店确认，酒店与客人之间便达成了一种具有法律效力的预期使用客房的协议，酒店有义务根据预订的价格、房型为客人提供所需的客房。所以，预订部已向客人确定的房间，包括房价，是酒店对客人的重要承诺，应按规定保留至最后期限，否则，就要失信于客人。孟子曾说："诚者，天之道也；思诚者，人之道也。"不管是酒店还是客人，一旦预订达成，都应当遵守承诺。履行诺言是人与人交往最基本的原则。酒店一般都在前厅部设有预订处或预订部，专门受理客房的预订业务。有的酒店根据自身需要在销售部也设有预订处，专门负责受理包括客房、餐饮、会议等各方面的预订业务。

Knowledge link 1

To Know Room Reservation

The front office department is the department of the hotel that organizes guest sources, sells guest room products, organizes reception and customer service, and provides various comprehensive services for guests. It is the center of the entire hotel's business activities. It is the hotel's sales department and general manager to make business decisions of highest staff. The front office department, also known as the customer service department, front desk department, and lobby department, is the window of the hotel to the outside world, the hotel's brain and nerve center, the bridge and link that connects guests, and the key department of hotel management, which directly affects the overall service quality and management level, economic efficiency and market image. The management system and work procedures of the front office department, the service quality, professional ethics, knowledge structure, operation skills, adaptability, language ability and manners of the front office department and its employees all affect the image and reputation of the hotel.

The primary function of the front office department is to sell rooms. The number of rooms sold and the average price reached are important objective criterion for measuring its work performance.

Room Reservation is the pre-booking of hotel rooms by the guest before arrival. The hotel reserves the room for a certain period of time according to the status of the room, which is also called reservation. Room reservation is the central link of room merchandise sales. Once this kind of reservation is confirmed by the hotel, the hotel and the guest have reached a legally binding agreement on the expected use of the room. The hotel is obliged to provide the guest with the required room based on the booked price and room type. Therefore, the room that the reservation department has confirmed to the guest, including the room rate, is an important commitment of the hotel to the guest. It should be kept until the deadline according to the regulations, otherwise, it will be distrustful to the guest. Mencius once said: "Sincerity is the way of Heaven. The attainment of sincerity is the way of men." For both hotels and guests, once the reservation is made, the promise should be kept. Keeping promises is the most basic principle of human relations. Hotels generally have a reservation office department or reservation department in the front office department, which specializes in handling guest room reservations. Some hotels also have a reservation office in the sales department according to their own needs, which is responsible for accepting reservations in various aspects including guest rooms, catering, and conferences.

一、客房预订的意义

（一）客房预订适应现代旅游者的需求

旅游者在出行前通常都会安排好自己的行程，其中最重要的环节就是自己下榻处所的安排。因为酒店就是客人的"家外之家"，有了这个"家外之家"，客人才会觉得安稳和踏实，酒店开展预订业务，正好满足了客人这一基本需求，使他们免遭酒店客满或自己所能接受客房已售完的风险，保证他们能及时入住理想的房间。

（二）客房预订适应现代酒店管理的需求

受理客人的客房预订是酒店一项重要的市场销售手段，科学的预订系统能为酒店提供长期的、稳定的客源。同时，有利于酒店更好地掌握客源动态，预测酒店未来业务，在激烈的酒店竞争中掌握主动权。通过客房预订，酒店可以预先了解客人的个人相关信息，事先做好对客服务的准备和协调，为客人提供有针对性的服务；也可以使酒店掌握未来一定时段内的业务量情况，合理安排各部门和各岗位的人力、物力资源，以及协调各部门业务，从而提高工作效率和服务质量。

I　The Significance of Room Reservation

（1）Room reservation adapts to the needs of modern travelers

Travelers usually arrange their own itinerary before traveling, the most important part of which is the arrangement of their own place to stay. Because the hotel is the guests' "home away from home", with this "home away from home", the guests will feel safe and sound. The hotel reservation business meets the basic needs of the guests, so that they are protected from the hotel being full or the risk of rooms being sold out and ensure they can stay in the ideal room in time.

（2）Room reservation meets the needs of modern hotel management

Accepting the guest room reservation is an important marketing tool for the hotel and scientific reservation system can provide the hotel with a long-term, stable source of customers. At the same time, it is helpful for the hotel to better grasp the customer source dynamics, predict the hotel's future business, and seize the initiative in the fierce hotel competition. Through room reservation, the hotel can know the personal information of the guests in advance, prepare and coordinate the guests service in advance, and provide targeted service for the guests; it can also make the hotel master the business volume in a certain period of time in the future, reasonably arrange the human and material resources of each department and each post, as well as coordinate the business of each department, so as to improve the work efficiency and service quality.

二、客房预订的任务

酒店的预订处是服务于客人的超前部门。其工作任务主要有接受、处理客人的订房要求，记录、储存预订资料，检查、控制预订过程，完成客人抵店前的各项准备工作。

（一）接受、处理客人的订房要求

酒店的预订处负责酒店的订房业务，接受客人以电话、网络、传真或面谈等方式的预订，并受理客人的各种订房要求。

（二）记录、储存预订资料

酒店的预订处不仅要记录和储存预订资料，还要制订预订报表（包括每月、半月、每周和翌日客人抵达的预报），参与制订全年客房的预订计划。

（三）检查、控制预订过程

酒店的预订处要规范酒店预订的服务流程，保证准确、及时地提供预订服务，向其他相关部门传递预订信息，提高酒店的服务质量，达到最佳的经济效益。

（四）完成客人抵店前的各项准备工作

前台预订与接待要密切联系，及时向前厅部经理以及其他相关部门提供有关客房的预订资料和数据，向上级提供 VIP 抵店的信息，以便酒店提前做好客人抵店前的各项准备工作，比如人员的安排、设施设备的更新或更换、客房的布置等。

II　The Tasks of Room Reservations

The hotel's reservation office is the advance department that serves guests. Its main tasks include accepting and dealing with guests' reservation requirements, recording and storing reservation information, checking and controlling the reservation process, completing various preparations before guests arrive in the hotel.

（1）Accept and deal with guests' reservation requirements

The hotel's reservation office is responsible for the hotel's room reservation business, accepting reservations made by guests via telephone, Internet, fax, or face-to-face meetings, and accepting all kinds of room reservation requirements from guests.

（2）Record and store reservation information

The hotel's reservation office not only records and stores reservation information, but also makes reservation reports（including monthly, semi-monthly, weekly, and next day guest arrival forecasts）, participates in making annual room reservation plans.

（3）Check and control the booking process

The hotel's reservation office shall standardize the hotel reservation service process, ensure accurate and timely provision of reservation services, transmit reservation information to other relevant departments, improve hotel service quality, and achieve the best economic benefits.

（4）Complete various preparations before guests arrive at the hotel

The front desk reservation and reception should be in close contact, promptly provide the front office manager and other relevant departments with the reservation information and data about the room, and provide the supervisors with VIP arrival information, so that the hotel can make all the preparations before the guest arrives in advance, such as the arrangement of personnel, the renewal or replacement of facilities and equipment, the layout of guest rooms, and so on.

三、客房的种类和价格

（一）客房的种类

一般酒店的客房种类设置大概有如下几种。

①单人间。

单人间的面积通常为 16 ～ 20 m²，内由卫生间和其他附属设备组成，房内设一张单人床。

②标准间。

房内设两张单人床的叫标准间，这样的房间适合住两位客人，适合旅游团体或会议团体使用。

③大床间。

大床间的房内设一张双人床，这样的房间适合夫妻同住。

④豪华间 / 高级间。

豪华间 / 高级间的房内设两张单人床或一张双人床，房间的面积、装修、房内设施比普通标准间和大床间档次高，价格也高一些。

⑤商务间。

商务间的房内设两张单人床或一张双人床，房内设施设备的配备考虑了商务客人的需求。

⑥行政间。

行政间的房内多为一张双人床，此类型房间单独为一楼层，并配有专用的商务中心、咖啡厅等，属于酒店中档次较高的客房类型。

⑦普通套间。

普通套间由两间或两间以上的房间组成。

⑧豪华套间。

豪华套间是指房间数量或面积较普通套间多或大的房间，装潢精美，设备高档，功能齐备，价格也较普通套间高。

⑨总统套间。

总统套间是最高级的客房，装饰讲究、造价昂贵，是酒店实力与档次的象征，甚至还是一个城市、一个地区接待能力的体现，通常由 5 个以上房间组成。

部分酒店也会根据其所处的地理位置推出海景房、山景房、江景房等，或根据房间的特性来命名，但一般房内配置不会发生太大变化，如海景房或山景房基本属于豪华间的范围。

Ⅲ　Types and Prices of Guest Rooms

（1）Types of guest rooms

The general hotel room types are set as follows.

① Single room.

The area of single room is usually $16 \sim 20$ square meters, with a bathroom and other ancillary equipment, and a single bed in the room.

② Standard room.

A room with two single beds is called a standard room, which is suitable for two guests and for tourist groups or conference groups.

③ Queen room.

The room with a double bed is suitable for couples to stay together.

④ Deluxe room/Superior room.

There are two single beds or a double bed in the room. The size, decoration and facilities of the room are higher than ordinary standard rooms and double rooms, and the price is also higher.

⑤ Business room.

The rooms are equipped with two single beds or a double bed, and the facilities and equipment in the rooms take into account the needs of business guests.

⑥ Executive room.

There is a double bed in it mostly. This type of room is on a separate floor equipped with a dedicated business center, coffee shop, etc., which belongs to the higher room type in the hotel.

⑦ Ordinary suite.

It is composed of two or more rooms.

⑧ Luxury suite.

The number or area of rooms is more or larger than that of ordinary suites, with exquisite decoration, high-grade equipment and complete functions, and higher prices than ordinary suites.

⑨ Presidential suite.

Presidential suite is the most advanced guest rooms, which is exquisitely decorated and expensive. They are a symbol of the strength and class of the hotel, and even the embodiment of the reception ability of a city or a region. It usually consists of more than five rooms.

Some hotels will also launch sea-view rooms, mountain-view rooms, river-view rooms, etc. according to their geographic location. Some name the room according to the characteristics of the room, but the general room configuration will not change much, such as sea-view rooms or mountain-view rooms. The room basically belongs to the scope of deluxe room.

（二）客房的价格

①标准价。标准价又称牌价、门市价、散客价，即在酒店价目表上明码公布的各类客房的现行价格，该价格不含任何服务费或折扣等因素。

②商务合同价。商务合同价是指酒店与有关公司或机构签订房价合同，并按合同规定向对方客人以优惠价格出租客房，以求双方长期合作。房价的优惠幅度视对方能够提供的客源量及客人在酒店的消费水平而定。

③团队价。团队价主要是针对旅行社的团队客人而定的折扣价格，其目的是与旅行社建立长期良好的业务关系，确保酒店长期、稳定的客源，提高客房利用率。团队价格可根据旅行社的重要性和所能组织的客源的多少以及酒店淡旺季客房利用率的不同而定。为了吸引团队客人，很多酒店给予团队客人的优惠价往往低于酒店标准价的50%。

④白天租用价。在下列情况下，酒店可按白天租用价向客人收取房费：客人凌晨抵店入住；客人离店超过了酒店规定的时间；入住与退房发生在同一天。大部分酒店

的白天租用价按半天房费收取，也有些酒店按小时收取。

⑤折扣价。折扣价是指酒店向常客或长住客或其他有特殊身份的客人提供优惠房价。

⑥家庭租用价。家庭租用价是指酒店为带小孩的父母提供的优惠价。

⑦免费。出于各种原因，酒店有时需要为某些特殊客人提供免费房。免费房的使用，通常只有总经理才有权批准。

⑧小包价。小包价是酒店为客人提供的一种报价方式，除房费外，还包括餐费、交通费、游览费（或其中的某几个项目）等，以方便客人。

⑨淡季价。淡季价是指在营业淡季，为了刺激消费，提高客房利用率，而为普通客人提供的折扣价。通常是在标准房价的基础上，下浮一定的百分比。

⑩旺季价。旺季价是指在营业旺季，为了最大程度地提高酒店的经济效益，而将房价在标准房价的基础上，上浮一定的百分比。

⑪团购价。团购价是随着电子商务的发展而兴起的，通过客人自行组团、专业团购网站、酒店组织团购等形式，提升客人与酒店的议价能力，并极大程度地获得房价让利。团购价实际就是根据薄利多销、量大价优的原理获得的折扣价。现在团购的主要方式是网络团购。

（2）Room Rates

① Standard price. The standard price is also known as the card price, market price, casual guest price, that is, current price of various guest rooms clearly announced on the hotel price list, and the price does not include any service fees or discounts and other factors.

② Business contract price. The business contract price refers to the hotel and the relevant companies or institutions signed a room rate contract, and the hotel rents rooms to each other's guests at a preferential price in accordance with the provisions of the contract, in order to seek long-term cooperation between the two parties. The extent of the room rate discounts depending on the number of customers that the other party can provide and the level of consumption of the guests in the hotel.

③ Team price. The team price is mainly a discounted price for the group guests of the travel agency. The purpose is to establish long-term good business relations with the travel agency, ensure long-term, stable source of customers and improve the utilization rate of rooms. Team price can be determined according to the importance of the travel agency and the number of guests that can be organized as well as the difference in the utilization rate of the hotel's rooms in the off-peak and peak seasons. In order to attract team guests, many hotels give team guests preferential price which is often less than 50% of the standard hotel price.

④ Daytime rental price. In the following cases, the hotel can charge the guests according to the daytime rental price: guests arrived in the early morning to stay; guests left the hotel more than the time specified by the hotel; check-in and check-out occurred on the same day. Most hotels charge half room rates during the day, and some hotels charge by the hour.

⑤ Discount price. The discount price refers to the hotel's preferential rates to regular or long-stay guests or other guests with special status.

⑥ Family rental rate. The family rental rate refers to the fact that the hotel offers a special rate for parents with children.

⑦ Free. For various reasons, hotels sometimes need to provide free rooms for certain special guests. The use of free rooms, usually only the general manager is authorized to approve.

⑧ Small package price. The small package price is a way of quotation provided by the hotel for guests. In addition to the room rate, it also includes meal expenses, transportation expenses, tour expenses（or some of these items）, etc., for the convenience of guests.

⑨ Off-season price. The off-season price is a discounted rate offered to regular guests during the low season of business in order to stimulate comsumption and improve room utilization, which is down a certain percentage based on the standard room rate.

⑩ Peak season price. Peak season price refers to the fact that in the peak season, in order to maximize the economic benefits of the hotel, the room rode is increased by a certain percentage on the basis of the standard price.

⑪ Group purchase price. Group purchase price rises with with the development of e-commerce. Through the guest group, professional group purchase website, hotel organization group purchase and other forms, the bargaining power between guests and the hotel is improved, and the price concession is greatly obtained. The group purchase price is actually the discount price obtained according to the principle of small profit and large quantity and good price. Now the main way of group purchase is network group purchase.

四、客房预订的渠道

（一）直接渠道

直接渠道是指客人或客户不经任何中间环节直接向酒店订房。客人通过直接渠道订房，酒店所耗成本相对较低，且能对订房过程进行直接有效的控制与管理。

直接渠道的订房大致有下列几类。

①客人本人或委托他人、单位直接向酒店预订客房。

②旅游团体或会议组织者直接向酒店预订客房。

③旅游中间商作为酒店的直接客户向酒店批量预订房间。

（二）间接渠道

间接渠道是指订房人由旅行社等中介机构代为办理订房手续。对酒店而言，将客房直接销售给消费者是最理想的选择，但是由于受到人力、资金、时间等的限制，酒店自身往往无法直接进行规模化的、有效的销售活动。因此，酒店往往通过利用中间商的专业特长、经营规模、与客源市场的联系等优势，实现更广泛、更顺畅、更快速的销售酒店客房的目的。

间接渠道订房大致有下列几类。

①通过旅行社订房。

②通过携程、同程、艺龙等国内在线旅游电商订房。

③通过连锁酒店或合同酒店订房。

④通过航空公司及其他交通运输公司订房。

⑤通过会议及展览组织机构订房。

Ⅳ　Channels for Room Reservation

（1）Direct channels

Direct channel means that guests or customers directly make reservations to the hotel without any intermediate links. When guests book rooms through direct channel, the cost of the hotel is relatively low, and the reservation process can be directly and effectively controlled and managed.

There are roughly the following types of direct channel reservations.

① The guest or their entrusted person/the commissioned unit books rooms directly with the hotel.

② Tourist groups or conference organizers directly book rooms directly with the hotel.

③ As a direct customer of the hotel, travel brokers book rooms in batches from the hotel.

（2）Indirect channels

Indirect channel means that the booker is handled by intermediary agencies such as travel agencies for the reservation procedures. For hotels, directly selling guest rooms to consumers is the most ideal choice. However, due to the constraints of manpower, capital, and time, the hotel itself is often unable to directly carry out large-scale and effective sales activities. Therefore, hotels often make use of the advantages of intermediaries, such as professional expertise, scale of operations, and connections with source markets, to achieve the goal of selling hotel rooms more extensively, smoothly, and faster.

There are roughly the following types of indirect channel reservations.

① Book a room through a travel agency.

② Make room reservations through domestic online travel e-commerce companies such as Ctrip, Tongcheng, and eLong.

③ Book a room through a chain or a contract hotel.

④ Book rooms through airlines and other transportation companies.

⑤ Make room reservations through conference and exhibition organizations.

五、客房预订的方式

客房预订的方式多种多样，各有特点。客人采用何种方式，受预订的紧急程度和预订设备条件的制约。

客人常采用的预订方式主要有下列几种。

（一）电话订房

电话订房是客人通过电话向酒店订房，这种方式应用最为广泛，尤其适用于离预期抵店日期较短的情况。其优点是直接、迅速、清楚地传递双方信息，可当场回复客人的订房要求。

（二）面谈订房

面谈订房是客人亲自到酒店与预订员面对面地洽谈订房事宜。这种订房方式能使预订员有机会详细地了解客人的需求，并当面解答客人提出的问题，有利于推销酒店产品。

与客人面谈订房事宜时应注意：

①仪表端庄、举止大方，讲究礼节礼貌，态度热情，语音、语调适当而婉转。

②把握客人的心理，运用销售技巧，灵活地推销客房和酒店其他产品。必要时，还可向客人展示房间及酒店其他设施与服务，以供客人选择。

③受理此方式预订时，应注意避免向客人做具体房号的承诺。

（三）传真订房

传真是一种现代通信技术，目前正得到广泛使用。其特点是操作方便，传递迅速，即发即收，内容详尽，并可传递发送者的真迹，如签名、印鉴等，还可传递图表，因此传真成为订房联系最常用的通信手段。

（四）国际互联网订房

互联网订房是最先进、目前最流行的一种订房方式。其优点是方便、快捷、先进、廉价、信息全、选择面广，越来越受到客人和酒店的青睐。

许多大型酒店已有自设网站，客人可直接向酒店订房，也可通过酒店连锁集团公司的订房系统向其所属的酒店订房，亦可通过携程、同程、艺龙等国际在线旅游网站订房。

（五）合同订房

酒店与旅行社或商务公司之间通过签订订房合同，达到长期出租客房的目的。

无论客人采取何种方式进行客房预订，预订员都应注意以下问题：

①无论是接受预订还是婉拒预订，都必须及时给客人以明确答复。一般来说，为尊重客人，客人以何种方式订房，酒店也应以同样的方式答复客人。

②不预先告知房号。预订员在接受预订时，不要给客人具体房间号码的许诺。因为房间的租用情况随时都在变化，一旦客人到达时所订房间没有空出或不能使用，将

失信于客人。

③为保证整个预订工作的严密性，应尽可能地掌握客人的离店日期。如果客人没有确定预订几天，酒店通常只为其预订一夜客房。

V　Method of Room Reservation

There are many ways to book rooms, each with its own characteristics. The method used by the guest is subject to the urgency of the booking and the condition of booking equipment.

Guests often use the following booking methods.

（1）Reservation by phone

Reservation by phone is when guest makes a reservation to the hotel by phone. This method is the most widely used, especially when the expected arrival date is short. Its advantage is that it can directly, quickly and clearly transmit the information of both parties, and the reservationist can respond to the guest's reservation request on the spot.

（2）Face-to-face reservation

Face-to-face reservation is that the guests goes to the hotel in person and negotiates the reservation with the reservation staff face-to-face. This way can give the reservation staff the opportunity to understand the needs of the guests in detail, and answer the questions raised by the guests face to face, which is conducive to the promotion of hotel products.

When discussing room reservation matters with guests face-to-face, the reservation staff should pay attention to:

① The appearance is dignified, the manner is generous, the manners and politeness are emphasized, the attitude is enthusiastic, and the pronunciation and intonation are appropriate and tactful.

② Grasp the guests' psychology, use sales techniques, and flexibly sell guest rooms and other hotel products. If necessary, the room and other hotel facilities and services can be shown to guests for their choice.

③ When the guests accept this method of booking, the reservation staff should avoid making promises of specific room numbers to guests.

（3）Fax reservation

Fax is a modern communication technology, which is now widely used. Its characteristics are convenient operation, fast delivery, detailed content, and can transmit the sender's authenticity, such as signature, seal, etc., and can also transmit charts, so fax has become the most commonly used communication method for booking contact.

（4）Internet reservation

Internet reservation is currently the most advanced and popular way to book a room. It is convenient, fast, advanced, inexpensive, complete in information, and wide in choice, making it more and more popular among guests and hotels.

Many large hotels have their own websites, and guests can book rooms directly with the hotel, or through the hotel chain group company's reservation system, or through the international online travel websites such as Ctrip, Tongcheng, and eLong.

（5）Contract room reservation

The hotel and the travel agency or business company sign a room booking contract to achieve the purpose of long-term rental of rooms.

No matter what method the guest takes to make a room reservation, the reservationist should pay attention to the following issues:

① Whether to accept a reservation or decline a reservation, the reservationist must give a clear answer to the guest in time. Generally speaking, in order to respect the guests, the hotel should respond to the guests in the same way in which the guests book the room.

② Do not tell the room number in advance. When accepting the reservation, the reservationist should not give the guest a promise of a specific room number. Because the rental situation of the room is changing at any time, once the room booked by the guest is not available or unavailable when the guest arrives, the hotel will lose trust.

③ In order to ensure the rigor of the entire booking process, the departure date of the guest should be grasped as much as possible. If the guest doesn't confirm the duration for the reservation, the hotel usually only books a room for one night.

六、客房预订的种类

客房预订的种类多种多样，以酒店应承担的责任为例，可以把预订分为非保证类预订和保证类预订。

①非保证类预订。

非保证类预订通常有以下 3 种具体方式。

a. 临时类预订。临时类预订是指客人的订房日期与抵店日期接近，甚至是抵店当天的订房。由于时间紧，酒店一般没有足够的时间给客人以书面确认，均以口头确认。当天的临时类订房通常会转由前厅接待处的员工受理。国际上的"取消预订时限"或称"截房时间"为下午 6 点，事先应注意告知客人。如果客人在取消预订时限内还未到达酒店，则该预订被取消。

b. 确认类预订。确认类预订是指客人提前较长时间向酒店提出订房要求，酒店以口头或书面方式给予确认，并答应为订房客人保留房间至某一事先声明的时间。

c. 等待类预订。等待类预订是指在客房预订已满的情况下，将一定数量的订房客人列入等候名单，如果有人取消预订，或有人提前离店，酒店就会通知等候的客人来店。

预订员在处理这类订房时，应征求客人的意见，是否可将其列入等候名单，并向客人说清楚，以免日后发生纠纷。

②保证类预订。

保证类预订（也称担保预订）是指客人通过使用信用卡、预付定金和订立商业合同等方式来保证酒店的客房收入，而酒店则必须保证为订房客人提供所需客房的预订。客人通过预付定金来保证自己的订房要求，即客人支付了至少一个晚上的客房费用后，酒店会保证在特定的日期内为其提供住宿服务。保证类预订以客人预付订金的形式来保护酒店和客人双方的利益，约束双方的行为，因而对双方都是有利的。

保证类预订在酒店与未来住客之间建立了更牢靠的关系。客人可能通过下列方法进行订房担保：

a. 信用卡。客人在订房时向酒店声明，使用信用卡为所预订的房间付款，并把信用卡的种类、号码、失效期及持卡人的姓名告诉酒店。如客人在预订日期未抵达酒店，酒店可以通过信用卡公司获得房费收入的补偿。

b. 预付定金。对于酒店来说，最理想的保证类预订方法是要求客人预付定金，如现金、支票、汇款等酒店认可的形式。预付金可以由预订处收取后交财务部，也可以由财务部收取后通知预订处。

c. 订立商业合同。订立商业合同是指酒店与有关客户单位签订订房合同。合同内容主要包括签约单位的地址、账号以及同意对因为失约而未使用的订房承担付款责任的说明，合同还应规定通知取消预订的最后期限，如签约单位未能在规定的期限通知取消预订，酒店可以向对方收取房费等。

VI Types of Room Reservations

There are various kinds of room reservations. According to the responsibility of the hotel, reservations can be divided into non-guaranteed reservations and guaranteed reservations.

① Non-guaranteed booking.

Non-guaranteed reservations usually have the following 3 specific methods.

a. Temporary reservation. Temporary reservation means that the guest's booking date is close to the arrival date, even the reservation made on the day of arrival. Due to the tight schedule, the hotel generally does not have enough time to give the guest a written confirmation, all of which are confirmed verbally. Temporary reservation on the day will usually be transferred to the staff at the reception desk in the front lobby. The international "cancellation time limit" or "cut-off time" is 6 o'clock in the afternoon. Guests should be notified in advance. If the guest has not arrived at the hotel within the cancellation time limit, the reservation will be cancelled.

b. Confirmation booking. Confirmation booking means that the guest makes a reservation request to the hotel a long time in advance, and the hotel confirms it verbally or in writing and promises to reserve the room for the reservation guest until a certain time stated in advance.

c. Waiting for reservations. Waiting for reservations means that when the room reservation is full, a certain number of booked guests will be put on the waiting list. If someone cancels the reservation, or if someone leaves the hotel in advance, the hotel will notify the guest to come to the hotel. When processing this type of reservation, the reservationist should seek the opinions of the guests, whether they can be put on the waiting list, and make it clear to the guests to avoid disputes in the future.

② Guaranteed booking.

Guaranteed booking refers to the use of credit cards, prepaid deposits, and commercial contracts to guarantee the hotel's room revenue, while the hotel must guarantee to provide reservations for the required rooms. Guests guarantee their reservation requirements by prepayment, that is, after the guest has paid for at least one night's room fee, the hotel will guarantee to provide accommodation services for them within a specific date. Guaranteed reservations protect the interests of both the hotel and the guests in the form of a guest's advance deposit, and restrict the behavior of both parties, which is beneficial to both parties.

Guaranteed booking establishs a stronger relationship between the hotel and future guests. Guests may guarantee the reservation through the following methods:

a. Credit cards. When booking a room, the guest declares to the hotel that the credit card will be used to pay for the room booked, and the type, number, expiration date and the name of the card holder will be informed to the hotel. If the guest does not arrive at the hotel on the reservation date, the hotel can obtain compensation from the room fee income through the credit card company.

b. Pay a deposit in advance. For hotels, the most ideal guarantee booking method is to require guests to pay a deposit in advance, such as cash, cheque, remittance and other forms approved by the hotel. The advance payment can be collected by the reservation office and then handed to the financial department, or it can be collected by the financial department and notified to the reservation office.

c. Commercial contracts. Establishing a commercial contract refers to a room reservation contract signed between the hotel and the relevant client unit. The content of the contract mainly includes the address and account number of the contracting unit, and the explanation of agreeing to bear the payment responsibility for the unused reservation due to the breach of the contract. The contract should also stipulate the deadline for notification of the cancellation of the reservation. If the contracting unit fails to notify the cancellation within the stipulated time limit, the hotel can charge the other party room fees, etc.

任务一 客房预订程序

【案例导入】

前厅预订员小王受理了一个韩国团队的客房预订，确定将团队房间安排在 5 楼。预订受理完后，小王出去接了个电话，待回到岗位后再将团队预订信息输入电脑。

其间，前厅预订员小夏接到了一位伍先生的预订电话。这位伍先生每次到这座城市都下榻该酒店，而且对 5 楼情有独钟。伍先生说，"伍"不仅与"5"同音，还是数字 5 的大写，住 5 楼有一种像住在自己家一样的心理满足感。同时，伍先生对 5 楼的客房陈设、布置、色调、家具也特别有亲切感，这些能唤起他对逝去岁月中一段美好而温馨往事的回忆。因为伍先生是酒店的常客，与预订员小夏相识，小夏便把 5 楼的506 房许诺给了他。

当发现客房被重复预订后，预订员小夏受到了严厉的批评。

酒店管理层认为，如果让伍先生住 5 楼，则要涉及一大批客人，很可能会产生新的矛盾。

后来，伍先生被告知因为韩国客人的预订才使自己不能如愿时，表现出了极大的不满，表示不同意换房……

［点评］

此案例中，由于预订员小王在受理团队预订中没有及时将预订信息输入电脑，预订员小夏在不知情的情况下将 506 房预订给了伍先生，最终造成了 506 房被重复预订的情况。

首先，预订员在接受预订时，一般不要给客人具体房间号码的许诺。因为房间的使用情况随时都在变化，一旦出现变化，就很可能出现客人到达时所订房间没有空出或不能使用的情况。这样酒店就会失信于客人，处于被动局面。

其次，预订员在受理预订工作中思想上要高度重视，要在第一时间录入预订信息，以免拖延或忘记。

再次，团队预订一般遵循集中排房的原则。

最后，当班领班应随时关注每位员工的操作情况，发现问题及时调整；平时多注意加强对员工工作程序的培训，尤其是责任心的培养。

Task 1   Room reservation Procedure

【Case Introduction】

Wang, a reservationist in the front office, accepted a reservation for a Korean group and confirmed that the group room will be arranged on the 5th floor. After receiving the reservation, Wang went out to answer a phone call and then imputed the group reservation information into the computer after he returned.

During that time, Xia, a reservationist the front office, received a reservation from a Mr. Wu by phone. Mr. Wu stays in the hotel every time he comes to the city, and has a fondness for the 5th floor. Mr. Wu said, "Wu" is not only the same sound as "5", but also the capitalization of the number 5 (in Chinse). Staying on the 5th floor gives him a sense of psychological satisfaction like living in his own home. At the same time, he also has a special intimacy with the furnishings, layout, color, and furniture of the rooms on the 5th floor, which can evoke his memories of a good and warm past in the past years. Because Mr. Wu was a regular customer of the hotel and knew Xia, the reservationist Xia promised him room 506 on the 5th floor.

When it was found that the room was booked twice, the reservationist Xia was severely criticized.

The hotel management thought, if Mr. Wu was allowed to stay on the 5th floor, a large group of guests would be involved and new conflicts would likely arise.

Later, when Mr. Wu was told that it was because of the Korean guests' reservation that he could not get what he wanted, he showed great dissatisfaction and said he did not agree to change the room ...

[Comment]

In this case, because the reservationist Wang did not input the reservation information into the computer in time when accepting the group reservation, the reservationist Xia booked room 506 to Mr. Wu without knowing it, which eventually caused room 506 booked twice.

First of all, reservationists should generally not give guests the promise of a specific room number when accepting reservations. Because the use of the room is changing at any time, once there is a change, it is likely that the room booked by the guest is not available or unavailable when the guest arrives. In this way, the hotel will lose trust in the guests, in a passive situation.

Secondly, the reservationist should pay great attention to the work of accepting reservations, and record the reservation information in time, so as not to delay or forget.

Thirdly, the team booking generally follows the principle of centralized room arrangement.

Finally, the foreman on duty should pay attention to the operation of each employee at any time, and make adjustments in time when problems are found; strengthen the training of work procedures, especially the responsibility cultivation.

【任务操作】

为了确保客房预订工作的高效运行，正常情况下，客房预订按照 8 个阶段进行操作：预订前的准备—通信联系—明确客人要求—受理预订或婉拒预订—确认预订—预订资料记录储存—修改预订—核对预订。

一、接受客房预订的程序

（一）预订前的准备

预订前的准备工作主要包括：检查预订报表和各种统计表；查阅交接班记录；准备好预订单和预订表格、用品；检查并调整电脑，使其处于待工作状态。

（二）通信联系

客人通常以电话、面谈、传真、互联网、信函等方式向酒店前厅部客房预订处提出订房要求。

（三）明确客人要求

预订员应主动向客人询问，以获悉客人的住宿要求，主要包括抵店时间、客房类型、用房数量、离店时间等。

【Task Operation】

In order to ensure the efficient operation of room reservations, normally, room reservations are operated in eight stages: preparation before booking—communication and contact—clarification of guest requirements—accepting or declining reservations—confirmation of reservations—reservation information storage—modification of reservations—checking the reservation.

I Procedures for Accepting Room Reservations

（1）Preparation before booking

The pre-booking preparations mainly include: checking the booking report and various statistical tables; checking the shift record; preparing the booking orders, forms, and supplies; checking and adjusting the computer so that it is in working condition.

（2）Communication and contact

Guests often make room reservation requests to the room reservation office of the hotel's front office by telephone, face-to-face interview, fax, Internet, and letter.

（3）Clarification of guest requirements

The reservationist should take the initiative to ask the guests to learn about the guests' accommodation requirements, which mainly include arrival time, room type, number of rooms, departure time, etc.

（四）受理预订或婉拒预订

预订员通过查看预订总表或电脑终端，以判断宾客的预订要求是否与酒店的实际提供能力相符，主要包括 4 个因素：抵店日期、客房类型、用房数量、用房夜次。

①接受预订。

若以上因素均符合，则接受预订，与客人确定房价，了解客人的相关信息，包括住店客人的姓名、人数、国籍、抵离店时间、车次或航班，所需客房的类型、数量、房价、付款方式、特殊要求，以及预订人姓名（或单位）及地址、电话号码等信息，并将预订信息填入客房预订申请单。

客房预订申请单				
申请单位		部　门		申请人
需求日期	自　　月　　日　　时起至　　月　　日　　时止共（　　　）天			
招待对象	客人单位			
	预订事由			
	入住人数	男：　　　　人　　　女：　　　　人　　共（　　）人		
	需房间数			
海湾酒店	□高级山景房□大床□双人床（　　　）间　　□高级海景房□大床□双人床（　　　）间			
	□豪华山景房□大床□双人床（　　　）间　　□豪华海景房（　　　）间			
	□高级海景套房（　　　）间　　　　　　　　□行政海景套房（　　　）间			
华骏酒店	□标准房□单人□双人（　　　）间　　　　□豪华房□单人□双人（　　　）间			
	□豪华套房单人大床（　　　）间			

续表

客房预订申请单			
城市客栈	□标准房大床（　　　）间		□高级房□大床□双人床（　　　）间
	□豪华房大床（　　　）间		□豪华双人房（　　　）间
	□商务套房（　　　）间		□行政套房（　　　）间
其他酒店	（请注明酒店名称）		
	（请注明订房标准及房间数）		
备注	费用承担　□客户付现　　□由公司承担住房费（其他费用客户自理）		
	□其他需求：＿＿＿＿＿＿＿＿＿＿＿＿＿＿＿（请注明）		
申请人		行政部	审　核

（4）Accepting or declining reservations

The reservationist will check the reservation master table or computer terminal to judge whether the reservation requirements of the guests are consistent with the actual capacity of the hotel, mainly including four factors: arrival date, room type, number of rooms and nights.

① Accept the reservation.

If the above factors are consistent, then accept the reservation, and confirm the room rate with guests. To know the guest's relevant information, including the name of the guest, the number of people, nationality, arrival and departure time, bus or flight, the type of rooms, the number, room rates, payment methods, special requirements, as well as the name（or unit）and address of the booker/applicant, telephone number and other information. Fill information in the room reservation application form.

Room Reservation Application Form					
Name of Applicant Comp.		Dept.		Name of Applicant	
Time Period	from	to		（　　　）days in total	
Guests	Comp.				
	Reason of Ordering				

Continued

Room Reservation Application Form				
Guests	No. of People	Male:	Female:	( ) in total
	No. of Rooms			
Haiwan Hotel	☐ Superior Mountainview Room ☐ Queen Room ☐ Double Room ( ) ☐ Superior Seaview Room ☐ Queen Room ☐ Double Room ( )			
	☐ Deluxe Mountainview Room ☐ Queen Room ☐ Double Room ( ) ☐ Deluxe Seaview Room ( )			
	☐ Superior Seaview Suite ( ) ☐ Executive Seaview Suite ( )			
Huajun Hotel	☐ Standard Room ☐ Single Room ☐ Double Room ( ) ☐ Deluxe Room ☐ Single Room ☐ Double Room ( )			
	☐ Deluxe Suite ( )			
City Inn	☐ Standard Room ( ) ☐ Superior Room ☐ Queen Room ☐ Double Room ( )			
	☐ Deluxe & Queen Room ( ) ☐ Double Room ( )			
	☐ Business Suite ( ) ☐ Executive Suite ( )			
Other Hotels	(Please write down the name of hotel)			
	(Please note booking standards and No. of rooms needed)			
Remark	Payment undertaker ☐ Individual ☐ Comp (Other expenses are at the customer's own expense)			
	☐ Other Issues: _____ (Please specify)			
Name of Applicant		Executive Dept		Examiner

②婉拒预订。

若客人的预订要求与酒店的实际提供能力不符，则应当婉拒客人。婉拒预订时应首先对客人选择本酒店表示感谢，可主动提出一系列供客人选择的建议，并希望今后能再有机会为客人提供服务。

a. 如果只是客人预订的房间类型与酒店的实际提供能力不相符，可建议客人预订其他类型的客房，操作话术参考如下：

"×× 女士 / 先生，很感谢您能预订我们酒店的房间！实在抱歉，您所需的套房目前已被订完了。不过，幸运的是现在我们还有一间 ×× 类型的客房，其面积和您所需的套房一样，而且朝向庭院，很安静……"

b. 当客房不接受预订时，建议客人作等候预订。将客人的预订要求、电话号码等记录在等候预订名单上。随后每日检查落实，一旦出现空房，就立即通知客人。

如果客人采用的是信函、电邮等书面方式订房，也应以致歉信等书面形式礼貌复函，以表歉意。

致歉信

_____ 小姐 / 女士 / 先生：

　　由于本酒店_____年_____月_____日的客房已经订满，我们无法接受您的订房要求，深表歉意。

　　感谢您对本店的关照，希望以后能有机会为您服务。

×× 酒店前厅预订处
____年___月___日

② Decline the reservation.

If the guest's reservation requirements do not match the actual hotel's offer, the guest should be declined. When declining a reservation, you should first express your gratitude to the guests for choosing this hotel, and put forward a series of suggestions for the guests to choose and hope that we will have the opportunity to provide services for the guests in the future.

a. If only the type of room booked by the guest does not match the actual capacity of the hotel, it is recommended that the guest book other types of rooms. The operating terms are as follows:

"Ms. / Mr. × ×, thank you for booking a room in our hotel! I'm really sorry, the suite you need has been booked out. Fortunately, we now have a × × type room with the same size as yours which faces the courtyard and is very quiet ..."

b. When the guest room is not accepted, it is recommended that guests make a waiting reservation. Record guest's reservation requirements, phone numbers, etc. on the waiting reservation list. Then check daily and notify the guest as soon as a room becomes available.

If the guest made the reservation in writing, such as by letter or email, you should also send a polite reply in writing, such as an apology letter, to express your apologies.

Apology Letter

_____ Ms./Madam/Mr.

Due to the fact that our hotel is fully booked for the date of... We apologize that we are unable to accept your reservation request.

Thank you for your interest in our hotel and we hope to have the opportunity to serve you in the future.

× × Hotel front office reservation desk

Date

（五）确认预订

如果接受客人的预订，预订员就要立即对客人的预订加以确认。

确认预订的方式通常有两种：口头确认（包括电话确认）和书面确认。如果条件允许，酒店一般应采用书面确认的方式，向客人发放预订确认函或确认邮件。

预订确认函

× × 酒店	客房类型：_____ 数量：_____ 房价：_____
地址：_____	预订日期：_____ 抵达日期：_____
电话：_____	抵达时间：_____ 住宿天数：_____
您对 _____	离店日期：_____
_____	结账方式：_____ 订金：_____
的预订已被确认。	客户地址：_____
	客户姓名：_____ 电话：_____

本酒店愉快地确认了您的订房。由于客人离店后，需要有一定的时间整理客房，因此，请于抵店当日 14:00 后办理入住，请见谅。另外，未付订金或无担保的订房，如未事先说明，所订房间只保留到抵店当日 18:00。

（5）Confirmation of reservations

If the guest's reservation is accepted, the reservationist should confirm the guest's reservation immediately.

There are usually two ways to confirm the reservation: oral confirmation（including telephone confirmation）and written confirmation. If the conditions permit, the hotel should generally use the way of written confirmation, issuing a reservation confirmation letter or confirmation e-mail to the guests.

Reservation Confirmation Letter

× × Hotel Address：_____ Tel：_____ Your _____ _____ reservation has been confirmed	Room type: _____ Number: _____ Room rate: _____ Booking date: _____ Arrival date: _____ Arrival time: _____ Number of days of stay: _____ Departure date: _____ Payment: _____ Deposit: _____ Address: _____ Name: _____ Tel: _____

Our hotel happily confirms your reservation. As we need some time to organize the rooms after guests' departure, therefore please check in after 14:00 on the day of arrival. In addition, if a reservation is made without a deposit or guarantee, the room will only be reserved until 18:00 on the day of arrival without a statement in advance.

（六）预订资料记录储存

当预订确认书发出后，预订资料必须及时、正确地记录和储存，以防疏漏。预订资料一般包括客房预订单、确认书、预付定金收据、预订变更单、预订取消单、客史档案卡及客人原始预订凭证等。有关同一客人的预订资料装订在一起，将最新的资料存放在最上面，依次顺推，以便于查阅。预订资料的记录储存可采用下列两种方式：

①按客人预订的抵店日期顺序储存。以便随时掌握未来每天的客人抵店情况。

②按客人姓氏字母顺序储存。按照客人姓氏第一个字母的顺序，将预订单归档储存，以便随时查找出客人的预订资料。

（七）修改预订

详见"2.1.2 客房预订的变更和取消"。

（八）核对预订

核对预订，又称订房再确认，是指订房部员工定期或不定期与订房者联系，以确定订房信息的准确性。为了提高订房信息的准确性与酒店客房的出租率，以及便于做好接待准备，在客人到店前，尤其是在旅游旺季，预订人员要通过电话等方式与客人进行多次核对，问清客人是否能够如期抵店，住宿人数、时间、用房数等是否有变化。核对工作通常要进行 3 次：第一次是在客人抵店前一个月；第二次是在客人预订抵店前一周；第三次是在客人预订抵店前一天。

（6）Reservation information storage

When the reservation confirmation is issued, the reservation information must be recorded and stored in a timely and correct manner to prevent omission. The reservation information generally includes room reservation order, confirmation letter, prepaid deposit receipt, reservation change order, reservation cancellation order, guest history file card and guest original reservation voucher, etc. The reservation information about the same guest is bound together, and the latest information is stored at the top for easy reference. The record storage of reservation information can be done in the following two ways:

① Stored in the order of the guest's scheduled arrival date in order to keep track of the future daily arrival of guests.

② Stored in alphabetical order according to the guest's last name. According to the order of the first letter of the guest's surname, the reservation order will be filed and stored, so that the reservation information of the guest can be found at any time.

（7）Modification of reservation

See "②① 2 Change and cancellation of room reservation" for details.

（8）Checking the reservation

Checking the reservation, also known as room reservation reconfirmation, refers to the staff of the reservation department contacting with the bookers regularly or irregularly to determine the accuracy of the booking information. In order to improve the accuracy of booking information and hotel room occupancy rate, as well as to facilitate good reception preparation, before the arrival of guests, reservation staff should check with the guests by telephone and other means for several times especially in the tourist season, asking whether the guests can arrive as scheduled and whether the number of people, time and the number of rooms, etc. have changed. The check is usually done for three times: the first time is one month before the guest arrives; the second time is one week before the guest arrives; and the third time is one day before the guest arrives.

二、各类客房的预订流程

（一）电话预订流程

第一步：铃响 3 声以内接起电话，礼貌问候："您好，这里是 × × 酒店前厅预订部，有什么可以帮助您？"

第二步：询问客人的抵离日期、用房数量、房间类型。

第三步：通过电脑查看客房的预订情况，确认能否接受此预订，并礼貌地告诉客人："您好，请您稍等，我正在为您查询……"

第四步：接受订房时，按"客房预订单"上的项目问清客人姓名、抵离日期、到达时间、房间类型等情况。向订房者说明房价，并在"客房预订单"上注明。询问客人有无特殊要求，如是否需要接机服务、是否需要无烟客房、是否需要房内做特殊布置等。

若客人需要的房间类型已订满，可建议客人住其他类型客房，并说明房价。

第五步：凡与酒店有协议或合同的公司、旅行社订房时，须在"客房预订单"上注明合同号码。

第六步：告知客人办理入住和离店的时限。

第七步：复述预订内容，与订房者进行核对，确保预订信息准确无误。

第八步：结束电话交流，向客人致谢，表示对其光临的期待。等客人挂断电话后再挂。

第九步：预订员在"客房预订单"下方签名，填上日期，并及时把预订内容输入电脑。

第十步：整理预订单，然后归档存放。

Ⅱ　Various Processes of Room Reservation

（1）Reservation process by phone

Step 1: Answer the phone within three rings, and politely greet: "Hello, ×× Hotel Front Office Reservation Department, how can I help you?"

Step 2: Ask the guest about the arrival and departure date, the number of rooms, and the type of room.

Step 3: Check the room reservation status through the computer to see if this reservation can be accepted, and politely tell the guest: "Hello, please wait a moment, I am checking for you..."

Step 4: When accepting the reservation, please check the items on the reservation form including guest name, arrival and departure date, arrival time, room type, etc. Explain the room rate to the guest and indicate it on the "room reservation form". Ask the guests if they have special requirements, such as whether they need airport pick-up service, non-smoking rooms, and special decorations in the room, etc.

If the room type requested by the guest is fully booked, the reservationist can suggest the guest to stay in other types of rooms, and explain the room rate.

Step 5: If the company or travel agency has an agreement or contract in the hotel book rooms, the reservationist must indicate the contract number on the "room reservation form".

Step 6: Inform guests of the time limit for check-in and check-out.

Step 7: Retell the reservation content and check with the booker to ensure that the reservation information is accurate.

Step 8: Finish the telephone conversation by thanking the guest and expressing your anticipation of his or her visit. Wait for the guest to hang up.

Step 9: The reservationist signs at the bottom of the "room reservation order", fills in the date, and inputs the reservation into the computer in time.

Step 10: Organize and file the reservation form.

（二）传真或 e-mail 预订流程

第一步：接到订房传真或 e-mail 后，从头到尾仔细看一遍，划线标注重要信息，如客人姓名、抵离日期、房间数量、房间类型和特殊要求等。

第二步：通过电脑查看客房预订情况，决定是否接受预订。

第三步：决定接受预订后，即刻填写"客房预订单"。

第四步：如果一份传真或 e-mail 同时订几个房间，并且不是同一日期到达，应按不同的到达日期分别填写"客房预订单"。

第五步：凡与酒店签有协议、合同的公司或旅行社预订，要在"客房预订单"上注明合同号。

第六步：如遇订房传真或 e-mail 资料不完整、字迹不清楚，应立即给对方去电（传真），得到正确信息后再填"客房预订单"；在未得到对方最终准确信息的传真或 e-mail之前，应将来电与复电合订在一起，放入指定地方存档。

第七步：接到的订房传真或 e-mail，必须在 24 小时之内予以回复，加急预订传真或 e-mail，应即刻回复。

第八步：确认预订内容完整，笔迹清晰，并使用酒店统一的"传真发文稿"回复；回复 e-mail 订房应通过 e-mail 形式。

第九步：如收到发给酒店领导或部门经理接收的预订传真或 e-mail，应先交有关部门批示后再签复确认预订。

第十步：将客人发来的预订和酒店回复的确认预订传真底稿或 e-mail 底稿合订一起存档。

（2）Reservation process by fax or e-mail

Step 1: After receiving the fax or e-mail, read it carefully from beginning to end and underline important information, such as guest's name, arrival and departure date, number of rooms, room type and special requirements, etc.

Step 2: Check the room reservation status through the computer and decide whether to accept the reservation.

Step 3: After deciding to accept the reservation, fill in the "room reservation form" immediately.

Step 4: If there are various reservations in one fax or e-mail with different dates of arrival, the reservationist should fill in the "room reservation form" according to the different arrival dates.

Step 5: If company or travel agency has an agreement or contract in the hotel book rooms, the reservationist must indicate the contract number on the "room reservation form".

Step 6: If the booking information is incomplete or the handwriting is not clear, the reservationist should call (fax) him/her immediately and fill in the "room reservation form" after getting the correct information; in the absence of the last accurate information from the fax or e-mail, the reservationist should combine the incoming call and re-call, put in the designated place to file.

Step 7: The received reservation fax or e-mail must be replied within 24 hours, and the urgent reservation fax or e-mail should be replied immediately.

Step 8: Confirm the reservation, make sure the content complete and handwriting clear; and use the hotel unified "fax document" to reply; reply e-mail booking by e-mail.

Step 9: If the reservationist receives a fax or e-mail sent to the hotel leader or department manager to accept the reservation, it should be sent to the relevant department for approval before signing the confirmation reservation.

Step 10: The reservation sent by the guest and the confirmation of the hotel's reply by fax or e-mail are combined and filed together.

（三）网络预订流程

第一步：装有网络连接终端机的酒店，必须每天定时查看预订信息，获得订房信息后，应标注客人姓名、抵离日期、房数和特殊要求等。

第二步：填写"客房预订单"。

第三步：若房间客满，必须事先通知网络中心。

第四步：每个网络订房都须予以确认。

第五步：将预订单输入电脑，做好相应记录，以便月底统计，最后将确认同预订单一起存档。

（3）Reservation process by the Internet

Step 1: The hotel equipped with network connection terminal must check the reservation information regularly every day. After getting the reservation information, the guest's name, arrival and departure date, the number of rooms and special requirements, etc. should be marked.

Step 2: Fill in the "room reservation form".

Step 3: If the room is full, the network center must be notified in advance.

Step 4: Each network reservation must be confirmed.

Step 5: Input the reservation into the computer, make the corresponding records for the month statistics, and finally file the confirmation together with the reservation order.

（四）重要客人（VIP）的预订流程

第一步：持有酒店 VIP 卡，经酒店领导、部门经理确认的预订和酒店高额消费的常客，应予确保。

第二步：接受预订后，发现是首次来店的重要客人，应将客人姓名、公司、职务等身份资料上报前厅部经理审批。

第三步：以前来过，享受过重要客人待遇的预订，应在"客房预订单"上注明重要客人及 VIP 代号等级，仍将其作为 VIP 客人接待。

第四步：接受 VIP 客人预订，尽可能获得客人的到达时间，以便大堂副理或领导迎接，使接待工作顺利进行。

第五步：将 VIP 客人信息输入电脑，填入"客房预订单"。

第六步：根据客人要求应事先控制、安排好其喜欢或指定的房间。

第七步：VIP 客人预订，须填写"VIP 客房布置单"，由前厅部经理批签后，将此单发往各有关部门。

（4）Reservation process for VIP guests

Step 1: Guests who hold the hotel VIP card and regular guests with high consumption, confirmed by the hotel leadership and department manager should be ensured.

Step 2: After accepting the reservation and discovering important guests who come to the hotel for the first time, the reservationist should submit their name, company, position and other identity information to the front office manager for approval.

Step 3: For guests who have been to the hotel before and have enjoyed the treatment as important guests, the reservationist should indicate the "important guests" and VIP code level on the "room reservation form", and treat them as VIP guests.

Step 4: When accept VIP guest reservation, try to get the guest's arrival time, so the assistant manager or leader in the lobby can greet them, making the reception work smooth.

Step 5: Input the VIP guest information into the computer and fill in the "room reservation form".

Step 6: According to the requirements of the guests, the rooms they like or designated should be arranged in advance.

Step 7: For VIP guest bookings, the reservationist must fill in the "VIP Room Arrangement Form" after the front office manager approves the form, and then sends this form to the relevant departments.

（五）团队、会议预订流程

第一步：问清预订人姓名、单位、人数、房间种类、数量、抵离日期等，确认是否为协议单位。

第二步：查看电脑客房预订情况，确定是否能接受预订。

第三步：填写"团队、会议接待通知单"。

团队、会议接待通知单

会议名称：		公司／单位名称：	
会议时间：		会议人数：	
会议负责人姓名：		联系电话：	
酒店接待人：		电话：	

	会　议　内　容　安　排					
客房部						
餐饮部	日期	用餐时间	用餐形式	人数／桌数	餐标	地点
	备注：					
会议部	日期	时间	会议室名称		价位	会场要求：
财务部	会议定金：			结算方式：		
	备注：					
工程部			安保部			
制表人			下单日期			

抄送：总经理　餐饮总监　浴场总监　财务总监　营销部　行政部经理　工程部经理　保安部经理（共 8 份）

批准人：

餐饮总监＿＿＿＿＿＿＿＿　　财务总监＿＿＿＿＿＿＿＿　　总经理＿＿＿＿＿＿＿

第四步：由于团队或会议订房数量通常较大，应完成定金交纳或合同签订手续，并确认预订。

第五步：根据"团队、会议接待通知单"内容，将信息输入电脑并打印，以控制客房流量和房号。

第六步：客人到达的前一天上午与预订单位联系，再一次确认是否有变动，如信息不全，应联系补全。

第七步：客人到达前一天由总台负责将"团队、会议接待通知单"送发各有关部门，要有签收手续。

第八步：将预订资料收集齐全，存档。

（5）Reservation process Group and conference

Step 1: Ask the name, company, number of people, room type, quantity, arrival and departure date of the reservation, and confirm whether it is an agreement unit.

Step 2: Check the computer room reservations to determine whether the reservation can be accepted.

Step 3: Fill in the "Group and Meeting Reception Notice".

Step 4: As the number of rooms booked for groups or meetings is large, the reservationist should complete the deposit payment or contract signing procedures and confirm the reservation.

Step 5: According to the content of the "Group and Meeting Reception Notice", input the information into the computer and print it to control the flow of rooms and room numbers.

Step 6: Contact the reservation company in the morning before the guest's arrival to confirm whether there are changes. If the information is incomplete, contact the reservation company to complete it.

Step 7: The day before the guests arrive, the reception desk will be responsible for sending the "Group and Meeting Reception Notice" to all relevant departments with sign-off procedures.

Step 8: Collect all the reservation information and file it.

Group and Meeting Reception Notice

Group Name：		Comp. Name：	
Time：		No. of People：	
Person in Charge：		Contact No：	
Reception Staff：		Telephone No：	
Meeting Issues			
Guests Dept			

续表

Food and Beverage Dept	Date	Time	Way of Dining	No. of Dining Room / Table (DRT).	Catering Tandards	Location	
	Remark：						
Meeting Dept	Date	Time	Room Name		Price	Room Requirement：	
	Remark：						
Financial Dept	Deposit：				Payment Method：		
	Remark：						
Engineering Dept					Security Dept		
Form Designer					Issued Date		

Copy to：General Manager, Catering Director, Director of Bathing, Financial Controller, Sales Dept., Executive Office, Engineering Dept., Security Dept.(8 in total)

Approval：

Catering Director _____ 　　Financial Controller _____ 　　General Manager _____

任务二　客房预订变更和取消

【案例导入】

在飞机场没有接到客人

一日，酒店机场代表与车队司机按预订单到机场迎接客人，当预订单上标示的航班客人都走完了也没有见到要接的客人，经机场代表与预订部联系才获悉预订已取消，但预订员忘记通知有关人员。

［点评］

接受预订和取消预订都有严格的操作程序，如果不严格执行规定，就会出现上述差错，为酒店造成直接经济损失或不必要的人力和物力浪费。

①前厅部接侍员、预订部预订员接到取消预订通知后，应根据该预订所涉及的部门、

岗位和人员，及时通知客房部、餐饮部、礼宾部、车队、大堂副理等有关部门、岗位和领导。

②接到取消预订通知后，有关人员应做好文字记录，在通知有关部门和预订人员该预订取消后，也应及时做好备注。

③接受预订和取消预订都需要高度的工作责任心，任何时候都不得马虎。此事虽未涉及客人，也未给酒店带来任何不良影响，但反映出员工工作的粗心大意与内部的协调配合工作不到位，存在沟通障碍。如果对此问题不引起重视，不采取措施加以解决，很可能在其他方面也表现出来，影响对客服务，造成客人投诉。

Task 2
Room Reservation Changes and Cancellations

【Case Introduction】

No Guest Received at the Airport

One day, the hotel airport representatives and fleet drivers arrived at the airport to pick up the guests according to the reservation form. When the flight guests have all gone and they have not seen the guests, the airport representative contacted the reservation department to know that the reservation had been cancelled but the reservationist had forgotten to notify the person concerned.

[Comment]

There are strict operating procedures for accepting reservations and canceling reservations. If not strictly enforced, the above error will occur, causing direct economic losses or unnecessary waste of manpower and material resources for the hotel.

① After receiving the cancellation notice, the receptionist of front office department and the reservationist of reservation department should notify the relevant departments, positions and personnel involved in the reservation, such as housekeeping department, catering department, concierge department, fleet, lobby deputy and other relevant departments in time.

② After receiving and notifying the notice of reservation cancellation, the personnel concerned shall make a good record. After notofying the relevant authorities and reservation personnel of the cancellation, a book should also be prepared in a timely manner.

③ Both accepting and canceling reservations require work responsibility, and must not be sloppy at any time. Although this matter did not involve guests, nor did it bring any adverse effects to the hotel, it reflects the carelessness of the staff and the lack of internal coordination and cooperation, and there are communication barriers. If this problem is not paid attention to and measures are not taken to solve it, it is likely to be manifested in other aspects, which may affect customer service and cause guest complaints.

一、预订变更的概念

预订变更是指预订客人在实际抵店前出于某种原因要对原预订信息做出补充或修改，甚至取消原预订。

在补充或修改预订信息、接受订房取消时，预订员不能表露出不愉快，而应使客人感觉到今后无论何时光临本酒店他都是受欢迎的。正确处理订房的取消，对于酒店巩固自己的客源市场具有重要意义。在国外，取消订房的客人中有90%以后还会来预订。

I　The Concept of Reservation Changes

Reservation changes refer to guest making additions or modifications to the original reservation information, or even canceling the original reservation for some reason before their arrival.

When adding or modifying reservation information and accepting the cancellation of the reservation, the reservationist should not show unhappiness but make the guest feel that he is welcome to visit the hotel at any time in the future. Handling the cancellation of reservations correctly is of great significance for the hotel to consolidate its customer source market. In foreign countries, 90% of the guests who cancel the reservation will come to book later.

二、预订变更的处理程序与标准

（一）预订更改的处理程序与标准

①接到客人更改预订信息后，询问要求更改预订客人的姓名及原定到达日期和离店日期，找出原始预订单。

②询问客人现在要更改的订房信息。

③确认更改预订，在确认新的预订信息之前，先要查询客房出租情况：在有客房的情况下，可以为客人确认更改预订，并重新填写"客房预订单"或"预订变更表"。

④将更改的预订单放在原预订单上面订在一起。

⑤按日期或客人姓名存档。

⑥如果客人的预订变更要求酒店无法满足，应及时向客人解释，并告知客人预订暂时放在等候预订名单上，酒店一旦有空房就会及时与客人取得联系。

⑦更改预订完成后，要感谢客人的及时通知，并感谢客人的理解与支持。

⑧如果此客人的预订涉及酒店其他部门的工作，还应将预订变更情况及时通知相关部门并做好记录。

预订更改表

姓名：_____	预订编号：_____
地址：_____	电话：_____
公司：_____	联系人：_____

更改日期：_____

到达日期：_____ 过夜数：_____ 离店日期：_____

人数：_____

预订客房类型及数量：_____ 每夜房费：_____元

需付订金：_____元

应付日期：_____ 收到日期：_____

结账方式：_____

备注：

原预订编号：_____ 原抵达日期：_____ 原房价：_____

II Procedures and Standards for Booking Changes

（1）Procedures and standards of reservation changes

① After receiving the change of the reservation information from the guest, ask the guest's name and the original arrival date and departure date, and find out the original reservation order.

② Ask the guest about the reservation information that he/she wants to change now.

③ Confirm the reservation change and check the room availability before confirming the new reservation information: if there is a room available, you can confirm the reservation change for the guest and fill out the "Room Reservation Form" or "Reservation Change Form" again.

④ Place the changed reservation form on top of the original reservation form and staple it together.

⑤ File by date or guest's name.

⑥ If the guest's reservation change request cannot be met by hotel, explanation should be made to the guest promptly. Tell the guest that the reservation is temporarily put on the waiting list, the hotel will contact with the guest as soon as there is vacancy.

⑦ After the change of reservation is completed, we should thank the guest for the timely notification and thank the guest for his/her understanding and support.

⑧ If the guest's reservation involves the work of other departments of the hotel, the reservation should also be changed in a timely manner to inform the relevant departments and make a record.

Reservation Change Form

Name: _____	Reservation No: _____
Address: _____	Contact No: _____
Comp: _____	Contact person: _____
Change date: _____	
Arrival date: _____ No. of overnight stays: _____ Departure date: _____	
No. of guests: _____	
Guest room type: _____ Price: _____ RMB	
Deposit: _____ RMB	
Due date: _____ Received on: _____	
Payment method: _____	
Remark:	
Original reservation No.: _____ Original arrival date: _____ Original price: _____	

（二）预订取消的处理程序与标准

①接到客人取消预订信息后，询问要求取消预订客人的姓名及原定到达日期和离店日期，找出原始预订单。

②尽可能地了解客人取消预订的原因。若可协调解决，尽量进行协调，以保住此单预订。

③协调无果的情况下，在原预订单上盖上"取消"的印章，并在备注栏内注明取消日期、原因、取消人。

④将盖有"取消"印章的预订单从原档案夹中取出，放入取消预订的专门档案夹中。

⑤在电脑上或者预订控制表上将其注销。

⑥如果此客人的预订涉及酒店其他部门的工作，还应将预订取消情况及时通知相关部门并做好记录。

（2）Procedures and standards for booking cancellation

① After receiving the cancellation information of the guest, ask for the name of the guest requesting cancellation and the original date of arrival and departure to find out the original booking form.

② Try to understand the reasons for cancellation of the reservation. If it can be resolved through coordination, try to coordinate as much as possible to keep this reservation.

③ If the coordination fails, stamp the "Cancel" seal on the original booking form, and indicate the cancellation date, reason, and cancellation person in the comment column.

④ Take out the reservation form with the "Cancel" seal from the original file folder and put it into the special file folder for canceling the reservation.

⑤ Log it out on the computer or on the booking control form.

⑥ If the guest's reservation involves the work of other departments of the hotel, the cancellation of the reservation should be notified to the relevant department in time and a record should be made.

任务三　预订"失约"管理

【案例导入】

在旅游旺季，各酒店的出租率均较高，为了保证经济效益，一般酒店都实行超额预订。五一长假的第一天，某酒店 2305 房为预离房，可该房一直未退房，大堂副理及前台多次打电话联系 2305 房的预离客人，但未联系成功。直至 18:00 时，客人才来前台办理延住手续。

而此时，2305 房的预抵客人也到达酒店，正要办理入住手续。

大堂副理试图向刚刚到达的客人解释情况，并保证将他安排在其他酒店，一旦本酒店有房间，再将其接回。但客人态度坚决，称这是酒店的问题，与他无关，他哪儿也不去。鉴于客人态度十分坚决，而且多次表示哪怕房间小一点也没关系，他不愿意到其他酒店。在值班经理的允许下，大堂副理将客人安置到了值班经理用房，客人对此表示满意。

Task 3　Reservation Failure Management

【Case Introduction】

In the tourist season, the occupancy rate of hotel is high. In order to ensure economic efficiency, general hotels are overbooked. On the first day of the May Day holiday, room 2305 of a hotel was a pre-leaving room, but the room has not been checked out. The lobby assistant manager and the front desk called the guest in room 2305 many times, but failed. The guest didn't come to the front desk to ask for extension procedures until 18:00.

At this time, the pre-arriving guest in room 2305 just arrived and was about to check in.

The assistant manager tried to explain the situation to the guest who had just arrived and promised to arrange him in another hotel. Once the hotel has a room, he will be picked up again. But the guest was firm, saying that it was a problem with the hotel and had nothing to do with him, and he would not go anywhere. Since the guest was determined and said that even if the room is small, it doesn't matter and he just doesn't want to go to other hotels. With the permission of the manager on duty, the assistant manager placed the guest in the manager's room, and the guest expressed satisfaction.

［点评］

客人向酒店订房，并不是每位客人都作出保证类订房。经验告诉我们，即使酒店的订房率达到100%，也会有订房者因故虽有预订而不到、临时取消或者住店客人提前离店等情形，使酒店出现空房。因此，酒店为了追求较高的住房率，争取获得最大的经济效益，往往实施超额预订。超额预订是订房管理艺术的最高体现，处理得好会提高客房出租率，增加酒店的经济效益。但是如果超额过度，预订客人又都在规定时限内抵达酒店，而酒店却因客满无法为他们提供所订住房，必然会引起客人的不满，这无疑将会给酒店带来很大的麻烦。因为接受并确认了客人的订房要求，就是酒店承诺了订房客人具有得到"自己的住房"的权利。发生这种情况属于酒店的违约行为，因此，必须积极采取补救措施，千方百计地调剂房间，开拓房源，最大限度地满足客人的预订要求，妥善安排好客人住宿，以消除客人的不满，挽回不良影响，维护酒店的声誉。

①凡有预订的客人一般都愿意按自己的预订需求入住，出于种种原因一般不愿被安排到其他酒店，因此满足客人的要求就成为最重要的问题。上述案例中由于客人不愿意去其他酒店，而超额预订又成为一道难题，经过有关人员的共同努力，终于让客人入住到了值班经理的用房，满足了客人的要求。既消除了客人的不满，挽回了不良

影响，维护了酒店的声誉，又为酒店增加了收入，这种做法值得提倡。

②在处理超额预订时，酒店只有在内部实在挤不出房间时，才可以考虑将客人安排至其他酒店。因为，有时客人入住其他酒店后就有可能成为其他酒店的回头客，这对于送出客人的酒店来说，有可能永远失去这位客源，将是一个损失。

[Review]

When a guest makes a reservation at a hotel, not every guest makes a guaranteed reservation. Experience tells us that even if the hotel's reservation rate reaches 100%, the guest may not arrive, cancel temporarily, or leave in advance, etc. Therefore, in order to pursue higher occupancy rates and maximize economic benefits, hotels are often overbooked. Overbooking is the highest manifestation of the art of booking management, and handling it well will increase the room occupancy rate and increase the economic benefits of the hotel. However, if the overbooking is excessive, the booked guests will arrive at the hotel within the prescribed time limit, and the hotel cannot provide them with the booked accommodation due to full capacity, which will inevitably cause dissatisfaction of the guests and bring great trouble to the hotel undoubtedly. Because it accepts and confirms the guest's reservation request, the hotel promises that the guest has the right to get their "own room". The occurrence of this situation is a breach of contract by the hotel. Therefore, it is necessary to take remedial measures actively and do everything possible to adjust rooms, seek rooms, maximize the satisfaction of guests' reservation requirements, properly arrange guest accommodation to eliminate guest dissatisfaction, minimize adverse effects and maintain the reputation of the hotel.

① Those who have a reservation are generally willing to check in according to their own reservation requirements, and are generally unwilling to be arranged to other hotels for various reasons, so meeting the requirements of the guests becomes the most important issue. In the above case, because the guests were unwilling to go to other hotels, overbooking became a problem. After the joint efforts of relevant personnel, the guests were finally allowed to stay in the room of the on-duty manager to meet the requirements of the guests. It not only eliminates the dissatisfaction of the guests, minimizes the adverse effects, maintains the reputation of the hotel, but also increases the income of the hotel. This approach is worthy of promotion.

② When dealing with overbooking, the hotel can only consider arranging guests to other hotels when it is really unable to squeeze out the room, because sometimes guests may become regular customers of other hotels after staying in other hotels. For the hotel sending out the guests, it is possible to lose the source forever, which will be a loss.

知识链接

对于酒店而言，客人在抵达酒店之前突然取消了预订，或者比预订的时间晚到，或者减少订房数量，都会减少酒店的收入。事实上，这样的事情在酒店每天都有发生。为了降低客人抵达的不确定性，酒店采取了核对预订、增加保证类预订等方法，但依然无法完全保证所有预订客人都信守预订。实际上也无法真正做到这一点，正因为如此才有了超额预订。

Knowledge Link

For the hotel, if the guest suddenly cancels the reservation before arriving at the hotel, or arrives later than the booked time, or reduces the number of reservations, the hotel's revenue will be reduced. In fact, such things happen every day in hotels. In order to reduce the uncertainty of guest arrival, the hotel has adopted methods such as checking reservations and adding guarantee reservations, but still cannot fully guarantee that all reservation guests will abide by their reservations. In fact, there is no way to do this, which is why there is overbooking.

一、超额预订

超额预订是指酒店在订房已满的情况下，再适当增加订房数量，以弥补少数客人因预订不到、临时取消或提前离店而出现的客房闲置。

对于超额预订，从实践上虽然是可以理解的，但从法律意义上讲，却不能得到法律的支持和认可。因为酒店接受了客人的预订，就意味着酒店与客人建立了客房出租的某种合同关系，如果超额预订控制失败，客人到店却没有事先预订的房间可住，这就相当于酒店单方面违约，客人有权利向司法部门起诉。对此，酒店管理者应当有清醒的认识，处理好两个关键问题：一是如何确定超额预订数量；二是一旦超额预订过度如何补救。

（一）超额预订数量的计算

超额预订应该有一个"度"的限制。根据酒店行业的经验，这个"度"的确定可以根据对市场的预测和对客情的分析计算得来。

计算超额预订数量，需要统计的数据包括预订取消率、预订而未到率、提前退房率、延期住店率等。假设，$X=$ 超额订房数；$A=$ 酒店客房总数；$C=$ 续住房数；$r_1=$ 预订取消率；$r_2=$ 预订而未到率；$D=$ 预期离店房数；$f_1=$ 提前退房率；$f_2=$ 延期住店率，则它们之间存在如下关系式：

$$X=(A-C+X)\cdot r_1+(A-C+X)\cdot r_2+C\cdot f_1-D\cdot f_2$$

$$X=\frac{C\cdot f_1-D\cdot f_2+(A-C)(r_1+r_2)}{1-(r_1+r_2)}$$

假设超额预订率为 R，则

$$R = \frac{X}{A-C} \times 100\%$$

I Overbooking

Overbooking refers to the fact that when the hotel is fully booked, reservation should be increased appropriately to make up for a small number of guests who have unused rooms due to no availability, temporary cancellation or early departure.

For overbooking, although it is understandable in practice, it cannot be supported and recognized by law. Because the hotel accepts the guest's reservation, it means that the hotel has established a certain contractual relationship with the guest for room rental. If the overbooking control fails, the guest arrives at the hotel but does not have the pre-booked room available, which is equivalent to unilateral breach of contract by the hotel. The guest has the right to sue the judicial department. In this regard, hotel managers should have a clear understanding and handle two key issues: one is how to determine the number of overbookings; the other is how to remedy the overbooking in case of overbooking.

（1）Calculation of overbooked quantity

There should be a "degree" limit for overbooking. According to the experience of the hotel industry, the determination of this "degree" can be calculated based on the prediction of the market and the analysis of customer conditions.

To calculate the number of overbookings, the statistics that need to be counted include booking cancellation rate, no-show rate, early check-out rate, postponed stay rate, etc. Suppose, X=number of overbooked rooms; A=total number of hotel rooms; C=number of renewed rooms; r_1=reservation cancellation rate; r_2=no-show rate; D=expected departure room; f_1=early check-out rate; f_2=extended stay rate, then there is the following relationship between them:

$$X = (A-C+X) \cdot r_1 + (A-C+X) \cdot r_2 + C \cdot f_1 - D \cdot f_2$$

$$X = \frac{C \cdot f_1 - D \cdot f_2 + (A-C)(r_1+r_2)}{1-(r_1+r_2)}$$

Assuming the overbooking rate is R, then

$$R = \frac{X}{A-C} \times 100\%$$

【实训练习题】

某酒店有可供出租的客房 400 间，未来 11 月 25 日续住客房数为 140 间，预期离店客房数为 75 间。根据以往预订统计资料分析，通常该酒店预订取消率为 7%，预订而未到率为 5%，提前退房率为 4%，延期住店率为 6%。试问，就 11 月 25 日而言，该酒店：

①应该接受多少间房的超额预订？

②超额预订率多少为最佳？

[Practical Training Exercise]

A hotel has 400 rooms available, and the number of renewal rooms will be 140 on November 25, and the expected number of guest rooms will be 75. According to the analysis of previous booking statistics, the cancellation rate of this hotel is usually 7%, no-show rate is 5%, the early check-out rate is 4%, and the extended stay rate is 6%. Questions: on November 25th, the hotel:

① How many rooms should be overbooked?

② What is the best overbooking rate?

（二）超额预订还应考虑的其他因素

根据之前的公式计算出来的结果只能作为确定超额预订数量的一个参考，因为它是依据酒店以往的经营统计数据计算的，未来状况会怎样，还要考虑其他各种影响因素。

①掌握好团队订房和散客订房的比例。

团队订房是事先有计划安排的，预订不到或临时取消的可能性很小，即使有变化，一般也会提前通知。而散客订房的随意性很大，因各种原因不能如约抵店又不事先告知酒店的可能性较大。因此，在团队预订多而散客预订少的情况下，超额预订的比例要掌握小些，反之，则超额预订的比例就可大些。

②根据客房预订种类分析订房动态。

酒店通常采用 3 种预订种类，即临时性预订、确认性预订和保证性预订。临时性预订的客人如在当天取消预订时限（18:00）还没到达酒店，则该预订即被取消，故超额预订的弹性较大。确认性预订有充分的时间给予书面确认，向他们收取欠款的风险较小，同时酒店在失诺时的责任也相对较大，故超额预订的弹性较小。保证性预订能确保酒店在出现预订客人不来入住的情况下仍有客房收益，因此，对待保证性预订的房间，酒店不应该再超订。

③酒店的自身情况。

酒店超额预订的数量还受酒店自身类型、市场信誉度、周边环境等的影响。一般来说，连锁酒店凭借完善的统一预订系统和庞大的分店数量，可以适当地提高超额预订率以提高利润；独立经营的酒店则应相对保守一点。在社会公众中影响力不大的酒店，超额预订的比例可适当放宽，而声誉较高的酒店超额预订的比例则应小些。另外，如果酒店所处的区域内还有其他同等级、同类型的酒店，可适当提高超额预订比例，万一因超订过量而无房提供，也可以介绍客人到其他酒店。

④其他特殊情况。

恶劣的天气常造成航班取消、渡轮停驶。如果这种天气出现在预订到达当天，那么"预订而未到率"肯定会大幅提高，对天气情况的预测便成为超额预订比例制订的重要依据之一。

又如，倘若在客人的预订到达期前两三天，其所在地发生不利的突发性事件（如强烈地震），较大可能会影响客人的行程。但往往由于事发突然，客人来不及取消预订。对酒店来说，则可适当增加到达当天的预订量。

总之，通过对上述几方面因素的分析，各酒店可根据自己的实际情况，做好资料收集、积累工作，认真总结经验，合理地确定超额订房的数量或比例，既使酒店最大限度地销售产品，增加收益，又能满足客人的订房需要，不致产生订房纠纷。

（2）Other factors that should be considered for overbooking

The result calculated according to the previous formula can only be used as a reference for determining the number of overbookings, because it is calculated based on the hotel's past operating statistics. What will happen in the future, various other factors must be considered.

① Grasp the ratio of group bookings and individual guest bookings.

Group reservations are planned in advance, and there is little possibility of unreserved or temporary cancellation. Even if there is a change, it will generally be notified in advance. However, individual guest reservations are very random, and it is more likely that they cannot arrive at the hotel as scheduled and do not inform the hotel in advance due to various reasons. Therefore, in the case of a large number of group bookings and a few individual bookings, the overbooking ratio should be smaller. On the contrary, the overbooking ratio can be greater.

② Analyze the booking dynamics according to the type of room booking.

Hotels usually use three types of reservations: temporary reservations, confirmed reservations and guaranteed reservations. If the guest who makes a temporary reservation does not arrive at the hotel within the cancellation time limit（18:00）that day, the reservation will be cancelled, so the flexibility of overbooking is also great. Confirmed reservations have sufficient time to give written confirmation, and the risk of charging them is relatively small. At the same time, when the promise is lost, the hotel's responsibility is relatively large, so the flexibility of overbooking is small. Guaranteed reservations can ensure that the hotel still has room revenue even if the reservation guests do not come. Therefore, the hotel should not overbook those rooms that are guaranteed.

③ The hotel's own situation.

The number of hotel overbookings is also affected by the hotel's own type, market credibility, and surrounding environment. Generally speaking, a chain hotel with a perfect unified reservation system and a large number of branches can appropriately increase the overbooking rate to increase profits while independently operated hotels should be conservative. For hotels with little influence among the public, the overbooking ratio can be appropriately expanded, while the overbooking ratio for hotels with higher reputation should be smaller. In addition, if there are other hotels of the same level and type in the area where the hotel is located, the overbooking ratio can be appropriately increased. In case there is no room available due to overbooking, guests can also be introduced to other hotels.

④ Other special circumstances.

Bad weather often results in cancellation of flights and suspension of ferries. If this kind of weather occurs on the day of arrival, the "no-show rate" will definitely increase significantly. The forecast of weather conditions will become one of the important bases for formulating the overbooking ratio.

If an unfavorable unexpected event（such as a strong earthquake）occurs at the location of the guest two or three days before the arrival date of the guest's reservation, it is more likely to affect the guest's itinerary. Because the incident happened suddenly, the guests did not have time to cancel. For hotels, it is appropriate to increase the reservation on the day of arrival.

In short, through the analysis of the above-mentioned factors, each hotel can do a good job of collecting and accumulating data according to its actual situation, conscientiously sum up experience, and reasonably determine the number or proportion of overbooking, which not only maximize the hotel sales products, increase revenue, but also meet the needs of the guests booking, not to generate booking disputes.

二、超额预订过度的处理

超额预订的量是根据过去的经营统计资料和酒店主观分析的结果，未来情况无法完全准确预测。因此，超额订房的失败也时有发生。如果出现超额预订过度，客人到店后无法使客人入住，酒店必须积极采取补救措施，妥善安排好客人的住宿，以消除客人的不满，挽回不良影响，维护酒店的声誉。

按照国际惯例，酒店方面的一般做法是：

第一，诚恳地向客人道歉，请求客人谅解。

第二，立即与另一家相同等级的酒店联系，请求援助。同时，派车将客人免费送往这家酒店。如果联系不到同级酒店，可安排客人到另一家级别稍高的酒店入住，高出部分的房费由原酒店承担。

第三，如属连住，则店内一有空房，在客人愿意的情况下，再把客人接回来，并对其表示欢迎，入住期间享受 VIP 待遇。

第四，对提供了援助的酒店表示感谢。

如客人属于保证类预订，则除采取以上措施以外，还应视具体情况，为客人提供以下帮助：

第一，支付其在其他酒店住宿期间的第一夜房费，或客人搬回酒店后可享受一天免费房的待遇。

第二，免费为客人提供一次长途电话费或传真费，以便客人能够将临时改变地址的情况通知有关方面。

第三，次日排房时，首先考虑此类客人的用房安排。大堂副理应在大堂迎候客人，并陪同客人办理入住手续。

II Handling Overbooking

The amount of overbooking is based on past operating statistics and the result of subjective hotel analysis while the future situation cannot be accurately predicted. Therefore, the failure of overbooking also happens from time to time. If there is excessive overbooking and the guest cannot check in after arriving, the hotel must actively take remedial measures and properly arrange the guest's accommodation to eliminate the guest's dissatisfaction, minimize the adverse effects, and maintain the hotel's reputation.

According to international practice, the general practice in hotels includes:

First, apologize sincerely to the guests and ask for their understanding.

Second, contact another hotel of the same level to request assistance immediately. At the same time, sent the guest to the hotel for free. If you cannot contact a hotel of the same level, you can arrange for the guest to check in at another hotel of a higher level and the pay for the excessive expenses.

Third, for continuous stay, the guest would be picked up if they like as soon as there is a vacancy in the hotel, and they would enjoy VIP treatment during the stay.

Fourth, express gratitude to the hotels that provide assistance.

If the guest is a guaranteed booking, in addition to the above measures, the following assistance should be provided to the guest depending on the specific situation:

First, pay for the first night of staying in other hotels, or guests can enjoy a free room for one day after they move back to the hotel.

Second, provide guests with a free long-distance telephone fee or fax fee so that they can notify the relevant parties of the temporary change of address.

Third, consider the arrangement of such guests the next day. The assistant manager of the front office should greet guests in the lobby and accompany them to check in.

三、订房纠纷的处理

酒店因客满不能安排预订客人入住，或客人抵店时所提供的房间不能尽如人意等情况时有发生。一旦发生订房纠纷，酒店应根据不同情况妥善处理。

日常发生的订房纠纷，除如前所述因酒店实施超额订房引起的外，还有以下几个主要原因：

第一种，客人通过信函或邮件要求订房，因客满，酒店在回信时只同意列为候补。

第二种，客人抵店时间已超过规定的截房时间，或是未按指定的航班、车次抵达，事先又未与酒店联系，酒店无法提供住房。

第三种，客人打电话到酒店要求订房，预订员同意接受，但事后并未发出确认信息，客人抵店时无房提供。

第四种，客人声称自己办理了订房手续，但接待处没有订房记录。

第五种，在价格上发生争执或因不理解酒店入住和住房方面的政策及当地法规而产生不满。

酒店在处理上述订房纠纷时，既要分清责任，维护自身的合法利益，又要耐心、诚恳，设身处地为客人着想，帮助客人解决问题。注意"情、理、法"三者兼顾。

第一种情况，不能视为准确订房。第二种情况虽为确认订房，但已超过了酒店规定的留房时限。显然，因前两种情况发生纠纷，责任不在酒店。但是对客人同样要热情接待，耐心解释，并尽力提供帮助，绝不可与客人争吵。如果酒店没有空房，可与其他酒店联系安排客人入住，但酒店不承担任何费用。

第三种情况，虽无书面凭证，但从信义上讲，口头承诺应同书面确认一样生效。遇到这种情况，应向客人表示歉意，尽量安排客人在本酒店住宿，实在无房提供，可安排客人在附近酒店暂住，次日接回并再次道歉。最忌讳的是，有的酒店处理此类问题时借口未确认而对客人失礼。

遇到第四种情况，接待处要与预订处联系，设法找到客人的订房资料，看是否放错或丢失，或是其他原因。如经查找，确认客人是有订房，但早到了或迟到了，前台接待人员应尽力提供各种帮助，为客人解决面临的困难。如经查找，确认客人有当日预订，但酒店此时已无法提供客房，那么则应按超订过度的补救方法处理。

遇到第五种情况，前台接待人员必须耐心且礼貌地向客人做好解释工作，使其既接受现实又不致产生不满情绪，无论如何不能与客人发生争执。

总之，处理订房纠纷是一件复杂、细致的工作，有时甚至很棘手。前台服务人员要注意平时多积累经验和技巧，善于把握客人心理。为了做好善后工作，防止类似纠纷的不断发生，还应记录酒店负有失约责任的住客名单，呈报管理部门，并注入有关客史档案。

客房预订工作业务量大，渠道多、方式多样且经常出现订房变更，所以很容易出现工作失误。预订人员在订房的全过程中要认真负责，按规范、要求细致地处理每一个问题，以保证预订工作的准确性，减少差错和纠纷。

Ⅲ　Dealing with Room Reservation Disputes

It may happen when the hotel cannot arrange for guests to check in due to full capacity, or the rooms cannot satisfy them when they arrive. Once a dispute occurs, the hotel should handle it properly according to different situations.

Daily room booking disputes, in addition to the hotel's overbooking as mentioned above, are caused by several main reasons:

The first type is that the guest makes reservation by letter or email, and hotel only agrees to put in waiting list because fully booked.

The second type is that the guest's arrival time has exceeded the stipulated cut-off time, or the guest has not arrived in accordance with the designated flight or train number, and has not contacted the hotel in advance, so the hotel cannot provide accommodation.

The third type is that the guest called the hotel for room reservation, and the reservationist agreed to accept it, but no confirmation was sent afterwards, and no room was provided when the guest arrived.

The fourth type is that guests claim that they have completed the booking procedure, but there is no booking record at the reception desk.

The fifth type is that there are disputes over prices or dissatisfaction caused by not understanding the policies and local laws and regulations regarding hotel accommodation and housing.

When dealing with the above-mentioned room reservation disputes, the hotel must distinguish between responsibilities and safeguarding its own legitimate interests, but also be patient and sincere, put itself in the shoes of the guests, and help the guests solve their problems. Pay attention to the three aspects of "feeling, truth, and law".

In the first case, it cannot be regarded as an accurate reservation. In the second case, although the reservation is confirmed, it has exceeded the time limit for staying in the hotel. Obviously, for the disputes in the first two cases, the responsibility does not lie with the hotel. But the reservationist should also treat guests warmly, explain patiently, and try his/her best to help, and never quarrel with guests. If there is no room available in the hotel, the assistant manager can contact other hotels to arrange for guests to check in, but the hotel will not pay for the expenses.

In the third case, although there is no written evidence, in terms of trust, an oral commitment should be effective as a written confirmation. In this case, the assistant manager should apologize to the guest and try to arrange the guest to stay in this hotel. If there is no room to provide, the assistant manager can arrange for the guest to stay in a nearby hotel temporarily, pick him/her up the next day and apologize again. Some hotels are rude to the guests with no confirming excuses when dealing with such problems.

In the fourth situation, the receptionist should contact the reservation office to try to find the guest's reservation information to see if it is misplaced or lost, or for other reasons. If it is confirmed that the guest has booked a room, but arrived early or late, the receptionists should try their best to provide all kinds of assistance to solve the difficulties faced by the guests. If it is confirmed that the guest has a reservation on the same day, but the hotel is no longer able to provide rooms at this time, it should be handled as an overbooking remedy.

In the fifth situation, the receptionist must explain to the guests patiently and politely, so that they can accept the reality without being dissatisfied. In any case, staff of hotels cannot dispute with the guests.

In short, dealing with room reservation disputes is a complicated and meticulous task, sometimes even tricky. Front desk staff should accumulate more experience and skills and be good at grasping the psychology of guests. In order to do a good job in the aftermath and prevent the occurrence of similar disputes, the hotel should also record the list of guests who are responsible for the failure of the reservation, report to the management department, and record into the customer history files.

Due to a large number of channels and methods and frequent changes in reservation work, it is easy to make mistakes. The reservation staff must be serious and responsible during the whole process of booking, and deal with every problem meticulously in accordance with the specifications to ensure the accuracy of the reservation and reduce errors and disputes.

项目二

礼宾服务

任务一　迎送服务

【案例导入】

一天傍晚，一辆轿车向酒店驶来，停靠在酒店门口。刚参加工作的门童小王看清车上坐着 3 位欧美国家的客人，两位男士坐在车后，一位女士坐在前排副驾驶座位上。小王上前一步，以迅速规范的动作，打开车后门，做好护顶，并向客人致意问候。关好后门后，小王又迅速地走向前门准备迎接那位女士下车。但女士满脸不快地自行拉开车门下车了，这让小王不知所措。事后小王意识到，是否后为女客人开车门，怠慢了客人而招致不满。

10 分钟后，又有一辆小轿车停在了酒店门口。这次是两位中国客人，一位年轻女士坐在副驾驶座位上，一位年纪稍长的男士坐在后座。吸取了上次的教训，这次小王迅速地先为女客人提供了迎接服务，再向男客人提供服务。而此时，小王又注意到，年轻的女客人在整个过程中，表情相当尴尬。小王糊涂了，到底自己哪里又做错了。

【案例思考】

①小王做错了吗？为什么？

②一名前厅部礼宾人员应该具备怎样的素质？

Project 2

Concierge Service

Task 1　Pick-up Service

【Case Introduction】

A car drove towards the hotel and stopped at the entrance of the hotel on an evening. Wang, a new concierge, saw three guests from western countries sitting in the car. Two men were sitting in the back of the car, and a woman was sitting in the front passenger seat. Wang took a step forward, opened the back door of the car with a quick and standardized action, protected guests from roof, and greeted the guests. After closing the back door, Wang quickly walked to the front door to welcome the lady. But the lady pulled the car door by herself and got out of the car with an unhappy expression, which left Wang at a loss. Afterwards, Wang realized that he opened the door for the female guest later, which neglected the guest and incurred dissatisfaction.

Ten minutes later, another car stopped in front of the hotel. There were two Chinese guests. A young lady was sitting in the passenger seat and an older man was sitting in the back seat. Learned from last time, Wang quickly welcomed the female guest first, and then provided services for the male guest. At this time, Wang noticed that the young female guest had a rather awkward expression throughout the process. Wang was confused and wondered what he had done wrong again.

【Thinking About the Case】

① Did Wang make a mistake? Why?

② What qualities should a front office concierge possess?

【案例分析与问题解决措施】

（一）问题原因分析

本案例中服务人员没有及时从预订处取得需要接站的客人名单，掌握客人的姓名、所乘的航班（车次）、到达的时间、车辆要求及接待规格等情况。

（二）问题解决办法

①及时从预订处取得需要接站的客人名单，掌握客人的姓名、所乘的航班（车次）、到达的时间、车辆要求及接待规格等情况。根据预订航班、车次或船次时间提前做好接站准备，写好接站的告示牌，安排好车辆，整理好仪容仪表，提前半小时至1小时到站等候。

②当客人乘车抵达或离开酒店时，门童应为客人开车门、护顶（佛教和伊斯兰教徒则不用，但需提醒"当心碰头"）。为客人开车门时，门童应站在所开车门的铰链位置，侧身朝向车门，用远离车门的那只手拉开车门，靠近车门的手为客人护顶，并问候客人"您请！"或"您好！欢迎光临！"或"请慢走！"

③若客人分别在车的前后门上（下）车，两位门童需同时将车门开启、护顶。若有3位客人要上（下）车，一位门童将同一侧的两个车门同时打开，不需护顶，但要提醒"当心碰头"；另一位门童则须小跑到另一侧打开车门、护顶。若有两辆或以上的车辆到店，两位门童则一人负责一辆车，必要时呼叫礼宾部附近岗位增援。门童在

一人负责一辆车时，应按照服务对象的国籍、礼仪规范要求确定服务的先后顺序及方式。当客人乘车离店时，需向宾客行恭送礼（15°、30°的鞠躬）。

【Case Analysis and Problem-solving Measures】

（1）Analysis of the cause of the problems

In this case, the service staff did not obtain the list of guests who needed to be picked up from the reservation office in time, the name of the guest, the flight（train）they took, the time of arrival, the vehicle requirements and the reception specifications, etc.

（2）Solutions to the problems

① Obtain the list of guests who need to be picked up from the reservation office in time, and know the name of the guest, the flight（train）they took, the time of arrival, the vehicle requirements and the reception specifications, etc. Prepare for pick-up in advance according to the scheduled flight, train or ship time, write down the pick-up sign, arrange the vehicle, keep a good appearance, and wait at the station half an hour to one hour in advance.

② When a guest arrives or leaves the hotel by car, the doorman should open the door for the guest and protect guest from the roof（not for Buddhists and Muslims, but need to remind "beware of your head"）. When opening the door for the guest, the doorman should stand at the hinge position of the door, turn sideways toward the door, use the hand far from the door to open the door, and the hand near the door to protect guest from the roof, and greet the guest "Please!" or "Hello! Welcome!" or "Please take care!"

③ If the guests get on（get off）the car at front and rear doors respectively, the two doormen need to open the car door and protect guest from the roof at the same time. If three guests want to get on（get off）the car, a doorman will open the two doors on the same side at the same time without roof protection and remind "beware of your head"; the other doorman must open the door and protect guest from the roof on the other side. If two or more cars arrive at the hotel, the two doormen will be in charge of one car respectively, and if necessary, call for reinforcements near the concierge. When a doorman is in charge of a car, the order and method of service should be determined according to the nationality and etiquette requirements. When the guests leave the hotel by car, they should give the guests a bow（15° or 30°）.

【解决问题需要具备的知识和技能】

门厅迎送服务是指对客人进出酒店正门时所进行的一项面对面的服务。门厅应接员或门童是代表酒店在大门口迎送客人的专门人员，是酒店的"门面"，也是酒店形象的具体体现。因此，门厅应接员必须服装整洁，仪容仪表端正、大方，体格健壮，精神饱满，与保安员、行李员相互配合，保证迎客、送客服务工作的正常进行。

【小结】

门童上岗前应整理好个人仪容仪表，调整好工作心态，精神饱满地进入良好的工作状态。配备对讲机、白手套、笔、记事簿、零钱袋等物品，提前半小时到岗交接工作。门童，也称为迎宾员或门厅应接员，是代表酒店在大门口迎送客人，为客人提供相关服务的专门人员，是酒店形象的具体表现。门童的主要职责包括迎宾、指挥门前交通、做好门前保安工作、回答客人问询、送客等。为做好门童工作，酒店通常选择形象高大、魁梧，记忆力强、目光敏锐、接待经验丰富的人担任门童。目前，有的酒店为了别树一帜，提高吸引力，也会聘用女性、长者或外国人做门童。

【Knowledge and Skills Needed to Solve Problems】

The pick-up service refers to a face-to-face service for guests when they enter and exit the hotel's front entrance. The receptionist or doorman in the lobby is a special person who greets guests at the gate on behalf of the hotel. It is the "facade" of the hotel and a concrete manifestation of the image of the hotel. Therefore, the reception staff in the hall must be clean, fit, keep good appearance, full of spirit, and cooperate with security guards and porters to ensure the normal progress of welcoming and pick-up services.

【Summary】

The doorman should keep good appearance, adjust his/her work attitude, and be ready to work with energy. Equipped with walkie-talkie, white gloves, pens, note pads, coin pockets and other items, he/she should arrive half an hour in advance to hand over the work. The doorman, also known as the greeter or the receptionist in the hall, is a professional person who greets guests at the gate on behalf of the hotel and provides relevant services to the guests, which manifests the hotel's image. The main responsibilities of the doorman include welcoming guests, directing traffic in front of the door, doing a good job of security in front of the door, answering guest inquiries, and seeing off guests. In order to do a good job, the hotel usually chooses an experienced receptionist who is tall, strong, has good memory and sharp eyes as the doorman. At present, in order to be unique and attractive, some hotels also employ women, the elderly or foreigners as doormen.

一、门童服务准备

门童上岗前应整理好个人仪容仪表，调整好工作心态，精神饱满地进入良好的工作状态。配备对讲机、白手套、笔、记事簿、零钱袋等物品，提前半小时到岗交接工作。

站立于酒店前厅大门一侧，面朝大门前方。站立时，挺胸抬头，左手握右手手腕上放于小腹区域，脚后跟并拢，两脚分开约 45° 或两手背于身后，两脚张开与肩并齐。

眼睛平视前方，用眼角的余光注意周边动态，随时提供服务，面部表情自然。

I Service Preparation for Doorman

The doorman should keep good appearance, adjust his work attitude, and be ready to work with energy. Equipped with walkie-talkie, white gloves, pens, note pads, coin pockets and other items, he/she should arrive half an hour in advance to hand over the work.

Stand on the side of the front door of the hotel, facing the front of the door. When standing, keep the chest and head up with left hand holding the wrist of the right hand on the abdomen. Keep heels together with feet apart about 45°, or keep hands behind back with feet at the same level as shoulders. Look straight ahead, and pay attention to the surrounding dynamics through the corner of eye and provide services at any time with a natural facial expression.

二、门童服务内容

（一）问候

客人进出酒店时，门童应向客人表示问候。迎接客人时，通常说："您好！欢迎光临"。送别客人时，通常说："谢谢光临！请慢走！"。若是酒店常客，则应带上客人的姓氏，如"您好！××先生（小姐/女士）欢迎光临！"。现在很多酒店在问候客人时一般没有要求固定的问候语言，反而强调带有个性化和针对性的问候。比如对连住的旅游者，其外出时，可问候"您好！××先生（小姐/女士），祝您愉快！"；对商务客人，则可问候"您好！××先生（小姐/女士），祝您工作顺利！"，或是在客人外出时给予一些温馨的提示。

对客人进行问候时，门童应声音洪亮，面带微笑，注视宾客眼眉三角区域，最好按姓氏称呼！客人进店时，做好手臂手心斜朝上"请"的手势。若酒店前厅大门为闭合的玻璃门，客人进出时，还应提前为客人推门。问候酒店管理层、政府部门领导、VIP客人、常住客等需按时段问候"早上/中午/晚上好！"，以姓氏及职位问候。

II Job Description of Doorman

（1）Greeting

When guests enter and leave the hotel, the doorman should greet the guests. When greeting guests, they usually say: "Hello! Welcome." When seeing off guests, they usually say: "Thank you for coming! Please take care!". If greet a regular guest, they should bring the guest's last name, such as "Hello! Mr.（Miss/Madam）×× welcome!". Nowadays, many hotels generally do not require a fixed greetings but emphasize personalized and targeted greetings. For example, for tourists who stayed in a row, when they go out, can say "Hello! Mr.（Miss/Ms.）××, have a good day!"; for business guests, can say "Hello! Mr.（Miss/Ms.）××, I wish you success in your work!", or give some warm reminders when guests are out.

When greeting the guests, the doorman should have a loud voice and a smile, looking at the triangle area of the guests' eyebrows, addressing the last name best! When guests enter the hotel, make a gesture of "please" with the palms of their arms facing upwards. If the front door of the hotel is a closed glass door, doormen should push the door in advance when entering or leaving. When greeting hotel management, government department leaders, VIP guests, frequent residents, etc., doormen need to say "Good morning/afternoon/evening!" according to the time of day with their surname and position.

（二）开车门服务

当客人乘车抵达或离开酒店时，门童应为客人开车门，护顶（佛教和伊斯兰教徒则不用，但需提醒"当心碰头"）。为客人开车门时，门童应站在所开车门的铰链位置，侧身朝向车门，用远离车门的那只手拉开车门，靠近车门的手为客人护顶，并问候客人"您请！"或"您好！欢迎光临！"或"请慢走！"。

若客人分别在车的前后门上（下）车，两位门童需同时将车门开启、护顶。若有 3 位宾客要上（下）车，一位门童将同一侧的两个车门同时打开，不需护顶，但要提醒"当心碰头"；另一位门童则须小跑到另一侧打开车门，护顶。若有两辆或以上的车到店，两位门童则一人负责一辆车，必要时呼叫礼宾部附近岗位增援。门童在一人负责一辆车时，应按照服务对象的国籍、礼仪规范要求确定服务的先后顺序及方式。当客人乘车离店时，需向客人行恭送礼（15°、30° 的鞠躬）。

（2）Opening Door Service

When a guest arrives or leaves the hotel by car, the doorman should open the door for the guest and protect guest from the roof（not for Buddhists and Muslims, but need to remind "beware of your head"）. When opening the door for the guest, the doorman should stand at the hinge position of the door, turn sideways toward the door, use the hand far from the door to open the door, and the hand near the door to protect guest from the roof, and greet the guest "Please!" or "Hello! Welcome!" or "Please take care!".

If the guests get on（get off）the car at front and rear doors respectively, the two doormen need to open the car door and protect guest from the roof at the same time. If three guests want to get on（get off）the car, a doorman will open the two doors on the same side at the same time without roof protection and remind "beware of your head"; the other doorman must open the door and protect guest from the roof on the other side. If two or more cars arrive at the hotel, the two doormen will be in charge of one car respectively, and if necessary, call for reinforcements near the concierge. When a doorman is in charge of a car, the order and method of service should be determined according to the nationality and etiquette requirements. When the guests leave the hotel by car, they should give the guests a bow（15° or 30°）.

（三）出租车服务

若客人需要安排出租车离店，门童有义务协助安排，竭尽所能。门童可以通过联系出租车公司叫车，或到邻近酒店的公路上为客人叫车，或以其他方式为客人预约出租车或叫车。出租车到达后，在车牌卡上记录好车牌号，递送给客人，提醒客人物品不要落在车内，开车门护顶，行恭送礼。

若客人是乘出租车抵达酒店，门童应为客人开车门护顶，协助行李员卸下行李，提醒客人带齐随身物品或行李，并应快速记录车牌号，备注好客人信息及抵达时间，以防客人遗落物品在车内。

（3）Taxi Service

If the guest needs to arrange a taxi to leave the hotel, the doorman is obliged to assist in the arrangement and do his best. The doorman can call a taxi company, or call a taxi on the road adjacent to the hotel, or book a taxi in other ways. When the taxi arrives, record the license plate number on the license plate and deliver it to the guests, reminding guests not to leave their belongings in the car. Open the door and protect guest's head from the roof.

If the guest arrives at the hotel by taxi, the doorman should open the door for the guest, assist the bellman to unload the luggage, remind the guest to bring his belongings or luggage, record the license plate number and note the guest's information and arrival time in case guests leave their belongings in the car.

（四）雨天服务

如遇雨天，门童当班时需准备好酒店租借专用雨伞、伞套、"小心地滑"牌。客人进店携带湿的雨伞，门童必须将雨伞套好，并且向客人做好解释工作，不寄存客人雨伞。

向客人提供雨伞租借服务，有以下几种情况：

第一种，对住店客人，原则上免费提供租借服务。客人必须出示房卡，门童在雨伞租借本上做好相关记录，包括日期、房号、数量等，最后客人签名确认。还伞时只需要客人报出房号，核对数量，检查有无损毁后，在雨伞租借本上进行注销。

第二种，对非住店客人，原则上不享受雨伞租借服务，若要借出，必须收取相应的押金。还伞后便可退还其押金，收回押金联。

第三种，对于VIP客人、常住客、酒店行政管理层等可以免掉以上借伞程序，直接借出，但必须在雨伞租借本上记录。

提供借伞服务要注意，借出的雨伞必须是完好的雨伞，有破损、使用不方便的雨伞一律不外借。每个班次交接时必须将雨伞外借总数和押金总数交接清楚。

雨天门童进行服务时，还应注意地面积水，若地面积水较多，应及时联系保洁部门进行清理，以防地滑影响客人的行动和自身行走。客人未打伞到店时，要及时为客人打伞，迎接客人归来。

（4）Service in Rainy Day

In case of rainy day, the doorman on duty must prepare special umbrellas for rent, umbrella covers, and "CAUTION WET FLOOR" cards. When guests enter the hotel with wet umbrellas, the doorman must cover the umbrellas, and explain to the guests, and do not store the guests' umbrellas.

Umbrella rental services are provided to guests in the following situations:

The first one is to provide free rental services for in-house guests. Guests must present their room card, and the doorman will make relevant records in the umbrella rental book, including date, room number, quantity, etc., then the guest signs to confirm finally. When returning the umbrella, guests only need to report the room number, then the doorman check the quantity, damage, and log off on the umbrella rental book.

Second, for non-resident guests, in principle, they do not enjoy the umbrella rental service. If they want to lend it, the doorman must charge a deposit. After returning the umbrella, the deposit can be refunded, and the deposit coupon can be recovered.

The third one, for VIP guests, regular guests, hotel executives, etc., the doorman can dispense the above procedures and lend them directly, but must record in the umbrella rental book.

When lending umbrellas, please note that the umbrellas must be in good condition. Umbrellas that are damaged and inconvenient to use will not be borrowed. The total number of umbrella and the deposit must be counted clearly at each shift.

When the doorman provides services in rainy days, he/she should also pay attention to the water on the ground. If there is a lot of water on the ground, the doorman should contact the cleaning department to clean it up in time to prevent guests from the slippery ground. When guests arrive at the hotel without an umbrella, the doorman must open an umbrella for the guests in time to welcome them.

（五）问询服务

作为酒店的形象、窗口岗位，门童应随时保持热情友好、乐于助人，及时响应客人的合理需求。这就要求门童要熟悉酒店的产品知识，各营业场所的营业时间、价格等；熟悉酒店周边环境，包括高档的商场、特产店、道路信息、交通信息、餐馆、休闲娱乐场所；熟悉本地的著名旅游景点及交通线路等，做好城市的"活地图"。不断丰富自己的知识，以便更好地应对客人的问询，为客人提供个性化的服务。

［思考题］

在门厅迎客服务中，需要注意哪些细节？

（5）Inquiry Service

As the image and window of the hotel, the doorman should be warm, friendly and helpful at all times, and respond to the reasonable needs of guests in a timely manner. This requires doormen to be familiar with hotel product knowledge, business hours, prices, etc.; familiar with the surrounding environment of the hotel, including high-end shopping malls, specialty stores, road information, traffic information, restaurants, leisure and entertainment venues; familiar with local famous tourist attractions and traffic routes as a "living map" of the city. Enrich knowledge in order to better respond to customer inquiries and provide customers with personalized services constantly.

[Question]

What details need to be paid attention to in the welcoming service?

任务二　行李服务

【案例导入】

情人节的礼物

2月14日是西方人的情人节。这一天恰好也正是 H 城一家五星级酒店首届美食节的开幕式之日。酒店在《中国日报》《大上海》及本地报纸、电台、电视台都做了大量的广告，酒店外部及大堂内都做了漂亮的装饰。美食节期间，酒店还有住房赠送餐券、累积消费抽奖等活动，因此慕名前来消费的顾客络绎不绝。

下午 3:00 左右，酒店广场上搭起了各式餐台进行厨艺表演，彩旗飘飘、人头攒动，充满了节日气氛。这时，一辆红色桑塔纳停在了酒店大门口，行李员快步上前为客人拉开车门、护顶。车上下来一对年轻男女，看样子像是一对情人。那位小姐说："亲爱的，这儿人这么多，我们先进去吧。"男的说："好吧，玛丽，我们先进去。"接着他对酒店行李员说："麻烦你，帮我们拿一下车后面的行李。"说着，两人步入了酒店大堂。行李员打开后盖，拿出行李，一共是两件，此外，车上没有其他箱包。这时，他抬头看见又有两辆出租车过来了，赶紧关上车盖，并迅速在提示卡上记下桑塔纳车号，提着行李来到了总台。客人已在登记，玛丽转身看到了行李员提着自己的行李，立刻惊呼起来："上帝！大卫，你送给我的礼物不见了。"大卫赶紧转身，看到果然只有两件行李，他赶忙问行李员："我们还有一件行李呢？"行李员答道："先生，您车上只有这两件行李。"大卫说："怎么可能？我们还有一件东西在车上，你怎么这么不仔细呢？我要找你们大堂经理投诉。"

大堂经理海伦闻讯赶来，对发生的情况立即做出分析。她知道有两种可能：一种是客人自己遗失了一件行李；另一种则确实是行李员少拿了一件行李……这时，玛丽又叫了起来："大卫，那可是你送给我的情人节礼物啊！"海伦见此情形，问客人："请问先生，您还有一件行李是什么样的？"大卫说："啊，是一个圣婴雕塑，用麻布包着的，是我送给玛丽的礼物。"海伦立刻明白了，一定是行李员忽略了这件用麻布包着的行李。这时大堂里的客人越来越多，大卫和玛丽焦急地看着海伦……

试问大堂经理海伦该如何处理这件事情？

Task 2　Luggage Service

【Case Introduction】

Valentine's Day Gift

February 14 is Valentine's Day for Westerners. This day also coincides with the opening ceremony of the first food festival of a five-star restaurant in H city. The hotel made a lot of advertisements in China Daily, Great Shanghai and local newspapers, radio and TV stations. The exterior of the hotel and the lobby were decorated. During the food festival, the hotel also had activities such as meal coupons and lottery, which attracted a lot of customers.

At around 3:00 p.m., various dining tables were set up in the hotel square for cooking performances, with flags flying and crowds gathering, which was full of festive atmosphere. At this time, a red Santana parked at the front door of the hotel, the bellman quickly stepped forward for the guests to open the door and protect guest from the roof. A young man and woman who seemed to be lovers got out of the car. The lady said, "Honey, there are so many people here, let's go inside first." and the man said, "Okay, Mary, let's go." Then he said to the bellman: "Please help us take the luggage in the back of the car." They stepped into the hotel lobby. The bellman opened the trunk lid and took out the luggage. There were two pieces in total and no other bags in the car. At that moment, he saw two cabs coming, then closed the trunk lid, wrote down the Santana number on the reminder card, and carried the luggage to the main desk. The guest was already checking in. Mary turned to see the bellman carrying her own luggage and immediately exclaimed, "God! David, the gift you gave me is missing". David hurriedly turned around and saw that there were indeed only two pieces of luggage, and asked the bellman, "Where is the other piece of luggage we have?" The bellman replied, "Sir, there are only these two pieces of luggage in the car." David said, "How is that possible? We have one more thing in the car, how can you be so careless? I'm going to complain to your manager."

Helen, the front office manager, arrived and immediately made an analysis of the situation. She knew there were two possibilities: one was that the guest himself had lost a piece of luggage; the other was that the bellman had overlooked a piece of luggage... At this moment, Mary called out again, "David, that's the gift you gave me on Valentine's Day!" Helen asked the guest, "Excuse me, sir, what kind of luggage do you have left?" David said, "Ah, it's a sculpture of the Holy Child, wrapped in linen. It was a gift from me to Mary." Helen immediately realized that the bellman must have overlooked the linen-wrapped luggage. At this time, there were more and more guests in the lobby, and David and Mary looked at Helen anxiously...

How should Helen, the front office manager, deal with this matter?

【案例分析与问题解决措施】

（一）分析问题原因

①本案例中因大门口人多，客人先一步进入酒店，行李员没有与客人确认行李件数，结果引起了这场投诉。

②行李员在取行李时没有仔细检查每个部位，并且没有特别注意一些小件行李，将其遗留在车内。

③在没让客人确保自己的行李全部取齐前，立即关上车后盖，使出租车先行离开。

（二）解决问题的方法

①利用行李员记下的出租车号，请求出租车调配中心以最快速度找到出租车司机，并立即将礼物送至酒店。酒店在当天找到行李并交还客人，同时向客人致歉并赠送水果。事已至此，当务之急是立即找到客人的礼物，使客人能如愿以偿。在出租车司机密切配合的前提下，这个办法应该是处理此事的最佳选择。

②告诉客人，出租车已经开走了，我们虽然有车牌号，但寻找需要一定的时间，我们会尽力而为。请客人先进房休息并赠送水果。

这个办法虽然能一时平息客人的焦虑，但不是解决问题的最好方法。因为这件行李不同于其他行李，它有特殊的意义和特殊的时间界限。也许，第二天找到了，但玛丽却不能在情人节这天收到礼物，会留下遗憾和对酒店服务的不满印象。

③在一时无法联系上出租车司机，而在客人又急又气的情况下，可请客人详细描述礼物的细节，酒店出钱立即买一个礼物给客人。若能买到一模一样的礼物，那么这个办法尚可行，客人也会比较满意，但这种可能性很小。更何况酒店要支出一笔不必要的费用，因此不是最好的办法。

④若与出租车司机联系上之后发现礼物不见了，而一时又买不到同样的或其他合适的礼物还给客人，则可利用酒店美食节的一些活动，给客人安排一个特别的节目，

如在情人节烛光晚餐时请钢琴师演奏一支特别的曲子，给客人一个惊喜，尽量让客人忘记礼物丢失的不愉快。次日，再将礼物丢失的消息告诉客人，同时致歉并给予房价的减免，尽可能减少客人节日当天的不满意。

这个做法迫于无奈，相信客人虽然会留下一些遗憾，但最终也会被酒店的良苦用心和真诚态度所感动，故此法尚可借鉴。

【Case Analysis and Problem-solving Measures】

1. Analysis the cause of the problem

① In this case, due to the large number of people at the gate, the guests went into the hotel first, and the bellman did not confirm the number of pieces of luggage with the guests, which resulted in a complaint.

② The bellman did not check every part carefully when taking the luggage, and did not pay special attention to small pieces of luggage, leaving them in the car.

③ The bellman closed the trunk lid and let the taxi leave first before letting the guest make sure all the luggage was taken.

2. Problem-solving methods

① Use the taxi number recorded by the bellman to request the taxi distribution center to find the taxi driver as quickly as possible, and send the gift to the hotel immediately. The hotel found the luggage on the same day and returned it to the guests. At the same time, the hotel apologized to the guests and presented fruit. Since it happened, the top priority is to find the gift of the guest immediately. With the close cooperation of taxi drivers, this method should be the best choice for handling this matter.

② Tell the customer that the taxi has already left. Although we have the license plate number, it's gonna take some time. We will try our best. Please go to the room to rest and give fruit in the room.

Although this method can calm the anxiety of the guests for a while, it is not the best way to solve the problem. Because this piece of luggage is different from other luggage, it has a special meaning in a special time. Maybe, we will find it the next day, but Mary couldn't receive the gift on Valentine's Day, leaving an impression of regret and dissatisfaction with the hotel's service.

③ When the taxi driver cannot be contacted for a while, and the guest is anxious and angry, we may ask the guest to describe the details of the gift, and the hotel will pay for one and return it to the guest immediately. If we can buy exactly the same gifts, then this method is still feasible and the guests will be more satisfied, but this possibility is very small. What's more, the hotel has to spend an unnecessary expense. Therefore, it is not the best way.

④ If you contact the taxi driver and find that the gift is gone and you can't buy the same or other suitable gift to return to the guest, you can use some activities of the food festival to arrange a special program for the guest. For example, in the Valentine's Day candlelight dinner, the pianist is invited to play a special music to surprise the guests, and try to make the guests forget the unpleasantness of missing gifts. On the next day, tell the guests the news of the missing gift, and at the same time apologize and give a reduction in the room rate, so as to minimize the dissatisfaction of the guests on the holiday day.

This approach can be used when there is no other way. I believe that although the guests will leave some regrets, they will eventually be moved by the hotel's good intentions and sincere attitude. Therefore, this method can still be used for reference.

【解决问题需要具备的知识和技能】

①出门迎接。

散客乘车抵店时，行李员应主动上前迎接，向客人表示欢迎，帮助客人卸下行李，并请客人清点过目，准确无误后帮客人提携。易碎物品和贵重物品不必主动提携，如客人需要帮助时，行李员应特别小心，注意轻拿轻放，以防丢失破损。

②引领入店。

行李员提着行李走在客人的侧前方，引领客人至前台接待处办理入住登记手续，如属大件行李，则需要行李车推送。到达前台后，行李员应放下行李，手背于身后直立站在客人侧后方 1.5 m 处，等待客人办理入住登记。等候时不可左顾右盼，并随时听候前台接待员及客人的召唤。

入住行政楼层的客人需引导他们至行政楼层办理入店手续，并需帮助客人搬开并放好登记台前的座椅，请客人入座，退后 1.5 m，站立等候客人办完手续。

③领客入房。

客人办完入住手续后，应主动上前从接待员手中接过房卡，引领客人进入客房。引领客人到达电梯门时，应放下行李，按电梯按钮。当电梯门打开时，用一只手扶住电梯门，请客人先进入电梯，然后进入电梯靠右侧站立并按楼层键。电梯到达后，请客人先出，行李员随后提行李跟出，继续引领客人到所在房间。行李员引领时走在客人侧前方两三步远，用右手指示方向。边走边向客人介绍酒店的设施和服务项目，到达楼层后介绍安全通道。

到达客房门口时，行李员先放下行李，按酒店既定程序敲门、开门，以免碰到重复卖房给客人造成不便。房内无反应再用房卡开门。打开房门后，将房卡插入取电盒、开灯，然后请客人进入。

如果是几位客人同时入店，应在办理完手续后，请每位客人逐件确认行李，在行李牌上写清客人的房间号码，并礼貌地告诉客人在房间等候，然后迅速将行李送入房间。

④介绍客房。

进房后，行李员将行李放在客房行李柜上，然后简要地介绍房间设施、设备及使用方法。介绍时手势不能太多，时间不能太长，应控制在 2 分钟以内，以免给客人造成索取小费的误解。如果客人以前曾住过本店，则不必再介绍。房间介绍完毕，应征求客人是否还有其他吩咐，在客人无其他要求时，应礼貌地向客人道别，并祝客人在本店住得愉快。离开时，将房门轻轻拉上。

【Knowledge and Skills Needed to Solve Problems】

① Go out to greet.

When individual passengers arrive at the hotel by car, the bellman shall greet the guests, welcome the guests, help them unload their luggage, and ask the guests to check it and help the guests to carry them. However, it is not necessary to carry fragile and valuable items. If guests need help, the bellman must be especially careful, and handle the luggage with care in case of loss or damage.

② Lead guests into the hotel.

The bellman walks in front of the guest with his luggage, and leads the guest to the reception desk for check-in. If it is a large piece of luggage, it needs to be pushed by a luggage cart. After arriving at the front desk, the bellman should put down his luggage, stand upright with the back of his hand 1.5 meters behind the guest, and wait for the guest to check in. Don't look around while waiting, and always listen to the call of the receptionist and guests at any time.

For guests staying on the executive floor, the bellman needs to guide them to the executive floor to complete the check-in procedures, and help guests move away and put the seats in front of the registration desk. Ask guests to take a seat, stand back 1.5 meters, and wait for the guests to complete the procedures.

③ Lead guests into the room.

After the guest completes the check-in procedure, the bellman should take the room card from the receptionist and guide the guest into the room. When guiding guests to the elevator, the bellman should put down the luggage and press the elevator button. When the elevator door is open, the bellman should hold the elevator door with one hand, ask the guest enter the elevator first, then enter the elevator, stand on the right side and press the button. After the elevator arrives, ask the guest to leave first, then pick up the luggage, follow the guest and continue leading them to the room. When leading, walk two or three steps in front of the guest and indicate the direction with right hand. Introduce the hotel's facilities and services to the guests while walking, and introduce the safe passages after arriving on the floor.

When arriving at the door of the guest room, the bellman should put down his/her luggage, knock on the door and open the door according to the established hotel procedures, so as not to encounter repeated sales of the room and cause inconvenience to the guests. If there is no response in the room, use the room card to open the door. After opening the door, the bellman should insert the room card into the power box, turn on the lights, and then invite guests to come in.

If several guests enter the hotel at the same time, after completing the procedures, confirm each guest's luggage one by one, write the guest's room number on the luggage tag, and tell the guest to wait in the room politely, and then send the luggage to the room quickly.

④ Introduce the guest room.

After entering the room, the bellman puts luggage on the luggage cabinet in the guest room, and then briefly introduces the room facilities, equipment and usage. During the introduction, there should not be too many gestures and the time should not be too long, and controlled within 2 minutes, so as not to give the guest the misunderstanding of asking for a tip. If the guest has stayed in hotel before, it is not necessary to introduce. After the room introduction, you should ask the guests whether there are any orders. When the guests have no other requirements, you should say goodbye to the guests politely and wish them a pleasant stay in our hotel. When leaving, pull the door gently.

【小结】

行李员在取行李时一定要仔细检查每个部位，并特别注意不要将一些小件行李遗留在车内。取出行李后，不要立即关上后盖，这样可以牵制出租车司机。要待客人确认他的行李全部取齐、行李员记下车号后，才可关上后盖，给司机放行。这样做的目的是避免将小件行李及一些容易被忽略的物品（如本例中的礼物）遗留在车内，以及有足够的时间给客人确认行李件数及行李的完好程度，不至于让酒店为出租车司机承担不必要的责任。记下车号，便于酒店追查客人遗留在车上的物品。

对已制定的服务操作流程要严格遵守，不可出于某种原因而忽略其中的几个环节，如本案例中因大门口人多，客人先一步进酒店，行李员没有与客人确认行李件数，结果就引起了投诉。

在处理某些具有时间限定的事件时，要当机立断，采取果断措施。

在因酒店工作失误而引起客人不满意的情况下，酒店为了留住客人或考虑到下次生意及酒店的长远利益，可采取一些对客补偿措施，如减免房价、赠送消费券等，总之，要让客人乘兴而来，称心而归。

行李服务工作由前厅部专设的行李处承担。行李处设在大门入口处的内侧，既易于被客人发现，又便于行李服务员观察客人抵离店的情况以及与前台的入住接待和收银处联系。行李处主管负责指挥、调度行李服务工作。每天一早，行李处主管要认真阅读和分析由预订处和接待处送来的"当日抵店客人名单"及"当日离店客人名单"，掌握进出店的客流量，以便安排人力。特别要掌握重要客人和团体客人抵离酒店的情况，做好充分的准备。在此基础上，做出当日的工作计划，召集全体所属人员进行布置安排。

【Summary】

The bellman must check every part carefully when picking up the luggage, and pay special attention not to leave some small pieces of luggage in the car. After taking out the luggage, do not close the trunk lid immediately, so as to restrain the taxi driver. After the customer confirms that all his/her luggage has been collected and the bellman has recorded the vehicle number, he can close the trunk lid and let the driver pass. The purpose of this is to avoid leaving small pieces of luggage and some easily overlooked items（such as gifts in this example）in the car, and to have enough time for guests to confirm the number of luggage and the integrity of the luggage, so as not to make the hotel bear unnecessary responsibility for the taxi driver. Writing down the car number enables the hotel to trace the items left by the guests in the car.

Abide by the established service operation procedures strictly, and do not ignore several links for some reason. For example, in this case, due to the large number of people at the gate, the guests went into the hotel first, and the bellman did not confirm the amount of luggage with the guests, which resulted in a complaint.

When dealing with certain time-limited events, act decisively and take some decisive measures.

In the case of guest dissatisfaction caused by hotel work errors, in order to retain guests or consider the next business and the long-term benefits of the hotel, the hotel can use some compensation measures for the guest, such as reduction or exemption of room prices, gift coupons, etc. In short, let the guests come and return with joy.

The luggage service is handled by the luggage office which is specially set up within the front office. The luggage area is inside the gate entrance, which is easy to be found by guests, and it is also convenient for the luggage attendant to observe the arrival and departure of guests and to contact the check-in reception and cashier at the front desk. The luggage office supervisor directs and dispatches luggage services. Every morning, the luggage office supervisor must carefully read and analyze the "list of guests arriving on the same day" and "list of guests leaving on the same day" sent by the reservation and reception desks, and track the flow of passengers entering and leaving in order to arrange manpower. In particular, the luggage office surpervisor must grasp the arrival and departure of important guests and group guests, and make full preparations. On this basis, a work plan for the day was made, and all affiliated personnel were summoned to make arrangements.

● **行李员职责**

①听从领班的工作安排。

②按照行李服务工作程序，为散客及团体客人的抵离提供最佳的服务。

③随时注意前台接待员的召唤，迅速接受带房任务。

④负责分送住店客人的物品、邮件、报纸、留言及总台通知函件等。

⑤回答客人提出的有关询问，尽量满足客人要求。

⑥保管寄存物品，帮助住店客人包扎行李物品。

⑦保养运输、搬卸工具，使之随时处于良好状态。

⑧关照来访的客人，协助维持大厅的秩序。

⑨门童忙时顶替门童站门。

⑩为客人打包物品。

⑪按规定控制酒店大厅内的灯光和喷泉。

⑫保持工作区域的清洁卫生。

● **Responsibilities of bellman**

① Follow the work arrangements of the foreman.

② In accordance with the baggage service procedures, provide the best service for individual passengers and group guests.

③ Pay attention to the call of the receptionist at any time, and quickly accept the task of guiding guests to the room.

④ Distribute items, mails, newspapers, messages and notification letters from the reception desk of the guests in the hotel.

⑤ Answer relevant inquiries raised by guests, and try to meet guests' requirements.

⑥ Take care of the hotel items and help the in-house guests to wrap up their luggage and items.

⑦ Maintain transportation and unloading tools to keep them in good condition at all times.

⑧ Take care of visiting guests and help maintain order in the hall.

⑨ When the doorman is busy, stand in for the doorman.

⑩ Pack items for guests.

⑪ Control the lights and fountains in the hotel lobby according to regulations.

⑫ Keep the work area clean and hygienic.

（三）散客行李离店服务

①接收通知。

当礼宾部接到客人离店搬运行李的通知时，问清客人的房号、姓名、行李件数及搬运行李的时间，并决定是否要带上行李车，然后指派行李员按房号收取行李。

②收取行李。

行李员在 3 分钟之内到达客人房间，轻敲三下，并告知客人"行李服务"。在征得客人同意后进入房间，并与客人核对行李件数，检查行李是否有破损情况，如有易碎物品，则应贴上易碎物品标志。

③助客离店。

弄清客人是否直接离店，若客人需要行李寄存，则填写行李寄存单，并将其中的一联交给客人作为取物凭证，向客人道别，将行李送回行李房寄存保管。待客人取行李时，核对并收回寄存单。

若客人需直接离店，装上行李后，应礼貌地请客人离开房间，主动为客人叫电梯，为客人提供电梯服务，引领客人到前厅收银处办理退房结账手续。客人离店时协助行李装车，向客人道别，并祝客人旅途愉快。

④返回登记。

完成行李运送工作后，将行李车放回原处，填写"散客行李离店登记表"。

散客行李离店登记表

日期

房号	收取行李行李员	收取行李时间	客人离店时间	送客离店行李员	是否结账	行李存放卡号码	行李件数	车号	备注

制表人：

【思考题】

一对老夫妻在该城市旅游一周后办理退房时需搬运行李，你该怎么做？

（2）Check out service for individual luggage

① Receive notifications.

When the concierge receives a notice from the guest to leave the hotel to carry luggage, they should ask the guest's room number, name, number of luggage, and time to carry the luggage, and decide whether to bring a luggage cart, and then assign a porter to collect the luggage according to the room number.

② Collect luggage.

The bellman will reach the guest's room within 3 minutes, knock it three times, and inform the guest of "luggage service". After obtaining the consent of the guest, the bellman can enter the room and confirm the number of pieces of luggage with the guest and check whether the luggage is damaged. If there are fragile items, a fragile item mark should be affixed.

③ Help customers leave the hotel.

Find out whether the guest is leaving the hotel directly. If the guest needs luggage storage, fill in the luggage storage form and give a copy of it to the guest as a proof of pick-up. Say goodbye to the guest and store the luggage to the luggage room. When the guest comes and gets luggage, check and take back the deposit slip.

If the guest needs to leave the hotel directly, after loading his/her luggage, the bellman should politely ask the guest to leave the room, call the elevator for the guest, provide elevator service for the guest, and lead the guest to the front office for check-out. When the guests leave the hotel, the bellman should assist in loading their luggage into the car, say goodbye to the guests, and wish them a pleasant journey.

④ Return to registration.

After completing the luggage delivery put the luggage cart back to the original place, and fill in the "Check-out Form for Individual Luggage".

Check-out Form for Individual Luggage

DATE:

RM No.	UP BELL MAN	UP TIME	DEPT TIME	OUT BELL MAN	BILL PAID	B/C No.	PIECES	CAR No.	REMARKS

Formulated by

【Question】

An old couple needs to carry their luggage when checking out after a week in the city. What should you do?

任务三　"金钥匙"服务

【案例导入】

订婚的故事

1月21日，大堂孙经理在大厅遇见6017房金卡申先生，礼貌地上前问好，看出申先生一脸愁云，便主动问道："请问有什么可以帮忙的吗？"申先生便把周三要订婚的事情告诉孙经理，因为家人都不在郑州，很多事情都不清楚，找个商量的人都没有。孙经理关切地问："有什么困难可以和我们说，我们一定会尽力帮助您的。"申先生说："到时要送礼金，想让帮忙找个小盒子，大概装6万元现金。"孙经理满口答应，告别客人后，很快从精品屋找来一个装茶杯的盒子，但盒子颜色是白色的，好像和喜庆的气氛不合，孙经理又找来一张红色的礼品包装纸，并找到前厅部张经理，与其商量能否帮助客人包装一下。张经理马上安排礼宾部李殿陆包装礼盒，她自己则到商务中心下载了一张精美的卡通图片（两只可爱的小老鼠身着结婚礼服步入婚礼殿堂），交给李殿陆贴在礼盒内侧，很快，一个包装精美、象征吉祥和祝福的礼盒呈现在大家眼前。

当申先生拿到礼盒时，非常高兴，一个劲地说"谢谢"。这时，申先生又不好意思地说，还有两件事需要麻烦一下："一件是刚买的十斤糖果想让帮忙分装一下，装成22袋；另一件事就是送的彩礼定为66666.6（6个6比较吉利），想让帮忙换一下零钱。"孙经理和闫副理一商量，爽快地答应了申先生的要求。两人分头行动，一边协调礼宾部的同事，利用工作空闲时间帮助客人包装糖果，一边联系财务部帮忙换零钱。很快，糖果包好了，并送到客人房间。可是换零钱时又遇到了麻烦，因为按老风俗，送彩礼的钱面值应尽量为双数，可财务出纳那里只有3张20元的，而3张2元的和3张2角的都没有。刚下班的闫副理决定去银行看看是否能换，跑了几家银行只换到3张2角的，没有换到3张2元的，只好用6张新的1元代替。第二天上午，两人帮忙将申先生的礼金用红丝带全部扎好，正准备出发时，申先生同行的一位长者说道："按风俗，最好能用一块红布把礼盒包起来。"可是哪里有红布呢，眼看时间就快到了，孙经理马上联系礼宾部田珂外出给客人购买，申先生说："时间快到了，我们先去，如果买回来了，麻烦让他直接给我们送去。"说着留下了中午用餐的地点，田珂马上出发，用最快的时间买到红布，并送到申先生订婚的酒店，当申先生看见小田冻红的脸，对酒店的服务表示由衷的感谢！16:40，申先生一行订婚宴结束回到酒店，第一件事就是来大堂表示感谢，孙经理微笑着说："没事的，我们只是做了一些小事，只要能帮助您解决问题，对我们来说就足够了。"

试问酒店是如何解决顾客问题的？

Task Three "Golden Key" Service

【Case Introduction】

Engagement Story

On January 21st, the front office manager Sun met Mr. Shen, with gold card for room 6017 in the lobby, and greeted him politely. Seeing that Mr. Shen looked sad, he asked: "Is there anything I can help please?" Mr. Shen told Manager Sun about his engagement on Wednesday. Because his family was not in Zhengzhou, many things were not clear, and there was no one to discuss. Manager Sun asked with concern: "If you have any difficulties, you can tell us, and we will try our best to help you." Mr. Shen said, "I will give gifts at that time. I would like to help find a small box with about 60,000 yuan in cash." Manager Sun promised, after saying goodbye to the guests, he quickly found a box for teacups from the boutique, but the white color of the box seemed inconsistent with the festive atmosphere. Manager Sun found another piece of red gift-wrapping paper and asked Manager Zhang from the front office whether she can help the guest to pack it. Manager Zhang immediately arranged for Li Dianlu in the concierge department to pack the gift box. She downloaded a beautiful cartoon picture (two cute little mice walking into the wedding hall in wedding dresses) at the business center and gave it to Li Dianlu to past it on the inside of the gift box. Soon, a beautifully packaged gift box full of auspiciousness and blessings appeared in front of everyone.

When Mr. Shen got the gift box, he was very happy, and he kept saying "Thank you". At this time, Mr. Shen was embarrassed and said that he needed help with two things: "Ont thing is that, I just bought ten kilos of sweets and wanted to divide them into 22 bags; the other thing is the betrothal gift is 66,666 yuan (6 is more auspicious), and I wanted to ask for some change." Manager Sun and Deputy Manager Yan negotiated and agreed to the guest's request. The two managers moved separately, coordinating colleagues in the concierge department, using their free time at work to help the guest pack candy, and contacting the finance department to help with the change. Soon, the candy was wrapped and delivered to the guest's room. There occurred trouble again when changing the change, because according to the old custom, the money for the betrothal gift should be as double as possible, but there are only three 20 yuan, and three 2 yuan and three 2 cents are not. Deputy Manager Yan, who just got off work, decided to go to bank to see if he could change it. After visiting a few banks, hc only exchanged three 20 cents, and there were no three 2 yuan, so he had to use six new ones with 1 yuan instead. The next morning, the two helped tie up all of Mr. Shen's gift money with a red ribbon. When they were about to set off, an elder who accompanied Mr. Shen said: "According to the custom, it's better to wrap the gift box with a piece of red cloth." But where is the red cloth? Seeing that the time is almost up, Manager Sun immediately contacted Tian Ke from the concierge department to go out and buy it for the guest. Mr. Shen said, "The time is almost up. Let's go first. If you buy it back, please let him send it to us directly." After getting the address of lunch venue, Tian Ke set off immediately, bought the red cloth as quickly as possible, and sent it to the restaurant where Mr. Shen was engaged. When Mr. Shen saw Tian's red face from the cold, he expressed his heartfelt gratitude to the hotel's service! At 16:40 in the afternoon, Mr. Shen returned to the hotel after the engagement banquet. The first thing was to come to the lobby to express his gratitude. Manager Sun just smiled and said, "It's okay. We just did some small things, as long as we can help you solve the problem, it is enough for us."

How do hotels solve customer's problems?

【案例分析与解决问题的措施】

（一）分析问题原因

迅速快捷地将顾客的问题及时反馈给工作经验丰富的"金钥匙"服务人员，及时作出反应，准确无误地解决顾客要求。

（二）解决问题的方法

国际金钥匙组织的蓬勃发展是以其先进的"金钥匙"服务理念为引导的。"金钥匙"服务理念的精髓是：

①价值观：先利人、后利己。只有有了全新的服务意识和先人后己的价值观才能做好酒店服务工作，特别是"金钥匙"服务工作。

②方法：用心极致，满意加惊喜。它要求酒店的所有服务人员和工作人员，都要全力以赴、竭尽所能地为住店客人提供高质量、全方位、个性化的服务，不能有丝毫懈怠。在竭尽所能为住店客人提供高质量、全方位服务的同时，尽可能地让客人有超值享受或者额外的惊喜。

③目标：在客人的惊喜中找到自己富有的人生。在客人的惊喜和满足中，在客人满意的眼神和赞许声中实现自己的人生价值。

"金钥匙"服务理念具有共同的价值观、人性化的科学方法和共同的追求目标，"金钥匙"们在为客人带来方便、欢喜和自信的同时，也给自己带来欢喜、自信和方便。"金钥匙"服务理念是"金钥匙"们长期实践和总结的成果，没有这个服务理念，就没有"金钥匙"的成功。

"金钥匙"服务理念给酒店带来了清新的服务理念和服务价值观，它对原有的服务思想和服务观念产生了强烈的影响和冲击，可以说，"金钥匙"服务理念是星级酒店服务的最高境界，是所有酒店人孜孜追求的最高目标。"金钥匙"服务是新形势下高星级酒店服务的新形式和新发展！

【Case Analysis and Problem-solving Measures】

1. Analyze the cause of the problem

Report customer problems to the experienced "Golden Key" service personnel quickly, make timely responses, and solve customer requests accurately.

2. Problem-solving methods

The vigorous development of the International Golden Key Organization is guided by its advanced "Golden Key" service concept. The essence of the "Golden Key" service concept is:

① Value: Benefit people first, then yourself. Only with a brand-new sense of service and the value of putting people first can we do a good job in hotel service, especially "Golden Key" service.

② Method: The ultimate intention, satisfaction and surprise. It requires that all service personnel and staff in the hotel must go all out and do their best to provide high-quality, comprehensive, and personalized services to the hotel guests, without the slightest slack. While doing everything we can to provide high-quality, full-service services to hotel guests, we try our best to provide guests with enjoyment or extra surprises.

③ Goal: Find your own rich life in the surprise of the guests. In the guest's surprise and satisfaction, in the guest's satisfied eyes and applause, to realize one's life value.

The service concept of "Golden Key" has common values, humanized scientific methods and common pursuit goals. "Golden Key" bring convenience, joy and self-confidence to guests, but also bring joy, self-confidence and convenience to themselves. The service concept of "Golden Key" is the result of long-term practice and summary of "Golden Key". Without this service concept, there would be no success of "Golden Key".

The "Golden Key" service concept has brought fresh service ideas and values to the hotel, and it has had a strong influence and impact on the original service ideas and ideas. It can be said that the golden key service concept is the highest level of star hotel service. It is the highest goal pursued by all hotel staff. "Golden Key" service is a new form and development of high-star hotel service under the new situation!

【解决问题需要具备的知识和技能】

对中外旅游者而言，酒店金钥匙是酒店内外综合服务的总代理，一个在旅途中可以信赖的人，一个充满友谊的忠实朋友，一个解决麻烦问题的人，一个个性化服务的专家。酒店金钥匙服务对高星级酒店而言，是管理水平和服务水平的一种成熟标志，是在酒店具有高水平的设施、设备以及完善的操作流程基础上，更高层次酒店经营管理艺术的体现。酒店金钥匙服务对城市或地区旅游业而言，将对其服务体系的形象产生深远的影响。在我国，中国酒店金钥匙是由一群富有服务经验、对中国旅游业发展和酒店发展负有历史使命感和责任感的人组成的，他们共同的任务是使中国旅游业、酒店业能够和国际接轨，同时能够在国际上树立起一块牌子。这样，中国可以吸引更多客人的光顾，企业就有效益，行业就有发展。酒店金钥匙不仅给各城市的旅游酒店业创新服务注入了新的活力，而且对各城市旅游服务业的健康良性互动发展也是一种动力。

【Knowledge and Skills Needed to Solve Problems】

For Chinese and foreign tourists, Golden Key is the general agent of comprehensive services inside and outside the hotel, a person who can be trusted during the trip, a loyal friend full of friendship, a trouble-shooter, and an expert in personalized service. For high-star hotels, hotel's Golden Key service is a mature sign of management level and service level, is the embodiment of higher-level hotel management art based on the hotel's high-level facilities, equipment and complete operating procedures. The hotel golden key service will have a profound impact on the image of its service system for the city or regional tourism industry. In China, the Golden Key is composed of a group of people with rich service experience and a sense of historical mission and sense of responsibility for the development of China's tourism and hotel industry. At the same time, it can establish a brand internationally. In this way, China will attract more customers, enterprises will benefit, and the industry will develop. It not only injects new vitality into the innovative services of the tourism and hotel industry in various cities, but also is a driving force for the healthy and interactive development of the tourism service industry in various cities.

【小结】

金钥匙服务是一种专业化的酒店服务，又是一个国际化的民间专业服务组织，此外还是对具有国际金钥匙组织会员资格的酒店礼宾部职员的特殊称谓。国际金钥匙组织（UICH）始创于 1929 年 10 月 28 日，源于法国著名的香榭丽舍大道，由斐迪南·吉列为首的一群法国礼宾司开创的努力追求极致、演绎尽善尽美、倡导个性化服务的全新的酒店服务理念，近一个世纪以来，广泛地在全世界范围内传递发展着。其标志是两把金光闪闪的交叉金钥匙，它代表着酒店金钥匙的两种职能：一把金钥匙用于开启酒店综合服务的大门，另一把金钥匙用于开启该城市综合服务的大门。

　　"金钥匙"的原型是 19 世纪初期欧洲酒店的"委托代办"（Concierge），而古代的 Concierge 是指宫廷、城堡的"钥匙保管人"。

　　国际"金钥匙"是一个全球性的协会，目前已分布在全球 30 多个国家和地区，拥有数千名会员。我国于 1997 年加入该协会。

　　"金钥匙"的口号是："先利人，后利己；用心极致，满意加惊喜。在客人的惊喜中，找到富有乐趣的人生。"对中外商务旅游者而言，"金钥匙"是酒店内外综合服务的总代理，一个在旅途中可以信赖的人，一个充满友谊的忠实朋友，一个解决麻烦问题的人，一个个性化服务的专家。

　　在"中国酒店金钥匙"的蓝图中，始终有一个明晰的目标：使中国的旅游酒店业能够和国际接轨，同时在国际上竖起一块牌子，证明"中国的旅游酒店服务是优质的"。

　　欧洲人早在 70 年前就已经认识到"金钥匙"服务的重要性，美国人在 40 年前就开始学习和运用"金钥匙"服务并体会到其价值所在。在美国，一家很受人欢迎的酒店，往往是"金钥匙"服务十分到位的酒店。20 年前，新加坡和香港迅速在亚洲的酒店中推广这种个性化的品牌服务。

　　"金钥匙"的服务很广泛：向客人提供市内最新的流行信息、时事信息和举办各种活动的信息，并为客人代购歌剧院或足球赛的入场券；为团体会议制订计划，满足客人的各种个性化需求，包括安排正式晚宴；为一些大公司设计旅程；照顾好客人的子女；甚至可以为客人把金鱼送到地球另一边的朋友手中。

　　在中国的一些大城市里，"金钥匙"委托代办服务往往被设置在酒店大堂，他们除了管理和协调好行李员和门童的工作，还负责其他的礼宾服务等。

【思考】

"金钥匙"服务是因为什么而存在的？

【Summary】

Golden Key Service is a kind of professional hotel service and is also an international non-governmental professional service organization. In addition, it is also a special name for the staff of the hotel concierge with the membership of the International Golden Key Organization. The International Golden Key Organization（UICH）was founded on October 28, 1929. It originated from the famous Champs Elysees in France. A group of French concierges led by Ferdinand Gillette made efforts to pursue the ultimate and perfect interpretation. The brand-new hotel service concept that advocates personalized service has been widely spread and developed around the world for nearly a century. Its logo is two crossed golden keys, which represent the two functions of the hotel's golden key: one golden key is used to open the door of the hotel's integrated service, and the other golden key is used to open the door of the city's integrated service.

The prototype of the "Golden Key" was the "Concierge" of European hotels in the early nineteenth century. Concierge in ancient times refers to the "key custodian" of the palace and castle.

International "Golden Key" is a global association, currently distributed in more than 30 countries and regions around the world, with thousands of members. China joined the association in 1997.

The slogan of the "Golden Key" is: "First benefit others, then yourself; the ultimate intention, satisfaction and surprise; find your own rich life in the surprise of the guests." For Chinese and foreign tourists, golden key is the general agent of comprehensive services inside and outside the hotel, a person who can be trusted during the trip, a loyal friend full of friendship, a trouble-shooter, and an expert in personalized service.

In the blueprint of the "Golden Key of Chinese Hotels", there is always a clear goal: to enable China's tourist hotel industry to be in line with international standards, and at the same time to erect a sign internationally to prove that "China's tourist hotel services are of high quality."

Europeans recognized the importance of "Golden Key" services as early as 70 years ago. Americans began to learn and use "Golden Key" services 40 years ago and realized the value of this credible organization. In the United States, popular hotels are often those offering good "golden key" service. 20 years ago, Singapore and Hong Kong quickly promoted this personalized brand service in hotels in Asia.

The service of "Golden Key" is very extensive: to provide guests with the latest popular information in the city, current affairs information and information on various events held, and to purchase tickets for the opera house or football games for guests; to make plans for group meetings to satisfy various personalized needs of the guests, including arranging formal dinners; designing journeys for some large companies; take care of the guests' children; and even send goldfish to friends on the other side of the world for the guests.

In some large cities in China, "Golden Key" concierge agency services are often set up in the hotel lobby. In addition to managing and coordinating the work of the bellman and doorman, they are also responsible for other concierge services.

【Think】

Why does the "Golden Key" service exist?

项目三

总台服务

【学习目标】

明确前厅部总台服务工作的重要地位及主要工作内容；理解客房状态、行政楼层的基本概念并熟记常见的房态类型；熟练掌握总台办理散客入住登记、团队入住登记、VIP 入住登记、访客留言、住客留言、散客结账、团队结账等总台服务及行政楼层入住接待的程序和标准；掌握总台接待处、问询处、收银处对客服务工作中常见问题的处理方法。

任务一　前台入住登记

【案例导入】

重复卖房之后

某天晚上 12 点以后，酒店大堂来了两男两女，他们要求开两个双人标准间，前厅接待员小刘查阅了房态后，忙碌起来。查预订单—选房—入机—住宿登记—交迎宾卡—做钥匙卡等各个环节都很快捷，四位客人很快就拿到分配的房间 1201、1203 房钥匙，愉快地登上了电梯，向下榻的客房走去⋯⋯

可是当他们走出电梯出示房卡时，楼层服务人员发现，1201 房间已经有客人入住，应该是接待员将房间开重了。客房服务员立即表示歉意，并请客人稍等，待她询问清楚再说。四位客人非常生气，立即乘电梯返回大堂，径直走向接待处，质问是怎么回事。当客人在大堂大吵大闹时，保安走过来阻止，客人更生气了，上前跟保安拉扯，这时酒店经理也来了⋯⋯

Project Three
Main Desk Service

【Learning Objectives】

Clarify the important position and main job duties of the front office reception desk service; understand the basic concepts of guest room status and executive floors and memorize common room types; master the procedures of reception desk services for individual check-in, group check-in, VIP check-in, visitor messages, guest messages, individual guest check-out, group checkout, and executive floor check-in procedures and standards; master the handling methods of common problems in customer service work at reception desks, information desks, and cashiers .

Task 1　Check in at the Front Desk

【Case Introduction】

After Double Check-in

Two men and two women came to the hotel lobby after midnight. They asked for two standard rooms. After checking the room status, Liu, the receptionist in the lobby, got busy. From checking the reservation form, choosing a room, boarding-accommodation registration, handing in a welcome card-making a key card and so on, all the steps were compeleted quicklyh. The four guests quickly got the keys to the assigned rooms 1201 and 1203, took the elevator and walked to the guest room happily...

Unexpectedly, when they walked out of the elevator and showed the room card, the floor service staff found that there were guests in room 1201, and the receptionist must have overbooked the room. The room attendant immediately apologized and asked the guest to wait until she asked about it. The four guests were very angry and took the elevator back to the lobby immediately, went straight to the reception, and asked what was going on. When the guest was making a lot of noise in the lobby, the security guards came to stop him. The guest became even more angry and stuck the security guards, and at this time the hotel manager also came ...

【案例分析】

双重卖房是酒店前厅最容易发生，也是较严重的一种工作失误，它往往给客人造成极其不好的影响。因此，我们都应对容易出现双重卖房的几个操作环节严格把关，特别是要核对房卡、预订单、电脑房态、实际房态等显示的资料是一致的。

本案例是一次因前厅、楼层、客房服务中心三方对房态不清、沟通不力而酿成的一次管理与服务上的失误。具体是前厅接待员粗心大意直接导致了开重房的严重后果，使客人产生自己被忽略、被愚弄的感觉。归根结底，这是有关部门员工服务意识淡薄及工作上不认真负责的表现。此案例也暴露了前厅、客房部门工作衔接之间存在的问题，值得我们深思。

【Case Analysis】

Double check-in is the most common and serious work error in the front hall of the hotel, It often causes extremely bad effects on guests. Therefore, we should strictly check the several operational links that are prone to double selling, especially checking that the information displayed by the room card, reservation form, computer room status, and actual room status is consistent.

This case is a management and service error caused by the unclear and poor communication between the front hall, the floor, and the room service center. Specifically, the carelessness of the front office staff directly led to the serious consequences of double-booking the double room, causing the guests to feel neglected and misled. In the final analysis, this is due to the indifferent service consciousness of the staff of the relevant departments and the performance of not being serious and responsible in their work. The case also exposed the problems existing in the connection between the front office and the guest room department, which is worthy of our deep consideration.

【解决问题的措施】

①接到报告后，管理人员应迅速赶到楼层，向客人表示歉意。

②通知前厅重新安排房间，房间尽量安排在本楼层，不离原房间太远，房间的格调、大小、方向尽量与原来的相同。

③房间安排好后，让行李员将房间钥匙和重新填好的迎宾卡送上楼层，带领客人到新的房间。

④换出客人原来的迎宾卡和房间钥匙。

⑤帮助客人将行李拿到新换的房间。

⑥如果客人没有特别提出折扣的优惠，酒店无须特别提示，只需在客人入住后，对此房间多加以重视，给予更多的关注，切不能再出现问题。

⑦查清重复卖房的原因，登记入档，吸取教训。

【Problem-solving Measures】

① After receiving the report, the management staff should hurry to the floor quickly and apologize to the guests.

② Inform the front office to rearrange the room. Try to arrange the room on this floor not too far from the original room, and the style, size, and direction of the room should be the same as the original one.

③ After the room is arranged, ask the bellman to deliver the room key and the refilled welcome card to the floor and escort the guests to the new room.

④ Replace the guest's original welcome card and room key.

⑤ Help guests take their luggage to the assigned room.

⑥ If the guest does not specifically propose a discount, the hotel does not need to give special reminders. After the guest checks in, pay more attention to this room and ensure there must be no more problems.

⑦ Find out the reasons for repeated house sales, register them in files, and learn from them.

一、总台服务认知

（一）总台服务工作的重要地位

总服务台又称为总台、前台，它在酒店整体服务工作中的地位和作用至关重要。它是酒店对内、对外联系的总渠道、总枢纽，是酒店接待服务工作的指挥中心，是客人入住酒店期间接触最频繁的部门，酒店内部的各个部门都要通过总服务台进行沟通、协调才能做好服务工作。因此，总台接待工作是酒店对客服务工作的重要组成部分。

（二）总台服务工作的内容

一般而言，总台服务工作的主要内容包括 3 个基本方面，即接待、问询和收银。

①接待。

总台接待工作主要包括客房销售、入住登记、修改客单、沟通协调、房态管理等。

②问询。

总台问询工作主要包括提供信息咨询、访客留言、住客留言、邮件处理等。

③收银。

总台收银工作主要包括客账管理、外币兑换、贵重物品寄存等。

客房状态又叫客房状况，可简称为房态，是指对每一间客房在一定时段上正在占用、清理或待租等情况的一种标示或描述。准确控制房态是做好酒店客房销售工作以及提高接待服务水准的前提。酒店的客房随着客人入住和离店等活动而处于各种不断变化的状态中。

I　To Know General Service Desk

（1）The important position of the general service desk

The general service desk is also called the main desk and the front desk, and its position and role in the overall service work of the hotel is crucial. It is the main channel and hub for the hotel's internal and external contacts, and the command center for the hotel's reception service work. It is the department most frequently contacted by guests during their stay in the hotel. All departments within the hotel must communicate and coordinate through the general service desk. Therefore, reception at main desk is an important part of the hotel's guest service work.

（2）Job description of the general service desk

Generally speaking, the general service desk work includes three basic aspects: reception, inquiry, and cashier.

① Reception.

The reception work of the main desk mainly includes room sales, check-in registration, modification of guest orders, communication and coordination, room status management, etc.

② Inquiry.

The inquiries work of the main desk mainly includes providing information consultation, guest messages, visitor messages, mail processing, etc.

③ Cashier.

The cashier work of the main desk mainly includes customer account management, foreign currency exchange, and storage of valuables.

The guest room status is also called room condition which can be referred to as the room status for short. It refers to a kind of indication or description of the situation of each guest room being occupied, cleared or waiting to be rented in a certain period of time. Accurate control of room status is a prerequisite for doing a good job in hotel room sales and improving reception service standards. The hotel rooms are constantly changing in various states as guests check in and check out.

酒店的常见房态通常有以下类型。

酒店的常见房态

房态	英文	中文	备注
Occupied	Occupied	住客房	住店客人正在使用的客房
Vacant	Vacant	空房	暂时未出租的房间
OC	Occupied & Clean	已清洁住客房	
OD	Occupied & Dirty	未清洁住客房	
VC	Vacant & Clean	已清洁空房	已完成清扫整理工作，尚未检查的空房
VD	Vacant & Dirty	未清洁空房	
CO	Check out	走客房	客人刚离店，房间尚未清洁
OOO	Out of Order	待修房	硬件出现故障，正在或等待维修的房间
OOS	Out of Service	停用房	出于各种原因，已被暂时停用的房间
BL	Blocked Room	保留房	为团体客人、预订客人以及重要客人等预留的房间
S/O	Sleep Out	外宿房	住店客人外宿未归的房间
LL	Occupied with Light Luggage	携少量行李的住客房	
NB	No Baggage	无行李房	
DND	Do Not Disturb	请勿打扰房	客房的请勿打扰灯亮着，或门把手挂有"请勿打扰"牌
DL	Double Locked	双锁房	酒店（或客人）出于安全等目的而将房门双锁

The common room status of hotels usually are as follows.

Common Room Status in Hotels

Status	English	Remarks
Occupied	Occupied	Rooms being used by guests
Vacant	Vacant	Temporarily unrented rooms
OC	Occupied & Clean	
OD	Occupied & Dirty	
VC	Vacant & Clean	Rooms that have been cleaned and tidied but not yet checked
VD	Vacant & Dirty	
CO	Check out	Rooms that have not been cleaned and guests have just left the hotel
OOO	Out of Order	Hardware malfunctioning and waiting for repair rooms
OOS	Out of Service	The room has been temporarily suspended due to various reasons
BL	Blocked Room	Rooms reserved for group guests, reserved guests, and important guests
S/O	Sleep Out	The in-house guests did not return
LL	Occupied with Light Luggage	
NB	No Baggage	
DND	Do Not Disturb	The Do Not Disturb light is on in the room, or the Do Not Disturb sign is on the door handle
DL	Double Locked	The hotel（or the guest）double locks the door for security

差异房态是指前厅部记录显示的客房状态同客房部查访结果不符合的情况。差异房态有两种，一种是逃账房（Skippers），另一种是沉睡房（Sleepers）。前者是指前厅部显示为住客房，而客房部查访报告则显示为空房；后者恰好相反，前厅部显示为走客房或空房，而客房部则发现房内有人。

客房差异状况表

差异房态	前厅部	客房部
逃账房（Skippers）	住客房	空房
沉睡房（Sleepers）	走客房或空房	住客房

为了防止差异房态的出现，应采取以下措施：

第一，制订完善的空房状态检查和控制制度，杜绝可能的漏洞，尽量避免客房状态差异。

第二，加强管理，通过系统培训提高员工的业务素质和业务技能，加强管理人员对一线员工工作的监督与检查，减少可能出现的工作差错，保证正确显示客房状态。

第三，认真分析，确认差异的原因，迅速采取有效措施加以解决，保证客房状态的正确显示。

The discrepancy room status refers to the situation where the room status shown in the front office records does not match the results of the inspection by the room department. There are two types of discrepancy room status, one is Skippers, the other is Sleepers. The former means that the front office department shows as occupied rooms, while housekeeping inspection report is shown as vacant rooms; the latter is the opposite, the front office department shows as vacant rooms, while the housekeeping department found the rooms occupied.

Discrepancy Room Status Table

Discrepancy room status	Front office department	Housekeeping department
Skippers	Occupied	Vacant
Sleepers	Check out or vacant	Occupied

In order to prevent the appearance of discrepancy room status, the following measures should be taken:

First, develop a perfect system for checking and controlling the status of vacant rooms to eliminate possible loopholes and avoid room status discrepancies as much as possible.

Second, strengthen management, improve staff's business quality and business skills through systematic training, and strengthen managers' supervision and inspection of front-line staff's work to reduce possible work errors and ensure correct display of room status.

Third, carefully analyze and confirm the causes of the discrepancies, and quickly take effective measures to solve them, so as to ensure the correct display of room status.

（3）客房状况显示系统

目前，酒店的客房状况显示系统一般有两种：客房现状显示系统和客房预订状况显示系统。

客房现状显示系统，又称客房短期状况显示系统，可显示每一间客房的状态，前台接待处的排房和房价等工作完全依赖此系统提供的状况。营业中的酒店，其客房处于以下几种状态：空房、住客房、整理房或走客房、待修房等。

客房预订状况显示系统，又称长期状况显示系统，可显示未来某一时间内，某种类型客房的可销售量。

酒店电脑互联网系统，是用电脑设备系统综合显示客房状态的最先进的一种方法，目前广泛适用于客房数量多、种类复杂、客流量大的大型和中型酒店，在前台接待处、前台收银处及客房值班中心配有互联网的电脑终端机。各部门可通过操作终端机来了解、掌握、传递有关客房状况的信息，这不仅加快了互相沟通、联络的速度，更能提高工作效率，避免工作差错。同时，酒店电脑联网系统不仅用于显示客房状况，还具有各种功能帮助进行客史档案的建立、客账管理、各种表的形成、营业收入汇总等，可用于前台及整个酒店的管理工作。

（3）Display system of guest room status

At present, there are generally two types of hotel room status display systems: guest room status display system and room reservation status display system.

The guest room status display system, also known as the guest room short-term status display system, can display the status of each guest room. The arrangement of rooms at the front desk and the room rate are completely dependent on the status provided by this system. The guest rooms of a hotel in operation are in the following states: vacant, occupied, clean or check out, out of order, etc.

The room reservation status display system, also known as the long-term status display system, can display the saleable volume of a certain type of room in a certain period of time in the future.

The hotel computer Internet system is the most advanced method of comprehensively displaying the state of guest rooms with a computer equipment system. It is currently widely used in large and medium-sized hotels with large number of guest rooms, complex types and large passenger flow, and there are Internet computer terminals at the reception desk, cashier at the front desk, and guest room duty center. Various departments can understand, master, and transmit information about the condition of the guest room by operating the terminal, which not only speeds up the speed of mutual communication and contact, but also improves work efficiency and avoids work errors. At the same time, the hotel computer networking system is not only used to display the guest room status, but also has various functions to help establish guest history files, guest account management, formation of various tables, business income summary, etc., which can be used at the front desk and the entire hotel management system.

二、办理入住登记手续的目的

办理入住登记手续是总台接待工作的一个重要环节，其工作效果将直接影响前厅部功能的发挥。不论酒店的规模和档次如何，客人入住酒店前，都必须先出示有效证件并办理入住登记手续。

（一）办理入住登记手续可以和客人签订住宿合同

客人在办理入住登记手续时，必须填写一张由酒店提供的临时住宿登记表，这张表相当于酒店和客人签订的住宿合同。登记表上明确了客人入住酒店的房号、房价、住宿期限、付款方式等项目，以及酒店告知客人的退房时间、贵重物品保管等注意事项。最后，酒店接待员和客人都必须在这张临时住宿登记表上签名确认，这标志着酒店与客人之间正式、合法的经济关系的确立。因此，只有完成入住登记手续，酒店与客人之间的责任与义务、权利与利益才能明确。同时，从客房预订的角度来说，只有客人办理了入住登记手续，才使酒店的潜在客人变成了现实的客人。

II The Purpose of Check-in

The check-in procedure is an important part of the reception work, and its work effect will directly affect the function of the front office. Regardless of the size and grade of the hotel, guests who want to stay in a hotel must first show a valid certificate to check in.

（1）When checking in, sign an accommodation contract with the guest

When checking in, the guest must fill in a temporary accommodation registration form provided by the hotel, which is equivalent to the accommodation contract signed by the hotel and the guest. The registration form specifies the room number, room rate, period of stay, payment method and other items of the guest staying in the hotel, as well as the check-out time and the storage of valuables that the hotel informs the guest. Finally, both the hotel receptionist and the guest must sign and confirm this temporary accommodation registration form, which marks the establishment of a formal and legal economic relationship between the hotel and the guest. Therefore, only by completing the check-in procedures, the responsibilities and obligations, rights and interests between the hotel and the guests can be clarified. At the same time, from the perspective of room reservations, only when guests have checked in can the potential guests of the hotel become real guests.

（二）办理入住登记手续是遵守国家有关户籍管理法律的规定

我国有关法律明确规定，在我国的外国人及国内流动人口，在宾馆、酒店、招待所临时住宿时，应当出示护照或身份证等有效证件，并办理入住登记手续，才能住宿。酒店管理人员若不按规定为客人办理入住登记手续，是违反国家法律有关户籍管理规定的行为，视情节严重程度会受到相应的处罚。所以，办理入住登记手续既是酒店遵守有关法律的行为，也是酒店对国家应尽的义务。

（三）办理入住登记手续时可以获得客人的个人资料

客人办理入住登记手续，填写临时住宿登记表，酒店可以获得住店客人的有关个人资料，如客人的姓名、性别、国籍、住所、工作单位、抵离店日期、付款方式等基本信息。这些资料对做好酒店的服务与管理至关重要，它为前厅部向酒店其他部门提供服务信息、协调对客服务提供依据，同时也为酒店研究客情，特别是创造个性化、人性化的服务，建立客人历史档案提供了依据。

（2）Going through the check-in procedures is to comply with the provisions of the relevant laws on household registration management

The relevant laws of China clearly stipulate that foreigners and domestic migrants in China, when temporarily staying in hotels, restaurants, and guest houses, must present valid documents such as passports or ID cards and go through the check-in procedures before they can stay. If hotel managers fail to check in for guests as required, it is a violation of the relevant household registration management laws and regulations of the state, which will result in corresponding penalties for serious circumstances. Therefore, the check-in procedure is an act of the hotel to abide by the relevant laws, and it is also an obligation of the hotel to the state.

（3）Personal information of guests can be obtained after check-in

The guest checks in and fills in the temporary accommodation registration form. The hotel can obtain the relevant personal information of the guest, such as the guest's name, gender, nationality, residence, workplace, arrival and departure date, payment method and other basic information. These data are essential for the service and management of the hotel. It provides a basis for the front office to provide service information to other departments of the hotel and to coordinate customer service. At the same time, it also provides a basis for the hotel to study guest conditions, especially to provide personalized and humanized service. It provides a basis for the establishment of guest historical archives with customized services.

（四）办理入住登记手续可以满足客人对房间及房价的要求

办理入住登记手续时，前台接待员通过回答客人的各种问题，让客人了解本酒店的各种客房类型和相应的房价，并且可以推荐一些有特色和优惠价格的房间，客人就可以根据自身不同的情况，选择自己满意的房间和房价。所以，通过办理入住登记手续不仅推销了客房，而且满足了客人对房间和房价的要求。

（五）办理入住登记手续可以向客人推销酒店的其他服务与设施

许多客人在入住酒店前并不十分了解该酒店的服务项目和设施设备情况，这会影响他们的购买行为。接待员在为客人办理入住登记手续时，可以在推销客房的基础上，抓住时机积极地向客人介绍酒店提供的各种服务项目与设施设备，以迎合客人的心理需求，方便客人选择，从而为酒店带来较高的经济效益和社会效益。例如：看见客人抱着小孩，可以推荐"托婴服务"；看见客人的衣服有污渍，可以推荐"洗衣服务"。需要注意的是，推销要根据客人的实际情况，并要有适度的原则，以免客人产生厌烦情绪。

（4）Check-in procedures can satisfy the guest's requirements for room and price

At the time of check-in, the receptionist can answer various questions from guests, so that guests can understand the hotel's various room types and corresponding rates, and can recommend rooms with distinctive features and preferential rates. Guests can choose the room and price they are satisfied with according to their own different situations. Therefore, the check-in procedure not only promotes the rooms, but also satisfies the guests'requirements for rooms and prices.

（5）Check-in procedures can promote other hotel services and facilities to guests

Many guests do not fully understand the service items and facilities of the hotel before they check into the hotel, which affects their consumption. When checking in for guests, the receptionist can, on the basis of selling rooms, seize the opportunity to actively introduce the various services and facilities provided by the hotel to the guests to cater to the psychological needs of the guests and facilitate their choices, so as to bring higher economic and social benefits to the hotel. For example, if the receptionist sees a guest holding a child, he/she can recommend a "baby care service"; if he/she see stains on their clothes, he/she can recommend a "laundry service". It should be noted that the sales promotion should be based on the actual situation of the customers, and there should be an appropriate principle, so as to avoid the customers' boredom.

【知识拓展】

有效证件的种类

①护照：外交护照；公务护照；官员护照；普通护照；特别护照；团体护照；联合国护照。

②身份证件：海员证；回美证；返日证；香港特别行政区护照；港澳居民来往内地通行证；台湾居民来往大陆通行证；中华人民共和国旅行证；中华人民共和国外国人拘留证；中华人民共和国外国人临时拘留证；中华人民共和国居民身份证；中国人民解放军三总部制发的现役军人身份证件；武警总部制发的警察身份证件。

③签证种类及代码：外交签证（W）；公务签证（U）；礼遇签证（Y）；团体签证（T）；互免签证（M）；定居签证（D）；职业签证（Z）；学习签证（X）；访问签证（F）；旅游签证（L）；乘务签证（C）；过境签证（G）；常驻我国的外国记者签证（J-t）；临时来华的外国记者签证（J-2）。

【Knowledge Expansion】

Types of Valid Documents

① Passports: Diplomatic Passport; Service Passport; Official Passport; Passport; Special Passport; Group Passport; United Nations Passport.

② Identity documents: Seamans Passport; Permit To Reenter The United States; Reenter Permit To Japan; Hong Kong Special Administrative Region Passport; Mainland Travel Permit for Hong Kong and Macao Residents; Taiwan Residents' Mainland Travel Permit; People's Republic of China Travel Permit; People's Republic of China Foreigners' Detention Certificate of the People's Republic of China; People's Republic of China Temporary Detention Certificate for Foreigners; People's Republic of China Resident Identity Card; Identity Document for Active Military Personnel issued by the Three Headquarters of the Chinese People's Liberation Army; Identity Document for Police Officers issued by the Armed Police Headquarters.

③ Types and codes of visas: diplomatic visa（W）; official visa（U）; courtesy visa（Y）; group visa（T）; mutual exemption visa（M）; permanent visa（D）; occupation visa（Z）; study visa（X）; visit visa（F）; tourist visa（L）; flight attendant visa（C）; transit visa（G）; visa for foreign journalists based in China（J-t）; visa for foreign journalists temporarily coming to China（J-2）.

三、客房预分

客房分配需要根据酒店空房的类型、数量及客人的预订要求和客人的具体情况进行。为了提高工作效率，减少客人住宿登记时间，对于预订客人（尤其是团队客人）

应在客人抵达酒店前提前预分房间——通常在客人抵达的前一天晚上进行。分好后，将客房钥匙、房卡装在写有房号和客人姓名的信封内，等客人抵店并填完住宿登记表后交给客人。团体客人的房间存在两次分配，由于接待员不了解团员之间的关系，因此，不便提前确定哪两位客人住在哪个房间，所以在装有钥匙的信封上只能注明房号或团名，而不能写上客人姓名。对于每个房间的具体安排要等到团队到达后，由熟悉团队情况的领队或陪同人员落实。

（一）排房的顺序

接待员在排房时，应根据客人的特点及轻重缓急顺序进行排房，应优先安排贵宾和团体客人等，通常可按下列顺序进行：贵宾、有特殊要求的客人、团队会议客人、有订房的散客、未经订房而直接抵店的散客。

（二）排房的艺术

为了提高酒店开房率和客人的满意程度，客房分配应讲究一定的艺术。

① VIP 客人应是相对较好的客房。

VIP 客人在房间的选择上应是同类客房中方位、视野、景致、环境、房间保养等方面处于最佳状态的客房，并注意客房的保密性与安全性。

②尽量使团体客人住在同一楼层或相近的楼层。

团队客人住在同一楼层或相近的楼层，一是便于同一团队客人之间的联系和管理；二是团队离店后，空余的大量房间可以安排给下一个团队，既便于管理，也利于提高入住率。此外，散客由于怕干扰，一般不愿与团队客人住在一起。另外，团队客人的用房一般安排在较低楼层，一是电梯很容易坐满，二是高层房间可以留给出高价的散客。

③残疾人和老人应安排在离服务台和电梯较近的房间。

对于身患残疾以及行动不便的老人，应尽量安排在离服务台和电梯较近的房间，方便通行。

④应尽量把内宾和外宾分别安排在不同的楼层。

内宾和外宾有不同的语言和生活习惯，因此，应分别安排在不同的楼层，以方便管理，提高客人的满意程度。

⑤不要把敌对国家的客人安排在同一楼层或相近的房间。

如美国客人和伊拉克等中东国家的客人，一般不宜安排在同一楼层或相近的客房。

⑥要注意房号的忌讳。

如西方客人忌"13"，我国港澳及沿海等地的客人忌"4""14"等带有"4"（同"死"）字的楼层房号，因此，不要把这类房间分给上述客人。考虑到这些忌讳，目前很多酒店在楼层设置上没有"13""14"楼层，而用"12A""12B"层来代替。

⑦淡季要集中排房。

淡季时入住率较低，要集中排房，比如尽量排一栋，尽量同一层，排状态相对好的房间。同时淡季也要注意房间的平均使用，保持客房设施新旧程度均匀。

III　Room Pre-arrangement

Room pre-arrangement should be based on the type and number of rooms available in the hotel, as well as the guest's requirements and the guest's specific situation. In order to improve work efficiency and reduce the time for guest registration, reservation guests（especially group guests）should be pre-assigned rooms the night before their arrival. After arrangement, put the room key and room card in the envelope with the room number and guest's name, and hand it to the guest after the guest arrives at the hotel and fills out the accommodation registration form. There are two allocations of rooms for group guests. Because the receptionist does not understand the relationship between the group members, it is inconvenient to determine in advance which two guests share the same room, so the room number or group can only be indicated on the envelope with the key without the guest's name. The specific arrangements for each room will be decided by the group leader or escort who is familiar with the group's situation after the group arrives.

（1）The order of room arrangement

The receptionist should arrange the rooms according to the characteristics of the guests and the order of priority. Priority should be given to VIPs and group guests, etc., usually in the following order: VIPs, guests with special requirements, group meeting guests, individual customers with reservations, individual customers who arrive directly at the hotel without making a reservation.

（2）The art of room arrangement

In order to improve the hotel occupancy rate and guest satisfaction, room arrangement should pay attention to a certain degree of art.

① VIP rooms should be relatively better rooms.

VIP should be assigned the best room in terms of orientation, view, scenery, environment, and room maintenance among similar rooms, and pay attention to the confidentiality and safety of the rooms.

② Try to make group guests live on the same floor or similar floors.

Having group guests live on the same floor or similar floors is convenient for contact and management between guests within the group; second, after the group leaves the hotel, a large number of vacant rooms can be allocated to the next group, which is convenient for management and is also conducive to improving the occupancy rate. In addition, individual guests are generally unwilling to live with group guests because they are afraid of interference. In addition, rooms for group guests are generally arranged on lower floors since the elevator is easy to fill up, and high-rise rooms can be reserved for high-priced individual guests.

③ The disabled and the elderly should be arranged in a room close to the service desk and elevator.

For the elderly who are disabled and have limited mobility, try to arrange them in a room close to the service desk and elevator to make movement easier for them.

④ Try to arrange domestic and foreign guests on different floors.

Domestic guests and foreign guests have different languages and living habits, so they should be arranged on different floors to facilitate management and improve guest satisfaction.

⑤ Do not arrange guests from hostile countries on the same floor or adjacent rooms

For example, American guests and guests from Middle East countries such as Iraq are generally not suitable to arrange rooms on the same floor or close to each other.

⑥ Pay attention to the taboo of the room number.

For example, Western guests should avoid "13". Guests from Hong Kong, Macao and coastal areas in China should avoid "4" "14" and other floor room numbers with the "4" (sound like "dead" in Chinese). Therefore, do not assign such rooms to the above guests. Considering these taboos, many hotels do not set "13" and "14" floors currently, and use "12A" and "12B".

⑦ Arrange rooms centrally in the off-season.

The occupancy rate is low during the off-season, so it is necessary to arrange the rooms together, such as arranging one building as much as possible, trying to be on the same floor, and arranging rooms in relatively good condition. And also pay attention to the average use of the room in the off-season, and keep the room facilities in the same condition.

四、入住接待的程序

（一）散客入住接待

①迎候客人。

接待员应随时做好待客准备，在距客人 3 m 处开始关注，2 m 处热情礼貌地打招呼；若正在接待其他客人，应向后来的客人致歉，并予以目光关注。

②询问预订。

礼貌地问清客人是否预订。

a. 有预订客人：查找预订，与客人确认预订房间类型、房数、入住天数、房价，是否含早餐，是否需要无烟房及其他特殊要求，在电脑中输入入住信息。

b. 无预订客人：向客人推销，通过观察或问询了解客人来店的目的，并针对客人的类型进行适当的推销和介绍房型。

③登记资料。

请客人出示相关证件进行登记，办理入住手续。登记时实行"一房一证"，对证对人。回头客核对证件后，直接在电脑中链接客户档案。确认客人姓名后，至少在对话中使用一次。填写"临时住宿登记表"。

④受理预付款。

a. 询问客人付款方式，是否需要签单消费，提醒客人如果签单消费较多，需适当多交纳相应的定金。

b. 请客人核对入住登记相关信息并签名认可。

需要注意的是：第一，客人现付时需唱收唱付，现场点清，避免不必要的麻烦和误会；第二，做信用卡预授权时，需核对信用卡持有人是否为登记客人本人；第三，外币需由收银员签收；第四，支票验证需有担保人；第五，转账需核对签单人签名。

⑤交付。

将客人的身份证件、房卡、押金收据的顾客联（如是信用卡支付，还应加上信用卡和回单），一并交还给客人。如有多位客人可准备房号联络表。

⑥相关提示。

a. 告知客人其房间的方位、电梯位置、用餐地点、优惠等信息，并提醒客人退房的截止时间及贵重物品的保存事宜。

b. 询问客人是否有其他要求，如是否需要行李员引领至房间，并预祝客人入住愉快。

⑦存档。

当客人离开后，将相关信息录入计算机，建立客户资料，更改房态，将相关单据在接待部、前台收银分别存档。

旅客临时住宿登记表

姓名		性别		出生日期		职业	
工作单位				籍贯		省　市（县）	
证件名称				证件号码			
从何处来		到何处去		住店日期		离店日期	

同行人数（人）	姓名	性别	出生日期	证件名称	证件号码

客房类型	单人间	双人间	三人间	豪华间	套房
用房数量					
客房单价					
房号					
付款方式	□现金　　□信用卡　　□旅行支票　　□公司账户　　□旅行社凭单　　□其他				
备注					

请注意：

①退房时间是中午 12：00 时整。中午 12：00 以后至下午 6：00 前退房将加收半天房费，如果延时超过下午 6：00 将加收一天房费。

②前台免费提供贵重物品保险箱供住店客人使用。

③访客请在晚上 11：00 前离开客房。

④结账后请交回客房钥匙。

顾客签名：

接待员：

年　月　日

Ⅳ　Check-in and Reception Procedures

（1）Individual check-in and reception

① Welcome guests.

The receptionist should be ready to welcome guests at any time, start paying attention to guests from a distance of 3 meters, and greet them warmly and politely at a distance of 2 meters; if the receptionist is receiving other guests, he/she should apologize to waiting guests and pay attention to them.

② Ask about reservation.

Ask whether the guest has a reservation politely.

a. Guests with reservations: find the reservation, confirm with the guests the type of room, the number of rooms, the staying days, the room rate, whether breakfast is included, whether non-smoking rooms are required and other special requirements, then enter check-in information in the computer.

b. Guests without reservations: recommend rooms to the guests, understand the purpose of the guest's visit through observation or inquiry, and promote and introduce room types accordingly.

③ Registration information.

Ask guests to present relevant documents for registration and check-in procedures. When registering, implement "one room, one card" and check the information of the person. After checking the documents of the regular guests, link the customer files directly in the computer. After confirming the guest's name, use it at least once in the conversation. Fill out the "temporary accommodation registration form".

④ Accept advance payment.

a. Inquire about the payment method of the guests, whether it is necessary to sign for consumption, and remind the guests that if they exceed a certain amount, they should pay the corresponding deposit appropriately.

b. Ask guests to check the information related to check-in registration and sign for approval.

It should be noted that: first, read it out when guests pay in cash, and check them on the spot to avoid unnecessary troubles and misunderstandings; second, when doing credit card pre-authorization, check whether the credit card owner is the registered guest; Third, the foreign currency must be signed by the cashier; fourth, a guarantor is required for check verification; fifth, the signature of the signer must be checked for transfer.

⑤ Delivery.

Return the ID, room card, and deposit receipt to the guest (if the payment is made by credit card, credit card and return receipt should be added). If there is more than one guest, prepare a room number contact form.

⑥ Relevant tips.

a. Inform guests of the location of their room, elevator location, dining location, discounts and other information. And remind guests of the check-out deadline and the preservation of valuables.

b. Ask the guests if they have other requirements, such as whether a bellman is needed to lead to the room, and wish the guests a pleasant stay.

⑦ Archive.

When the guest leaves, input the relevant information into the computer, create the customer profile, and change the room status. File the relevant documents in the reception department and the front desk cashier respectively.

Temporary Accommodation Registration Form

Name		Gender		Date of Birth		Occupation	
Workplace				Native place			
ID type				ID number			
From		To		Arrival date		Departure date	
Companions	Name	Gender	Date of Birth	ID type		ID number	
Room type	Single room		Double room		Triple room	Deluxe room	Suite
Number of rooms							
Room rate							
Room number							
Payment	☐ cash ☐ credit card ☐ travel's cheque ☐ company account ☐ travel agent voucher ☐ others						
Remark							

Please note:

① Check-out time is 12:00 at noon. Check-out after 12:00 to 6:00 p.m will be charged a half-day room rate. If the delay exceeds 6:00 p.m, an additional day room rate will be charged.

② The front desk provides safe box for in-house guests for free.

③ Visitors should leave the guest room before 11 p.m.

④ Guests should return the room key after check-out.

Customer signature:

Receptionist:

Date:

（二）团队入住接待

①引领团队。

a.每个班次指定专人进行团队接待，指定的接待员需要随时关注团队是否到达酒店。

b.当团队到达酒店时，指定的接待员应及时将团队引领至专门进行团队接待的区域。

②接待入住。

a.与团队陪同人员确认团队团号、人数及房间数，确认无误后，即可将已准备好的钥匙交与陪同人员，并让其在"团队入住登记单"上签字，留下联系方式。

b.与陪同人员联系，确认叫醒、用早餐、出行李的时间，并询问客人当日从哪里来，离店后到哪里去。

c.向陪同人员索要已分好房的客人资料，填写"团队人员住宿登记表"并查看资料是否齐全，其中，内宾团需要宾客姓名、性别、证件号码；外宾团需要宾客姓名、性别、年龄、证件号码、有效期、入境口岸和日期、地址。拿到资料后进行复印。

d.没有团队资料的，将护照收齐，让客人在登记单上签字，先让客人入住，登记完之后再送回房间。

e.付款方式。如果是房费或餐费由组织单位转账，杂费自理的情况，则需收取杂费押金；如果所有费用现付，则需收取全额押金或信用卡。

③通知其他部门。

a.第一时间通知客房部团队入住，并在电脑中更改房态为"入住"。

b.将叫醒时间通知总机，用餐时间通知餐厅，出行李时间通知行李部。

④电脑输单。

将客人姓名、性别、出生年月输入电脑，并在电脑中更改房费，电脑中团队房费不能为零，需根据实际房费调整。

⑤资料存档。

将房费算好写在团队单上，第一联交收银，第二联交前台留存。

团队入住登记单

团队名称			国籍		人数	
抵店时间		离店时间		住宿天数		
客户名称		陪同姓名	陪同房号	领队姓名		领队房号
客房类型	单人间	双人间	三人间	豪华间		套房
用房数量						
客房单价						

续表

房号				
合计用房数		叫醒时间		
结账方式	□现金　□旅行支票　□信用卡　□公司账户　□旅行社凭单　□其他			
备注：				

陪同签名：　　　　　　　　　　　接待员：

年　月　日　　　　　　　　　　年　月　日

团队人员住宿登记表

团队名称							
客户名称							
抵店日期				离店日期			
姓名	性别	职业	国籍	证件名称	证件号码	房号	

制表人：

年　月　日

（2）Group check-in reception

① Lead the team.

a. Each shift designates a person for team reception, and the designated receptionist needs to stay informed about whether the team arrives at the hotel.

b. When the team arrives at the hotel, the designated receptionist will lead the team to the area dedicated to the group check-in area promptly.

② Reception check-in.

a. Confirm the group number, the number of people and the number of rooms with the team escort. After confirming the correct number, hand the prepared key to the escort, and ask the escort to sign on the "Group Check-in Registration Form", leaving the contact details.

b. Contact the escort to confirm the time of wake-up call, breakfast and luggage, and ask the guest where they come from and where they will go after leaving the hotel that day.

c. Ask the escort for the information of the guests who have been arranged rooms, fill out the "Registration Form for Group Members". For domestic groups, need to check guest's name, gender, and ID number; for foreign groups, need to check the guest's name, gender, age, certificate number, expiration date, port of entry and date, address. Make a copy after getting the information.

d. If there is no team information, all passports should be collected and the guests should sign on the registration form. The guests will be sent to the room first, and then sent passports back to the room after registration.

e. Payment method. If the room fee and meal fee is transferred by the company account, and other expenses are paid by themselves, a deposit for other charges is required; if all costs are paid in cash, either a full deposit or credit card is required.

③ Notify other departments.

a. Notify the housekeeping department at the first time and change the room status to "check-in" in the computer.

b. Notify the switchboard of the wake-up call time, the restaurant of the meal time, and the baggage department of the departure time.

④ Input information into computer.

Input the guest's name, gender and date of birth into the computer, and change the room charge in the computer. The group room charge in the computer cannot be zero, and should be adjusted according to the actual room charge.

⑤ File the information.

Write the room charge on the group list, give the first part to the cashier and the second part to the front office to keep.

Group Check-in Registration Form

Group name			Nationality		Number of people	
Arrival time		Departure time		Number of days of stay		
Cuest name		Escort name	Escort room number	Group leader name		Group leader room number

Continued

Room type	Single room	Double room	Triple room	Deluxe room	Suite
Number of rooms					
Room rate					
Room number					
Total number of rooms			Call-up time		
Payment	☐ cash ☐ credit card ☐ travel's cheque ☐ company account ☐ travel agent voucher ☐ others				
Remark					

Escort signature：　　　　　　　　Receptionist：

Date:　　　　　　　　　　　　Date:

Registration Form for Group Members

Group name						
Cuest name						
Arrival time				Departure time		
Name	Gender	Occupation	Nationality	ID type	ID number	Room number

Formulated by

Date:

（三）VIP 入住接待

VIP 是 Very Important Person 的简称。VIP 是酒店给予在政治、经济以及社会各领域有一定成就、影响和号召力的人士的荣誉，是酒店完善标准的接待规格和服务对象，是酒店优质服务体系的集中体现。VIP 客人的入住接待程序如下。

①准备工作。

a. 从预订处或销售部接到 VIP 接待通知单或每天预计到店名单中获知贵宾的姓名、到达时间、职务等资料后，应立即报告总经理，填写 VIP 申请单（即重点客人呈报表），请示酒店是否派管理人员接待及接待规格等。

VIP 接待通知单

No.

姓名（团体）		身份		国籍	
人数	男 / 女		房号		
抵店日期			班次		
离店日期			班次		
拟住天数			接待标准		
客人要求					
接待单位			陪同人数身份		男 / 女
特殊要求					
审核人			经手人		
备注：					
				年　月　日	

b. 根据接待规格安排相应的房间，提前准备好房间钥匙、欢迎卡和住宿登记单及有关客人信件等。

c. VIP 客人到达酒店前将装有房卡、钥匙等的欢迎信封及登记卡放至大堂经理处，同时通知有关部门按照接待规格做好准备。

d. 大堂经理在客人到达前 1 小时检查房间；客人抵达前半小时，大堂经理应准备好客房门卡、欢迎卡及住宿登记单，在门厅迎候客人抵店。

②办理入住手续。

a. 准确掌握当天预抵 VIP 客人姓名；以客人姓名称呼客人，对不同级别的 VIP 客人，通知相应的酒店总经理、驻店经理、前厅部经理及大堂经理等亲自迎接。

b. 不同级别的管理人员分别将不同级别的 VIP 客人亲自送至房间，并向客人介绍酒店设施和服务项目。

③储存信息。

a. 总台接待人员复核有关 VIP 客人资料，并准确输入电脑；在电脑中注明"VIP"以提示其他各部门或人员注意。

b. 为 VIP 客人建立客史档案，并注明身份，以备查询。

（3）VIP reception

VIP is the abbreviation of Very Important Person. VIP is the honor given by the hotel to the people who have certain achievements, influence and appeal in the political, economic and social fields. It is the perfect standard reception specification service object of the hotel, which is the centralized embodiment of the hotel quality service system. The VIP guests' check-in reception procedure is as follows.

① Preparation.

a. After receiving VIP reception notice from the reservation office or sales department or daily list, know VIP's name, arrival time, position and other information. Report to the general manager immediately, fill out the VIP application form（key guest report form）and ask whether the hotel should send managers for reception and follow the reception specifications.

VIP Reception Notice

No.

Name（group）		Identity		Nationality	
Number of people	Male/Female		Room number		
Arrival time			Flight（train）		
Departure time			Flight（train）		
Number of days to stay			Reception standard		
Guest request					
Reception unit			Number of escort male female		
Special requirements					
Reviewer			Handler		
Remark：					
				Date	

b. Arrange the appropriate room according to the reception specifications, and prepare the room key, welcome card, accommodation registration form and relevant guest letters in advance.

c. Before the VIP guests arrive at the hotel, place the welcome envelope containing the room card, key, etc the registration card to the lobby manager, and at the same time inform the relevant departments to prepare according to the reception specifications.

d. The lobby manager should check the room one hour before the guest arrives, prepare the guest room, room card, welcome card and accommodation registration form and wait for guests in the lobby half an hour before the guest arrives,

② Check-in.

a. Know the names of VIP guests who are expected to arrive on the day; address the guests by their names. For VIP guests of different levels, notify the hotel general manager, resident manager, front office manager and lobby manager to personally greet them correspondingly.

b. Management personnel of different levels will send VIP guests of different levels to the room in person, and introduce the facilities and services of hotel to the guests.

③ Store information.

a. The reception staff at the reception desk should review the relevant VIP guest information and input it into the computer accurately; indicate "VIP" in the computer to mention other departments or personnel.

b. Establish guest history files for VIP guests and indicate their identities.

【知识拓展】

某星级酒店 VIP 客人的分类及接待规格

级别	定义	礼品	客房物品	欢迎级别
A 级	国家元首、中央领导、警卫任务接待等	果篮、花篮、酒店纪念品、欢迎信	专用洗浴品、浴衣、五巾	董事长、总经理、总监、各部门经理迎接
B 级	部级、省级、大公司总裁、名人明星等	果篮、花篮、欢迎信	专用洗浴品、五巾	总经理、总监、各部门经理迎接
C 级	市级领导、酒店同行等	果盘、盆花或盆景、欢迎信	专用洗浴品	总监、各部门经理迎接

【思考】

部分客人为了减少麻烦，出于保密或显示自己特殊身份和地位等目的，住店时不愿登记或登记时有些项目不愿填写。身为前台接待员的你应当如何做？

【Knowledge Expansion】

Classification and reception specifications of VIP guests of a star hotel

Level	Definition	Gifts	Items in Room	Welcome Level
Level A	Head of state, central leadership, security task reception, etc.	Fruit basket, flower basket, hotel souvenirs, welcome letter	Special bath products, bathrobe, five towels	Chairman, general manager, director, managers of various departments to meet
Level B	Ministerial leader, provincial leader, president of large companies, celebrities, etc.	Fruit basket, flower basket, welcome letter	Special bath products, five towels	General manager, director, managers of various departments to meet
Level C	Municipal leaders, hotel colleagues	Fruit basket, potted flowers or bonsai, welcome letter	Special bath products	Director, managers of various departments to meet

【Thinking】

Some guests do not want to register for confidentiality or to show their special status and position. As a receptionist, what should you do?

任务二　入住接待常见问题处理

【案例导入】

事先预订的房间被告知没有了

宋先生是一家大公司驻某市的代表，最近他的上司要来该市视察业务开展情况，为了做好接待工作，宋先生提前10天在市内一家高档酒店预订了一间商务套间。宋先生是个办事谨慎的人，虽然预订了房间，但是次日他还是打电话到酒店总台与接待员再次确认，当得知房间已安排妥当后，宋先生总算放心了。哪知天有不测风云，就在宋先生与总台接待员电话确认订房的第二天，他接到了总台预订员的电话，被告知商务套间已满，建议其入住豪华套间。因存在房费差价，宋先生拒绝了酒店的建议，并取消了在该酒店的订房，改住到其他酒店。

Task 2　Handling Common Problems of Check-in and Reception

【Case Introduction】

A room booked was told that it was not available

Mr. Song is a representative of a large company in a city. Since his boss will come to the city to inspect its business development recently, in order to do a good job of reception, Mr. Song booked a business suite at a high-end hotel in the city 10 days in advance. Mr. Song is a cautious person. Although he booked a room, he called the hotel reception desk the next day to reconfirm with the receptionist. When he learned that the room had been arranged, Mr. Song was finally relieved. Unexpectedly, the day after Mr. Song phoned the receptionist to confirm the reservation, he received a call from the receptionist, who informed him that the business suite was full and suggested that he stay in the deluxe suite. Due to the room rate difference, Mr. Song rejected the hotel's suggestion and cancelled the reservation at the hotel and chose another hotel.

【案例分析】

　　酒店客房是很脆弱的特殊商品，具有不可储存性，为了获取最大的利益，经营者总是希望住店客人越多越好。但是，一年365天，哪天盈，哪天缺，酒店很难了如指掌，这就给客房预订增加了难度。客人提前订好了房间，因客满而住不上房的现象时有发生，但是酒店却不能以此为由，把不便留给客人，应该热情相待，妥善处理。按照国际旅游协会的规定，客房预订是受法律保护的，客人一般不会因预订问题起诉酒店，但是信誉是酒店最重要的东西，面对客满，订房客人可能不声不响地离去，表面上看异常纠纷平息了，但酒店却很可能永远失去了一位顾客，这个损失用眼前利益是无法衡量的。因此，对预订某类型房间而无此类型房住的客人，理应无条件地留下，比如可以将客人的房间升级，从表面上看这种做法使酒店损失了几百元钱，但酒店因此却可以保住信誉，并赢得了一位客人。钱损失了还可以赚回来，但是信誉受损了就难恢复了。

　　分析宋先生预订纠纷的原因主要是酒店预订处与接待处沟通不良，接待员未能正确掌握可租房的数量，造成了订房差错；预订处发现订房差错后，没有妥善处理好宋先生的订房事宜，最终使酒店失去了这位客人。

　　为避免类似现象，酒店应做好以下几方面工作：总台设预订总表并由专人负责统计每日客房预订总数；建立和健全预订组与开房组间的有效沟通制度；管理人员加强对预订工作的日常检查；妥善处理预订纠纷，努力达到客人和酒店同受益、共满意。

【Case Analysis】

Guest rooms in hotels are perishable commodities that cannot be stored like regulawr goods. In order to obtain the maximum benefit, the operator always hopes that the more guests staying in the hotel, the better. As there are 365 days in a year, it is difficult to predict when the hotel can make profit and when gain nothing, which makes room reservation difficult. It happens sometimes that the guest has booked the room but cannot live in the room because it is full. However, the hotel cannot use this as an excuse, should treat each other warmly and deal with it properly. According to the regulations of the International Tourism Association, room reservation is protected by law. Generally speaking, guests will not sue the hotel for reservation problems, but reputation is the most important thing in a hotel. When rooms are full, guests may leave the hotel quietly. It seemed that dispute has subsided, but the hotel is likely to lose its guests forever. This loss cannot be measured with short benefits. Therefore, for guests who book a certain type of room, there is no more room for them. Hotel can upgrade their room. Although this approach has caused the hotel to lose hundreds of dollars, the hotel kept its promise and won the guest's trust. Money can be earned back someday, but it is difficult to recover its reputation.

Mr. Song's reservation dispute is mainly due to poor communication between the hotel's reservation office and reception, and the receptionist failed to correctly determine the number of rooms available for rent, resulting in a reservation error. After the reservation office found a reservation error, the hotel did not properly handle the reservation. This issue eventually made the hotel lose this guest.

In order to avoid similar phenomena, the hotel should do the following things: establish a reservation summary table at the front desk and assign a dedicated person to track the total number of daily room reservations; establish and improve an effective communication system between the reservation group and the room opening group; management personnel strengthen daily inspection of the reservation work; handle reservation disputes properly, and strive to achieve mutual benefit and satisfaction of guests and hotels.

一、客人因等候办理入住手续的时间过久而引起抱怨

繁忙时刻，会有许多客人急切地等候办理入住登记手续，在办理的过程中，他们会提出很多问题与要求，大厅内可能会出现忙乱的现象，前台服务人员必须保持镇静，不要慌乱。

①客人抵店前，接待员应熟悉订房资料，检查各项准备工作。

②根据客情，合理安排人手，客流高峰到来时，保证有足够的接待人员。

③繁忙时刻保持镇静，不要想着在同一时间内完成好几件事。

④保持正确、整洁的记录。

I The guest waits for too long to check in, which causes complaints

There will be many guests eagerly waiting to check in during rush hour. During the process, they will ask many questions and requirements. There may be turmoil in the lobby. The front desk staff must keep calm.

① Before the guest arrives, the receptionist should be familiar with the reservation information and check all preparations.

② According to the guest flow, arrange the staff reasonably, and ensure that there are enough receptionists during peak hours.

③ Keep calm during busy times and don't try to accomplish several things at the same time.

④ Maintain correct and neat records.

二、客人不愿翔实登记

部分客人为了减少麻烦，出于保密或显示自己特殊身份和地位等目的，住店时不愿登记或登记时有些项目不愿填写。

①耐心地向客人解释填写住宿登记表的必要性。

②若客人出于怕麻烦或填写有困难，则可代其填写，只要求客人签名确认即可。

③若客人出于某种顾虑，担心住店期间被打扰，则可以告诉客人，酒店的计算机电话系统有"DND"（请勿打扰）功能，并通知有关接待人员，确保客人不被打扰。

④若客人为了显示其身份地位，酒店也应努力改进服务，满足客人需求。比如充分利用已建立起的客史档案系统，提前为客人填妥登记表中的有关内容，进行预先登记，在客人抵店时，只需签名即可入住。常客、商务客人及 VIP 客人可先请客人在大堂休息，为其送上茶（或咖啡），然后再为客人办理登记手续，甚至可让客人在客房内办理手续，以显示对客人的重视和体贴。

II The guest does not want to register in detail

In order to avoid unnecessary trouble, some guests do not want to register when staying in the hotel or do not want to fill in some information for confidentiality or to show their special identity and status.

① Patiently explain to the guests the necessity of filling in the accommodation registration form.

② If the guest is afraid of trouble or has difficulty in filling in, fill in the form on his behalf, and only require the guest to sign for confirmation.

③ If guests are worried about being disturbed during their stay, tell them that the hotel's computer telephone system has a "DND"（Do Not Disturb）function, and notify the relevant receptionists to ensure that the guests are not disturbed.

④ If guests want to show their status, the hotel should also strive to improve services to meet the needs of the guests. For example, make full use of the established guest history file system, fill out the relevant content in the registration form for the guest in advance, and perform pre-registration. When the guest arrives, only need to sign to check in. For regular guests, business guests and VIP guests, ask the guests to rest in the lobby first, bring them tea（or coffee）, and then handle check in for the guests, or even check in for the guests in the guest room to show consideration to the guests.

三、遇到有不良记录的客人

接待员遇到有不良记录的客人光顾酒店时，要凭以往经验或客史档案，认真、机智、灵活地予以处理。

①对于信用程度低的客人，通过确立信用关系、仔细核验、压印信用卡、收取预付款等方式，确保酒店利益不受损失，及时汇报有关处理的情况。

②对于曾有劣迹、可能对酒店造成危害的客人，则应以"房间已全部预订"等委婉的说法，巧妙地拒绝其入住。

Ⅲ Encountering guests with bad records

When a receptionist encounters a guest who has a bad record, he/she should deal with it seriously, tactfully, and flexibly based on past experience or guest history files.

① For customers with low credit, establishing credit relationships, carefully verifying, imprinting credit cards, and receiving prepayments, etc., ensure the hotel's interests and report the relevant processing in a timely manner.

② For guests who have had bad deeds and may cause harm to the hotel, the receptionist should refuse to check in with euphemisms such as "all rooms have been booked".

四、酒店提供的客房类型、价格与客人的要求不符

接待员在接待订房客人时，应复述其订房要求，以获得客人的确认，避免客人误解。房卡上填写的房价应与订房资料一致，并向客人口头报价。如果出现无法向订房客人提供所确认的房间，则应向客人提供一间价格高于原客房的房间（也就是进行客房升级），按原先商定的价格出售，并向客人说明情况，请客人谅解。

IV The types and prices of guest rooms provided by the hotel do not meet the requirements of the guests

When receiving guests who booked a room, the receptionist should repeat their reservation requirements to obtain confirmation from the guests and avoid misunderstandings. The room rate filled on the room card should be consistent with the room reservation information, and an oral quotation should be made to the guest. If the confirmed room cannot be provided to the guest who booked the room, the guest should be provided a higher-category room than the original guest room（that is, a room upgrade）. Sell the room at the originally agreed price, explain the situation to the guest and ask for his understanding.

五、在房间紧张的情况下，客人要求延住

照顾已住店客人的利益为第一要义，宁可为即将来店的客人介绍别的酒店，也不能赶走已住店的客人。

①可以先向已住店客人解释酒店的困难，征求其意见，是否愿意搬到其他酒店延住。

②如果客人不愿意，则应尽快通知预订处，为即将来店的客人另寻房间，或联系其他酒店。

V The guest asks for an extension when rooms are full

Take care of the interests of the guests who have stayed in the hotel is the first priority. It is better to introduce other hotels to the guests who are coming to the hotel rather than to drive away the guests who have already stayed in the hotel.

① Explain the difficulties of the hotel to the guests, ask whether they are willing to move to another hotel for their extended stay.

② If the guest is unwilling to move, inform the reservation office as soon as possible to find another room for the guest who is coming, or contact other hotels.

六、客人要求用一个证件同时开两间客房

按照现行酒店业的管理制度，入住酒店必须实行"一人一证"的登记制度。

①与客人商量是否可以请其朋友出示证件办理入住登记；若客人表示其朋友要随后到达酒店，则应请客人先开一间房，另一间作保证类预订处理。

②若客人坚持要办理入住手续，则应请客人提供其朋友的有关信息，查看客史档案，若有，则办理入住；若没有，为客人办理入住手续后，钥匙保留在总台，提醒客人请其朋友到达酒店后到总台取钥匙或通知接待员送到房间并补办手续。

③对客人表示感谢，并做好跟进服务工作。

VI The guest requests to open two rooms at the same time with one certificate

According to the current management system of the hotel industry, the hotel must implement the registration system of "one person one card".

① Discuss with the guest whether he/she can ask his/her friends to show his/her certificates to check in; if the guest indicate that his/her friend will arrive at the hotel later, the recepionist should ask the guest to open one room first, and the other room for guarantee booking.

② If the guest insists on the check-in procedure, the guest should provide the relevant information of his friend. The reception should check the guest history file, and if there is a record, proceed with check-in. If not, after checking in for the guest, the key will be kept at the reception desk to remind their friends to pick up the keys at the front desk or notify the receptionist to send them to the room and complete the procedures.

③ Express gratitude to the guests, and do a good job of follow-up service.

七、住店客人要求保密

接待员对于客人入住时提出的"不接听电话""不接待来访客人""房号保密"等特殊要求,应予以高度重视,立即在电脑中做特殊标记,并通知总机、客房部、保安部等部门和岗位,不应草率行事,避免客人的投诉。

①确认客人的保密程度,例如是只接长途电话,只有某位客人可以来访,还是来访者一律不见、来电话一律不接听等。

②在值班日志上做好记录,记下客人姓名、房号及保密程度。

③当有人来访问要求保密的客人时,一般以客人没有入住或暂时没有入住为理由予以拒绝。

④通知电话总机做好客人的保密工作。例如外来电话查询要求保密的客人时,电话总机室的接线员应告诉来电者该客人未住店。

VII Staying guests require confidentiality

The receptionist should attach great importance to special requirements such as "not answering phone calls" "not receiving visitors" "room number confidentiality" and other special requirements put forward by guests during check-in. Departments such as the switchboard, housekeeping, and security should not act hastily and to avoid complaints from guests.

① Confirm the confidentiality of the guests, such as answering long-distance calls only, allowing only specific vistors, or refusing all visitors and incoming calls.

② Make a record in the log book, noting the guest's name, room number and level of confidentiality.

③ When someone visits a guest who requires confidentiality, it is generally refused on the grounds that the guest did not check in or did not check in right now.

④ Inform the telephone switchboard to do a good job of keeping guests confidential. For example, when someone calls a guest who requires confidentiality, the operator in the telephone exchange room should tell the caller that the guest is not staying in the hotel.

八、住店客人换房

换房有两种可能：一种是客人主动提出，另一种是酒店的要求。换房往往会给客人和酒店带来麻烦，必须慎重处理；若不能马上满足客人的换房要求，应向客人说明，请其谅解并做好记录。一旦有空房，则按客人提出换房的先后顺序予以满足。若属酒店过错（超额订房、设施故障等），应向客人道歉，必要时，可让客人入住规格较高的客房。

①接到换房要求时应问清（解释）换房原因，根据客人要求（酒店客房实情）选择适当的房间。

②填写房卡和换房通知单，将相关信息输入电脑；将换房要求及时通知各有关部门，并分发换房单。

<table>
<tr><td colspan="2" align="center">换房通知单</td></tr>
<tr><td>日期： _____</td><td>时间： _____</td></tr>
<tr><td colspan="2">客人姓名： _____</td></tr>
<tr><td>由客房： _____</td><td>换至客房： _____</td></tr>
<tr><td>房价由： _____</td><td>变更为： _____</td></tr>
<tr><td colspan="2">原因： _____</td></tr>
<tr><td colspan="2">备注： _____</td></tr>
<tr><td>客房服务员： _____</td><td>批核： _____</td></tr>
<tr><td colspan="2" align="right">年　　月　　日　　时</td></tr>
</table>

③客房部将客人原住房的房态改为结账房；礼宾部及时协助客人提拿行李；洗衣房及时将客人送洗的衣物送到新房间；收银处将换房信息输入电脑。

④更换客人的档案栏（更改房间号码），将登记卡及有关文件放入新房间的档案中。

VIII   Change rooms of in-house guests

There are two possibilities for changing rooms: one is the guest's request, and the other is the hotel's request. Room change will often cause trouble to guests and the hotel, and it must be handled carefully; if the guest cannot meet the guest's room change request immediately, explain to the guest and make a record. Once there is a vacant room, it will be satisfied according to the order in which the guest proposes. If the hotel is wrong (overbooking, facility failure, etc.), apologize to the guest, and if necessary, allow guests to stay in rooms with higher specifications.

① Upon receiving a request for a room change, ask (explain) the reason for the room change, and choose an appropriate room according to the guest's request (the actual situation of the hotel room).

② Fill in the room card and the room change form, input the relevant information into the computer; notify the relevant departments of the room change requirements in time, and distribute the room change form.

Room Change Form	
Date： _____	Time： _____
Guest name： _____	
From room： _____	To： _____
From room rate ： _____	To： _____
Reason： _____	
Remark： _____	
Room Attendant： _____	Approval： _____
	Date

③ The housekeeping department will change the guest's original room to the checkout; the concierge department will promptly assist the guest to pick up the luggage; the laundry room will promptly deliver the laundry to the new room; the cashier will input the room change information into the computer.

④ Change the guest's file column (change the room number), and put the registration card and related documents into the file of the new room.

九、客用钥匙丢失

①发生客用钥匙丢失，应马上检查丢失原因，并采取必要措施及时处理以保证客人的人身、财产安全。

②客房部经理应亲自查找，并报告值班经理，更改 IC 卡密码，修改电脑程序，并

督促服务员仔细回忆，做好记录。

③若酒店客房是机械锁，如未找到钥匙，应通知大堂副理，由其出面与客人交涉有关索赔事宜。

④报前厅部经理，由其签发配换钥匙的通知，下单请工程部人员进行换锁。换锁原因及钥匙号码须在钥匙记录簿中记录备案。

十、团队离店退房并回收钥匙

①团队离店前一天，接待员须打印次日离店的团队表单。

②离店当日，由早班接待员负责将离店团队的钥匙收回。

③如发现钥匙有未退回的，应马上与团队陪同人员取得联系，请其协助追回钥匙。

④若钥匙丢失，须马上通知收银员、大堂副理，由大堂副理与客人交涉索赔事宜。

⑤团队钥匙全部收回后，通知收银员将钥匙押金退还陪同人员或领队。

IX　The guest key is lost

① If the guest key is lost, the reason for the loss should be checked immediately, and necessary measures should be taken to deal with it in time to ensure the personal and property safety of the guest.

② The manager of the housekeeping department should check personally and report to the manager on duty, change the IC card password, modify the computer program, and urge the waiter to recall carefully and make records.

③ If the hotel room has a mechanical lock and key is not found, the assistant manager in the lobby should be notified, who will negotiate with the guest about the claim.

④ Report to the front office manager, who will issue a key replacement notice, and place an order to ask the engineering department personnel to change the lock. The reason for changing the lock and the key number must be recorded in the key record book.

X　The team checks out and collects the keys

① The day before the team leaves the hotel, the receptionist must print out the team form for the next day's departure.

② On the day of departure, receptionist on the morning shift is responsible for taking back the keys of the departure team.

③ If you find that the key has not been returned, contact the escort immediately and ask for their assistance in retriving the keys.

④ If the key is lost, the cashier and assistant manager in the lobby must be notified immediately, and the assistant manager in the lobby negotiates the claim with the guest.

⑤ After all the team keys are collected, notify the cashier to return the deposit to the escort or team leader.

任务三　前台问询服务

访客问询时，如何当着访客面灵活请示？

【案例一】

一位先生入住 1808 房，要求为保密房。第二天一位自称为该客人妻子的女士到酒店前台问询处查询这位客人，问询员 A 通过电脑得知客人申请保密，便礼貌告知查无此人，但该女士说其丈夫肯定在这里住，现在找他有急事，而且非常紧急，要求问询员仔细查找。

此时问询员 A 灵机一动，说："我现在到办公室帮您详细核查一下住客资料。"问询员 A 来到后台，通过电话告知 1808 客人前台有人找他，此客人问明情况后表示要求回避。于是问询员 A 来到前台再次对该女士说查无此人，该女士见问询员不厌其烦地找了几遍都没有结果也就离开了。

Task three　Inquiry Service of the Front Office

How to ask for instructions flexibly in front of visitors when they ask questions?

【Case 1】

A gentleman stayed in room 1808 and requested a confidential room. The next day a lady who claimed to be the guest's wife went to the hotel's front desk to investigate the guest. Information clerk A learned that the guest had requested confidentiality through the computer, and politely informed the lady that there was no such person. However, the lady said her husband must be here and was looking for him in an urgent matter, and asked the information clerk to check carefully.

At this time, information clerk A had an idea and said: "I will help you check the guest information in detail in the office." information clerk A came to the backstage and told 1808 guest by phone that someone was looking for him at the front desk. The guest refused to see the lady. information clerk A came to the front desk again and said to the lady that there was no such person. As the information clerk had checked several times without result, the lady left.

【案例二】

一位客人在前台登记入住，并说自己是酒店总经理的朋友，要求房价打 6 折，接待员 B 拨通总经理电话，当着客人面向总经理请示，结果总经理碍于情面只好同意，其实该客人与总经理只是一面之交。

【Case 2】

A guest checked in at the front desk and said that he was a friend of the hotel's general manager and asked for a 40% discount on the room rate. Receptionist B called the general manager and asked the general manager in front of the guest. As a result, the general manager had no choice but to agree. In fact, the guest and the general manager are just acquaintance.

【案例三】

一位先生来到迎宾台前说要找总经理，迎宾员 C 有礼貌地问道："好的，先生，请问您是哪个单位的？怎么称呼您？"客人报上了自己的单位与姓名。迎宾员 C 又说："先生请稍等，我为您联系一下。"于是迎宾员 C 拨通了行政办公室的电话，可是没有人接听，接着迎宾员 C 只好直接拨通总经理办公室电话，正是总经理接听，由于当着客人的面，迎宾员 C 灵活地对总经理说："你好，我是酒店迎宾员，请问总经理在吗？有某单位某某先生找他。"总经理一听，明白了迎宾员的用意，于是从容地决定是否接见这位客人。

【Case 3】

A gentleman came to the front desk and looked for the general manager. The usher C asked politely: "Okay, sir, which company do you work for? How can I address you?" The guest reported to his company and name. The usher C said: "Sir, please wait a moment, I'll contact him for you." The usher C dialed the phone number of the administrative office, but no one answered it. Then C had to dial the phone number of the general manager's office directly, and it was the general manager who answered it. In front of the guest, usher C said to the general manager: "Hello, I am the usher. Is the general manager here? Mr. × × from × × company is looking for him." The general manager understood after hearing this, so he could decide whether to meet the guest calmly.

【案例分析】

这是一组反映如何当着客人面灵活请示的技巧案例。

案例一中有访客要求找保密房的客人，并且情况特殊是住客妻子。问询员处理得当，灵活地避开访客向住客请示，否则难免出现一场误会和冲突。

案例二中接待员的处理方式不对，正确的方式应该是按规定程序通知大堂副理来处理，如超出大堂副理的职权范围，再由大堂副理以适当的方式通知总经理或值班经理。

案例三中该迎宾员处理规范，表现灵活，作为酒店的总经理日理万机，不可能随时接待所有来访客人，一般客人先由行政办公室或涉及相关职能部门来接待，还有些客人由于某些原因，总经理不便于接待，所以本例中迎宾员灵活的处理让访客和总经理都能较好地接受，不至于尴尬。

【Case Analysis】

This is a set of technical cases that reflect how to ask for instructions flexibly in front of guests.

In the first case, a visitor asked to find a guest in a confidential room. It was the wife of the guest in a special situation. The information clerk handled it properly and flexibly. Ask the residents for instructions avoiding visitors, otherwise there would be misunderstanding and conflict.

In the second case, the receptionist's handling method is wrong. The correct way should be to notify the deputy manager in the lobby according to the prescribed procedures. If necessary, the deputy manager in the lobby will notify the general manager or the manager on duty in an appropriate manner.

In the third case, The usher handles the issue in a standard and flexible manner. As the general manager of the hotel, it is impossible to receive all visitors at any time. Generally, guests are received by the administrative office or related functional departments first. The general manager is inconvenient to receive some guests for some reasons, so the flexible approach in this example allows the visitor and the general manager to be better accepted without embarrassment.

一、查询住客情况

①查询一般客人的信息。

查询住店客人情况的主要内容：客人的房号，客人是否在酒店，有无他人来访问客人。对这些查询，问询员应先问清来访者的姓名，与住店客人的关系等。然后打电话到被查询者的房间，经该客人允许后，才可以让来访者去找住店客人；如果住客不在房内，切不可将住客的房号及电话号码告诉来访者，也不可以让来访者到房间找人，以保证客人的隐私权，避免出现差错和纠纷。

如果查明客人尚未抵店，请对方在客人预订抵店的日期再来询问；如果查明客人已退房，则向对方说明情况。除已退房客人有委托外，一般不可把客人离店后的去向和地址告诉来访者。

Ⅰ　Check the situation of guests

① Check general customer information.

The main content of inquiring about the guest in the hotel includes: the guest's room number, whether the guest is in the hotel, and whether there is anyone visiting the guest. For these inquiries, the information clerk should ask about the name of the visitor, the relationship with the guest, etc. Then call the room of the person to be queried, and only after the guest's permission can the visitor go to the hotel; if the guest is not in the room, do not tell the visitor the guest's room number and telephone number. Visitors are not allowed to find someone in the room to ensure the privacy of guests and avoid disputes.

If it is found that the guest has not yet arrived, ask the visitor to check again on the date the guest is supposed to arrive; if it is found that the guest has checked out, explain the situation to the visitor. Except for the entrustment of the guests, it is generally not allowed to tell the visitors where the guests will be after they have left the hotel.

②住店客人要求房号保密处理。

有时住店客人出于某种原因，会要求酒店对其房号进行保密。做好这项服务工作，小则可防止住客受到不必要的干扰，大则可以保证客人的住店安全和预防各类案件的发生。问询员在未征得客人的同意时，不可泄露其房号。具体处理办法如下：

a. 接受房号保密要求时，问清客人的保密程度，例如，是绝对保密，还是只接听某些电话、只接待某位客人的来访等。

b. 准确记录需保密的房号、起止时间和特殊要求。

c. 通知电话总机做好保密工作。例如来电查询要求保密的客人时，接线员应告诉来电者该客人未住在本店。

d. 在电脑上设保密标记。

e. 当有人访问要求保密的客人时，一般以客人没有入住为理由予以拒绝。

f. 当客人要求解除保密或改变保密程度时，要认真做好记录，取消或更改电脑上的标记，并通知电话总机。处理方法：先问清访客情况→打电话告知住客→按住客要求处理。

② Dealing with the confidentiality of the room number requested by the hotel guests.

Sometimes the resident asks the hotel to keep their room number secret for some reason. To do a good job of this service, not only prevents unnecessary interference to the guests, but also ensures the safety of the guests and prevent such cases. The information clerk must not reveal the room number without the client's consent. The specific measures are as follows:

a. When accepting the confidentiality request of the room number, the information clerk must ask the guest to what extend they require confidentiality. For example, is it absolutely confidential, or only answering certain calls and only receiving visits from a certain guest, etc.?

b. Record the room number, time and special requirements that need to be kept confidential.

c. Inform the telephone switchboard to do a good job of keeping guests confidential. For example, when someone calls a guest who requires confidentiality, the operator in the telephone exchange room should tell the caller that the guest is not staying in the hotel.

d. Set a security mark on the computer.

e. When someone visits a guest who requires confidentiality, it is generally refused on the grounds that the guest did not check in.

f. When the guest requests to lift the confidentiality or change the degree of confidentiality, it is necessary to make a careful record, cancel or change the mark on the computer, and notify the telephone switchboard. Handling method: ask for the visitor's information → call the guest → handle the guest's request.

二、有关酒店内部的问询

①餐厅、商场所在的位置及营业时间。

②宴会、会议举办场所及时间。

③酒店提供的其他服务项目、营业时间及收费标准。

问询员要做出令客人满意的答复，必须熟悉本酒店所有的服务设施、服务项目和经营特色，以及酒店的各项有关政策，并积极、热心地向客人宣传和推销酒店产品。

Ⅱ Inquiries about the interior of the hotel

① The location and opening time of restaurants and shopping malls.

② The venue and time of the banquet and meeting.

③ Other service such as business hours and charges provided by the hotel.

In order to give a satisfactory answer to the guests, the inquirer must be familiar with all the service facilities, service items and operating characteristics of the hotel, as well as various related policies of the hotel, and actively and enthusiastically promote and sell the hotel's products to the guests.

三、酒店外部情况介绍

客人对酒店外部信息的问询涉及面非常广，这就要求问询员必须有较广的知识面，掌握大量的信息。但是，即使是最优秀的问询员，也不可能完全回答客人的问题，也不可能把客人所需的资料全部记忆在脑子里。因此，问询处必须准备大量的书面资料，并根据客人的需求和具体情况的变化，对资料不断地更新、补充。问询处应准备的书面资料主要有：

①国内、国际航空线的最新时刻表和票价，以及航空公司名称。

②最新铁路时刻表、里程表和票价。

③最新轮船时刻表、里程表和各级舱位的票价。

④出租汽车市内每公里收费标准。

⑤酒店所在地至周围主要城市的距离及抵达方式。

⑥酒店所在地的市内交通情况。

⑦酒店所在地影剧院、歌舞厅的地址和即将上演的节目及时间。

⑧酒店所在地展览馆和博物馆的地址、电话号码、开放时间及上展项目。

⑨酒店所在地主要银行的名称、地址、电话号码。

III　External information of the hotel

The inquiries from guests to the hotel's external information involve a wide range of areas, which requires that the information clerk must have a wide range of knowledge and a large amount of information. However, even the best information clerk cannot fully answer the guest's question, and it is impossible to remember all the information the guest needs in his/her head. Therefore, the information office must also prepare a large amount of written information, and constantly update and supplement the information according to the needs of the guests and the changes in the specific situation. The written materials that the information office should prepare mainly include:

① The latest timetables and fares of domestic and international airlines, as well as the name of the airline.

② The latest railway timetable, distance and fare.

③ The latest ship schedules, distance and fares for all classes of service.

④ Taxi rates in the city.

⑤ The distance between the location of the hotel and the surrounding major cities and the way of arrival.

⑥ Traffic conditions in the city.

⑦ The address of the theater and dance hall and the program and time of the day.

⑧ Address, telephone number, opening hours and exhibition items of the exhibition hall and museum.

⑨ The name, address, and telephone number of the main bank.

四、问询服务要求

为客人提供及时周到的问询服务，要求提供服务的人员掌握大量的信息，并且有很好的服务意识和对客技巧。在服务过程中需要做到：

①对待客人礼貌热情、彬彬有礼并且一视同仁，避免让客人产生厚此薄彼的感觉。

②对酒店的各项服务项目要非常熟悉，记清酒店各服务部门的电话号码，以便能及时联系，减少客人等待的时间。

③性急的客人或是因着急询问而语无伦次、词不达意的客人，要帮助他们稳定情绪，然后迅速、简明扼要地回答客人的问题。

④问询员要随时补充、修改、更新自己掌握的信息和资料，以便解答客人的各种问题。

⑤对于熟知的问题，回答时应简明扼要，不要模棱两可、含糊其词，使客人无法理解。

⑥不太了解的问题，应向客人道歉并说明，请客人稍等然后迅速借助手中资料或互联网等进行查找；如果一时查找不到，请求客人给予谅解，并将客人的姓名、房号及问询内容记录下来，事后再迅速进行查阅，一旦查到就立即告知客人；如果经过努力查找仍无结果，也应向客人取得联系，如实向客人说明情况，并请客人谅解。

● 问询员在回答客人问询时，必须准确无误，态度温和，不能使用不确定的语言，如"我想可能""大概""也许"等。

● 当几位客人同时进行询问时，应该遵循先问先答、急问急答、有问有答的原则，尽可能使每位客人都能得到热情的接待和满意的解答。

● 问询员要耐心、细致地回答客人的任何询问，做到百问不厌。

IV Inquiry service requirements

Provide customers with timely and thoughtful inquiry services, requiring the service personnel to master a lot of information, and have a good sense of service and customer-oriented skills. During the service process:

① Treat guests politely, warmly, courteously and equally, to avoid giving them a feeling of favoring one over the other.

② Be very familiar with the various service items of the hotel, and remember the telephone numbers of the various service departments of the hotel in order to be able to contact them in time and reduce the waiting time for guests.

③ For impatient guests or guests who are incoherent or inconsistent due to anxious inquiries, help them stabilize their emotions, and then answer the guests' questions quickly and concisely.

④ The information clerk should increase, modify, and update the information and materials he/she has at any time in order to answer various questions from guests.

⑤ For familiar questions, the answer should be concise. Don't be ambiguous or vague, so that guests cannot understand.

⑥ For questions that are not well understood, the information clerk should apologize and explain to the guests. Ask guests to wait for a while and then quickly search on the Internet; if can't find it for a while, ask the guest for understanding, record the guest's name, room number and inquiries content and check it quickly afterwards. Once it is found it, inform the guest immediately; if there is no result after searching, get in touch with the guest, explain the situation to the guest truthfully, and ask the guest for understanding.

● When answering a guest's question, the information clerk must be accurate and gentle, and cannot use uncertain words, such as "I think it's possible" "probably" "maybe", etc.

● When several guests make enquiries at the same time, the principles of "answering questions according to the order; answering urgent questions quickly; answering every question" should be followed, so that every guest can receive a warm reception and satisfactory answer.

● Answer any enquiries from guests patiently and meticulously, and not to get bored.

五、在问询服务中，如何保证客人的隐私权

①接待员应主动热情地回答客人所提出的问题，对国内外客人要一视同仁。

②只回答自己权限内的问题，对自己不了解的事情应当向客人表示歉意，同时尽可能请示有关方面的负责人。

③每位客人的姓名、房号、国籍、活动、房价等资料均属保密范围，接待员不得随意泄露，对他们的来访和来电都应委婉拒绝。

④对来电、来访者，接待员要先从电脑中查明被访者是否住在本酒店，如被访者不住酒店应礼貌告诉客人。如被访者有预订，可建议来电、来访者留言。

⑤保密服务流程。

a. 当客人要求在要求保密办理入住时，要重新在系统中确认他们的身份，并再次和客人确认他们的全名和房号。

b. 和客人解释提供的保密服务内容，即无论是电话还是在前台询问客人信息时，酒店都会以客人没有入住回答。

c. 和客人核对他们是否有例外的情况，如可以告知特定的人其入住酒店的信息。

d. 再次和客人确认客人保密入住的要求和可以透露信息的例外情况。

e. 询问客人是否需要其他的服务，并预祝客人有一个愉快的入住体验。

f. 作为参考，告知客人你的名字并提出如果在入住期间需要服务，非常欢迎再次联系你。

g. 把客人要求保密的要求非常清楚地标识在系统中，并注明所有的细节，包括例外情况。

h. 通知服务中心、礼宾部、保安部、客房部和送餐部所有要求保密入住客人的情况。

i. 如果有人通过电话或在前台问询保密入住客人的信息，标准回答是："非常遗憾我们酒店没有客人使用该名字登记入住。"

j. 如果是保密入住客人允许的特定人，非常清楚地表明身份后询问保密客人的信息，可以帮助联系这位客人。

V How to ensure the privacy of guests in the inquiry service

① The receptionist should answer questions raised by guests actively and enthusiastically, and treat domestic and foreign guests equally.

② Only answer questions within their own authority, apologize to the guests for things they don't understand, and ask the person in charge of relevant things as much as possible.

③ Each guest's name, room number, nationality, activities, room rate and other information are confidential. The receptionist shall not arbitrarily disclose, and shall tactfully refuse their visitors and calls.

④ For incoming calls and visitors, the receptionist must first find out from the computer whether the interviewee is staying in this hotel. If the guest does not live in the hotel, tell the guest politely. If the guest has a reservation, it is recommended to call and leave a message for the guest.

⑤ Confidential service process.

a. When guests request to check in confidentially, reconfirm their identity in the system and reconfirm their full name and room number with the guest.

b. Explain to the guest the confidential service content, that is, whether it is the phone or at the front desk to ask for the guest information, the hotel will not check in the guest answer.

c. Check with guests whether they have any exceptions. For example, can tell a specific person that he/she is staying in a hotel.

d. Reconfirm with the guests the confidentiality of the check-in requirements and the exceptions to which the information can be disclosed.

e. Ask the guests if they need other services, and wish them a pleasant stay.

f. As a reference, tell the guest your name and suggest that if guest needs service during the stay, you are very welcome to be contacted again.

g. Mark the guest's request for confidentiality in the system clearly with all the details including exceptions.

h. Notify the service centre, concierge, security, housekeeping, and meal delivery departments of all requests for confidentiality of guests.

i. If someone asks for information about confidential check-in guest by phone or at the front desk, the standard answer is: "We regret that we do not have any guests checking in under that name".

j. If there is specific person allowed by the staying guest, the receptionist can contact the guest after the person shows the identity clearly.

【小结】

酒店问询服务最主要的任务就是解答客人有关酒店服务、设施及酒店所在城市的交通、游览等内容的询问。

酒店所提供的服务包括客人查询、问询、代客留言、物品转交、找人、联系旅游等。

【Summary】

The main task of the hotel information service is to answer guests' inquiries about hotel services, facilities, and transportation and excursions in the city.

The services provided by the hotel include guest inquiries, leaving messages, transferring items, finding people, contacting to travel, etc.

任务四　客账管理

【案例导入】

替朋友垫付押金

某天，王先生和他的两个朋友谈笑风生地步入一家四星级酒店。他们一共开了 3 间房。在总台办理入住手续时，收银员请他们支付押金。王先生说："我来、我来。"两个朋友也没推让，故当时 3 间房的押金全部是由王先生一人支付的。但是到第三天上午，王先生来到总台收银处退房结账时，却对总台出具的账单大为不满："为什么我朋友的账都算在了我的账上呢？我们可是各付各的。"收银员告诉他，他的两个朋友因有事已先走一步了，也未主动到总台结账，因为王先生付的是 3 个房间的押金，所以按惯例，所有消费款项都算到了王先生的账上。王先生告诉收银员，他只是给其朋友垫付押金，结账时各自的费用应由各自承担，并要求将押金退还给他。此时，收银员该如何处理这件事呢？

Task 4　Customer Account Management

【Case Introduction】

Advance deposit for friends

One day, Mr. Wang and his two friends walked into a four-star hotel, chatting and laughing. They had a total of three rooms. When checking in at the front desk, the cashier asked them to pay a deposit. Mr. Wang said: "Let me do it. I'll pay." The two friends did not refuse, so at that time, the deposit of the three rooms was all paid by Mr. Wang. But on the third morning, when Mr. Wang came to the front desk to check out, and he was very dissatisfied with the bill issued by the front desk: "Why is my friend's account counted on my account? We each pay separately." The cashier told him that his two friends had already left for something. They did not take the initiative to check out at the front desk. Because Mr. Wang paid the deposit for three rooms, so according to the usual practice, all the consumption of the accounts was counted on Mr. Wang's account. Mr. Wang told the cashier that he only paid the deposit for his friends, and the respective expenses should be borne by each at the time of checkout and requested that the deposit should be returned to him. In this situation, how should the cashier handle this matter?

【案例分析】

①按照王先生的意思处理，先把他的费用结清，并退还剩下的押金，他的两个朋友的费用等他的朋友来时再付。此法是收银员不成熟的表现，很有可能王先生的两个朋友不再来付费，那这笔费用是应由酒店来承担还是该由收银员来承担呢？不管怎样，收银员是负有主要责任的。在没有任何保障的前提下，将押金先退给客人的做法是收银员没有责任心的表现。

②告知王先生，其朋友已离店，酒店没有办法联系，他朋友的费用必须由他来承担，并让王先生去向他的朋友讨还这笔由他垫付的费用。这个办法收银员虽不承担风险，酒店也没有损失，但很可能使矛盾激化。客人付钱后气愤地离去会给其他客人留下不好的印象，另外该客人可能从此不会再来这个酒店，酒店无形中失去了一个客户。

③和王先生商量，请王先生当场与他的朋友取得联系，由收银员对他的朋友说清楚由谁付费的问题。若他的朋友在电话中答应日后来付费，可请王先生先刷信用卡作为抵押，在一定期限内若他的朋友未来结账，酒店将以信用卡的方式取得这笔费用。这个处理办法比较灵活，弥补了前两者的不足，由收银员与王先生的朋友沟通，也给他们双方留足了面子，不至于使他们之间为了钱的问题伤了和气。

④若王先生未带信用卡，暗示王先生在本酒店部门经理级以上有无熟人，若有，可找他们签字担保。签字担保后即可将押金退还给王先生。此办法在客人与酒店有良好信誉关系的情况下也是可以的，有了高级管理人员的担保，收银员也可放心了，而且管理人员与客人之间也比较容易保持沟通，同时也增强了客人对酒店的信任与好感。但此办法千万不可滥用，过于随便和频繁地接触类似事件，只会给管理人员带来麻烦，也降低了酒店在处理此类问题上的严肃性。

⑤请王先生先将全部账款结清，同时请他与其朋友联系，约定他们来付账的日期。如酒店收到其朋友的账款，则把王先生为他们垫付的费用退还其本人，退款方式可以是邮汇或下次入住时再退。这也是一种较为妥善的解决方式，既保证了酒店的账务安全，又给客人以承诺，但承诺的前提条件是由客人先垫付。

【Case Analysis】

① Follow Mr. Wang's intentions, first settle his expenses and refund the remaining deposit. The expenses of his two friends will be paid when his friends return to the hotel. This method is a manifestation of the immaturity of the cashier. Likely, Mr. Wang's two friends will no longer come to settle the accounts. Should this cost be borne by the hotel or by the cashier? In any case, the cashier takes the main responsibility. In the absence of any guarantee, the practice of returning the deposit to the customer first is an indication that the cashier has no sense of responsibility.

② Tell Mr. Wang that his friends has left the hotel and the hotel cannot contact them. He has to bear the expenses of his friends and let Mr. Wang claim the expense from his friends. Although the cashier does not take risks with this method, and the hotel has no losses, it is likely to intensify the conflict. The guest who pays and leaves angrily will leave a bad impression on other guests. In addition, the guest may never come to the hotel again, and the hotel has virtually lost a customer.

③ Discuss with Mr. Wang, ask Mr. Wang to get in touch with his friends on the spot, and let the cashier clarify to his friends who are responsible for the payment. If his friend agrees to pay in the future on the phone, they can ask Mr. Wang to swipe his credit card as collateral. If his friends do not settle the bill in the future within a certain period, the hotel will obtain the fee by credit card. This method is more flexible and makes up for the shortcomings of the first two. The communication between the cashier and Mr. Wang's friends would not embarrass the guests so that there would not be a conflict between them over the money issue.

④ If Mr. Wang does not bring a credit card, the cashier could ask whether Mr. Wang has any acquaintances at the department manager level or above in the hotel. If so, you can ask he/she to sign a guarantee. After signing the guarantee, the deposit can be returned to Mr. Wang. This method is also possible when the guest has a good reputation relationship with the hotel.

With the guarantee of the senior management, the cashier can rest assured, and it is easier to maintain communication between the manager and the guest. At the same time, it also enhances the trust and impression of the guests towards the hotel. But this method must not be misused. Too casual and frequent contact with similar incidents will only cause trouble to the management staff and reduce the seriousness of the hotel in dealing with such issues.

⑤ Suggest that Mr. Wang settle all the accounts first, and at the same time let him contact his friends and set a date for them to pay the bills. If the hotel receives the payment from the friends, it will refund the fee which Mr. Wang paid for them. The refund method can be a postal transfer or a refund upon their next check-in. This is also a more appropriate solution, which not only guarantees the security of the hotel's accounts, but also promises the guests, but the prerequisite for the promise is that the guest pays in advance.

【思考与启示】

通过此例，我们应从中吸取教训，并再次强调酒店在收取押金时一定要向客人说明，押金是用来扣除消费款的，在结账的时候多退少补。若遇到为朋友垫付押金的情况，更要问清楚最后的结账方式，同时在每一份入住登记单上注明该房的付款人，并请该付款人签字生效，以保证客人消费款的顺利结算。

若因故暂时无法收到应收款项须请人担保时，应有代他人付费的书面凭证，如担保单，以利于日后追账。前厅收银员在维护酒店原则的同时，也要考虑到客人的切身利益，必要时为了维护应付款人与实际付款人之间的和睦关系，收银员应挺身而出，做好协调工作。

（案例来源：孙丽坤等.《前厅客房服务与管理》.东北师范大学出版社，2007 年 2 月第 1 版 .）

【Thinking and Enlightenment】

Through this case, we should learn and emphasize that the hotel must explain the purpose of collection deposits to the guests, the deposit is used to deduct consumption, during the checkout it will be a refund for any overpayment or a supplemental payment for any deficiency. If you encounter a situation where a guest pays a deposit for a friend, you must ask about the final checkout method, and at the same time indicate the payer of the room on each check-in form, and ask the payer to sign it to ensure the smooth settlement of customer consumption.

If for some reason, the receivable cannot be received, for the time being, a guarantee must be obtained, written proof of payment on behalf of another person shall be required, such as a guarantee slip. To collect the receivable in the future, the front desk cashier should take into account the vital interests of the guests while upholding the principles of the hotel. If necessary, to maintain the harmonious relationship between the payer and the actual payer, the cashier should come forward and do a good job of coordination.

（Case source: Sun Likun, etc. Front Office Room Service and Management. Northeast Normal University Press, 1st edition, February 2007.）

一、结账服务工作内容

①为客人办理结账手续。

②更新前厅相关资料信息（房态、客史档案、住客资料信息）。

③在客人心目中树立良好的最后印象。

I　Work content of checkout service

① Handle checkout procedures for guests.

② Update the relevant information of the front hall（room status, guest history files, guest information）.

③ Establish a good last impression in the minds of guests.

二、结账服务程序

（一）散客结账服务程序

①准备工作：审核客人账单。

②向客人问好。

③确认房号和姓名。

④主动收回房间钥匙。

⑤通知相关部门：客房楼层、总机、其他相关部门（提前退房的客人）。

⑤询问客人是否有即时消费，并即时录入电脑。

⑦打印账单，客人确认账单。

⑧确认最后付款方式，开具发票。

⑨善后服务。

a. 提醒客人是否有贵重物品寄存。

b. 对客人住店及结账表示感谢，并征求客人对酒店的意见。

c. 与客人道别，并祝客人旅途愉快。

d. 行李员提供离店行李服务。

e. 将"消费账单""宾客入住登记单""预收订金收据"等各种凭证，汇总归类交审计员审核。

f. 修改客史档案。

⑩注意事项：延时退房。

II Checkout service procedures

(1) Individual checkout service procedures

① Preparation: review guest bills.

② Greeting to the guests.

③ Confirm the room number and name.

④ Take the initiative to take back the room key.

⑤ Notify relevant departments: guest room floor, switchboard, other relevant departments (for guests who check out early).

⑥ Ask the guests whether they have instant consumption and record it into the computer immediately.

⑦ Print the bill, and the guest confirms the bill.

⑧ Confirm the final payment method and issue an invoice.

⑨ After-care service.

a. Remind guests whether they have valuables in storage.

b. Thank guests for staying in the hotel and check-out, and ask for their opinions on the hotel.

c. Say goodbye to the guests and wish them a pleasant journey.

d. The bellman provides the check out baggage service.

e. Collect and classify all kinds of vouchers such as "consumption bill" "guest check-in form" "advance deposit receipt" and other vouchers to the auditor for review.

f. Modify the guest history file.

⑩ Matters needing attention: late check-out.

(二)团体客人结账服务程序

①通知楼层查团体走房。

②打印账单，做到团体总账和客人自付分开。

③如预订单上标明付款方式为转账，则请付款单位陪同人员在转账单上签字认可，并注明报账单位以便将来结算。凡不允许挂账的单位，其团体到店付账时费用一律付现，团体客人的房价不可透露给其他客人。

④为有自付账目的团体客人打印账单、结账。

⑤收回房卡和钥匙。

(2) Group guests checkout service procedures

① Notify the floor to check and confirm the group rooms.

② Print the bills, and separate the group account from the guest's own payment.

③ If the payment method is indicated on the booking form as transfer, then the person accompanying the paying company is required to sign on the transfer slip for approval and indicate the payment company for future settlements. For a company that does not allow payment on credit, the fee will be paid in cash when the group comes to the hotel, and the room rate of group guests cannot be disclosed to the other guests.

④ Print bills and settle accounts for group guests who have self-paid bills.

⑤ Take back the room card and key.

三、快速结账服务

①宾客房内结账（现金除外）

②客人填写"快速结账委托书"办理结账手续（信用卡结账）：离店前一天填写

Ⅲ　Quick checkout service

① Checkout in the guest room（except cash）

② The guest fills in the "Quick Checkout Delegate" to go through the checkout procedures（credit card checkout）：fill out the day before leaving the hotel

四、特殊情况的处理

（一）当住店客人的欠款不断增加时

有些客人在住店期间所交预付款（押金）已经用完，还有的客人住进酒店后，长期未决定离店日期，而其所欠账款在不断上升。在这种情况下，为了防止客人逃账，或避免引起其他不必要的麻烦，必要时可通知客人前来付款。催促客人付款时，要注意方式方法和语言艺术，可用电话通知，也可用印备的通知书，将客人房号、姓名、金额、日期等填妥后，装入信封，放入客人房间内。一般客人见此通知后会主动前来付款，如遇特殊情况，客人拒而不付时，应及时处理。

Ⅳ　Handling of special circumstances

（1）When the arrears of in-house guests continue to increase

Some guests have used up the prepayment（deposit）during their stay in the hotel, and some guests have not decided the date of check out for a long time after staying in the hotel, and the amount owed by them is constantly rising. In this case, to prevent the guest from evading the account or causing other unnecessary troubles, the guest can be notified to pay if necessary. When urging guests to pay, pay attention to the methods and language art. You can notify by phone or by a printed notice-after filling in the guest room number, name, amount, date, etc., place it in the envelope and deliver it to the guest room. Generally, guests will take the initiative to settle after seeing this notice. In case of special circumstances, if the guest refuses to pay, then staff should deal with it in time.

（二）当客人甲的账由客人乙支付时

若干人一起旅行，由一人付款，或者甲的账由乙支付，而甲已先行离去，人多事杂，这时往往会发生漏收的情况，给酒店带来损失。为了防止出现这种情况，应在交接记录上注明，并附纸条在甲、乙的账单上，这样，结账时就不会忘记，接班的人也可以看到。处理这种情况还有一种较为简单的办法：如乙替甲付款，甲先走，可将甲的账目全部转入乙的账单上，甲账变为零来处理，但此时必须通知乙，并有乙的书面授权，以免出现不必要的纠纷。

（2）When guest A's account is paid by guest B

When several people travel together and one person pays, or a guest A's bill is paid by a guest B, and guest A has left first, there are many people and many things are prone to disorder. At this time, there will often be missed collections, which will bring losses to the hotel. To prevent this from happening, it should be noted on the handover record, and a note should be attached to the bill of A and B, so that they will not forget it when they check out, and the shift staff can also see it. There is a simpler way to deal with this situation: if a guest B pays for a guest A, and A goes first, A's accounts can all transfer to a guest B's bill, and A's account becomes zero for processing. At this time, guest B must be notified and have written authorization from B to avoid unnecessary disputes

（三）如过了结账时间仍未结账

如过了结账时间（一般为退房当天中午 12：00）仍未结账，应催促客人。如超过时间，可根据酒店规定，加收房费，例如，有的酒店的做法是 15:00 以前结账者，加收一天房费的 1/3；15:00—18:00 点结账的，加收房费的 1/2；18:00 以后结账的，则可加收全天房费。

关于加收房费的问题，如果客人是常客或者该公司为酒店提供的间夜量很大，只要客人给前台打电话说一声推迟 2 ~ 3 小时退房，而且不是酒店的旺季，酒店通常不向客人收取任何费用。

（3）If the account has not been settled after the check-out time

If the bill has not been settled after the check-out time（usually at 12:00 on the day of check-out）, the guest should be urged. If the time has passed, an additional room fee can be charged according to the hotel's regulations. For example, some hotels will charge 1/3 of the day's room rate if they check out before 15:00; 1/2 of the day's room rate if they check out from 15:00 to 18:00; and the whole day's room rate if they check out after 18:00.

Regarding the issue of additional room charges, if the guest is a regular guest or the company rents a large number of rooms in the hotel, as long as the guest calls the front desk to inform that the check-out will be delayed by 2 to 3 hours, and it is not the peak season of the hotel, the hotel usually does not charge any fee to guests.

（四）退账处理

客人在结账时才提出要折扣优惠，而且也符合优惠条件的；或者结账时收银员发现该房间的某些费用是某种原因输入错误造成的。在这种情况下，收银员应填写一份"退账通知书"，一式两联，第一联交财务，第二联留结账处。然后，由前厅部经理签名，并注明原因，最后在电脑上将差额做退账。

（4）Processing of refunds

The guest only asked for a discount at the checkout, and it also meets the conditions of the discount; or at the checkout, the cashier found that some of the room's fees were caused by an input error for some reason. At this time, the cashier should fill in a "Refund Notice" in two copies, the first copy is for finance, the second copy is kept at the checkout office. Then, the front office manager must sign off and approve it, and the reason must be indicated, and finally on the computer will do the difference in the refund account.

五、前厅账务处理方法与要求

（一）账户清楚

①个人账户与团体账户的区别。

②账单内容。

（二）转账迅速

①账单处理。

②将账目款项及时挂到相关账户。

（三）记账准确

各项费用明细应准确记入客人账户。

V　The front office accounting processing methods and requirements

（1）Clear account

① The difference between individual accounts and group accounts.

② Bill content.

（2）Quick transfer

① Bill processing.

② Link the account funds to the relevant account in time.

（3）Accurate accounting

All expenses details should be accurately credited to the guest account.

六、宾客的支付方式

①现金支付 - 预付押金（实际住宿费用的 2 倍）。

②支票支付 - 外宾旅行支票、国内公司支票（验证）。

③信用卡支付（验卡）。

④转账（挂账）。

⑤其他人代付。

VI Guest payment methods

① Cash payment deposit in advance（2 times the actual accommodation fee）.

② Cheque payment-foreign guests traveler's cheque, domestic company cheque（verification）.

③ Credit card payment（card verification）.

④ Transfer money（pay on credit）.

⑤ Other people pay on your behalf.

【知识拓展】

信用卡是由银行或信用卡公司提供的一种供客人赊欠消费的信贷凭证，上面印有持卡者的姓名、号码、初签等。

①美国运通公司的运通卡。

②香港汇丰银行的东美卡（签证卡）和万事达卡。

③香港麦加利银行的大来卡。

④日本 JCB 国际公司和三和银行的 JCB Card。

⑤我国发行的信用卡，现有长城卡、牡丹卡、太平洋卡等。

【Knowledge Expansion】

A credit card is a credit certificate provided by a bank or a credit card company for guests to spend on credit, with the cardholder's name, number, initial sign, etc. printed on it.

① American Express Card.

② Hong Kong HSBC East American Card and MasterCard.

③ Diner Club Card of Hong Kong Macquarie Bank.

④ JCB Card of Japan JCB International Corporation and Sanwa Bank.

⑤ Credit cards issued by China, existing Great Wall Card, Peony Card, Pacific Card, etc.

【小结】

客人在办理离店手续过程中对酒店产生的最后印象是至关重要的，它可以决定客人是否再度光临并带来新的客人。因此，在为客人办理离店手续时，收银员应热情、礼貌、快捷而准确地提供服务。

【Summary】

The guest's last impression of the hotel during the check-out procedure is very important. It can determine whether the guest will visit again and bring in new guests. Therefore, the cashier should provide services enthusiastically, courteously, quickly, and accurately when handling check-out procedures for guests.

项目四
行政楼层服务

【案例导入】

一日，酒店即将到店的客人中，有两位是日本某跨国公司的高级行政人员。该公司深圳方面的负责人员专程赴酒店为这两位客人预订了行政楼层的客房，并要求酒店安排 VIP 接待，该公司其他客人的房间则安排在普通楼层。客人到店之前，相关部门均做好了准备工作。管家部按客人预订要求，提前清洁行政楼层及普通楼层的客房；前台及行政楼层接待处准备好客人的钥匙及房卡；大堂副理部则通知相关部门为 VIP 客人准备鲜花和水果，并安排专人准备接待。然而，就在一切准备就绪，等待 VIP 客人到店之际，其中一位 VIP 客人出现在酒店，并声称已入住在普通楼层的客房。

经过一番查证，发现客人确已下榻酒店普通楼层的客房，但这并非客人要求。VIP 客人与其他客人一行三人抵达酒店时，前台接待员 A 只核实了第一位客人的姓名与预订单上客人姓名相符，未进一步在电脑系统中查询另外两位客人的预订，而这三位客人自称来自同一公司，又是一起抵达酒店，接待员 A 主观判断是预订单上标示的客人名字出现了偏差，于是安排三位客人入住。接待员 A 在只核实到其中一位客人入住普通楼层的情况下，未经进一步核实就将本应入住行政楼层客房的客人与其他客人一同安排在普通楼层。

接待员 A 认为是预订单上将客人姓名写错，将预订单上的客人名字更改成已入住客人之后，实际应入住普通楼层的客人在抵店时，其中一位接待员 B 无法查到该客人的预订。接待员 B 虽然让客人出示该公司名片后确认客房为该公司员工，并马上安排此客人入住，但已使客人对酒店的服务水平产生质疑。

Project 4
Executive Floor Service

【Case Introduction】

One day, two of the hotel's upcoming guests were senior executives from a Japanese multinational company. The person in charge of the company in Shenzhen made a special trip to the hotel to book rooms on the executive floor for the two guests and asked the hotel to arrange a VIP reception, while the rooms of other guests of the company are arranged on ordinary floors. Before the guests arrive at the hotel, the relevant departments had made preparations. The butler department has cleaned the guest rooms on the executive floor and ordinary floors in advance according to the guest's reservation requirements; the front desk and the executive floor reception desk have prepared the guest's keys and room card; the assistant manager department has informed the relevant departments to prepare flowers and fruits for VIP guests and has arranged someone to prepare the reception. However, just when everything was ready and waiting for the VIP guests to arrive at the hotel, one of the VIP guests showed up at the hotel and claimed that he had been assigned in a room on an ordinary floor.

After some investigation, it was found that the guest had indeed stayed in a room on the ordinary floor of the hotel, but this was not what the guest requested. When a VIP guest arrived at the hotel with two other guests, receptionist A only verified that the first guest's name matches the guest's name on the reservation form, and did not further check the reservations of the other two guests in the computer system. These three guests claimed to be from the same company and arrived at the hotel together. Receptionist A subjective judgment is that the guest's name on the booking form was incorrect, and three guests are arranged to check-in. Receptionist A only verified that one of the guests is staying on an ordinary floor, without further verification, the guest who was supposed to stay on the executive floor rooms has been arranged with other guests on the ordinary floor.

Receptionist A believes that the guest's name was incorrectly written on the reservation form. After changing the name of the guest on the reservation form to the guest who is already checked in, the receptionist B cannot check the guest's reservation when the guest should be staying on the ordinary floor arrives. Although receptionist B asked the guest to show the company's business card, confirm that the guest is an employee of the company, and arrange for the guest to check-in immediately, it has caused the guest to question the hotel's service level.

【大堂副理处理结果】

在查清造成上述错误的原因之后，当值大堂副理马上与客人联系，但当致电客人房间时，客人均已外出。于是酒店一方面在行政楼层为客人保留了房间，另外在 VIP 客人房间内留下一封致歉信，就此事向客人致歉。在接到 VIP 客人回到酒店的通知后，大堂副理亲自向他致歉，并询问是否愿意转回行政楼层。客人在接受酒店道歉之后，表示对下榻的客房比较满意，无须再转去其他房间。第二天当 VIP 客人离开酒店之时，当值大堂副理又专程向客人当面致歉。客人表示并不介意此次不愉快的经历，并对酒店对于他的重视很满意。

【The Process Result of the Assistant Manager】

After finding out the cause of the above error, the assistant manager on duty immediately contacted the guests, but when he called the guest room, the guests had already gone out. So the hotel reserved a room for the guest on the executive floor and left a letter of apology in the VIP guest room to apologize to the guests for this matter. After receiving the notice from the VIP guest returning to the hotel, the assistant manager apologized to him personally and asked if he would be willing to transfer back to the executive floor. After accepting the hotel's apology, the guest said that he was satisfied with the room he stayed in and did not need to transfer to another room. When the VIP guest left the hotel the next day, the assistant manager apologized to the guests in person. The guest said that he did not mind the unpleasant experience and was very satisfied with the hotel's attention to him.

【评析】

由于此客人为酒店重要商务客人——某跨国大公司的 VIP 客人，酒店接待工作因疏忽给客人留下不愉快的印象，使客人对酒店的信心产生动摇，很有可能因此而失去这位重要客户，而对酒店产生不可估量的经济损失，酒店的声誉和形象也随之受到负面影响。

酒店存在以下问题：

对 VIP 客人的接待，每个当班员工未能引起足够的重视，当值主管未尽其监督之职。

工作不细致，未在客人抵店时仔细查询客人预订。VIP 客人未入住已准备好的房间，使酒店相关部门为此次接待工作所做的一切准备付之东流，虽然经酒店方的努力，客人接受了道歉，但此次接待任务的失败势必使客人对酒店的印象打了折扣。

工作准确性不够。接待员在客人名字与预订单不符时，主观判断是预订单上名字写错，造成其他员工无法查到已预订普通楼层房间但随后到店客人的名字，使该客人无法按预订入住。

"差之毫厘，谬以千里"，因为前接待员工作中一个环节的疏忽，造成客人到店后产生一系列的问题，影响后续各个工作部门的工作；所谓"100-1＝0"，由于一位员工的疏忽，酒店所有部门所做的工作都在客人心目中大打折扣。

【Comment and Analysis】

Because this guest is an important business guest of the hotel——a VIP guest of a large multinational company, the hotel reception work left an unpleasant impression on the guest due to negligence, which shakes the confidence of the guest in the hotel, and is likely to lose this important customer. As a result of the immeasurable economic loss of the hotel, the reputation and image of the hotel are also negatively affected.

The hotel has the following problems:

Each employee on duty failed to pay enough attention to the reception of VIP guests; the supervisor on duty did not perform his duty of supervision.

The work is not meticulous, and the guest's reservation is not checked carefully when the guest arrives. The VIP guest did not check into the prepared room, which made all the preparations made by the relevant hotel department for the reception work in vain. Although the guest accepted the apology through the efforts of the hotel, this reception failure will inevitably make the guests' impression of the hotel be diminished.

The working accuracy is not enough. When the guest's name does not match the reservation form, the receptionist's subjective judgment is that the name on the reservation form is wrong. As a result, other staff could not find the name of the guest who had booked a room on an ordinary floor but then came to the hotel, so the guest could not check in as reserved. "A tiny lapse can lead to a huge mistake". The negligence of a link in the work of the former receptionist caused a series of problems after the guests arrived in the hotel, which affected the work of various subsequent departments; the so-called "$100-1=0$", due to an employee's negligence, the work done by all departments of the hotel was greatly reduced in the minds of the guests.

酒店住客王先生 10 月 4 日在酒店商务中心订了一张 10 月 5 日从上海去大连，然后 10 月 6 日从大连返回上海的来回机票，并无任何其他特殊要求，商务中心员工小张按客人要求，为客人订了票。王先生要求票到后将票送至他的房间。傍晚，票到后员工小张把票送到了王先生房间。晚上王先生持票来到商务中心投诉，说为何把往返票开在同一票上，因为公司只给报销返回那张票的钱。于是员工小张立即与票务人员联系，但因为票务中心下班了，所以无法即时更改机票。小张向王先生解释后，王先生恼怒，要求第二天一早给予更改。中班员工小张做了交班，第二天早上早班人员小李了解事情后，再次与票务中心联系，请求给予更改与解决，但票务中心人员无法更改，提出两个办法，一是为客人出两张（一来一回）证明；二是退票，但退票费由客人付，经联系后都被客人拒绝了。

【案例思考】

①出现问题的原因是什么？

②酒店应该如何处理此事？

③如何避免此类问题的发生？

Hotel guest Mr. Wang booked a round-trip air ticket from Shanghai to Dalian on October 5th at the hotel business center on October 4th, and then back to Shanghai from Dalian on October

6th. There were no other special requirements. Business center employee Xiao Zhang booked a ticket for the guest according to the request of the guest. Mr. Wang asked for the ticket to be sent to his room after the ticket arrived. In the evening, when the ticket arrived, Xiao Zhang delivered the ticket to Mr. Wang's room. In the evening, Mr. Wang came to the business center with a ticket to complain, saying why the round-trip ticket was issued as a single ticket because his company only reimbursed the money of the return ticket. So employee Xiao Zhang immediately contacted the ticketing staff, but because the ticketing center was off work, he could not change the ticket immediately. After Xiao Zhang explained to Mr. Wang, Mr. Wang was annoyed and asked to make changes the next morning. The middle shift employee Xiao Zhang made the shift. After the morning shift employee Xiao Li learned about the matter the next morning, he contacted the ticketing center again, requesting change and resolution, but the ticketing center staff could not change it and proposed two methods, one is to provide the guests with two proofs (one departure and one return), the second was a refund, but the refund fee was paid by the customer. After contacting the guest, he refused.

【Case Thinking】

① What is the cause of the problem?

② How should the hotel handle this matter?

③ How to avoid such problems?

现代高档、豪华酒店一般都设有行政楼层，专门接待往来于国内及世界各地从事商务活动的客人、名人和高级人士。该楼层提供有别于普通客房楼层的贵宾式服务，因此，被人们誉为"店中店"。

行政楼层设有专用电梯和接待处，为客人提供方便快捷的入住手续办理及多项免费服务。专用的商务中心及客房内的私人传真机使客人与公司同事和家人保持密切联系；另有尊贵独享的行政酒廊为客人提供免费早餐、下午茶和晚间鸡尾酒。

Modern high-end and luxury hotels generally have an executive floor, which specializes in receiving business guests, celebrities, and senior-level guests at home and abroad. This floor provides VIP-style services that are different from ordinary guest floors, so it is known as a "hotel-in-hotel".

The executive floor is equipped with a dedicated elevator and reception desk to provide guests with convenient and quick check-in procedures and several free services. The dedicated business center and the private fax machine in the guest room keep guests in close contact with company colleagues and family members. In addition, the exclusive executive lounge provides guests with free breakfast, afternoon tea, and evening cocktails.

一、服务设施布局特色

行政楼层与普通客房楼层在布局上有明显不同。它可以向商务客人提供更多、更细致、更具个性的专业化服务。

（一）单独设接待处

凡预订行政楼层的客人都可以在进店后直接在楼层快速登记入住，以及离店时在本层结账退房。接待处设计制作精巧，环境氛围轻松，旁边设置有沙发等休息座位，使得这种"一对一"式的轻松、开放专用的服务接待方式更显个性化，使客人备感温馨。

（二）单独设酒廊

在行政楼层设置环境幽雅、独具匠心的专用酒廊，并提供冷饮、热饮、早餐、午茶，还可以安排鸡尾酒会及会晤朋友，是行政楼层吸引商务客人的重要场所。这种酒廊的设置，提高了行政楼层客人始终被尊重的"身份感"，使客人体会到"家"的感受。

（三）单独设商务中心

行政楼层一般设有专用商务中心及规格不等的会议室、洽谈室等设施，以供商务客人随时召开会议，或与客户会晤及洽谈生意。商务中心设备先进、种类齐全，从文件打印、复印、分拣至装订等一应俱全，而且服务效率高。

I　Layout features of service facilities

The layout of the executive floor is obviously different from the ordinary floor. It can provide business guests with enhanced, more detailed, and more personalized professional services.

（1）Separate reception desk

All guests who book the executive floor can check-in directly on the floor after entering the hotel, and check out on this floor when leaving the hotel. The reception area is exquisitely designed and made, the environment is relaxed, and there are sofas and other rest seats next to it, making this "one-to-one" dedicated service more relaxed, open, personalized, and warm.

（2）Separate lounge

Set up an elegant and unique dedicated lounge on the executive floor, and provide cold drinks, hot drinks, breakfast, afternoon tea, and can also arrange cocktail parties and meet friends. It is an important place for the executive floor to attract business guests. The setting of this kind of lounge improves the "sense of identity" that the guests on the executive floor have always been respected, and enables guests to experience the feeling of "home".

（3）Separate business center

The executive floor generally has a dedicated business center, conference room, meeting rooms, and other facilities of varying specifications for business guests to hold meetings at any time, or to meet and talk business with the customers. The business center has advanced equipment and a complete range of products, from document printing, copying, sorting to binding, etc., and the service efficiency is high.

二、管理及服务模式特色

行政楼层的管理为一套相对独立运转的接待服务系统，在行政管理上通常隶属于前厅部，在人员素质和服务内容上，均有不同于总台的特殊要求。

（一）人员的专业素质和特殊素质要求

在行政楼层从事接待服务的管理人员及服务人员，在形体、形象、气质、知识、技能及外语等方面表现突出，均接受过严格、系统的专业培训。

他们在熟练掌握了前台预订、接待、结算等技能的同时，还应掌握商务中心、餐饮方面的服务技能和技巧，尤其善于与客人交往、沟通，能够圆满地处理客务关系，合作性、协调性强。

（二）个性化的私人管家服务

商务客人之所以优先选择行政楼层，设施及环境的舒适条件固然是重要因素，但是他们更看重的是行政楼层所提供的细致入微、个性化的私人管家服务。

①对客人一见如故。

行政楼层的接待服务人员只要见过客人一次，第二次再见面时就可以称呼客人的姓名和头衔，客人由此产生被重视和被特别关照的心理满足感与荣誉感。

②对客人体贴入微。

行政楼层的接待服务人员对每一位在此下榻的客人都要作详尽的客史档案记录，记录客人的喜好、癖好、偏好，使客人每次下榻时都会惊喜地看到按自己的习惯和喜爱的方式所布置的房间，甚至连所喜爱的某种品牌或特殊规格的物品都已放在熟悉的位置。因此，行政楼层的房价虽然大大高出普通客房的房价，却不断吸引着众多的回头客及商务客人。

II Characteristics of management and service model

The management of the executive floor is a relatively independent operation of the reception service system, which usually belongs to the front office in terms of administrative management, and has special requirements different from the front office in terms of personnel quality and service content.

（1）Professional quality and special quality requirements of personnel

The management and service personnel engaged in reception services on the executive floor have outstanding conditions in terms of physique, image, temperament, knowledge, skills, and foreign languages, and they have all received strict and systematic professional training.

While they are proficient in the front desk booking, reception, settlement, and other skills, they should also master the service skills and techniques of business centers and catering, especially good at interacting and communicating with guests and successfully handling customer relations, cooperation, and coordination.

（2）Personalized butler service

The reason why business guests prefer to choose the executive floor is that the facilities and the comfort environment are important factors, but what they value more is the meticulous and personalized butler service provided by the executive floor.

① Treating guests like old friends.

As long as the reception service staff on the executive floor have met the guest once, they can call the guest by their name and title when they meet the second time. This creates a sense of psychological satisfaction and honor for the guest to be valued and cared for.

② Being considerate to guests.

The reception service staff of the executive floor must make a detailed guest history file for each guest staying here, record the guest's likes, hobbies, and preferences. Every time guests stay, they will be pleasantly surprised to see the rooms arranged according to their habits and favorites, and even their favorite brands or special specifications have been placed in familiar locations. Therefore, although the price of the executive floor is much higher than the price of ordinary rooms, it continues to attract many repeat customers and business guests.

三、行政楼层的主要服务项目

（一）轻松入住

由专人负责办理入住登记手续，气氛轻松。

（二）丰盛早餐

自助餐台上各种食品、饮品丰富，任客人自选，就餐酒廊环境幽雅，接待人员态度热情、动作敏捷、服务意识极强。

（三）时事动态

附设多种中外报刊，供客人选择浏览，同时播放国际卫星传输的电视新闻、专题节目等，使客人随时了解世界各地要闻及商业经济动态。

（四）悠闲下午茶

每天下午按时布置好茶水台，各种茶饮、茶具、软饮及点心免费供客人选用。

（五）鸡尾酒会

行政楼层在晚间还精心安排免费为本层客人提供结识新老朋友、沟通关系的鸡尾酒会，使客人度过美好之夜。

（六）商务洽谈

行政楼层设置的各种会议室和洽谈室及配置的复印机、传真机、电脑工作台、多功能投影仪等设备一应俱全，并提供打印、翻译、装订文件、发送文稿等商务秘书服务。

（七）委托代办

行政楼层为商务客人出行、中转提供票务、订房、订车等代办服务，使客人足不出户便可享受快捷、方便的服务。

（八）快速结账

行政楼层接待服务人员可以为客人在本层或房间办理离店结账手续，并提前安排行李员或代订交通工具，最终给客人留下美好的印象。

Ⅲ The main service items of the executive floor

（1）Easy check-in

Designated personnel is responsible for the check-in procedures, and the atmosphere is relaxed.

（2）Hearty breakfast

The buffet table is rich in various foods and beverages, and guests can choose from them. The dining lounge environment is elegant and the reception staff are enthusiastic, agile, and have a strong sense of service.

（3）Current affairs

A variety of Chinese and foreign newspapers and periodicals are attached for the guests to choose to browse. At the same time, the broadcast TV news and special programs are transmitted by international satellites, so that guests can keep abreast of key news, business, and economic trends from all over the world.

（4）Relaxing afternoon tea

The tea station is arranged on time every afternoon, and all kinds of tea, tea sets, soft drinks, and snacks are free for guests to choose.

（5）Cocktail party

In the evening, the executive floor also arranges a free cocktail party for guests on the floor to meet new and old friends and communicate with each other, so that guests can spend a good night.

（6）Business meeting

Various conference rooms and meeting rooms are set up on the executive floor, as well as copiers, fax machines, computer workstations, multi-function projectors, and other equipment. It also provides business secretarial services such as printing, translation, binding documents, and sending documents.

（7）Entrusted agent

The executive floor provides ticketing, room reservation, car reservation, and other agency services for business guests to travel and transfer so that guests can enjoy fast and convenient services without leaving the room.

（8）Quick checkout

The reception service staff on the executive floor can handle the check-out procedures for the guests on this floor or in the room and arrange a bellman or book transportation on behalf of the guests in advance, and finally leave a good impression on the guests.

四、行政楼层日常工作流程

①行政楼层值早班的接待员在 7：00 到前厅部报到，取出客人邮件，与值夜班人员交接班。

②打印当日房况报表、预抵店客人名单、在店客人名单等，然后在预离店客人名单上标上记号，做好预离店客人结账等相关服务的准备工作。

③值班台负责接待、结账及商务中心服务等工作。

④ 7:10 备好自助餐台、餐具等，提供早餐服务。

⑤准备并检查客房水果、鲜花篮、礼品，核对欢迎卡、总经理欢迎致辞等，并逐一核对抵店客人名单。

⑥早餐服务于 10：00 结束。

⑦主管召开当日工作例会，传达酒店有关信息并安排当日工作。

⑧接待入住客人，办理入住登记手续，并送上迎宾茶或咖啡，主动介绍行政楼层各种服务项目及酒店其他服务设施。

⑨为离店客人办理结账手续及代订车辆、安排行李员等事宜。

⑩检查是否有客人需要洗、烫衣服服务。

⑪受理并安排预订机票、预订酒店等委托代办服务。

⑫中班 13:30 上班，打印各种报表。

⑬中班 15:30 与早班交接班。

⑭提供下午茶服务（16:00—17:00）、鸡尾酒服务（18:00—19:30）。

⑮中班做好第二天的各项准备工作。

⑯中班 23:00 下班，并委托前厅总台代理夜间服务。

Ⅳ　The daily work process of the executive floor

① The receptionist on the morning shift on the executive floor will arrive at the front office at 7:00, take out the guests' mail, and hand it over to the night shift staff.

② Print out the room condition report of the day, the list of expected arrival guests, the list of in-house guests, etc., and then mark the list of expected departure guests, and make preparations for the checkout of expected departure guests and other related services.

③ The duty desk is responsible for reception, checkout, and business center services.

④ At 7:10, the buffet table, tableware, etc. are ready, and breakfast service is provided.

⑤ Prepare and check the room fruits, fresh flowers, gifts, check the welcome card, general manager's welcome speech, etc., and check with the list of arriving guests one by one.

⑥ Breakfast service ends at 10:00.

⑦ The supervisor convenes a daily work meeting, conveys relevant information about the hotel, and arranges daily work.

⑧ Reception of guests and check-in procedures, include delivering welcome tea or coffee and taking the initiative to introduce various service items on the executive floor and other service facilities of the hotel.

⑨ Handle checkout procedures and book vehicles on behalf of guests who leave the hotel, arrange bellman services and other matters.

⑩ Check if any guests need laundry services.

⑪ Accept and arrange entrusted agency services such as booking air tickets and booking hotels.

⑫ The middle shift staff work at 13:30 and print various reports.

⑬ The middle shift staff will take over from the morning shift staff at 15:30.

⑭ Provide afternoon tea service（16:00-17:00）, cocktail service（18:00-19:30）.

⑮ The middle shift staff do all the preparations for the next day.

⑯ Middle shift staff leave at 23:00 and entrust the front desk office to take charge of night service.

【知识拓展】

酒店里的"贴身管家服务"

目前，管家职业化程度最高的就是酒店行业。入住行政楼层的客人会享受到贴身的管家式服务。

管家服务出现于中世纪的欧洲，在英国得到极大的发展，不但完善了管家服务的内容和技巧，更形成了系统的理论和思维，各方面都带有英式烙印，自此，英式管家成了高贵、奢华的代名词。

所谓"贴身管家服务"，实际上是更专业和私人化的一站式酒店服务，它是集酒店前厅、客房和餐饮等部门的服务于一人的服务。下榻酒店的贵宾将得到一位指定的专业管家专门为他（她）服务。贵宾的一切服务需要，如拆装行李、入住退房、客房服务、清晨叫早、订餐送餐、洗衣、订票、安排旅游和秘书服务等，都由这位贴身管家负责。

【Knowledge Expansion】

"Personal Butler Service" in the Hotel

At present, the highest level of professionalization of butlers is in the hotel industry. Guests staying on the executive floor will enjoy personal butler service.

Butler's service appeared in medieval Europe and was greatly developed in the United Kingdom. It not only improved the content and skills of butler service but also formed a systematic theory and thinking, with British branding in all aspects. Since then, British butler has become synonymous with nobility and luxury.

The so-called "personal butler service" is a more professional and personal one-stop hotel service. It is a one-person service that integrates the front office, guest room, and catering departments of the hotel. The VIP staying in the hotel will get a designated professional butler to serve him or her. All the service needs of VIPs, such as unpacking and packing of luggage, check-in and check-out, room service, early morning call, meal delivery, laundry, ticket booking, travel arrangements, and secretarial services, etc., are taken care of by this personal butler.

贴身管家素质标准

①具有基层服务的工作经验，熟悉酒店各前台部门的工作流程及工作标准；熟悉餐饮部各个部门的菜肴，以及酒水搭配。

②具有较强的服务意识，能够站在顾客的立场和角度提供优质服务，具有大局意识，工作责任心强。

③具有较强的沟通、协调及应变能力，能够妥善处理与客人之间发生的各类问题，与各部门保持良好的沟通、协调。

④具有丰富的知识储备，了解酒店的各类服务项目、本地区的风土人情、旅游景点、土特产等，具有一定的商务知识，能够简单处理与客人相关的商务材料。

⑤形象气质佳，具有良好的语言沟通能力。

⑥有较强的抗压能力。

Personal butler quality standards

① Have working experience in grassroots service; familiar with the work process and working standards of the various front desk departments of the hotel; familiar with the dishes and wine pairings of each department of the catering department.

② Have a strong sense of service, be able to provide high-quality services from the customer's standpoint and perspective, have a sense of the overall situation and have a strong sense of work responsibility.

③ Have strong communication, coordination, and response capabilities, be able to properly handle various problems with guests and maintain good communication and coordination with various departments.

④ Have a wealth of knowledge reserve, understand the various service items of the hotel, local customs, tourist attractions, and local products, have certain business knowledge etc., and be able to simply process guest-related business materials.

⑤ Good appearance and temperament, with good language communication skills.

⑥ Have a strong ability to withstand pressure.

贴身管家的岗位职责

①负责检查客人的历史信息，了解抵离店时间，在客人抵店前安排赠品，做好客人抵达的迎候工作。

②负责客人抵达前的查房工作，客人抵店前做好客房间的检查工作，准备客人的房间赠品，引导客人至客房并适时介绍客房设施和特色服务。提供欢迎茶（咖啡、果汁）、行李开箱或装箱服务。

③与各前台部门密切配合安排客人房间的清洁、整理、夜床服务及餐前准备工作的检查和用餐服务，确保客人的需求在第一时间得到满足。

④负责客房餐饮服务的点餐、用餐服务，免费水果、当日报纸的配备，收取和送还客衣服务；安排客人的叫醒、用餐、用车等服务。

⑤征询客人住店期间的意见，了解客人的消费需求，并及时与相关部门协调沟通予以落实，确保客人的需求得以解决和安排。

⑥及时准备了解酒店的产品、当地旅游和商务信息等资料，适时向客人推荐酒店的服务产品。

⑦致力于提高个人的业务知识、技能和服务质量，与其他部门保持良好的沟通、协调关系，24小时为客人提供高质量的专业服务。

⑧为客人提供会务及商务秘书服务，根据客人的需求及时有效地提供其他相关服务。

⑨整理、收集客人住店期间的消费信息及生活习惯等相关资料，做好客史档案的记录和存档工作。

⑩客人离店前，为客人安排行李、出租车服务欢送客人。

Job responsibilities of a personal butler

① Responsible for checking the historical information of the guests, understanding the arrival and departure times, arranging gifts before the guests arrive, and welcoming the guests upon arrival.

② Responsible for the room rounds and check the guest rooms before the guests arrive, prepare the guest room gifts, guide the guests to the guest rooms and introduce the room facilities and special services promptly. Provide welcome tea (coffee, juice), and luggage unpacking or packing service.

③ Work closely with the front desk departments to arrange the cleaning, tidying up, turn-down service of guests' rooms, inspections of pre-dinner preparations and meal services to ensure that guests' needs are met at the first time.

④ Responsible for ordering and dining services of in-room catering services, free fruits, and newspapers of the day, collection and return of guest clothes; Arrange for guests' wake-up, meal, car, and other services.

⑤ Ask guests for their opinions during their stay in the hotel, understand the consumption needs of the guests, and promptly coordinate and communicate with relevant departments for implementation to ensure that the needs of the guests can be resolved and arranged promptly.

⑥ Be prepared to learn about the hotel's products, local tourism, and commercial information in time, and recommend the hotel's service products to guests on time.

⑦ Be committed to improving professional knowledge, skills, and service quality, maintaining good communication and coordination with other departments, and providing customers with high-quality professional services 24 hours a day.

⑧ Provide guests with conference affairs and business secretarial services, and provide other related services in a timely and effective manner according to the needs of the guests.

⑨ Sort out and collect relevant materials such as consumption information and living habits of guests during their stay, and do a good job in recording and archiving of guest history files.

⑩ Arrange luggage and taxi service for guests before leaving the hotel.

贴身管家须知

贴身管家并非寸步不离。贴身管家就像是一个"隐形人",贴身管家的"贴"是一种职业艺术,既要在最短时间内取得客人的信任,又要和客人保持合适的距离。因此,如何与客人保持适度的"贴身服务"很关键。最重要的是,贴身管家必须以真诚打动客人,同时又不能忘记这份工作代表酒店,再熟悉的客人也不能完完全全当作朋友。掺杂太多私人感情,贴身管家的服务就会变得随意。

Personal butler instructions

The personal butler will not be by the guests' side at all times. The personal butler is like an "invisible person", and the "personal" of the personal butler is a professional art. It not only needs to gain the trust of the guests in the shortest time, but also keep a proper distance from the guests. Therefore, how to maintain an appropriate "personal service" with guests is very important. The most important thing is that the personal butler must impress the guests with sincerity, and at the same time, he must not forget that this job represents the hotel, and even the familiar guests cannot completely be friends. With too many personal feelings, the service will become too casual.

【复习自测题】

①行政楼层的主要服务项目有哪些?

②案例分析:

酒店住客王先生 10 月 4 日在酒店商务中心订了一张 10 月 5 日从上海去大连, 然后 10 月 6 日从大连返回上海的来回机票, 其他并无任何特殊要求, 商务中心员工小张按客人要求, 为客人订了票。王先生要求票到后将其票送至他的房间。傍晚, 票到后员工小张把票送到了王先生房间。晚上王先生持票来到商务中心投诉, 说为何把往返票开在同一票上, 因为其公司只给报销返回那张票的钱。于是小张立即与票务人员联系, 但因为票务中心下班了, 无法即时更改机票。小张向王先生解释后, 王先生恼怒, 要求第二天一早给予更改。中班员工小张做了交班, 第二天早上早班人员小李了解事情后, 再次与票务中心联系, 请求给予更改与解决, 但票务中心人员无法更改, 提出两个办法, 一是为客人出两张 (一来一回) 的证明, 二是退票, 但退票费由客人付, 经联系后都被客人拒绝了。

【案例思考】

a. 出现问题的原因是什么?

b. 酒店应该如何处理此事?

c. 如何避免此类问题的发生?

【Review of Self-test Questions】

① What are the main service items of the executive floor?

② Case analysis:

Hotel guest Mr. Wang booked a round-trip air ticket from Shanghai to Dalian on October 5th at a hotel business center on October 4th, and then back to Shanghai from Dalian on October 6th. There were no other special requirements. Business center employee Xiao Zhang booked a ticket for the guest according to the request of the guest. Mr. Wang asked for the ticket to be sent to his room after the ticket arrived. In the evening, when the ticket arrived, Xiao Zhang delivered the ticket to Mr. Wang's room. In the evening, Mr. Wang came to the business center with a ticket to complain, saying why the round-trip ticket was issued as a single ticket because his company only reimbursed the money of the return ticket. So xiao Zhang immediately contacted the ticketing staff, but because the ticketing center was off work, he could not change the ticket immediately. After xiao Zhang explained to Mr. Wang, Mr. Wang was annoyed and asked to make changes the next morning. The middle shift employee xiao Zhang made the shift. After the morning shift employee xiao Li learned about the matter the next morning, he contacted the ticketing center again, requesting change and resolution, but the ticketing center staff could not change it and proposed two methods, one is to provide the guests with two proofs (one departure and one return), the second was a refund, but the refund fee was paid by the customer. After Contacting the guest, he refused.

【Case Thinking】

a. What is the cause of the problem?

b. How should the hotel handle this matter?

c. How to avoid such problems?

项目五
总机服务

【案例导入】

上午10点左右，总机接线员胡珊珊接到客人询问关于月饼事宜的来电。在电话铃响了多次以后该员工接起电话，直接询问客人得知吕先生在酒店购买了中秋月饼票25张，因在酒店附近故想在酒店提取月饼。但因两次在领货点领货时都没有现货，该员工在听清客人的问题后跟客人道歉，表示给客人造成的不便很抱歉，并告知客人此款月饼销售不错，临近佳节提货人员比较多导致供不应求，现酒店还有此货，先可以帮他预订下，以免到时白跑一趟。随后，和客人确定领货时间，客人告知下午3点左右。和客人结束通话后，该员工立即致电饮食中心告知此事情况。

Project 5
Switchboard service

【Case Introduction】

Around 10 a.m, the switchboard operator Hu Shanshan received a call from a customer asking about mooncakes. After the phone rang several times, the operator picked up the phone and directly asked the customer and learned that Mr. Lu bought 25 Mid-Autumn Mooncake tickets at the hotel. The customer wanted to pick up moon cakes because he was near the hotel. However, because there was no stock when picking up the goods at the pick-up point twice, the employee apologized to the customer after hearing the customer's complaint, saying that she was sorry for the inconvenience caused to the customer, and told the customer that this moon cake is selling well. This often leads to short supply. Now that the hotel still has the stock, and she could make a reservation for the customer first. Afterward, she confirmed the pick-up time with the customer, and the customer informs about 3 p.m. After finishing the conversation with the customer, the operator immediately called the food center to inform them of the situation.

【评析】

该员工在此次总机服务中，出现了以下问题：

①电话铃声多次响后才接听。

②未正确报位，问候客人。

③没有主动跟进解决。

正确的处理方法及程序：

①电话铃响三声以内接听。

②正确报位，问候客人。

③聆听客人要求并提供帮助。

④正确处理客人的投诉。

⑤主动提供帮助。

⑥结束通话并跟进解决。

【Comment and Analysis】

The employee didn't perform the following tasks well during this switchboard service:

① Answer the phone only after ringing several times.

② Incorrectly Introduce and greet guests.

③ Do not take the initiative to follow up to solve the problem.

Correct handling method and procedure:

① Answer the phone within three rings.

② Make a correct introduction and greet the guests.

③ Listen to customer requests and assist them.

④ Correctly handle guest complaints.

⑤ Take the initiative to provide help.

⑥ End the call and follow up to solve it.

任务一　总机服务认知

一、总机服务的重要性

电话是当今社会最主要的通信手段之一，也是酒店客人使用频率最高的通信设施，在对客服务过程中扮演着重要的、不可替代的角色。酒店客人所需要的几乎所有服务都可通过客房内的电话解决。总机是负责为客人及酒店经营活动提供电话服务的前台部门。

　　总机是酒店内外沟通联络的通信枢纽和喉舌，以电话为媒介，直接为客人提供转接电话、留言、叫醒、查询等服务，是酒店对外联系的窗口，其工作代表酒店的形象，体现酒店服务的水准。总机操作员即话务员被称为酒店中"看不到的接待员"。总台、餐厅及客房楼层的服务人员都是直接和客人面对面接触，对客人的种种反应、表情都可以及时观察，并依此作出即时的直接应对反应。而通过电话里向客人服务，其困难及局限性则多出许多，因为看不到客人的表情及种种行为反应，仅能从其言语的速度、音量、语调等来判断并作出相应的答复。因此，电话服务对操作人员来说，要求具备比较丰富的经验、纯熟的技巧，以及具有足够的耐心。

　　总机服务是一个看不到的对客服务的一个小分部，只要涉及对客，就关乎服务质量问题，关系到客人的满意度，进而对整个酒店的声誉产生影响。

Task 1　Switchboard Service Awareness

I　The importance of switchboard service

The telephone is one of the most important means of communication in today's society, and it is also the communication facility most frequently used by hotel guests. It plays an important and irreplaceable role in the process of customer service. Almost all services required by hotel guests can be handled through the telephone in the guest room. The switchboard is the front desk department responsible for providing telephone services for guests and hotel business activities.

The switchboard is the communication hub inside and outside the hotel. It uses the telephone as the medium to directly provide customers with transfer calls, message services, wake-up calls, inquiries, and other services. It is the window for the hotel to communicate with the outside world, and its work represents the image of the hotel and reflects the standard of hotel service. The switchboard operator, that is, the telephone operator can be called the "unseen receptionist" in the hotel. The service staff at the reception desk, restaurant, and guest room floors are in direct face-to-face contact with the guests. The various reactions and expressions of the guests can be observed timely, and immediate and direct responses can be made accordingly. Serving guests on the phone has more difficulties and limitations, because operators can't see the guests' facial expressions and various behavioral responses, and can only judge and respond accordingly from the speed, volume, and tone of their speech. Therefore, for operators, telephone service requires rich experience, proficient skills, and patience.

The switchboard service is a small branch of invisible customer service. As long as the customer service is involved, it is related to service quality issue and customer satisfaction, which in turn has an impact on the reputation of the entire hotel.

二、总机服务的规范

总机服务在酒店对客服务中扮演着重要角色，每一位话务员的声音都代表着酒店的形象，话务员是"只听其悦耳声，不见其微笑容"的幕后服务员。因此，话务员必须以热情的态度、礼貌的语言、甜美的嗓音和娴熟的技能，优质高效地为客人提供服务，使客人通过电话就能够感到微笑、热情、礼貌和修养，甚至感到酒店的档次和管理水平。

（一）话务员应具备的素质

①修养良好，责任感强。

②口齿清楚，音质甜美，语速适中。

③听写迅速，反应敏捷。

④专注认真，记忆力强。

⑤有较强的外语听说能力。

⑥有熟练的计算机操作和打字技术。

⑦有较强的信息沟通能力。

⑧掌握酒店服务、旅游景点及娱乐等知识与信息。

⑨严守话务机密。

⑩工作责任心强。

II　Specifications of the switchboard service

The switchboard service plays an important role in the hotel's guest service. Every operator's voice represents the image of the hotel, and the operator is the service provider behind the scenes whose "pleasant sound can be heard, but the smile cannot be seen". Therefore, the operator must provide high-quality and efficient services to the guests with a warm attitude, polite language, sweet voice, and adept skills, so make guests feel warmth, enthusiasm, politeness through the phone, and even "feel" the grade and management level of the hotel.

（1）The qualities that an operator should possess

① Good manners and a strong sense of responsibility.

② Clear speech, sweet voice quality, moderate speaking speed.

③ Quick dictation and quick response.

④ Concentration, strong memory.

⑤ Have strong foreign language listening and speaking skills.

⑥ Have proficient computer operation and typing skills.

⑦ Have strong information communication skills.

⑧ Master the knowledge and information of hotel services, tourist attractions, and entertainment.

⑨ Keep the call confidential.

⑩ Have a strong sense of responsibility.

（二）总机服务的基本要求

①话务员必须在总机铃响三声之内应答电话。

②礼貌规范用语不离口，坐姿端正，不得与客人过于随便。

③话务员应答电话时，必须礼貌、友善、愉快，且面带微笑。客人虽然看不到话务员，但能够感觉到她／他的笑脸，因为只有在微笑时话务员才会表现出礼貌、友善和愉快，她／他的语音才会甜美、自然，有吸引力。

④接听电话时首先用中英文熟练准确地自报家门，并自然亲切地使用问候语。接听内线电话，应先报岗位。

⑤客人的留言内容，应做好记录，不可单凭大脑记忆，复述时应注意核对数字。

⑥应使用婉转的话语建议客人，不可使用命令式的语句。

⑦若对方讲话不清，应保持耐心，要用提示法来弄清问题，切不可急躁地追问或嘲笑、模仿等。

⑧话务员应能够辨别主要管理人员的声音，接到他们的来电时，话务员需给予恰当的尊称。

⑨话务员应清楚记忆酒店内所有岗位分机号及店外常联系的单位，如上级主管单位、兄弟酒店、重要客户单位等的电话。

⑩结束通话时应主动向对方致谢，待对方挂断电话后，再切断线路，切忌因自己情绪不佳而影响服务态度与质量。

（2）Basic requirements for switchboard service

① The operator must answer the call within three rings of the switchboard.

② Be polite and use standardized language, sit upright, and not be too casual with guests.

③ When the operator answers the call, she/he must be polite, friendly, cheerful, and smiling. Although the guests cannot see the operator, they can feel her/his smiling face, because the operator will be polite, friendly, and cheerful only when smiling, and her/his voice will be sweet, natural, and attractive.

④ When answering the phone, first use Chinese and English proficiently and accurately to introduce the hotel, and use greetings naturally and kindly. To answer an internal call, the operator should report your position first.

⑤ The content of the guest's message should be recorded, not just remembered mentally, and the numbers should be checked when retelling.

⑥ Advise guests with tactful words instead of imperative sentences.

⑦ If the other party can't speak clearly, the operator should be patient, use prompting methods to clarify the problem, and don't ask irritably, mock, imitate, etc.

⑧ The operator should be able to distinguish the voice of the main management personnel. When receiving their call, the operator should give an appropriate honorific title.

⑨ The operator should memorize the extension numbers of all posts in the hotel and the company frequently contacted outside the hotel, such as the telephone numbers of the department supervisor, sister company, important customer, etc.

⑩ When ending the call, the operator should take the initiative to thank the other party, and then cut off the line after the other party hangs up. Don't affect the service attitude and quality due to personal emotions.

任务二　电话应接服务

【案例导入】

周先生给酒店总机打电话，要求接到 921 房间，称有急事找客人。但是，房内客人正在通电话，电话长时间占线，总机话务员为周先生转接了几次仍然占线。由于周先生听不到占线的声音，每次电话打到总机时，总机话务员只能告诉周先生占线，由于等的时间太长，而且话务员总是称占线，周先生便以为总机话务员不愿意为他转接电话，便开始对总机话务员发火，说了一些不堪入耳的话。总机话务员感到十分委屈，虽然没有与周先生争吵，但向周先生表示将不再接他的电话，并在 921 客人挂断电话后仍然拒绝为周先生接通电话。最终导致周先生向酒店投诉。

Task two　Telephone Answering Service

【Case Introduction】

Mr. Zhou called the hotel's switchboard and asked to connect to room 921, saying that he was looking for the guest for an urgent matter. However, the guest in the room was talking on the phone, and the line was busy for a long time. The switchboard operator transferred several times for Mr. Zhou and it was still busy. Since Mr. Zhou was not certain whether the line is busy, every time a call was made to the switchboard, and the switchboard operator could only tell Mr. Zhou that the line was busy. Because the waiting time was too long and the operator always said that the line was busy, Mr. Zhou thought that the switchboard operator was unwilling to transfer the call for him, so he started to get angry with the switchboard operator and said something unbearable. The switchboard operator felt very aggrieved. Although he did not quarrel with Mr. Zhou, he told Mr. Zhou that he would no longer answer his calls and refused to connect with Mr. Zhou after the 921 guests hung up. Eventually, Mr. Zhou complained to the hotel.

【评析】

为客人接通电话是总机话务员义不容辞的工作职责，无论遇到什么情况都不应该拒绝为客人转接电话。在上述案例中，总机话务员虽然受到客人的误解，但不应该采取极端措施，变有理为无理。

①话务员本可以在周先生发火之前向其解释，也许能得到周先生的理解。同时提醒客人："您是否需要留言或稍后再拨？"若客人留言，应将留言单送至周先生房内。

②周先生在不了解真实情况下对总机话务员说了一些不适当的话，反映了他的素质还不够高。但是，总机话务员作为酒店的员工应具备相应的素质，正确地控制自己的情绪，不能以牙还牙，采取不正确的方式回应客人，损坏酒店的形象。

【Comment and Analysis】

It is the indispensable job responsibility of the switchboard operator to answer the call for the guest. No matter what the situation is, the operator should not refuse to transfer the call for the guest. In the above-mentioned case, although the switchboard operator was misunderstood by the guest, he should not take extreme behavior to make rationality unreasonable.

① The operator could have explained to Mr. Zhou before he became angry, maybe he/she could get Mr. Zhou's understanding. The guest should be reminded: "Do you need to leave a message or call later?" If the guest leaves a message, the message form should be sent to Mr. Zhou's room.

② Mr. Zhou said some inappropriate words to the operator of the switchboard without knowing the real situation, reflecting that he is ill-mannered. However, the switchboard operator, as a hotel employee, should have the appropriate manner, control his emotions correctly, and can't retaliate, use improper means to respond to guests, damaging the image of the hotel.

一、电话转接服务

（一）接听电话

电话铃声响起，要迅速接起电话，向对方问候，表明单位名称或部门名称，表达乐于提供帮助的意愿。

话务员应在铃声响起三声之内接听电话。应接外线电话时，应说："您好！（上午好！／下午好！／晚上好！）××酒店。有什么可以帮您的吗？"应接内线电话时，应说："您好！（上午好！／下午好！／晚上好！）总机。有什么可以帮您的吗？"若对方无应答，则应用英文再问候一遍。

当值时要精神集中，操作时要迅速、准确。必须以热情、礼貌和友好的态度应接每一个电话。说话时吐字清晰、语音柔和，使用"您好""对不起""请稍候""请问""谢谢"等礼貌用语。回答或解释问题时，语言简练、语气谦和；发生差错或耽搁时要道歉；当值时不能谈笑，不能咀嚼食物，不得顶撞客人。

I　Telephone transfer service

(1) Answer the phone

When the phone rings, answer the phone promptly, greet the other party, indicate the name of the company or department, and express willingness to help.

The operator should answer the call within three rings. When answering an external call, should say: "Hello! (Good morning! / Good afternoon! / Good evening!) × × hotel. Can I help you?" When answering the internal call, should say: "Hello! (Good morning!/Good afternoon!/Good evening!) Switchboard. What can I do for you?" If the other party does not answer, please greet again in English.

When you are on duty, you must concentrate and operate quickly and accurately. Every call must be answered with enthusiasm, courtesy, and friendliness. Speak clearly, speak softly, and use polite words such as "Hello" "Sorry" "Please wait" "Excuse me" "Thank you" and so on. When answering or explaining questions, keep your language concise and modest; apologize for mistakes or delays; you can't talk and laugh when you are on duty, you can't chew food, and you can't stand up to the guests.

（二）接驳电话

根据客人的要求把电话接驳至客房、租户办公室或酒店各个部门。要特别注意的是，接驳电话进客房前，应先核对电脑资料，确认来电者要求转接客房的客人姓名与登记相符才进行转接。在等候转接时，可按音乐键，播放悦耳的音乐。

转接之后，如对方无人听电话，铃响30秒后，应向客人说明："对不起，电话无人接听，您是否需要留言或过会儿再打来？"给住客留言的电话通常需转到前台问询处；需给酒店管理人员的留言（非工作时间或管理人员办公室无人时），一律接受下来，并重复确认，然后通过寻呼方式或其他有效方式尽快将留言转达给相关的管理者。

接驳电话时，除非是紧急事情，否则不能随便插线打扰客人通话。绝对禁止窃听客人通话。

（2）Connecting the phone

Connect the phone to the guest room, tenant's office, or various departments of the hotel according to the customer's request. It is important to note that before connecting the phone to the guest room, the operator should first check the computer information and confirm that the caller's request to transfer to the guest's room matches the registered name of the guest before proceeding. While the guest is waiting for the transfer, the operator can press the music button to play pleasant music.

After the transfer, if no one answers the phone, after 30 seconds of ringing, the operator should explain to the guest: "Sorry, no one answered the phone, do you need to leave a message or call back later?" Calls for which need to leave a message to guests are usually transferred to the information desk at the front desk; messages that need to be addressed to hotel managers （not during working hours or when there is no one in the manager's office）, are all accepted and double-check, and through paging or other effective methods to forward the message to the relevant managers as soon as possible.

When answering the phone, unless it is an emergency, the operator can't just plug in the line and disturb the guest on the phone. Eavesdropping on guest calls is prohibited.

二、免电话打扰（DND）服务

总机话务员在接到住店客人DND服务要求时，要将客人的姓名、房号、具体DND服务时间记录在交接班本上，并写明接受客人DND服务的时间。随后，在电脑上按客人要求的DND时段锁上该房间电话号码。

在免打扰期间，如来电者要求与住客通话，话务员应将礼貌地告知来电者相关DND服务信息，并建议其留言或待取消DND之后再来电话。

客人要求取消DND后，话务员应立即通过电脑释放被锁的电话号码，同时，在交接班本上标明取消记号及时间。

II Do Not Disturb（DND）service

When the switchboard operator receives the DND service request from the in-house guest, he/she shall record the guest's name, room number, and specific DND service time in the Logbook, and specify the time of receiving DND service from the guest. Then, lock the phone number of the room on the computer according to the DND period requested by the guest.

During the Do Not Disturb period, if the caller requests to talk to the guest, the operator shall politely inform the caller of the relevant DND service information, and suggest that he/she could leave a message or call after the DND is canceled.

After the guest requests to cancel the DND, the operator should immediately release the locked phone number through the computer, and at the same time, mark the cancellation mark and time on the logbook.

三、接听电话留言

（一）访客留言

①电话占线或无人接听时，应提醒客人："您是否需要留言或稍后再拨？"

②根据来电者所报的客人姓名、房号与电脑核对，若正确，将留言内容详细记录在留言单上。

③将留言内容复述一遍并与来电者核实，如有疑问应与来电者再次核实，保证留言内容的准确性。

④当电话占线时可采取口头留言的方式直接告知客人，要求语言表达清楚简练，有相应的礼貌敬语。同时将留言内容记录并留存总机，以备客人查询；如占线时间过长或无人接听，应将留言单送至客人房内。

⑤三分钟之内填写留言单及留言信封,应注意字迹工整,语句通畅、简洁,内容完整、准确,格式标准,使用敬语,不得用口语记录留言内容。

⑥要在第一时间通知礼宾部送留言单至客房，将留言的第一联送至客人房内，第二联送至总台，第三联由礼宾部签收后，留存总机备查。

Ⅲ　Take the phone message

（1）Caller message

① When the call is busy or no one is answering, the caller should be reminded: "Do you need to leave a message or call later?"

② Check with the computer according to the guest's name and room number given by the caller and record the content of the message on the message form if it is correct.

③ Retell the content of the message and verify it with the caller. If in doubt, check with the caller again to ensure the accuracy of the content of the message.

④ When the call is busy, the operator can inform the guests verbally, requiring clear and concise language, with corresponding polite and respectful words. At the same time, record the content of the message and keep it on the switchboard for customers to inquire; if the line remains busy for too long or no one answers, the message form should be sent to the guest room.

⑤ Fill out the message form and message envelope within three minutes, pay attention to neat handwriting, the sentences are clear, concise, complete and accurate, standard format, use honorifics, and do not record the content of the message in spoken language.

⑥ To inform the hotel concierge to send the message form to the guest room as soon as possible, send the first copy of the message to the guest's room, and send the second copy to the reception desk. After the third copy is signed by the hotel concierge, keep it on the switchboard for future reference.

（二）住客留言

将住客留言内容填写在留言单上，将客人房间的电话转至总机，并通知当班所有话务员，凡是转接该房的电话或内线分机拨此房间跳至总机的，一律转告住客的留言，要告知客人回房后取消留言，再将电话恢复正常。

（2）Guest message forwarding

Fill in the guest's message on the message form, transfer the guest's room phone to the switchboard, and notify all operators on duty. Anyone who transfers the room's phone or internal extension to the room and jumps to the switchboard must forward the guest's message, To inform the guest to cancel the message forwarding after returning to the room, and then restore the call to normal.

【实训练习题】

请补充下列几种情况的对话。

情况一：

（总机电话铃声响起）

话务员：＿＿＿＿＿＿＿＿＿＿＿＿＿＿＿＿＿＿＿＿＿＿＿＿＿＿＿＿。

来电客人：请帮我转接 1618 号房间。

话务员：＿＿＿＿＿＿＿＿＿＿＿＿＿＿＿＿＿＿＿＿＿＿＿＿＿＿＿＿。

来电客人：这个我不清楚。

话务员：＿＿＿＿＿＿＿＿＿＿＿＿＿＿＿＿＿＿＿＿＿＿＿＿＿＿＿＿。

情况二：

（总机电话铃声响起）

话务员：＿＿＿＿＿＿＿＿＿＿＿＿＿＿＿＿＿＿＿＿＿＿＿＿＿＿＿＿。

来电客人：请帮我转接 1618 号房间。

话务员：＿＿＿＿＿＿＿＿＿＿＿＿＿＿＿＿＿＿＿＿＿＿＿＿＿＿＿＿。

来电客人：王宁。

话务员：＿＿＿＿＿＿＿＿＿＿＿＿＿＿＿＿＿＿＿＿＿＿＿＿＿＿＿＿。

（无人接听）

话务员：＿＿＿＿＿＿＿＿＿＿＿＿＿＿＿＿＿＿＿＿＿＿＿＿＿＿＿＿。

要求

①应答语言符合话务员礼仪规范。

②正确处理来电客人的电话转接要求。

【Practical Training Exercises】

Please fill in the dialogues in the following situations.

Situation 1:

（The switchboard phone rings）

Operator: _____.

Caller: Please connect me to room 1618.

Operator: _____.

Caller: I am not sure about this.

Operator: : _____.

Situation 2:

（The switchboard phone rings）

Operator: _____.

Caller: Please connect me to room 1618.

Operator: _____.

Calling guest: Wang Ning.

Operator: _____.

（No one answer）

Operator: _____.

Requirements:

① The response language complies with operator eliquette rules.

② Hand call for warding requests from incoming guests correctly.

任务三　叫醒服务

【案例导入】

　　一天，酒店客人要求总台为他做一次第二天早上 6:30 的叫醒服务。总台服务人员马上通知了总机。然而，第二天早上 7:00 过后，客人非常气愤地来到大堂经理处投诉说，今天早上并没有人叫他起床，也没有听见电话铃声，以致他延误了国际航班。后经查实，总机在接到总台指令后，立刻就通过电话为他做了早晨叫醒服务并排除了线路及器械故障的可能。经过分析后认为，可能是由于客人睡得比较沉，没有听见。电话铃声响了几次之后就会自动切断，造成了最终结果。

Task 3 Wake-up service

【Case Introduction】

One day, the hotel guest asked the front desk to provide him with a wake-up service at 6:30 the next morning. The front desk service staff immediately notified the switchboard. However, after 7:00 am next morning, the guest came to the lobby manager very angrily and complained, no one came to wake him up this morning, nor did he hear the phone ringing, which caused him to miss the international flight. Later, it was verified that the switchboard immediately provided him with a morning wake-up service via telephone after receiving the command from the front desk and eliminated the possibility of line and equipment failures. After analysis, it was believed that the may have been in a deep sleep and did not hear it. The phone will automatically cut off after ringing several times, leading to the final result.

【评析】

上述案例从表面上来看，客人要求的服务，酒店也做了，但最终结果却没有达到服务的目的。从这里，我们也可以看出"宾客至上"并非一个简单的口号，这是一项细致、具体的工作。平时只要多一些人性化的服务，少一些公式化、程序化的服务，那么工作将做得更好。比如，客人要求是 6:30 叫醒，除了做一个电脑设置，在 6:40 可以再让服务员到房间做一次上门叫醒。这样，就可以避免此案例中所发生的不愉快。假如客人已醒，可以询问客人是否要退房，还可以征询客人是否要为他叫一辆出租车，以及是否帮他搬运行李，等等。总之，在服务过程中，能设身处地为客人多想一想，客人的投诉可能就不会发生了。

【Comment and Analysis】

The above case is taken at face value, the hotel did the service requested by the guest, but the final result did not achieve the service objective. From here, we can also see that "Guest First" is not a simple slogan; it is very detailed and specific work. Usually, as long as there are more people-oriented services and less formalized, programmatic services, then the work will be better. For example, the guest requests a wake-up call at 6:30. In addition to setting up the wake-up call on the computer, the staff can come to the room to wake up the guest again at 6:40. In this way, the unpleasantness that occurred, in this case, can be avoided. In addition, if the guest is awake, the staff can ask if the guest wants to check out, the staff can also ask if the guest needs a taxi, and does he/she need luggage service, and so on. In short, during the service, if you can put yourself in the guest's position and think more about the guests, the complaints of the guests may not happen.

叫醒服务，就是按照客人指定的时间打电话（也有直接敲门的）叫客人起床，一般的酒店都有。这样的服务可以让客人安安稳稳地睡觉而不用担心因睡过头而错过了要事。叫醒服务是总机服务中非常重要的一个服务项目，它涉及客人的计划和日程安排，尤其是关系到客人的航班、车次等。因此，不能出任何差错，否则会给客人和酒店带来不可弥补的损失。总机提供的叫醒服务是全天 24 小时服务，分为人工叫醒和自动叫醒两类。在采用功能齐全的程控交换机的酒店，多选择电话自动叫醒。

Wake-up service calls guests (or knocks on the door directly) to wake guests up at a designated time; it is available in most hotels. This kind of service allows guests to sleep peacefully without worrying about oversleeping and missing important things. Wake-up service is a very important part of switchboard service. It involves guests'plans and schedules, especially related to guests' flights and train numbers. Therefore, no mistakes can be made, otherwise, it will cause irreparable losses to the guests and the hotel. The wake-up service provided by the switchboard is 24-hour service, divided into two types: manual wake-up and automatic wake-up. In hotels that use fully functional program-controlled switches, most choose the automatic phone wake-up.

一、人工叫醒服务

总机的人工叫醒服务就是由话务员在客人指定的叫醒时间打电话到客人房间叫醒客人。这种叫醒方式亲切，具有人性化，叫醒成功率高。但此种方式容易因话务员工作疏忽而遗忘叫醒；并且，若当同一时间需要叫醒的客人较多时，话务员往往应接不暇，甚至耽误客人的时间。

I　Manual wake-up service

The manual wake-up service of the switchboard is that the operator calls the guest's room to wake up at the time specified by the guest. This kind of wake-up method is cordial, humanized, and has a high success rate. However, this method is easy to forget due to the negligence of the operator; and, if many guests need to wake up at the same time, the operator is often overwhelmed and even delays the guest's schedule.

人工叫醒服务的程序如下：

①接受客人叫醒服务要求。

②问清要求叫醒的具体时间和房号，并确认。

③填写"叫醒服务记录单"。

叫醒服务记录单

序号	房间号	客人姓名	叫醒日期、时间	经办人	是否按时叫醒	经办人	备注

④在定时钟上准确定时。

⑤定时钟鸣响，话务员接通客房分机，叫醒客人，并问候客人"××先生/小姐，您好！现在是×点×分，您的叫醒时间到了。"

⑥核对叫醒记录，以免出现差错。

⑦若房内无人应答，5分钟后再叫一次，若仍无人回话，则应立即通知客房服务中心，由服务员前往客房，实地察看，查明原因。

⑧记录叫醒情况。

The procedure for manual wake-up service is as follows:

① Accept guest wake-up service requests.

② Ask and confirm the specific time and room number of the wake-up call.

③ Fill in the "Wake-up Service Record Sheet".

Wake-up Service Record Sheet

No.	Room No.	Guest's Name	Wake-up date and time	Operator	Whether wake up the guest on time	Operator	Remark

④ Time accurately on the clock.

⑤ When the clock rings, the operator connects to the guest room extension, wakes up the guest, and greets the guest "Mr/Ms. ××, hello! It's ×× time, it is your wake-up time."

⑥ Check the wake-up records to avoid errors.

⑦ If there is no answer in the room, call again after 5 minutes. If there is still no answer, the operator should notify the room service center immediately, and the attendant will go to the guest room to check and find out the reason.

⑧ Record the wake-up situation.

二、自动叫醒服务

总机的自动叫醒服务是话务员将客人的房间号及要求叫醒的时间在电脑上进行设置，时间一到，电脑控制的自动叫醒系统就会自动拨通客人房间的电话，待客人接电话时，系统会自动播放事先录制好的统一问候语。

自动叫醒服务的程序如下：

①接受宾客叫醒服务要求。

②问清要求叫醒的具体时间和房号并确认。

③填写"叫醒服务记录单"。

④将该客人的叫醒信息输入电脑自动叫醒系统并启动。

⑤叫醒时间一到，自动叫醒系统就会自动拨号到房间，叫醒客人并播放问候语。如果客人没有接听，5分钟后（时间间隔可自行设定）会自动弹回来，此时应迅速进行人工叫醒。如果仍没有人接听，则立即通知客房服务中心，由服务员再次到房间进行叫醒服务。

⑥记录叫醒情况。

无论是人工叫醒，还是自动叫醒，话务员在受理时，都应认真、细致、慎重，避免差错和责任事故的发生。一旦出现失误，不管责任在酒店还是在客人都应给予高度重视，积极采取措施，而不要在责任上纠缠。同时，还应注意叫醒的方式。比如，用姓名称呼客人、对 VIP 客人派专人人工叫醒等，尽可能使客人感到亲切。若能在叫醒服务时将当天的天气变化情况通报给客人，并询问是否需要其他服务，则会给客人留下美好的深刻印象。

Ⅱ　Automatic wake-up service

The automatic wake-up service of the switchboard is that the attendant sets the guest's room number and the wake-up time on the computer. Once the time is up, the computer-controlled automatic wake-up system will automatically dial the guest's room phone and wait for the guest to answer. When the guest answers, the system will automatically play the unified greeting that has been recorded in advance.

The procedure for automatic wake-up service is as follows:

① Accept guest wake-up service requests.

② Ask and confirm the specific time and room number of the wake-up call.

③ Fill in the "Wake-up Service Record Sheet".

④ Input the guest's wake-up information into the computer's automatic wake-up system and start it.

⑤ When the wake-up time is up, the automatic wake-up system will automatically dial the guest room, wake up the guest and play a greeting. If the guest does not answer the call, it will automatically call back after five minutes（the time interval can be set）, at this time, a manual wake-up call should be made quickly. If there is still no one to answer, immediately notify the room service center, and the staff will go to the guest's room for a wake-up service.

⑥ Record the wake-up situation.

Whether it is manual or automatic wake-up, the operator should be serious, meticulous, and cautious when accepting the requests, to avoid the occurrence of errors and liability accidents. Once there is a mistake, no matter whether the responsibility lies in the hotel or the guest, we should attach great importance to it and take active measures instead of being entangled in responsibility. At the same time, the operator should also pay attention to the way he/she wakes up guests. For example, operators can call guests by their names, and assign someone to wake up VIP guests manually, etc., to make the guests feel cordial as much as possible. If the operator can inform the guests of the weather change of the day during the wake-up service, and ask if other services are needed, the guests will be impressed.

三、叫醒服务的问题与对策

叫醒服务是酒店为客人提供的一项基本服务内容，但常常发生叫醒失误的现象，引起客人投诉。

（一）叫醒失误的原因

叫醒失误的原因有以下几种。

①酒店方面。

a. 话务员漏叫。

b. 总机话务员做了记录，但忘了将叫醒信息输入电脑进行叫醒设置。

c. 记录的房号太潦草、笔误或误听，输入电脑时输错房号或时间。

d. 电脑出现故障。

②客人方面。

a. 报错房号。

b. 电话听筒没放好，无法振铃。

c. 睡得太熟，电话铃响没听见。

III　Problems and countermeasures of wake-up service

Wake-up service is a basic service provided by the hotel for guests, but wake-up errors often occur, causing guest complaints.

（1）Reasons for wake-up errors

There are several reasons for wake-up errors.

① Hotel.

a. The operator missed a call.

b. The switchboard operator made a record but forgot to input the wake-up information into the computer for the wake-up setting.

c. The recorded room number is too scribble, clerical error or misunderstanding, and the wrong room number or time is entered into the computer.

d. The computer is malfunctioning.

② Guests.

a. Report the wrong room number.

b. The phone cannot ring if the receiver is not placed properly.

c. The guest was sleeping too soundly and didn't hear the phone ring.

（二）叫醒失误的对策

为了避免叫醒失误或减少失误率，酒店方面可以从以下几方面着手，积极采取措施。

第一，经常检查电脑运行状况，及时通知有关人员排除故障。

第二，话务员应重复一遍客人所报的房号和叫醒时间，并得到客人的确认。

第三，遇到客人没有应答叫醒电话，应通知客房服务中心安排客房服务员敲门叫醒。

还有一种情况，就是客人虽然听到了叫醒电话，但没有及时起床，结果误了事，反而责怪酒店没有提供（或没有按时提供）叫醒服务，要求酒店对此负责，并赔偿损失。为了避免这类事件的发生，一种有效的办法就是安装一台录音电话，将叫醒服务的通话记录录下来，作为证据保存。

另外，需要说明的是，叫醒服务不同于叫早服务，它是全天候24小时服务，而不只限于早晨的叫醒。有些酒店，叫醒服务是电脑自动控制，客人要求下午或晚上某个时间叫醒，结果叫醒铃响后，拿起电话听到的第一句话仍然是："早上好，这是您的叫早服务"，令人啼笑皆非。

（2）Countermeasures for wake-up errors

To avoid wake-up errors or reduce the error rate, the hotel can start from the following aspects and actively take measures.

First, check the computer's operating status frequently and notify relevant personnel to troubleshoot in time.

Second, the operator should repeat the room number and wake-up time given by the guest and obtain the guest's confirmation.

Third, when the guest does not answer the wake-up call, the operator should notify the room service center to arrange for the room attendant to knock on the door to wake up the guest.

Another situation is that although the guest heard the wake-up call, did not get up in time, resulting a mistake, and then, he blamed the hotel for not providing（or failing to provide）the wake-up service, asking the hotel to be responsible for it and to compensate for the loss. To avoid such incidents, an effective way is to install a recording phone to record the call records of the wake-up service and save them as evidence.

In addition, it should be noted that the wake-up service is different from the morning service. It is available 24 hours a day, not just as a morning wake-up call. In some restaurants, the wake-up service is automatically controlled by a computer. Guests request to wake up at a certain time in the afternoon or evening. As a result, after the wake-up bell rings, the first sentence heard when picking up the phone is still: "Good morning, this is your morning call service"，which makes guests laugh.

【课堂讨论】

1月20日909房间客人昨晚11：00左右致电总机要设置叫醒服务，据当班话务员反映，客人当时称要一个明天12：50的叫醒，话务员还重复问了一句："是明天吗？"客人答复"是"。但今日一早客人到前台称他要的是凌晨12：50的叫醒。客人买了长沙到西安的火车票，但由于没有叫醒，导致睡过头，错过了火车。

这种情况下酒店应如何处理？在今后的工作中应如何避免同类问题的产生？

【参考意见】

酒店应道歉并安抚好客人做好解释工作，同时应立即协助客人改签火车票，将客人的损失降至最低。

酒店在接受客人叫醒服务要求时，应注意：

①客人可能会记错当天的日期，话务员与其确认时可能会出现时间上的误差，因此话务员在向客人确认时要加上"今天是 × 月 × 日，您是需要在明天也就是 × 月 × 日吗？"之类时间确认的话，以提醒客人。

②客人在晚上或凌晨提出叫醒服务要求时，可能会出现的时间差别是需要我们注意的。如客人在晚上10:00通知第二天6：00叫醒，话务员在确认时要注意问到底是上午6点还是下午6点等。

③记录好客人打电话和要求叫醒的具体时间，以便进行核对。

【Class Disscussion】

On January 20th, the guest in room 909 called the switchboard at around 11:00 to set up a wake-up service. According to the operator on duty, the guest said that he wanted a wake-up call at 12:50 tomorrow, and the operator repeatedly asked: "Is it tomorrow?" The guest replied, "Yes". But the guest came to the front desk early this morning and said what he wanted was a wake-up call at 12:50 in the morning. The guest bought a train ticket from Changsha to Xi'an, but because he did not wake up, he overslept and missed the train.

How should the hotel handle this situation? In the future work, how to avoid similar problems?

【Reference Suggestion】

The hotel should apologize and appease the guest to explain it well, and at the same time, they should immediately assist the guests to change the train ticket to minimize the loss of the guests.

When accepting guest wake-up service requests, the hotel should pay attention to:

① The customer may remember the date of the day incorrectly, and there may be a time error when the operator confirms it. Therefore, the operator should add "Today is × month × day, what you need is tomorrow, which is × month × day...?" such time confirmation to remind guests.

② In the evening or early morning, when a guest requests a wake-up service, the possible time difference is something to be aware of. If the guest is notified at 10:00 in the evening to wake up at 6:00 the next day, when confirming, the operator should pay attention to whether to ask at 6 a.m or 6 p.m.

③ It is necessary to record the specific time when the guest called and requested to wake up for verification.

【知识拓展】

叫醒服务中英文对话

客：你好，我要一个叫醒服务。

员：好的，没问题，××先生 / 女士，请问你需要几点的叫醒？

客：7点钟吧。（是早上七点还是晚上七点呢？所以要多加一句问候客人，如下）

员：请问是明天早上 7 点钟吗？

客：是的。

员：好的，没问题，请问您需要第二次叫醒吗？

客：需要，7 点 10 分吧。

员：好的，×× 先生 / 女士，您的房间号是 ×××，您需要一个叫醒服务，您的叫醒时间是明天的 7 点和 7 点 10 分，对吗？

客：是的。

员：好的，没问题，请问还有什么可以帮到您？

客：没有了。

员：感谢您的来电，×× 先生 / 女士，祝您晚安，再见。

【Knowledge Expansion】

Wake-up service Chinese and English dialogue

G: Hello, I need a wake-up call.（G=Guest; O=Operator）

O: Certainly, Mr./Ms. ××, may I know what time would you like?

G: 7 o'clock.

O: Tomorrow morning?

G: Yes.

O: Certainly, Mr./Ms. ××, would you like a reminder call?

G: Yes, 7:10, please.

O: Certainly, Mr./Ms. ××, your room number is ×××, and your wake-up call time is 7 a.m and 7:10 a.m, tomorrow, is that right?

G: Perfect.

O: OK. Anything else I can do for you?

G: No, thank you.

O: Thank you for calling. Mr./Ms. ××. Good night.

任务四　问询与计费服务

【案例导入】

凌晨 3:00，酒店的各个营业场所除了美容厅外都已经停止营业，此时对于酒店的总机来说已经不是很忙了，一般较多的是要求叫醒的内线电话，"滴滴"话务台显示有电话来了，是外线。话务员 A 接起电话，报酒店名。"帮我查询 ×× 的房间号。"话筒里传来了一名女子的声音。"请问您贵姓？"话务员 A 说。"你们真麻烦，姓吴，他给我打的电话，让我把资料送到房间，快点，耽搁了事情你们负责。"这名女子不高兴地说。话务员看此情况不大好，于是便把客人房号告知了这名女子。

Task 4　Inquiry and Billing Services

【Case Introduction】

At 3:00 in the morning, all the business premises of the hotel have been closed, except for the beauty salon, and the switchboard of the hotel was not very busy at this time. Generally, the internal calls for wake-up calls, "Didi" the switchboard indicated that there was a call coming, it was an outside line. Operator A answered the phone and introduced the name of the hotel."Check the room number of × × for me", a woman's voice came from the microphone, "May I ask your last name?" Operator A said. "You are really troublesome. My last name is Wu. He called me and asked me to send the document to the room. Hurry up, you are responsible for the delay," the woman said unhappily. The operator saw that the situation was not good, so he informed the woman of the guest's room number.

【分析】

话务员从事的是一项机要工作，酒店内部的信息和客人的私人情况是不能外泄的，这既是组织纪律，也是礼节、礼貌的基本要求。为了维护酒店的声誉，话务员不得向外界披露酒店和客人的情况，确保酒店客人不受打扰或发生意外。此案例中，如果话务员打电话至客人房间征求客人意见，按照客人的意思处理，也不会出现如此情况。

【Analysis】

The operator is engaged in a confidential job, and the information inside the hotel and the private situation of the guests must not be leaked. This is not only an organizational discipline but also a basic requirement of courtesy. In order to maintain the reputation of the hotel, the operator shall not disclose the situation of the hotel and its guests to the outside and ensure that the hotel guests will not be disturbed or accidents occur. In this case, if the operator calls the guest's room to ask for instruction from the guest, and handles it according to the guest's wishes, this situation will not happen.

一、问询服务

酒店内外的客人常常会向酒店总机提出各种问询，因此，话务员要像前台问询处员工一样，掌握店内外常用的信息资料，尤其是酒店各部门及本市主要机构的电话号码，以便对客人的问询和查询做出热情、礼貌、准确而迅速的问答。但要注意，涉及客人隐私的问题通常拒绝回答或谨慎回答。

（一）接到客人问询电话

在铃响三声之内接听电话，清晰地报出所在部门，表示愿意为客人提供服务。

（二）聆听客人问询内容

仔细聆听客人问询的问题。必要时，请客人重复某些细节或含混不清之处。重述客人问询内容，以便客人确认。

（三）回答客人问询

若能立即回答客人，应及时给客人满意的答复；若需进一步查询才能答复客人，则应请客人挂断电话稍候。然后，通过查询电脑中存储的相关信息或询问酒店相关部门等途径，找到准确答案。在机台进行操作，接通与客人房间的电话，清晰地报出自己所在部门及岗位，重复客人问询要求，获得客人确认后，将答案告诉客人。待客人听清后，征询客人是否还有其他疑问之处，表示愿意提供帮助。

I Inquiry service

Guests both inside and outside the hotel often ask various inquiries to the hotel's switchboard. Therefore, the operator, like the staff at the front desk, should master the information commonly used inside and outside the hotel, especially the telephone numbers of the various departments of the hotel and the main organizations in the city, providing enthusiastic, polite, accurate and quick answers to inquiries. But be aware that questions involving guest privacy are often refused or answered with caution.

(1) Received a guest's inquiry call

Answer the phone within three rings, clearly report to the department, and express willingness to provide services to the guest.

(2) Listen to the content of guest's inquiries

Listen carefully to the questions the guest says. If necessary, repeat some details or ambiguities. Restate the content of the guest's inquiry for confirmation.

(3) Answer guest's inquiries

If the operator can answer the guest immediately, he/she should give the guest a satisfactory answer in time; if the operator needs a further inquiry to answer the guest, he/she should ask the guest to hang up and wait. Then, find accurate answers by querying the relevant information in the computer or inquiring from the relevant departments of the hotel. Operate on the machine, connect the phone with the guest's room, clearly report the department and position, repeat the guest's inquiry request, and after the guest's confirmation, tell the guest the answer. After the guest hears it clearly, ask if the guest has any other questions, and express willingness to help.

二、长话计费服务

酒店向客人提供国内、国际直拨长途电话服务，也称 DDD、IDD。通话结束后，电脑会自动计算通话费用并打印出账单。目前，多数酒店的客房电话与酒店计算机管理系统接口，直接记入客房账户。

II　Long-distance call billing service

The hotel provides guests with domestic and international direct dial long-distance telephone services, also known as DDD and IDD. After the call is over, the computer will automatically calculate the call fee and print out the bill. At present, most hotel guest room telephones are interfaced with the hotel's computer management system and are directly credited to the guest room account.

【知识拓展】

如何处理接听电话时的具体问题

①接听电话时，动作要迅速，电话铃声不应超过三声，问候对方："您好"，表明自己的身份，不可用"喂，喂，喂……"

②打电话时，组织好讲话的内容，把有关资料放在电话旁边，问候对方，转入正题。

③用电话沟通时，话筒和嘴唇距离大约 25 cm，若靠得太近，声音效果不好，保持自然音调，不可大喊大叫，电话机旁常备便条纸和笔。

④客人要求房号保密，当有外线电话找该客人时，可问清来电者姓名、单位或所在地，然后告诉客人，询问客人是否接这个电话。如果客人表示不接任何电话，应立即通知总台在电脑中输入保密标志，若有问询，即答该客人未入住酒店。若客人有更具体的要求，如可接长途电话，可接某指定人的电话等，要问清并做记录，按客人要求执行。

⑤晚上客人打电话缠住话务员，要求陪其聊天时，要委婉告诉客人，当班时间有很多工作要做，如果不能按时完成，会影响对客人的服务质量；同时告诉客人，聊天会长久占用酒店的营业电话，招致其他客人的投诉；向客人介绍酒店的各类娱乐场所。

⑥如果对方要找的人不在，可以这样回答客人："他现在不在办公室，我能帮您的忙吗？"也可以告诉客人要找的人在何处及电话号码；或给对方准确的时间，请其再打电话；也可留下对方的号码，待要找的人回来时打电话给对方；或为对方留言。

终止电话时，应使用结束语："除了这些，还有什么事我可以帮忙的吗？"等对方先挂断之后再放下听筒。轻轻放下听筒，不可"砰"的一声猛然挂断。

【Knowledge Expansion】

How to deal with specific problems when answering the phone

① When answering the phone, answer quickly, and the phone should ring no more than three times, and greet the other party with "Hello", indicate your identity, and avoid "Hey, hello, hello..."

② When making a call, organize the content of the speech, put relevant materials next to the phone, greet the other party, and turn to the topic.

③ When communicating by telephone, the distance between the microphone and your mouth is about 25 centimeters. If it is too close, the sound effect will not be good. Keep a natural tone and do not yell. Keep some notepaper and pens next to the phone.

④ The guest requires the room number to be kept secret, when there is an outside call for the guest, the operator can ask the caller's name, company, or location, and then tell the guest and ask if the guest answers the call. If the guest indicates that he/she will not answer any phone calls, the operator should immediately notify the front desk to mark the guest's status as confidential sign in the system. If there is any inquiry, it will be answered that the guest has not checked into the hotel. If the guest has more specific requirements, such as being able to answer long distances calls, being able to answer the phone of a certain designated person, etc., ask them clearly and make records, and execute them according to the requirements of the guests.

⑤ At night, when guests call the operator and ask the operator to chat with them, the operator should euphemistically tell the guests that there is a lot of work to be done during the shift. If the work cannot be completed on time, the quality of service to the guests will be affected; at the same time, tell the guests that the chat will tie up the hotel's business line for a long time and cause complaints from other guests; introduce guests to various recreational places in the hotel.

⑥ If the person the caller is looking for is not there, the operator can answer the caller like this: "He is not in the office now, can I help you?" The operator can also tell the caller the location and the phone number of the person he is looking for; or give the other party an accurate time and ask them to call again; the operator can also take down the caller's number and call the caller back when the person he is looking for returns, or leave a message for the caller.

When terminating the call, the operator should use the concluding sentence: "Is there anything else I can help with?" Wait for the other party to hang up before putting down the receiver. Put down the handset gently, and don't hang it up abruptly.

任务五　临时指挥中心服务

【案例导入】

晚饭时分，日本客人山本次郎乘车回到下榻的上海某酒店，这是他在上海旅行的最后一天。美丽的上海给他留下了深刻的印象，但几天的旅行也使他感到十分疲惫。在回酒店的路上，他就想好回房后痛痛快快地洗个澡，再美美地品尝一顿中国佳肴，为他在上海的旅行画上一个圆满的句号。

山本兴冲冲地乘上酒店的 3 号客梯回房。同往常一样，他按了标有 30 层的键，电梯迅速上升。当电梯运行到一半时，意外发生了，电梯停在 15 楼不动了。山本一愣，再按 30 层键，没反应，山本被"关"在电梯里了。无奈，他只得打电话给总机，总机话务员问清事情发生的地点后，告诉山本马上派人立即处理。但 10 多分钟过去了，电梯仍然未动，再打总机电话，无人接听。无助的山本显得十分紧张，疲劳感和饥饿感一阵阵袭来，继而都转化为怒气。又过了 10 多分钟，电梯动了，电梯门在 15 楼打开。山本走了出来，心中十分不满，自己被关了 20 多分钟，没有得到酒店方任何解释和安慰，出了电梯又无人迎接，于是愤然直奔大堂投诉。

其实，当电梯发生故障总机话务员接到紧急情况后，就采取了抢修措施，一刻也没怠慢。电梯值班人员马上赶到楼顶电梯机房排除故障，但电梯控制闸失灵，无法操作。他又赶紧将电梯控制闸由"自动状态"转换为"手动状态"，自己赶到 15 楼。拉开外门一看，发现电梯停在了 15 楼至 16 楼之间，内门无法打开。为了使客人尽快出来，电梯值班员带上工具，爬到电梯厢顶，用手动操作将故障电梯迫降到位，终于将门打开，放出客人。

从发生故障到客人出电梯的 20 多分钟，电梯维修人员已经尽力了，但为什么酒店还是遭到了投诉？

Task 5　Temporary Command Center Service

【Case Introduction】

Puring the dinner time, the Japanese guest Jiro Yamamoto drove back to a hotel in Shanghai where he was staying. This was the last day of his trip in Shanghai. The beautiful Shanghai left a deep impression on him. However, a few days of travel made him feel very tired. On the way back to the hotel, he wanted to take a nice shower after returning to the room, and then have a delicious Chinese meal, which would make his travel to Shanghai a wonderful ending.

Yamamoto happily boarded the hotel's No. 3 passenger elevator back to the room. As usual, he pressed the button labeled 30th floor, and the elevator rose quickly. When the elevator was halfway up, an accident happened and the elevator stopped on the 15th floor. Yamamoto was startled and then pressed the 30th-floor button again. There was no response.

Yamamoto was "trapped" in the elevator. Helpless, he had to call the switchboard, and after the switchboard operator asked where the incident happened, he told Yamamoto to send someone to deal with it immediately. But more than ten minutes passed and the elevator still didn't move. He called the switchboard again, but no one answered. The helpless Yamamoto looked very nervous, feeling tired and hungry, and his fatigue and hunger soon turned into anger. About 10 minutes later, the elevator moved and the door opened on the 15th floor. Yamamoto walked out and felt very dissatisfied. He was trapped for more than 20 minutes without any explanation or comfort from the hotel. No one picked him up after he got out of the elevator, so he went straight to the lobby to complain.

In fact, when the elevator malfunctioned, the operator of the switchboard took emergency repair measures after receiving an emergency and did not neglect for a moment. The elevator personnel on duty immediately rushed to the elevator machine room on the roof to eliminate the fault, but the elevator control panel failed and could not be operated. He quickly changed the elevator control gate "automatic state" to "manual state" and rushed to the 15th floor by himself. When he opened the outer door and found that the elevator had stopped between the 15th and 16th floors, and the inner door could not be opened. In order to get the guests out as soon as possible, the elevator attendant brought tools, climbed to the top of the elevator car, and forced the faulty elevator down into place by manual operation, and finally opened the door to release the guests.

It took more than 20 minutes for the guest to get out of the elevator when the failure occured, the maintenance staff had tried their best, but why did the hotel still receive a complaint？

【评析】

这起电梯"关人"紧急情况事件引起客人投诉，问题在于酒店内各部门之间的协调配合度不够，未及时对客人进行安抚，稳定客人情绪。

①总机话务员应安抚客人，稳定情绪，不得擅自离岗，并保障线路通信的畅通。这样，在此案例中，客人第二次来电，电话未接听的情况就不会发生，客人也不会情绪失控。

②前台、后台配合不够默契。发生紧急情况时，总机应成为酒店管理人员采取相应措施的指挥协调中心。在上述案例中，前台通知工程部维修电梯后，并没有赶到现场与客人取得联系，也没有与工程部随时沟通。工程部修理人员虽然工作态度很积极，跑上跑下排除故障，但没有想到通过机房的对讲机与客人通话，或安慰或通报维修进展。如果后台负责修理电梯的工程部能与前台沟通，一面修电梯，一面与客人联系，随时通报修理情况，对客人适当进行安慰，共同处理好此次紧急事件，许多不愉快就不至于发生。

【Comment and Analysis】

This emergency incident of elevator "trapping" caused guest complaints. The problem is that the coordination between the various departments in the hotel is not enough, without pacifying the guest and stabilize his emotion.

① The switchboard operator should calm the guest, stabilize his emotion, not leave his posts without authorization, and ensure the smooth communication of the line. In this way, in this case, if the guest calls again, the missed call will not happen, and the guest will not lose control of his emotion.

② The cooperation between the frontstage and the backstage is not tacit. In the event of an emergency, the switchboard should become the command and coordination center for hotel managers to take corresponding measures. In the above case, after the front desk notified the engineering department to repair the elevator, he did not rush to the scene to get in touch with the guests, nor did he communicate with the engineering department at any time. Although the repair staff in the engineering department had a positive working attitude and ran up and down to troubleshoot, he did not talk to the guests through the intercom in the computer room, or comfort or report the progress of the maintenance. If the engineering department responsible for repairing the elevator backstage can communicate with the front desk, while repairing the elevator, contact the guests at any time, report the repair situation at any time, comfort the guest appropriately, and jointly handle the emergency, many unpleasant things will not happen.

一、临时指挥中心服务

总机除了提供上述服务，还有一项重要职责就是当酒店出现紧急情况时，应成为酒店管理人员采取相应措施的指挥协调中心。

酒店的紧急情况是指诸如发生火灾、水灾、伤亡事故、恶性刑事案件等情况。紧急情况发生时，酒店领导为迅速控制局面，必然要借助电话系统，话务员要沉着、冷静、不慌张，提供高效率的服务。

①接到紧急情况报告电话后，立即问清事情发生的地点、时间及简单情况，问清报告者姓名、身份，并迅速做好记录。

②即刻通报酒店领导和有关部门，并根据现场指挥人员的指令，迅速与市内有关部门（如消防、安全等）紧急联系，并向其他话务员通报情况。

③严格执行现场指挥人员的指令。

④在未接到撤离指示前，不得擅自离岗，需保障线路通信的畅通。

⑤继续从事对客服务工作，并安抚客人、稳定客人情绪。如有人打听情况（如火情），

一般不做回答，转大堂副理答复。

⑥完整记录紧急情况的电话处理细节，以备事后检查。

I Temporary command center service

In addition to the above-mentioned services, the switchboard also has an important duty to be the command and coordination center for hotel managers to take corresponding measures when an emergency occurs in the hotel.

Hotel emergencies refer to situations such as fires, floods, casualties, vicious criminal cases, etc. When an emergency occurs, in order to quickly control the situation, hotel managers must resort to the telephone system. Operators must be calm, not panicked, and provide efficient services.

① Upon receiving an emergency report call, immediately ask about the location, time, and simple circumstances of the incident, ask for the reporter's name and identity, and quickly make a record.

② Immediately notify the hotel leaders and relevant departments, and according to the instructions of the on-site commander, the relevant departments in the city（such as fire protection, safety, etc.）can be contacted urgently, and other operators can be notified of the situation.

③ Strictly implement the instructions of on-site commanders.

④ Before receiving the evacuation instruction, do not leave the post without authorization, and ensure the smooth communication of the line.

⑤ Continue to engage in customer service work, soothe customers and stabilize their emotions. If someone inquires about the situation（such as the fire）, generally do not answer and transfer to the assistant manager to answer.

⑥ Completely record the emergency telephone handling details for subsequent inspections.

二、紧急报警的处理

（一）客人及员工紧急报火警的处理

①接到紧急报警。

a. 首先告诉报警人要保持冷静。

b. 向报警人询问以下内容：报警人姓名、报警人所在部门、出事地点、何物燃烧、火势大小。

c. 迅速将有关内容准确记录在案。

d. 告诉报警人："我们会立即通知有关部门及人员，请您马上寻找紧急出口撤离。"

②通知消防控制中心。

a. 立即通知消防控制中心以下内容：报警人姓名、报警人所在部门、着火地点、燃烧物、火势大小、话务员姓名。

b. 记录受话人姓名。

③记录报警内容。

准确地将接到的报警内容记录在报警本上。

④等待消防中心报警。

消防控制中心会立即派人实地查询，若情况属实，会立即从出事地点向总机报警。

⑤接待消防中心紧急报警。

按"消防中心紧急报警处理"方法处理。

⑥通知有关部门。

按"消防中心紧急报警处理"方法处理。

⑦记录紧急报警内容。

按"消防中心紧急报警处理"方法处理。

Ⅱ　Emergency call handling

（1）Handling of an emergency fire report by guests and employees

① Receive an emergency call.

a. First tell the caller to keep calm.

b. Ask the caller for the following: the name of the caller, the department where the caller is located, the location of the incident, what is burning, and the size of the fire.

c. Quickly record relevant content accurately.

d. Tell the caller: "We will notify the relevant departments and personnel immediately. Please find the emergency exit and evacuate."

② Notify the fire control center.

a. Immediately notify the fire control center of the following: the name of the caller, the department where the caller is located, the location of the fire, the burning material, the size of the fire, and the name of the operator.

b. Record the name of the caller.

③ Record the report.

Accurately record the received call content in the report book.

④ Wait for the fire center to call the police.

The fire control center will immediately send someone to make an on-site inquiry. If the situation is true, it will immediately report the incident to the switchboard.

⑤ Receive the fire center emergency report.

Deal with according to the "fire center emergency service processing" method.

⑥ Notify relevant departments.

Deal with according to the "fire center emergency service processing" method.

⑦ Record emergency report.

Deal with according to the "fire center emergency service processing" method.

（二）消防中心紧急报警的处理

①接到紧急报警。

a. 认真、仔细听清报警地点、报警人姓名。

b. 重复报警地点及报警人姓名。

c. 把报警内容迅速、准确地记录下来。

②通知有关部门。

a. 白天需通知客务经理、保卫部值班室、总经理办公室及消防值班领班。

b. 夜间需通知值班店领导、客务经理、保卫部值班室及当日部门值班经理。

③填写报警记录。

a. 报警时间、报警地点及报警人姓名。

b. 记录所通知到的部门及相关领导、人员的姓名。

c. 话务员姓名。

d. 等待并记录消防中心通知的报警原因。

（2）Handling of the emergency report in the fire center

① Receive an emergency report.

a. Listen carefully to the caller's location and the name of the caller.

b. Repeat the caller's location and name.

c. Record the report content quickly and accurately.

② Notify relevant departments.

a. During the day, the guest manager, security department duty room, general manager's office, and the on-duty foreman from the fire department must be notified.

b. At night, the on-duty leader of the hotel, the customer service manager, the duty room of the security department, and the duty manager of the department must be notified.

③ Fill in the report record.

a. The time and place of the incident and the name of the caller.

b. Record the names of the notified departments and relevant leaders and personnel.

c. The name of the operator.

d. Wait for and record the report reason notified by the fire center.

【知识拓展】

总机房的环境

①位置便利。

有些小型酒店将电话交换机安装在前台，由前台接待员或问询员兼任话务员。中、大型酒店需要更多的外线、内线和专线，电话业务量大，必须由专职话务员提供服务，应有专门的总机房。由于话务与前台业务密切相关，因此，应考虑将总机房设置在前台附近，以便沟通联络。

②安全保密。

总机房设备复杂，必须有良好的隔音、防潮、防尘设施以保证话务质量。此外，在安全管理上，它属于酒店保安重地，无关人员未经许可不得进入总机房。

③洁净舒适。

总机房应配备空调和通风设备，以保持室内的温度和空气清新度。话务员使用的工作台和椅子舒适配套，可以降低或减少话务员工作疲劳感。在室内进行适当的装修及布置，可以保持室内光线的明亮和柔和度，使话务员在值班期间能够保持良好的精神状态，集中精力为客人提供服务。

【Knowledge Expansion】

The environment of the switchboard room

① Convenient location.

Some small hotels install the telephone exchange at the front desk, and the receptionist or inquirer also serves as the operator. Medium and large hotels need more external lines, internal lines, and dedicated lines. The volume of the telephone business is large, and full-time operators must provide services, and there should be a dedicated switchboard room. Since the call traffic is closely related to the front desk business, it should be considered to set up the switchboard near the front desk to facilitate communication.

② Safe and confidential.

The switchboard room is complex and must have good sound insulation, moisture-proof, and dust-proof facilities to ensure the quality of calls. In addition, in terms of safety management, it is an important place for hotel security, and irrelevant personnel are not allowed to enter the switchboard room without permission.

③ Clean and comfortable.

The switchboard room should be equipped with air-conditioning and ventilation equipment to maintain indoor temperature and air freshness. The work desk and chair used by the operator are comfortable, which can reduce the operator's work fatigue. Proper decoration and layout in the room can maintain the brightness and softness of the indoor light so that the operator can maintain a good mental state during the duty period and concentrate on providing services to the guests.

【本节实训练习题】

学生分组以角色扮演的方式模拟总机电话转接服务。

要求

①服务迅速，语音柔美，语言符合礼貌、礼节规范。

②电话转接准确，无人接听时，应对正确。

③严格遵守话务员职业道德。

【Practical Training Exercises in This Section】

Students are grouped in a role-playing way to simulate the switchboard telephone transfer service.

Requirements

① The service is fast; the voice is soft and the language conforms to the rules of courtesy and etiquette.

② The call transfer is accurate, and the response is correct when no one answers.

③ Strictly abide by the professional ethics of operators.

【复习自测题】

①为客人转接电话时应注意哪些问题？

②试述总机服务的基本要求。

③人工叫醒服务和自动叫醒服务的优缺点各是什么？

④当酒店发生紧急情况时，总机应如何发挥其临时指挥中心作用？

【Review of Self-test Questions】

① What issues should be paid attention to when transferring calls for guests?

② Describe the basic requirements of the switchboard service.

③ What are the advantages and disadvantages of manual wake-up service and automatic wake-up service?

④ When an emergency occurs in a hotel, how should the switchboard play its role as a temporary command center?

【案例分析】

一天深夜，"叮铃铃"的电话声惊醒了某酒店总机服务员小王，她立刻接起电话用英语说，"接线员"，话筒中一位中年女士用英文说："叫醒服务？""好的，我能帮您做些什么?"小王积极热情地问询。"您能在 6 点钟叫醒我吗?这是 408 房间。""当然,女士,408 房,6 点!""我熬夜会很晚才睡,请多叫我几次。""好的,晚安。"

切断电话,小王抬手看了一下手表,已是凌晨 2:00,客人既然要求多叫几遍,必定有急事需赶时间。酒店的话务台叫早时间只能每隔 5 分钟设定一次,且叫早的铃声响过,电话被提起后是无声的,没有电话语音,一般情况下,设两遍叫早。这位客人要求多设几遍,而话务系统只能连续设定 3 遍叫早,可最要命的是,要在客人规定的时间后 15 分钟才会响起,这对于时间观念很强的商务客人最致命。想到此,小王在电话记录本上记下:Room 408,6:00 叫早,电话系统设两遍,请于 6:06 人工进行一次叫早。

清晨,小王看看时间已是 6:00,过了 6:05,她查看 408 房的状态,两遍铃都已响过。此时小王想,客人起来了没有呢?如果起来了,再打电话,算不算打扰客人?如果没有起来,不打电话,万一客人误事了怎么办?

可是,客人的确并没有让人工叫早,也没有强调必须 6:00 叫醒她,但⋯⋯

小王的直觉认为应该打电话,如果客人起床了,就问声早,如果客人没起床,就算人工叫早。6:06 分,小王拨通了 408 房的电话,铃声响到第 6 次,客人才接:"Hello"声音有点发涩,估计客人没有完全清醒,小王连忙微笑着说:"早上好,女士,我是接线员,您现在起床吗?现在 6:06。""我马上就起,谢谢。""不客气,再见。"小王确认客人已经起床了,一颗悬着的心终于落了地。

请根据所学到的知识结合案例实际回答:小王的做法正确吗?我们能从中学到什么?

【Case Analysis】

Late one night, the sound of the phone ring awakened Xiao Wang, a hotel operator, and she immediately picked up the phone and said in English, "Operator", and a middle-aged lady in the microphone said in English: "Wake up service?" "Okay, what can I do for you?" Xiao Wang asked actively and enthusiastically. "Can you wake me up at 6 o'clock? This is room 408." "Of course, madam, room 408, 6 o'clock!" "I stay up late and go to bed late. Please call me a few more times." "Okay, good night."

After hanging up the phone, Xiao Wang looked at her watch. It was already 2 o'clock in the morning. Since the customer asked to call several times, there must be an urgent matter. The hotel's console wake-up time can only be set every 5 minutes, and the early call ring rang, the phone is silent after being picked up, and there is no voice. Normally, the call is set twice morning. The guest asked to set up several times, and the call system can only set three times in a row to call early, but the bad thing is that it will not ring until 15 minutes after the time set by the guest. This is lethal for business guests who have a strong sense of time. With this in mind, Xiao Wang wrote down in the phone log: Room 408, call morning at 6:00, and the telephone system is set twice. Please call morning at 6:06 manually.

In the early morning, Xiao Wang checked that the time was 6:00. After 6:05, she checked the status of Room 408, and the bell had rung twice. At this time, Xiao Wang thought, "Did the guest wake up?" If she wakes up, call again, will it be considered an interruption to the guest? If she doesn't get up and I don't call, what if the guest delay in work?

However, the guest did not request for manual wake-up service, and did not emphasize that she must be woken up at 6:00...

Xiao Wang's instinct told her that she should call. If the guest wakes up, she could greet her, and if the guest does not wake up, it is a manual wake-up. At 6:06, Xiao Wang dialed the phone in Room 408, and the ringer rang for the sixth time before the guest answered: "Hello" is a bit rough. It seemed that the guest is not fully awake. Xiao Wang quickly smiled and said, "Good morning, Madam, I'm the operator. Do you get up now? It's 6:06 now." "I'll get up soon, thank you." "You're welcome, goodbye." Xiao Wang confirmed that the guest had gotten up, and she was finally relieved.

Please answer the questions based on the knowledge you have learned: Is Xiao Wang's approach correct? What can we learn from it?

工作领域三　前厅管理工作

Work Area III　Front Office Management Work

项目一
服务质量管理

【学习目标】

了解前厅服务质量的具体内容和特点；正确理解优质服务的内涵，培养优质服务的意识；理解处理好宾客关系的意义，掌握处理宾客关系的原则与方法。

Project 1
Service Quality Management

【Learning Objective】

Understand the specific content and characteristics of the front office service quality; correctly understand the connotation of high-quality service and cultivate the awareness of high-quality service; understand the meaning of handling guest relations, and master the principles and methods of handling guest relations.

任务一　优质服务

【案例导入】

不要让疲倦的客人就这么走了

一天深夜，两位面容倦怠的客人来到前厅接待处，要求一间普通标准间。接待员表示标准间刚刚卖完，只有一间刚刚退房，楼层服务员准备清扫，请两位客人稍等片刻。

客人不禁皱起了眉头："不行，刚才机场代表告诉我们是有房间的。"

接待员："是有的，但请稍等一会儿，我们马上清理出来，请您在大堂吧略坐片刻，我们会通知您的。"

客人看了看接待员，一句话不说走向大堂吧。接待员赶紧催促客房中心立即清扫普通标准间。15 分钟后，其中一位客人来到接待处。

顾客："小姐，到底有没有房间，我们坐了 3 个多小时的飞机，真的很累，想休息……"

接待员连忙安慰客人，又立刻打电话到客房中心询问普通标准间是否准备好，客房服务员却说："刚清扫好了一间豪华标准间，其他房间还没有。"

接待员："你们在干什么呢，做房间那么慢，你们知道客人等得多焦急！"

服务员："房间总得一间间做吧，哪有那么快。"说完就挂断了电话。

接待员无奈地放下话筒。又过了 15 分钟，两位客人再次走向接待处，开口便高声责问接待员："你们到底有没有房间？让我们等这么久，又不提供房间，我们不在你们这儿住了。"说完，便向门外走去。这时，大堂副理过来想留住客人，可没等他说话，客人便愤然离去。

Task 1　Quality Service

【Case Introduction】

Don't let tired guests just leave

One night, two tired-looking guests came to the front desk in the lobby and asked for a standard room. The receptionist said that the standard rooms have just been sold out, and only one has just checked out. The floor attendant is ready to clean it. Please wait for a while.

The guest couldn't help frowning: "No, the airport representative just told us that there is a room."

Receptionist: "Yes, but please wait a while and we will clean it right away. Please sit in the lobby bar for a while and we will notify you."

The guest looked at the receptionist and walked towards the lobby bar without a word. The receptionist hurriedly urged the guest room center to clean the standard rooms immediately. 15 minutes later, one of the guests came to the reception.

Guest: "Miss, do you have a room? We have been on the plane for more than 3 hours. We are really tired and want to rest..."

The receptionist hurriedly comforted the guests, and immediately called the guest room center to ask if the standard room was ready, but the room attendant said: "I just finished cleaning a deluxe room, but the other room hasn't started yet."

Receptionist: "What are you doing? Cleaning the room so slowly, you know how anxious the guests wait."

Room attendant: "The rooms have to be done one by one, how can I do it quickly." After speaking, the phone hung up.

The receptionist reluctantly put down the receiver. After another 15 minutes, the two guests walked to the reception again, and they loudly asked the receptionist: "Do you have any room? Keeping us waiting for so long and not offering a room. We won't stay here anymore." Then they walked out the door. At this time, the assistant manager came over and wanted to keep the residents, but before he could speak, the guests left angrily.

【案例问题】

①案例中，前厅的服务与管理有漏洞吗？

②前厅服务员、客房服务员、大堂副理各自的问题是什么？

③从全面质量管理的角度出发，此事该补救吗？若能，如何补救？

【Case Questions】

① In this case, are there loopholes in the service and management of the front office?

② What are the respective problems of the front office staff, room attendant, and assistant manager?

③ From the perspective of comprehensive quality management, should this be remedied? If so, how?

【案例分析】

分析 1：美国心理学家马斯洛把人的需要分为 5 个基本层次：生理需要、安全需要、社交需要、尊重需要、自我实现需要。客人来到酒店吃住是最基本的生理需求，而当这一需求一而再、再而三地得不到满足时，不满的情绪就会油然而生，同时会给酒店带来很多负面的影响。案例中客人这一次不愉快的经历，将影响他们再次进入该酒店。案例中出现的问题，说明该酒店在管理与服务上有漏洞。

【Case Analysis】

Analysis 1: American psychologist Maslow divides human needs into 5 basic levels: physiological needs, safety needs, social needs, respect needs, and self-realization needs. The most basic physiological need is for guests to come to the hotel to eat and stay, and when this need is not met, again and again, dissatisfaction will arise inevitably. At the same time, it will bring many negative effects to the hotel. In this case, the guests' unpleasant experience will affect them to enter the hotel again. The problems in the case indicate that the hotel has loopholes in its management and services.

分析2：首先，前厅服务员在不了解酒店现实房态的情况下向客人许诺。俗话说：言必行，行必果。无论从事管理或是服务，都必须做到这一点。机场代表在接待前，就应了解房态，答应客人后，更应该及时联系酒店做出安排，使客人抵达后能够顺利入住。其次，客房服务员处事不够灵活。从客人的话语中，客房服务员就应该听得出客人的急切心理，在服务过程中，我们应急客人所急，想客人所想。当酒店一时满足不了客人的时候，要及时采取变通措施。楼层服务员的不配合是最根本的原因。从服务员回答的口气里我们可以看出其服务的意识与合作的态度是欠佳的。最后，大堂副理也有责任。大堂副理的职责是营业部门经理下班或不在场的情况下，监管各营业部门的运作，处理非正常运作导致的客人投诉，处理酒店发生的意外事件或紧急事件，最终使客人满意。案例中的客人已等候多时以至发脾气要离开了，大堂副理才姗姗出现，其行为是失职的。

Analysis 2: First of all, the front desk staff promises to the guests without knowing the actual state of the hotel room. As the saying goes: be faithful in your word and resolute in your actions. Whether engaged in management or service, this must be done. Before the reception, the airport representative should understand the room status, and after agreeing to the guest, he should contact the hotel in time to make arrangements so that the guest can check in smoothly after arrival. Then, the room attendant is not flexible enough. From the guest's words, the room attendant should hear the guest's eagerness. During the service, we respond to what the guest is anxious about and think about what the guest thinks. When the hotel cannot satisfy the guests for a while, it is necessary to take corrective measures in time. The non-cooperation of the room attendant is the most fundamental reason. From the tone of the staff's answer, we can see that his service consciousness and cooperative attitude are not good. Finally, the assistant manager is also responsible for this. The responsibility of the assistant manager is to supervise the operation of each department when the operation department manager is off duty or not present, handle guest complaints caused by abnormal operations, deal with accidents or emergencies that occur in the hotel, and ultimately achieve customer satisfaction. The guests in the case had waited for a long time until they lost their temper and were about to leave. The assistant manager only appeared then, and his behavior was a dereliction of duty.

分析3：从全面质量管理的角度出发，应对此事进行补救。希望受人重视是人的天性。有的顾客希望通过抱怨而引起服务员（前台）对他的注意和重视，或者由此引出酒店相关负责人或经理与其见面，使他感觉到自己很重要。酒店应尽量防止过失发生，防抱怨于未然。一旦出现抱怨，应及时、适当处理，消除顾客怨气，是最后的补救方法。

抱怨是一种痛苦的表达方式，人们不愿意抱怨，也避免去抱怨。只有 1/5 的客人愿意把抱怨说出来。抱怨是顾客发出的一种信号：我愿意再来，但请你改进，下次不要再发生问题，给我一个再次回来的理由。抱怨直接反映了酒店存在的问题，提供了改进及提高的建议。4/5 心存怨气的顾客会不做抱怨，不把问题提出来，这类客人的回头率很低，甚至再也不会来了。

"质量是企业的生命"这一观念已经成为当代企业的基本共识，对于酒店管理也同样如此。在市场竞争条件下，酒店经营成败的关键在于服务质量。前厅服务是酒店服务的重要组成部分，其质量高低直接影响酒店服务质量和酒店产品的销售。

被世界酒店业誉为"酒店之父"的斯塔特勒先生说过："酒店出售的商品只有一个，那就是服务。"有了良好的服务才能吸引并留住顾客，而顾客是酒店生存和发展的基础和条件。酒店的目标是向客人提供最佳的优质服务。随着酒店业的飞速发展和人民生活水平的日益提高，宾客对酒店服务的要求也越来越高，除了满足客人的物质需要，还必须满足客人的心理需求，才能实现这一经营宗旨。

Analysis 3: From the perspective of comprehensive quality management, this matter should be remedied. It is human nature to want to be valued by others. Some customers have caused the staff (front desk) to pay attention to them by complaining, or this leads to the relevant person in charge or manager of the hotel meeting with him, making him feel that he is important. The hotel should try to prevent negligence and prevent complaints before they happen. Once complaints arise, they should be dealt with promptly and appropriately to eliminate customer grievances, which is the best remedy. Complaining is a painful form of expression. People are unwilling to complain and avoid complaining. Only one-fifth of the guests complained. Complaining is a signal sent by the customer: I'd love to come again, but please improve, don't have problems next time, and give me a reason to come back again. Complaints directly reflect the problems of the hotel and provide suggestions for correction and improvement. Four-fifths of resentful customers will not complain or bring up the problem. The return rate of such customers is very low, and even they will never come again.

The concept of "quality is the life of an enterprise" has become the basic consensus of contemporary enterprises, and the same is true for hotel management. Under the conditions of market competition, the key to the success or failure of a hotel business is the quality of service. Front office service is an important part of hotel services, and its quality directly affects the quality of hotel services and the sales of hotel products.

Mr. Statler, who is known as the "father of hotels" in the global hotel industry, once said: "There is only one product a hotel sells, and that is service." A good service can attract and retain customers, and customers are essential for the survival of the hotel. And customers are the basis and conditions for development. The goal of the hotel is to provide guests with the best quality service. With the rapid development of the hotel industry and the ever-increasing improvement of people's living standards, guests have higher and higher requirements for hotel services. In addition to meeting the material needs of the guests, the psychological needs of the guests must also be met to achieve this business purpose.

【知识拓展】

"服务"的含义

西方人曾经将"服务"的英文写法"SERVICE"拆解开来，每个字母都有其相应的含义：字母"S"理解为"Smile"，即"微笑"，是指酒店员工在服务过程中应该带有真诚的微笑，也就是酒店所提倡的微笑服务；字母"E"是指"Excellent"，即"出色"，是指酒店员工不仅仅是一般地为顾客提供服务，而是要超出顾客的预想，在服务态度、服务标准、服务程序上要展现得非常出色，也就是个性化服务；字母"R"是指"Ready"，即"有所准备"，是指在为顾客提供服务前就准备好物质、心理、技能等条件，以便随时能满足顾客的需求，娴熟地为顾客提供周到的服务；字母"V"是指"Viewing"，即"看待"，是指酒店员工应当将每一位顾客视为贵宾，重视顾客所提出来的每一个要求，竭诚予以满足；字母"I"是指"Inviting"，即"邀请"，是指酒店员工在每一位顾客接受了一次完整的服务后，都应当礼貌地向顾客发出"欢迎再次光临"的邀请，或者向客人主动推荐酒店的服务项目，邀请顾客在酒店享受更多的服务项目；字母"C"是指"Creating"，即"创造"，是指酒店员工在为顾客提供服务的过程中，除遵守既定的服务程序外，还应当发挥自己的主观能动性，针对顾客的特点和顾客的需求，创造性地满足顾客，为顾客营造一个舒适愉快的氛围；字母"E"是指"Eye"，即"眼光"，是指酒店员工在服务过程中，应当注意自己眼睛的神态和指向，不应当漫无目的、左顾右盼，而应当随时注视顾客，让顾客感觉到酒店员工对自己的关注和重视。

【Knowledge Expansion】

The meaning of "SERVICE"

Westerners once disassembled the English wording "SERVICE", each letter has its corresponding meaning: the letter "S" is understood as "Smile", It means that the hotel staff should have a sincere smile in the service process, which is the smiling service advocated by the hotel; the letter "E" means "Excellent", which means that the hotel staff not only provide services to customers in general, but also exceed customer expectations, show excellent service attitudes, service standards, and service procedures, that is, personalized service; the letter "R" means "Ready", that is, "prepared", which means to prepare material, psychological, technical and other conditions before providing services to customers, to meet customer needs at any time, and to provide thoughtful service to customers. The letter "V" refers to "Viewing", which means that the hotel staff should treat every customer as a VIP, attach importance to every request put forward by the customer, and wholeheartedly meet it; the letter "I" refers to "Inviting", that is, "invitation", which means that after each customer has received a complete service, the hotel staff should politely issue a "welcome again" invitation to the customer, or the guest Actively recommend hotel service items and invite customers to enjoy more service items in the hotel; The letter "C" refers to "Creating", that is, "creating", which means that in the process of providing services to customers, hotel staff should not only comply with the established service procedures but also exert their own subjective initiative, according to customer characteristics and customer needs, creatively satisfy customers and create a comfortable and pleasant atmosphere for customers; the letter "E" refers to "Eye", which means that the hotel staff should pay attention to the eye expression and direction of their eyes during the service process, and shouldn't be aimless and look around. Instead, they should keep an eye on the customers, making them feel valued and attended to.

一、优质服务的概念

优质服务是指最大限度地满足客人的正当需求，为客人提供舒适、洁净的环境，并提供宾至如归的一流服务，主动提供个性化服务。酒店要在顾客市场中占有大量的份额，在市场竞争中立于不败之地，就必须强调优质服务，而对于优质服务的含义，不同的人有不同的理解。但是有一点是共同的，即优质服务含有一般性的服务内容，也有超出常规的服务，用一个公式来表示，那就是"优质服务 = 规范化服务 + 个性化服务"。

I The concept of quality service

High-quality service refers to meeting the legitimate needs of guests to the greatest extent, providing guests with a comfortable and clean environment, and offering first-class services that make them feel at home, and proactively delivering personalized services. In order for a hotel to occupy a large market share of the market and remain invincible in market competition, it must emphasize quality service. Different people have different understanding of quality service. But there is one thing in common, that is, high-quality services contain general service content, and there are also services beyond the conventional ones. This can be expressed by a formula: "High-quality service = standardized service + personalized service".

二、优质服务的内容

（一）良好的礼仪、礼貌

注重礼仪、礼貌是酒店前厅服务工作中最重要的职业基本功之一，它体现了酒店对客人的基本态度，也反映了从业人员的文化修养和素质。外表上，衣冠整齐，注意仪容仪表等；语言上，讲究语言艺术，谈吐文雅，应对自然得体；行动上，举止文明等；态度上，不卑不亢，真诚自然，微笑服务客人。

II　The content of high-quality services

（1）Good manners and courtesy

Paying attention to etiquette and courtesy is one of the most important professional basic skills in the front office service work of the hotel. It reflects the basic attitude of the hotel to the guests, and also reflects the cultural refinement and quality of the employees. In appearance, dress neatly and pay attention to your grooming etc.; in language, pay attention to language art, speak elegantly, and deal with nature appropriately; in action, behave politely, etc.; in attitude, neither humble nor overbearing, sincere and natural, and greet guests with smile.

（二）良好的服务态度

良好的服务态度会使客人产生亲切感。服务时要做到认真负责、积极主动、热情耐心、细致周到、文明礼貌。在服务中杜绝敷衍、搪塞、厌烦、傲慢等态度。

（2）Excellent service attitude

A good service attitude will make guests feel intimate. Service should be serious, responsible, proactive, enthusiastic, patient, meticulous, and courteous. Avoid perfunctory, behavior prevarication, indifference, arrogance, and other attitudes in service.

（三）丰富的服务知识

前厅服务涉及很多方面的知识，主要有语言知识、社交知识、旅游知识、法律知识、心理学知识、服务技术知识、民俗学知识、管理经营知识、生活常识等。只有具备了较为丰富的服务知识，才能很好地回答客人的各种问题，从而提供优质的服务。

（3）Rich service knowledge

Front office service knowledge involves many aspects, such as: language knowledge, social knowledge, tourism knowledge, legal knowledge, psychological knowledge, service technology knowledge, folklore knowledge, management knowledge, the common sense of life, etc. Only with relatively rich service knowledge can the staff answer guests' various questions well and provide high-quality service.

（四）娴熟的服务技能

娴熟的服务技能是决定服务质量水平的基础，包括服务技术和服务技巧两方面。

服务技术是指各种服务操作，例如前台员工的登记入住、行李员的行李服务、话务员的转接电话服务等。服务技巧在前厅服务中尤为重要。服务最大的特点就是面对人，而人是复杂的，规程只能提供指南，却不是判断某种服务方式是错或是对的绝对标准。因此服务技能十分重要，灵活处理非常重要，不管采用哪种合理的方式、方法，只要达到使客人满意的效果，就是成功的。

（4）Good service skills

Good service skills are the basis for determining the level of service quality, including service technology and service skills. Service technology refers to various service operations, such as check-in of front desk staff, baggage service of the bellman, and call transferring service of the operator. Service skills are particularly important in front office services. The most important feature of service is dealing with people, and people are complicated, and procedures can only provide guidelines, but they cannot provide absolute standards for judging whether a certain service method is wrong or right. Therefore, service skills are very important, and flexible handling is very important. No matter what reasonable way or method is adopted, as long as it satisfies the customer, it is successful.

（五）快捷的服务效率

服务效率是指为客人提供服务的时限。酒店中最容易引起客人投诉的有两个问题：一是服务态度，二是服务效率。解决好这两点，其他方面即使不尽完善，也会赢得客人的好感。讲究效率不等于瞎忙，要力求服务快而不乱，反应敏捷、迅速而准确无误。它不仅体现出前厅服务人员的业务素质，也体现了前厅的管理效率。

（5）Fast service efficiency

Service efficiency refers to the speed for providing services to guests. Two issues are most likely to cause guest complaints in hotels: service attitude and service efficiency. By addressing these two points, even if other aspects are not perfect, the hotel will win the favor of the guests. Paying attention to efficiency does not mean being busy, and we must strive to serve quickly and systematically, responding swiftly, quickly, and accurately. It not only reflects the professional quality of the front office service staff but also reflects the management efficiency of the front office.

（六）齐全的服务项目

服务项目的设置，一定要尽可能以适应、满足客人的需要为宗旨。只要客人有需要，前厅的服务项目就要不厌其多，只恐不足。当然，服务项目的设置要讲究实效，不要无需而设，以博其名。凡设置的项目，就要确保提供，名副其实。服务项目的设置，既要考虑细致周到，又要考虑客人便利。除前厅基本服务项目外，还要尽可能设立满足客人各种特殊需要的服务项目。

（6）Complete service items

The setting of service items must be aimed at adapting and satisfying the needs of customers as much as possible. As long as the guests have needs, the service items in the front office must be endless, and never insufficient. Of course, the setting of service items should pay attention to actual effect, and avoid offering unnecessary services. All items that are set up must be provided and worthy of the name. For the setting of service items, not only consider the meticulous and thoughtful, but also consider the convenience of guests. In addition to the basic service items in the front office, it is also necessary to set up service items that meet the special needs of guests as much as possible.

（七）灵活的服务方式

服务方式是指酒店热情、周到地为客人服务所采取的形式和方法，其核心内容是如何给客人提供各种方便。前厅服务方式主要包括适当的营业时间、简便的业务手续、舒适的休息场所、得力的应急措施、分外的主动服务、方便的规章制度、灵活的收费标准等。

（7）Flexible service method

Service method refers to the form and method adopted by the hotel to serve guests warmly and thoughtfully. The core concept is how to provide guests with various conveniences. Front office service methods mainly include appropriate business hours, simple operation procedures, comfortable resting places, effective emergency measures, extra attentive services, convenient rules and regulations, flexible charging standards, etc.

（八）科学的服务程序

服务程序是指接待服务的先后顺序和步骤，它看起来无关紧要，实际上也是构成前厅服务质量的重要内容之一。在服务过程中，既有大项顺序，也有小项顺序，顺序里面一项接一项，一环套一环。这就要求服务员在工作中严格按规程操作，既不能颠倒，也不能错漏。实践证明，娴熟的服务技能，加上科学的操作程序能使客人在满足需求的同时得到美的享受。前厅的服务程序和操作程序是根据客人的要求和习惯，科学地归纳、编排出来的规范化作业顺序，只要按照顺序工作就能保证服务质量；而杂乱无章，随心所欲，不按规程办事，除了给工作造成被动，还说明该前厅的服务人员、管理人员缺乏专业训练，从而影响了服务质量。

（8）Scientific service procedures

Service procedures refer to the order and steps of reception services. Although it may seem irrelevant, it is one of the important contents of the service quality of the front office. In the service process, there is both a major and minor item sequence, one after another in the sequence. This requires the staff to strictly follow the rules during work, that is, it cannot be reversed or missed. The practice has proved that skilled service skills and scientific operating procedures can enable guests to meet their needs while still enjoying the beauty of the service. The service procedures and operating procedures of the front office are based on the requirements and habits of the guests, according to the scientific summary, the standardized operation sequence that is compiled and discharged, and the quality of service can be guaranteed by working following the order. The disorganized and arbitrary work style, not following the rules, invites trouble. In addition to causing passive work, it also shows that the service staff and management staff in the front office lack professional training, which affects the quality of service.

（九）完善的服务设施

要保证所有的设施设备科学、合理地满足客人需求，并且随时处于良好的运行状况，使客人感到舒适愉快。如果大暑天空调失灵、复印机不能正常使用等只要发生一次，服务质量就会大打折扣。设施能否让客人感到舒适，与前厅的维修保养水平有密切关系。

（9）Complete service facilities

It is necessary to ensure that all the facilities and equipment meet the needs of the guests scientifically and reasonably, and are in good operating conditions at all times to make the guests feel comfortable and happy. If the air conditioner fails in the summer, the printer cannot be used normally, etc., the service quality will be greatly reduced even of it happens only once. Whether the facilities can make guests feel comfortable is closely related to the maintenance level of the front office.

（十）可靠的安全保障

"安全责任，重于泰山"，保证客人的生命财产安全是服务质量中重要的一环。前厅是客流密集且人员复杂的区域，应建立严密的保安制度，包括防火、防盗，应对电梯故障、断电等意外事件等一整套制度和规程。

（10）Reliable security

"Safety responsibility is more important than Mount Tai". Ensuring the safety of guests' lives and property is an important part of service quality. The front hall is an area with dense passenger flow and complex personnel. A strict security system should be established, including a complete set of systems and procedures for fire prevention, anti-theft, and handling of accidents such as elevator failures and power outages.

（十一）优雅的服务环境

前厅除了要有一种和谐、温暖、舒适的气氛，还要给客人创造一种干净、安静的环境，这也是服务质量的一种表现。服务人员在任何地方都要低声讲话，不可喊叫，以免打扰客人休息。保持前厅的高度清洁，酒店可以因设施豪华程度而划分成不同的档次，但却不可因级别的区别而降低基本的卫生标准。

（11）Elegant service environment

In addition to creating a harmonious, warm and comfortable atmosphere in the front hall, it is also necessary to create a clean and quiet environment for the guests, which is also a manifestation of the quality of service. The service staff must speak in a low voice in any place, avoiding sharing, so as not to disturb other guests. To maintain a high level of cleanliness in the front hall, the hotel can be divided into different grades due to the degree of luxury of the facilities, but the basic hygiene standards cannot be lowered due to the difference in grades.

三、个性化服务

【案例导入】

记住客人的生日

夏日，厦门某酒店大堂，两位外国客人向礼宾台走来，礼宾司小倪立即面带微笑地以敬语问候。客人忧虑地讲述起他们心中的苦闷："我们从英国来在这儿负责一项工程，大约要3个月，可是离开了翻译我们就成了睁眼瞎，有什么方法能让我们尽快解除这种陌生感？"小倪微笑地用英语答道："感谢两位先生光临指导我店，使我店蓬荜生辉。这座历史悠久的都市同样欢迎两位先生的光临，你们在街头散步的英国绅士风度也一定会博得市民的赞赏。"熟练的英语所表达的亲切情谊，一下子拉近了彼此间的距离，气氛变得活跃起来。随后外宾更加详细地询问了当地的生活环境、城市景观和风土人情。小倪无不一一细说。外宾中的马斯先生还兴致勃勃地谈道："早就听说中国的生肖十分有趣，我是1954年8月4日出生的，遇到过两三次大的意外都大难不死，一定是命中属相助佑。"说者无心，听者有意，两天之后就是8月4日。谈话结束之后，小倪立即在备忘录上做记录。

8月4日一早，小倪就买了鲜花，并代表酒店在早就预备好的生日卡上填好英语贺词，请服务员将鲜花和生日贺卡送到马斯先生的房间。马斯先生从珍贵的生日贺礼中获得了意外的惊喜，激动不已，连声答道："谢谢！谢谢贵店对我的关心，我深深体会到这贺卡和鲜花之中隐含着许多难以用语言表达的情意。我们在厦门逗留期间再也不会感到寂寞了。"

Ⅲ　Personalized service

【Case Introduction】

Remember the guest's birthday

In the summer, two foreign guests approached the concierge desk in the lobby of a hotel in Xiamen, and the concierge Xiao Ni immediately greeted them in honorifics with a smile on his face. The guests expressed their distress anxiously: "We came here from the UK to be responsible for a project for about three months, but after leaving the interpreter, we felt loss. Is there any way we can relieve this sense of strangeness as soon as possible?" Xiao Ni replied in English with a smile: "Thank you, two gentlemen, for visiting and providing advice to our hotel, so that the lobby is splendid. This historic city also welcomes you, your British gentleman's demeanor walking on the street will surely win the public's admiration." The cordial friendship brought by the concierge's proficient English suddenly narrowed the distance between each other and the atmosphere became active. Then, the foreign guests asked detailedly about the local living environment, urban landscape, and customs. Xiao Ni explained all of them in detail. One of the foreign guests, Mr. Mars, also talked enthusiastically, "I have long heard that the Chinese zodiac is very interesting. I was born on August 4, 1954. I have encountered two or three major accidents and survived the catastrophe. I think with help from the Chinese zodiac" The speaker has no particular intention in mentioning the birthday, but the listener reads his meaning into it. Two days later, it was August 4th. After the conversation, Xiao Ni immediately took notes on the memo.

On the morning of August 4th, Xiao Ni bought flowers and filled out the English blessing message on the birthday card prepared earlier on behalf of the hotel, and asked the staff to deliver the flowers and birthday card to Mr. Mars' room. Mr. Mars was surprised by the precious birthday gift. He was so excited that he replied repeatedly: "Thank you! Thank you for your concern for me. I deeply realize that many emotions are difficult to express in words in greeting cards and flowers. We will never feel lonely again during our stay in Xiamen."

【案例分析】

本案例中大堂副理对待两位客人的做法是站在客人的立场上，把客人当作上帝的出色范例。第一，他设身处地，仔细揣摩客人的心理状态。两位英国客人由于在异国他乡逗留时间较长，语言不通，深感寂寞。小倪深入观察，准确地抓住了外国客人对乡音的心理需求，充分发挥他的英语专长，热情欢迎外国客人的光临，还特别称赞了他们的英国绅士风度，进而自然而然地向客人介绍当地的风土人情等，使身居异乡的外国客人获得了一份浓浓的乡情。第二，大堂副理小倪富有职业敏感性，善于抓住客人的有关信息。客人在交谈中无意中透露生日。小倪及时敏锐地抓住这条重要信息，成功地策划了一次为外国客人赠送生日贺卡和鲜花的优质服务和公关活动，把与外国客人的感情交流推向了更深的层次。因此，善于捕捉客人有关信息的职业敏感也是酒店管理者和服务人员应该具备的重要素质。

【Case Analysis】

This case is an excellent example of regarding the guests as God. The assistant manager in the lobby treated two guests from the standpoint of the guests. First, he put himself on the ground and carefully figured out the mental state of the guests. The two British guests were deeply lonely because of their long stay in a foreign country and language barriers. Xiao Ni conducted in-depth observation and accurately grasped the psychological needs of foreign guests for the local accent, gave full play to his English expertise, warmly welcomed foreign guests, especially praised their British gentlemanly demeanor, and naturally introduced the guests to the local customs, so that foreign guests living in a foreign country would feel a strong sense of nostalgia. Second, Xiao Ni, the assistant manager, is professionally sensitive and good at capturing relevant information from guests. The guest unintentionally revealed his birthday during the conversation. Xiao Ni grasped this important information in a timely and perceptive manner, and successfully planned a high-quality service and public relations activity that presented birthday cards and flowers to foreign guests, and enhanced the emotional exchanges with foreign guests to a deeper level. Therefore, the professional sensitivity to be good at capturing guest-related information is also an important quality that hotel managers and service personnel should possess.

（一）个性化服务的含义

①个性化服务的概念。

个性化服务就是以顾客为中心，服务员以强烈的服务意识主动接近客人，了解客人，设身处地地为客人着想，有针对性地为客人提供服务。个性化服务的目的是使服务持续改进，进而使客人获得持续的满意。

由此定义我们可以发现传统服务与个性化服务的最大区别在于：传统服务是酒店有什么就向顾客提供什么，而个性化服务则是顾客需要什么酒店就为其提供什么，从而最大限度地满足顾客的需求。近年来，酒店行业中流传着这样一句口号："我们的产品就是顾客的满意。"将满意作为酒店的产品，这无疑是对个性化服务最清晰、最直接的诠释。因为不同的顾客有着不同的需求，要使每一位顾客都感到满意，显然仅仅靠"酒店有什么就向顾客提供什么"的传统服务模式是无法做到的。只有针对不同顾客的不同需求"对症下药"，提供个性化服务，才有可能使每位顾客都感到满意，酒店的价值才能得到实现。

（1）The meaning of personalized service

① The concept of personalized service.

Personalized service centers around the guest. The service staff actively approaches the guest with a strong sense of service, understands the guest, puts himself in the guest's shoes, and provides targeted services to the guest. The purpose of personalized service is to make the service continuously improve and make guests get continuous satisfaction.

From this definition, we can find that the biggest difference between traditional service and personalized service is: traditional service means that the hotel provides guests with what they have, while personalized service means the hotel provides guests with what they need, to meet the needs of guests to the greatest extent. In recent years, there has been a slogan in the hotel industry: "Our products are guest satisfaction." Regarding satisfaction as a hotel's product is undoubtedly the clearest and most direct interpretation of personalized service. Because different guests have different needs, and making every guest satisfied it cannot be achieved by the traditional service model of "providing guests with what the hotel has." Only by "prescribing the right medicine" for the different needs of different guests and providing personalized services can it be possible to satisfy every guest and the value of the hotel can be realized.

②个性化服务的必然性。

目前无论国内还是国外，在采用标准化服务还是个性化服务上达成了共识，即标准化是基础，个性化是趋势。

现代酒店的市场竞争已从最初的价格竞争上升到较高的质量竞争，最终要达到文化竞争。每一家酒店都有自己的特色、自己的文化。说到底，酒店竞争的关键是特色，特色的核心是品牌，品牌的保障是文化，文化的表现是服务。在市场竞争日益激烈的今天，要留住客人，赢得客人，单纯靠规范和笑脸是远远不够的，更重要的是能给客人实实在在的帮助，也就是说服务要更加有内涵。具体来说，就是把客人当成朋友，提供的服务不仅满足客人的期望，更应"雪中送炭，锦上添花"，给客人一个意外的惊喜，满意加惊喜。这种服务是在不违反法律和道德原则的前提下，使客人获得满意加惊喜的服务。

② The inevitability of personalized service.

At present, both at home and abroad, a consensus has been reached regarding the choice between standardized services and personalized services: standardization is the foundation, and individualization is the trend.

The market competition of modern hotels has risen from the initial price competition to the higher quality competition, and finally reaches the cultural competition. Each hotel has its own characteristics and its own culture. After all, the key to hotel competition is uniqueness, the core of uniqueness is brand, the brand guarantee is the culture, and the expression of culture is service. In today's increasingly fierce market competition, in order to retain and win guests, it is far from enough to rely solely on standards and a smile. More importantly, it can provide real help to guests, which means that the service must be more connotative. Specifically, it is to treat guests like friends. The services provided not only meet the expectations of guests but also "offer help when it's most needed, and add an extru touch of delinght" to give guests an unexpected surprise, which means delivering satisfaction and surprise. This kind of service is to provide guests with satisfaction and pleasant service without violating laws and ethical principles.

③个性化服务的特点。

个性化服务虽然因客人要求不同，服务员提供服务的方式、方法和手段也千差万别，但寻根究底，个性化服务仍具有以下特点：一是要求有更为主动的服务；二是要求有更为灵活的服务；三是要求有更细微的服务；四是要求有超常的服务；五是要求有更强的感情投入。

③ Features of personalized service.

Personalized service, although the ways, methods, and means of service provided by service staff vary widely due to different requirements of guests, personalized service has the following characteristics: first, it requires more initiative service; second, it requires more flexible service; third, more subtle services are required; fourth, extraordinary services are required; fifth, stronger emotional input is required.

（二）个性化服务的实施

①对客人给予绝对的重视，对客人的需求保持高度的敏感。

酒店是为客人提供物质享受和精神享受的场所，客人来到酒店不仅是为了吃一顿饭、住一宿店，同时还有精神上的要求。他们时时处处都要得到足够的重视。把对 VIP 客人的服务推广到对普通客人的服务中，学会理解客人，善于发现客人需求，包括客人在心里没有说出来的需求，同时尽最大的努力满足客人的需求。

（2）Implementation of personalized services

① Give absolute attention to guests and maintain a high degree of sensitivity to their needs.

A hotel is a place to provide guests with material and spiritual enjoyment. Guests come to the hotel not only for a meal or overnight stay but also for spiritual requirements. Guests must be given adequate attention at all times and in all situations. Provide the same level of service to both VIP guests and ordinary guests, learn to understand the guests, be good at discovering the needs of the guests, including guests' unspoken needs, and try best to meet the needs of the guests.

②提高服务效率，始终关注细节。

速度和细节是优质服务最重要的组成部分。没有任何一个客人愿意接受一个慢腾腾的服务。任何人的等待都是有限度的，酒店在所有的服务中必须始终保持高速、快捷，能量化的一定要量化，能缩短的一定要缩短。另一方面，服务要始终关注细节，不注重细节是服务中最大的天敌。员工之间交谈的声音是不是影响了客人，走路的声音是否影响了客人，与客人打招呼时的语气、声音、动作、眼神是否尊重了客人等，这些细节上都必须引起酒店的高度重视。细节就是企业文化，细微之处见精神，只有足够注重细节，客人才会感到由衷的满意。

② Improve service efficiency and always pay attention to details.

Speed and detail are the most important components of quality service. No guest is willing to accept a slow service. Anyone's waiting is time limited. The hotel must always maintain effciency in all services. What can be quantified must be quantified, and what can be shortened must be shortened. On the other hand, the service must always pay attention to details, and lack of attention to detail is the worst enemy in service. Whether the voice of the conversation between employees affects the guests, the sound of walking affects the guests, or the tone, voice, gestures and eye contact respect the guest, and so on. When greeting the guest, these details must be highly valued by the hotel. The details are the corporate culture, and the subtleties show the spirit. Only with enough attention to detail can the guests feel sincerely satisfied.

③增加一流微笑，扩展服务内容。

微笑是一种世界性的语言，它对客人、酒店都非常重要。服务的整个过程都应是微笑的过程，一流的微笑应是自然的、发自内心的、诚挚的，而不是普通的、呆板的、为了微笑而进行的微笑。与客人相处一定要坚持 3 m 之内用微笑、1 m 之内用敬语，让客人感到酒店的每一位员工都是"微笑天使"。前厅部主要向客人提供礼宾、客房预订、接待、问询、话务等服务，除此以外，前厅还应在国家法律、行业规范许可的范围内拓展服务项目，以满足客人多方面的需求。对客人提出的特殊要求，服务人员在法律规定的范围内应采取各种方法尽力满足顾客的需求，真正做到"永远不要说不"。

③ Add the first-class smile and expand service content.

Smile is a worldwide language, and it is very important for guests and hotels. The entire service process should involve smiling. A first-class smile should be natural, heartfelt, and sincere, rather than ordinary, rigid, smiling for the sake of smiling. When getting along with guests, we must insist on smiling within three meters and greeting within one meter, so that guests feel that every employee of the hotel is a "smiling angel." The front office mainly provides concierge, room reservation, reception, inquiries, telephone services, and other services to guests. In addition, the front office should also expand service items within the scope of national laws and industry regulations to meet the various needs of guests. For the special requirements of the guests, the service personnel shall adopt various methods to meet the needs of the guests within the scope stipulated by the law, and truly achieve "NEVER SAY NO".

④善于对下授权，欢迎客人投诉。

前厅的员工经常会遇到客人提出的服务要求超出员工管理权限的情况，这时由于服务人员不能及时满足客人的要求，造成客人的不满意。管理人员可将必要的权力赋予服务在一线的员工，让他们主观能动地、富有创新地工作，也就是授权。通过授权可以实现前厅内部有关的信息、知识和报酬的共享，使员工对酒店和客人有较充分的了解，让他们自己寻找解决问题的方法，并对自己的决定和行为负责。适当授权能唤起员工的工作责任感，打破常规，主动、灵活地为顾客做好服务，使客人满意度增加。

如果在服务过程中出现差错，引来客人的投诉，员工在及时采取服务补救的同时必须认真面对投诉、真诚接受投诉、合理处理投诉，让投诉的客人得到心理上的绝对尊重，同时要对客人的投诉表示感谢，让坏事变好事，让客人通过我们对待投诉的认真态度而产生对酒店的归属感。

④ Good at authorizing, welcome guest complaints.

The staff in the front hall often encounter things that the guest's service request exceeds their management authority. At this time, the guest's dissatisfaction is caused when the service staff cannot meet the guest's request in time. Managers can delegate necessary powers to front-line employees, allowing them to work subjectively and creatively, that is authorization. Through authorization, the relevant information, knowledge, and remuneration in the front office can be shared, so that employees have a deeper understanding of the hotel and guests, allowing them to find solutions to problems on their own, and be responsible for their own decisions and actions. Appropriate authorization can arouse employees' sense of responsibility, break the routine, actively and flexibly serve guests well, and increase guest satisfaction.

If there is an error in the service process, which attracts complaints from guests, employees must face the complaints seriously, accept the complaints sincerely, and handle the complaints reasonably while offering service remedies promptly, so that guests who complain can receive absolute psychological respect, and at the same time, we must express our gratitude to the guests for their complaints, turn bad things into good things, and let the guests have a sense of belonging to the hotel through our serious attitude towards complaints.

【知识拓展】

酒店员工应养成的 10 个习惯

第一个习惯：员工必须知道酒店的目标、价值观、信条和自己的工作范围。

酒店目标要靠全体员工的努力才能实现。只有管理层知道的目标是没有根的目标。员工最需要知道的是酒店对自己的期望和要求。他们对这些目标的认知和理解，直接影响酒店的服务质量。因此，每一位员工都有义务理解酒店的目标，并进一步知道围绕这个根本目标制订的各种酒店战略中和员工有关的工作。

【Knowledge Expansion】

10 habits that hotel employees should develop

The first habit: Employees must know the hotel's goals, values, creed, and scope of work.

The goal of the hotel can only be achieved by the efforts of all the staff. A goal that only management knows about is a goal without roots. What employees need to know most is the hotel's expectations and requirements of themselves. Their cognition and understanding of these goals directly affect the service quality of the hotel. Therefore, every employee is obligated to understand the hotel's goals and know more about the work related to employees in the various hotel strategies developed around this fundamental goal.

第二个习惯：员工必须做到尽量使用客人的名字称呼客人，预见并满足客人的需求，热情亲切地送别客人。

使用客人的姓氏称呼客人，表达对客人的尊重和关注。满足客人的需求是对服务的基本要求，但要做到宾至如归，就必须在实践中不断总结，做到预见客人的需求，在客人还没有提出或客人认为是额外的服务不好意思提出时，主动帮助客人解决困难。同样，员工不要忘记做好送客工作，直到把客人送走，整个服务过程才算结束。

The second habit: All employees must try to use their names to address guests, foresee and meet their needs, and send them off warmly and cordially.

Addressing guests by their surnames expresses respect and concern for the guests. Satisfying the needs of guests is the basic requirement for service, but in order to make guests feel at home, you must continue to summarize in practice and anticipate the needs of the guests. When the guest hasn't proposed it or the guest feels embarrassed to propose an extra service, staff need to take the initiative to help the guest solve the problem. Similarly, all employees must not forget to do a good job of sending guests off, the process is not over until the guest has left.

第三个习惯：员工在工作时间不应使用客用设施设备，在任何时间、地点，行动都应该以客为先。

员工应该培养酒店意识。酒店意识是指酒店员工的言行举止应该有酒店从业人员的职业素质和风度。应该做到：

礼貌：见到客人和同事应该打招呼、问好，并主动询问客人是否需要帮忙。

三轻：走路轻、讲话轻、操作轻。有客人在时应该停止内部的对话，转而关注客人的需求。如果在和另外的客人讲话或通电话时，应该用眼神和客人打招呼。由于工作需要乘客用电梯时应该保持安静，不要大声和同事或其他客人讲话。

回避：做客房清洁卫生时，如果住客回房间应该主动询问是否打扰客人，主动回避。

礼让：客人使用酒店公共设施时应该自觉礼让，让客人优先使用。如让客人优先出入电梯，在走廊通道礼让客人先走等。

方便：服务是为了方便客人。酒店服务员不应该因为正在为客人服务而使客人感到不便。如在清洁公共卫生间时，如果有客人使用，应该先让客人使用，然后再继续清洁；客人入住高峰期不应该安排大堂地板打蜡；客人使用电梯时不应该抢先在里面打扫；陪同客人到酒店内的目的地，而不是仅指明方向了事，等等。

The third habit: Employees should not use guest facilities and equipment during working hours. At all times and in all places, guests should be prioritized.

Employees should develop hotel professionalism. Hotel professionalism means that the words and deeds of hotel employees should have the professional quality and demeanor of hotel employees. Should do:

Politeness: When you see guests and colleagues, you should greet, say hello, and ask the guests if they need help.

Three lights: walk lightly, speak softly, work quietly. When there are guests, you should stop the internal dialogue and focus on the needs of the guests instead. If you are talking to another guest or talking on the phone, you should greet the guest with your eyes. As you need to take the guests' elevator for working use, you should keep quiet and do not speak loudly with colleagues or other guests.

Avoidance: When doing room cleaning and sanitation, if the guest returns to the room, the staff should ask if they are disturbing the guest and take the initiative to avoid it.

Courtesy: When guests use the hotel's public facilities, the staff should consciously be courteous and give priority to guests. For example, giving guests priority to enter and exit the elevator, politely letting guests go first in the corridor passage, etc.

Convenience: The service is for the convenience of the guests. Hotel attendants should not inconvenience guests because they are serving them. For example, when cleaning public toilets, if guests are using them, they should be used by guests first, and then the cleaning can continue; the lobby floor should not be waxed during peak check-in period; when guests use the elevator, the staff should not clean it first; accompany the guests to the destination in the hotel instead of just pointing out the direction and so on.

第四个习惯：保证对面前 3 m 内的客人和员工微笑致意，并让电话中的客人听到你的微笑。

微笑是酒店从业人员的重要习惯。微笑不仅可以使客人感到喜悦，而且可以化解客人的不满。酒店不仅要求员工保证向客人微笑，更重要的是使微笑成为员工生活的一部分。

The fourth habit: Make sure to smile at the guests and employees within 3 meters in front of you, and let the guests on the phone feel your smile.

Smiling is an important habit of hotel employees. Smiling will not only bring joy to the guests but also resolve their dissatisfaction with the guests. The hotel not only requires employees to promise to smile at guests but more importantly, make smiles a part of employees' lives.

第五个习惯：为满足顾客的需求，员工应充分运用酒店的授权，直至寻求总经理的帮助。

满足顾客的需求是酒店获取利润的源泉。只要是为了满足客人的需求，员工应该对自身的判断力充满信心，运用酒店的授权解决客人的困难。必要时，积极向其他部门的同事和上级管理者寻求支持和援助，甚至勇敢地直接向总经理寻求援助。酒店管理者应该鼓励和培养这种全心全意为顾客服务的精神和勇气。

The fifth habit: In order to meet the needs of guests, employees should use the hotel's authorization sufficiently, and, if necessary, seek the help of the general manager.

Satisfying the needs of guests is the source of profit for the hotel. As long as it is to meet the needs of guests, employees should have full confidence in their own judgment and use the hotel's authorization to solve guests' difficulties. If necessary, actively seek support and assistance from colleagues and supervisor managers in other departments, until bravely seek assistance directly from the general manager. Hotel managers should encourage and cultivate the spirit and courage to serve guests wholeheartedly.

第六个习惯：员工必须不断认识酒店存在的缺点，并提出改进意见和建议，使酒店的服务和质量更加完美。

任何一家酒店都或多或少地存在缺点，酒店只有不断改进才能适应不断变化的竞争环境。酒店管理层应该创造一个让员工消除畏惧心理的开放环境，用对待客人投诉的态度和方式对待所有员工的意见和建议。

The sixth habit: Employees must constantly recognize the shortcomings of the hotel and put forward opinions and suggestions for improvement to make the hotel's service and quality more perfect.

Any hotel has more or less shortcomings, and only through continuous improvement can the hotel adapt to the ever-changing competitive environment. The hotel management should create an open environment that allows employees to eliminate their fears, and treat all employee's opinions and suggestions in the same way and in the way that they treat guest complaints.

第七个习惯：积极沟通，消除部门之间的偏见。不要把责任推给其他部门或同事。在工作场所，不要对酒店做消极的评论。

当客人提意见时，员工把责任推到其他同事或者其他部门，甚至推到领导身上的事例屡见不鲜。他们不明白客人考虑的不是酒店中哪一个部门或哪一个人应该负责，而是酒店要负责任。员工这种推卸自身责任的态度会令客人更加不满，进一步损害酒店的整体形象。因此，酒店服务中内外有别是必要的。对内要分清责任，对外要维护酒店的整体形象。

The seventh habit: actively communicate and eliminate prejudice between departments.

Don't pass the responsibility to other departments or colleagues. In the workplace, do not make negative comments about the hotel.

It is not uncommon for employees to shift the responsibility to other colleagues or other departments, or even to the leader when guests make complaints. They don't understand that what the guest considers is not which department or person in the hotel should be responsible, but the hotel is responsible. This attitude of employees to shirk their own responsibilities will make guests more dissatisfied and further damage the overall image of the hotel. Therefore, it is necessary to distinguish the difference between the inside and outside of the hotel service. Responsibilities must be distinguished internally, and the overall image of the hotel must be maintained externally.

第八个习惯：把客人的每一次投诉都视作改善服务的机会。

倾听并用最快的行动解决客人的投诉，保证投诉的客人得到安抚。员工应该把客人的每一次投诉看成一次留住客人的机会，必须尽一切办法，快速回应，解决问题，再次赢得客人对酒店的信心。

The eighth habit: Regard every guest complaint as an opportunity to improve service.

Listen to guest complaints and take swift action to resolve them to ensure that the guest feels reassured. The staff should regard every complaint from the guest as an opportunity to retain the guest and must do everything possible to respond quickly and solve the problem, so as to win the confidence of the guest in the hotel again.

第九个习惯：制服要干净整洁、合身，鞋要擦亮，仪容仪表端正大方，上岗时要充满自信。

员工在上岗时精神饱满，着装整齐，充满自信，不仅表达了对客人的重视和尊敬，而且能够充分展示酒店的形象和管理水平。自信来源于对工作的驾驭能力、满意度和相关知识，自信的员工才会有工作的自豪感，自信的员工才会得到客人的尊重。

The ninth habit: Uniforms must be clean, tidy, well-fitted, shoes must be polished, appearance must be upright, and be confident when on duty.

The employees are full of energy, neatly dressed, and confident when they are on duty. They not only express the importance and respect for the guests but also fully demonstrate the corporate image and management level of the hotel. Confidence comes from the ability to handle the job, job satisfaction, and job-related knowledge. Only confident employees will have a sense of pride in their work, and confident employees will be respected by customers.

第十个习惯：爱护酒店财产，发现酒店设备设施破损时必须立即报修。

不爱护酒店的资产就等于增加酒店经营的成本。没有维修保养意识，不及时维修，新酒店也会很快陈旧。酒店不必追求豪华的装修和装饰，但必须有完好常新的设备，员工要努力创造一个让客人惊喜的居停环境。

The tenth habit: Take good care of the hotel property and report for repairs immediately when the hotel equipment and facilities are found to be damaged.

Heglecting the hotel's assets is tantamount to increasing the cost of hotel operations. Without maintenance awareness, the new hotel will quickly become obsolete if it is not repaired in time. The hotel does not need to pursue luxurious renovation and decoration, but the equipment must be in good condition and often new, and employees must strive to create a living environment that surprises guests.

任务二　宾客关系管理

【案例导入】

腰包不见了

某美籍华人旅行团到达某酒店的第二天上午 8:00 左右，该团的张女士急匆匆跑到大堂副理处投诉说，她的腰包不见了，内有 600 多美元，并非常肯定地说："我已经找遍了房间所有的地方和行李箱，都没有。我记得很清楚是放在房间内的桌子上的，刚才我还看到有客房服务员进我的房间。"该团 8:20 要出发到各个景点，陪同人员在一旁也帮客人讲话，非常着急，因为整车的客人都等着呢!

【案例问题】

大堂副理该如何处理呢?

Task 2　guest relationship management

【Case Introduction】

The pocket is gone

Around 8:00 am the next day after a Chinese-American tour group stayed in a hotel, Ms. Zhang hurried to the assistant manager in the lobby to complain that her pocket was missing and there were more than 600 dollars in it. And she said with certainty: "I have searched all the places and suitcases in the room, and there was no pocket. I remember clearly that it was placed on the table in the room. Just now I saw a room attendant entering my room." The group has to depart to various attractions at 8:20, and the companions are also very anxious to help the guests because all the guests in the car are waiting!

【Case Question】

How should the assistant manager deal with it?

【案例分析】

可能采取的做法及评析：

①立即拨打 110 报警，由当地公安机关调查、处理此事。向 110 报警，是一个查处的办法，但作为酒店，是要考虑给客人安全感的。若警车开到酒店门口，身穿制服的公安人员在酒店出入，住店客人看到后的第一感觉肯定是该酒店发生重大案件了，客人的安全感大大下降，会给酒店带来间接的损失。故此法不妥。

②向客人允诺我们一定查处那位服务员，追回失窃款。失窃现象在酒店难免会发生，有内盗，也有外盗，但作为酒店大堂副理，面对如此急躁又肯定的张女士，一定要有主见，千万不要当场轻易同意她的判断，在事情没有水落石出之前不要给客人任何承诺。设想如果是在客人房间内衣橱里的小件行李包中找到了腰包，那么对受怀疑被盘查的服务员的打击是多么大！故这样做法是不利于酒店内部管理的。

③安抚客人不要着急，我们一定尽力帮助查找，并让张女士仔细回忆她最后一次看到腰包的时间、地点，询问是否去过别的什么地方。告诉客人一有结果会立即通知她。客人走后立即通知酒店保安部和客房部进行查找。

可将事情的详情向保安部汇报，通过酒店自身的设备和能力解决问题。所以我们倡导第 3 种解决办法。大堂副理当时让陪同人员留下联系电话，而不是等她回酒店后再告知结果，这种做法也较周到。若事情很快有了结果可立即通知客人，张女士不至于在整日的行程中全无兴致，从而影响到整团客人的心情。

【Case Analysis】

Possible approaches and comments:

① Call 110 immediately, and the local public security bureau will investigate and deal with the matter. Reporting to 110 is a way to investigate and deal with it, but as a hotel, it is necessary to consider giving guests a sense of security. If the 110 police car arrives at the entrance of the hotel and public security personnel wearing uniforms enter and exit the hotel, the guests' first impression after seeing it is that a major incident must have occurred in the hotel, and the guest's sense of security will be greatly reduced, which will bring indirect losses to the hotel. Therefore, this method is inappropriate.

② Promise the customer that we will investigate the staff and recover the stolen money. Theft will inevitably occur in hotels, both internal and external, but as the assistant manager, when facing such an impatient and certain Ms. Zhang, you must have your own opinions. Do not easily agree to her judgment on the spot. Don't make any promises to guests before the conclusion is reached. Imagine if the pocket bag were found in the small luggage in the guest's underwear closet, what a blow it would be to the staff suspected of being interrogated! Therefore, this method is not conducive to the internal management of the hotel.

③ To appease the guests so that they do not worry, we will try our best to help find the pocket. We can ask Ms. Zhang to carefully recall the time and place when she saw her pocket for the last time and ask if she had been anywhere else. Tell the guest that she will be notified as soon as there is a result. After the guest leaves, immediately notify the hotel's security department and housekeeping department to search.

The details of the matter can be reported to the security department, and the problem can be solved through the hotel's own equipment and capabilities. So, we advocate the third solution. The assistant manager asked her companion to leave her contact number instead of waiting for her to return to the hotel to inform the result. It was also more thoughtful. If there is any feedback, the guests can be notified immediately, so that Ms. Zhang will not lose interest in the whole day's itinerary, which will affect the mood of the entire group of guests.

【案例启示】

①酒店应该加强安全保卫工作，杜绝失窃现象的发生。

②对服务员进行素质培训，使之具备一名酒店从业人员最基本的素质。同时制订一系列严格的规章制度及处罚制度。

③一旦有失窃现象发生，酒店管理人员要沉着冷静。应懂得最基本的失窃处理常识，如保护现场，及时请保安部会同破案等。

【Case Enlightenment】

① The hotel should strengthen its security work to prevent theft from happening.

② Quality training should be carried out for staff so that they have the most basic qualities of a hotel employee. At the same time, it is necessary to formulate a series of strict rules and regulations and punishment systems.

③ Once a theft occurs, the hotel management staff must remain calm. You should understand the most basic common sense of theft handling, such as protecting the scene and asking the security department to solve the case in time.

一、正确认识宾客，提供针对性服务

前厅服务人员需要与各种不同类型的客人打交道，因此服务人员应具备察言观色的能力，并能迅速从客人的举止、谈吐、神态中判断其情绪与要求，在注意自己的表情与言谈的同时，根据客人的特征，提供针对性服务。前厅服务人员应在日常的工作中重视培养自己待人处事的技巧。一名优秀的前厅服务人员在接待服务工作中要迅速、正确地理解客人，处理事情通情达理，有智有谋，并且善于自我约束。

I　Understand the guests correctly and provide targeted services

The front office service staff need to deal with different types of guests, so the service staff should have the ability to observe words and expressions, and can quickly judge their emotions and requirements from the behavior, conversation, and demeanor of the guests, pay attention to their own expressions and speeches at the same time, according to the characteristics of the guests, and provide targeted services. Front office service personnel should pay attention to cultivating their skills in dealing with others in their daily work. An excellent front office service staff should quickly and correctly understand the guests in the reception service work, deal with matters sensibly, wisely, and be good at self-discipline.

为了能向客人提供针对性的服务，服务人员必须了解不同类型客人的基本需求。

（一）客人类型与针对性服务

酒店的客人基本上可以分为 3 类：公务型客人、旅游型客人和贵宾。

In order to provide customers with targeted services, service personnel must understand the basic needs of different types of guests.

（1）Types of customers and targeted services

Hotel guests can be divided into three categories: business guests, tourist guests, and VIPs.

①公务型客人。公务型客人包括商人、前来参加会议的客人、长驻专家和具有公事目的的各种代表团。针对公务型客人，要求酒店的设施能达到家庭式的舒适及办公机构般的服务效率。他们的住房不仅是休息、睡觉的场所，而且还是工作、学习的地方。因此，要求房内隔音良好、光线充足、备有写字台与上网功能。此外，他们还希望酒店有一个完善的商业服务中心，能为他们提供传真、复印、秘书、打字及商业信息等服务；希望前厅接待员能快速为他们办理预订客房业务以及进店、离店手续；希望酒店能为其提供叫醒服务、预订出租车服务、房内用餐服务、快速洗衣服务、干洗熨烫服务以及信用卡结账服务。无论是在国内还是国外，公务型客人都是一个高消费群体，一般有较高的文化修养，公务繁忙，对服务方式、服务效率都很讲究，并希望得到更多的尊重。许多高档酒店为公务型客人开设了商务行政楼层，集中管理，提供有针对性的服务，很受客人欢迎。

① Business guests. Business guests include businessmen, guests who come to attend meetings, resident experts, and various delegations with official purposes. For the service of business guests, the hotel's facilities are required to achieve family-style comfort and office-like service efficiency. Their room is not only a place to rest and sleep but also a place to work and study. Therefore, the room is required to have good sound insulation, sufficient light, a writing desk, and Internet access. In addition, they also hope that the hotel has a complete business service center that can provide them with fax, photocopying, secretarial, typing, and business information services. They hope that the receptionist at the front desk can quickly handle the room reservation business and the formalities of entering and leaving the hotel for them. It is hoped that the hotel can provide wake-up service, taxi booking service, in-room dining service, express laundry service, dry cleaning, and ironing service, and credit card checkout service. Business guests are a high-expenditure group, both at home and abroad. Business guests generally have a high level of cultural accomplishment, are busy with business, are very particular about service methods and service efficiency, and hope to get more respect. Many high-end hotels have set up business executive floors for business guests, which are centrally managed and provide targeted services, which are very popular with guests.

②旅游型客人。旅游型客人包括前来我国旅游、探亲、度假的散客以及团体客人。他们在附近的旅游点游览，把酒店作为落脚的基地。在大部分旅游城市的酒店内，旅游型客人占很大的比例，他们的需求与公务型客人需求同样重要，应引起重视。他们希望居住的房间能观赏到优美景色，住店期间能品尝当地的风味佳肴，希望了解当地的风俗人情，购买当地的土特产及手工艺纪念品；希望酒店的前台能为他们提供介绍旅游景点情况的资料，各种交通工具时刻表以及购物指南；希望前厅服务员能为他们介绍娱乐场所的特点，当地餐馆的经营特色、天气预报，还能为他们解决行李搬运问题及代订机票、车票和各种文娱活动票等。

② Tourist guests. Tourist guests include individual travelers and group guests who come to our country for tourism, family visits, and vacations. They visit nearby tourist spots and use the hotel as a place for their stay. Tourist guests account for a large proportion of hotels in most tourist cities. Their needs are as important as those of business guests and should be taken seriously. They hope that their room offers a beautiful scenery, they can taste the local delicacies during their stay in the hotel, they hope to understand the local customs, buy local specialties and handicraft souvenirs; hope the front desk of the hotel can provide them with information about tourist spots, as well as various transportation timetables and shopping guides; hope that the front office attendant can introduce them to the characteristics of entertainment venues, the operating characteristics of local restaurants, weather forecasts, and solve the problem of baggage

工作领域三 / 项目一　服务质量管理

handling and book air tickets, bus tickets, and various entertainment tickets for them.

③贵宾。酒店面向贵宾的接待规格及待遇通常较高。比如，政府邀请的贵宾身份均很高，前厅服务人员不但要搞好服务工作，还要注意保密。还有一些商务性的贵宾，他们可能是一家航空公司或大旅行社的总裁，也可能是一名国际会议或旅游组织机构的代表，其在酒店所受到的待遇对酒店今后的客源影响很大，贵宾接待服务工作的质量与酒店的声誉和经营有很大的关系。酒店可以把接待贵宾的过程看作酒店最高接待水平的展示。

③ VIPs. The standard and treatment for VIPs reception are usually higher. For example, the status of VIPs invited by the government is regarded highly, and the front office service staff must not only do a good job of service but also pay attention to confidentiality. There are also some business VIPs. They may be the president of an airline or a big travel agency, or they may be a representative of an international conference or tourism organization. The treatment they receive in the hotel will have a great impact on the hotel's future customers. The quality of VIP reception services has a lot to do with the reputation and operation of the hotel. The hotel can regard the process of receiving VIPs as a demonstration of the hotel's highest hospitality level.

（二）客人个性与针对性服务

同类型的客人具有不同的个性。了解各种类型的客人共性后，还需要进一步了解客人的个性，为不同个性的客人提供个性化服务。

（2）Guest personality and targeted services

Guests of the same type also have different personalities. After understanding the commonalities of various types of guests, it is necessary to further understand the personalities of the guests and provide personalized services for the guests.

①交际型客人。这类客人热情、健谈，有时甚至过于热情。他们也许会请酒店人员外出或一起用餐。在为此类客人服务时，应保持镇静与幽默，应根据酒店的规章制度，有策略地回答客人的需求，必要时可请求领导的帮助。

① Sociable guests. Such guests are enthusiastic, talkative, and sometimes even too enthusiastic. They may invite hotel staff to go out or have a meal together. When serving such guests, you should remain calm and humorous, respond to the guests' needs strategically in accordance with the hotel's rules and regulations, and ask for help from the leader if necessary.

②急躁型客人。这类客人的特点是不管服务人员多么繁忙，他们都坚持要求立即提供服务。如果客人的要求是偶然的，服务人员可尽量提前为其服务，满足此类客人的要求，但这对其他客人来说是不公平的，因此，服务人员要设法走捷径，尽快把他们安顿下来，但应该注意态度和方式方法。

② Impatient guests. The characteristic of impatient guests is that no matter how busy

311

the service staff is, they insist on providing service immediately. If the request of the guest is accidental, the service staff can serve him as soon as possible to meet the requirements of such guests, but this is unfair to other guests. For this reason, the service staff should try to take shortcuts and settle them down as soon as possible, but you should pay attention to attitudes and methods.

③闲聊型客人。对于喋喋不休的客人，前厅服务人员要关心、体谅，注意礼貌。在适当的时候，向他们表示歉意，因为其他客人也需要得到服务。

③ Talkative guests. For the chattering guests, the front office staff should be caring, considerate, and courteous. When appropriate, apologize to them, because other guests also need to be served.

④抱怨型客人。抱怨型客人是指那些即使自己做错了事，也会把责任推给酒店的客人。当此类客人抱怨时，前厅服务人员应注意倾听，致以歉意，再设法解决问题。注意接待此类客人要热情，绝不能与之争辩。

④ Complaining guests. Complaining guests refer to those guests who will blame the hotel even if they do something wrong. When such guests complain, the front office staff should listen carefully, apologize, and then try to solve the problem. Pay attention to treating such guests with enthusiasm and never argue with them.

⑤易变型客人。易变型客人的特点是在做出选择前，不断地改变主意。接待此类客人，应注意保持耐心与礼貌，应留给客人充足的时间做决定。此外，还应根据客人的特点提供引导性的建议。

⑤ Hesitant guests. The characteristic of hesitant guests is that they constantly change their minds before making a choice. When receiving such guests, you should be patient and polite. Guests should be given plenty of time to make decisions. In addition, guiding suggestions should be provided according to the characteristics of the guests.

⑥胆怯型客人。由于胆怯型客人不轻易表示自己的不满，因此，服务人员应注意觉察此类客人的要求，否则很难了解他们真正的想法。此外，还应努力向此类客人提供良好的服务。

⑥ Shy guests. Because timid guests do not express their dissatisfaction easily, service personnel should pay attention to the requirements of such guests, otherwise, it is difficult to understand their real thoughts. In addition, efforts should be made to provide good services to such guests.

⑦要求型客人。应设法了解此类客人的真正需求，提供其急需的东西。在接待服务中要能忍耐、有礼貌，绝不能发脾气。

⑦ Demanding guests. We should try to understand the real needs of such guests and provide them with what they urgently need. Be patient and polite in reception services, and never lose your temper.

⑧敌意型客人。这类客人似乎对外界总怀有敌意，因此很难使他们高兴。前厅服务人员与此类客人打交道时，应注意容忍，要热情地为他们提供最好的服务，设法缓和局面，取悦客人。

⑧ Hostile guests. Such guests seem to be hostile to the outside world, so it is difficult to make them happy. When dealing with such guests, the front office staff should pay attention to tolerance, provide them with the best service enthusiastically, and try to ease the situation and please the guests.

⑨吵闹型客人。吵闹型客人通常喜欢在公共场所大叫大嚷，希望引起大家的注意，成为中心人物。前厅服务人员如遇到此类情况，应立即设法制止，以免影响他人。与此类客人打交道时，应尊重他们，小声地与他们讲话，尽量避免冲突。

⑨ Noisy guests. Noisy guests usually like to yell in public places, hoping to attract everyone's attention and become the focus of the crowd. If the front office service personnel encounter such a situation, they should try to stop them immediately, so as not to affect others. When dealing with such guests, you should respect them, speak to them quietly, and try to avoid conflicts.

⑩友善型客人。从表情上可以判断，友善型客人很乐意来酒店住宿，对酒店某些服务不周的疏忽之处，能予以谅解。大部分客人均属于此类型。我们应为他们提供最好的服务。

⑩ Friendly guests. Judging from the facial expressions, friendly guests are very happy to stay in the hotel and can forgive some of the hotel's inadequate service and negligence. Most guests fall into this category. They should be provided with the best service.

⑪特殊型客人。此类客人的喜好与大部分人有明显的区别。例如，对于客房的色调喜欢强烈的对比色，等等。前厅服务人员很难满足他们的全部要求。接待此类客人时，应耐心、礼貌，尽可能满足他们的部分要求。如果对此类客人的要求处理得比较恰当，他们下次还会光临。

⑪ Special guests. The preferences of such guests are clearly different from those of most people. For example, they prefer guest room with strong contrasting colors. It is difficult for the front office staff to meet all their requirements. When receiving such guests, they should be patient and polite, and try to meet some of their requirements as much as possible. If the request of such guests is handled appropriately, they will come again next time.

⑫价格敏感型客人。客人把房价与预估成本比较，若高于预估房价，便会抱怨房价太贵。前厅服务人员应以良好的服务态度、有效的销售技巧，向他们说明客房的特点

及客人能得到的利益。对此类客人应该耐心接待，但不能随意降价。

⑫ Price-sensitive guests. The guest compares the room rate with the expected cost. If the price is higher than expected, they complain that the room is too expensive. The front office service staff should explain to them the characteristics of the guest room and the benefits that guests can get with a good service attitude and effective sales skills. You should be patient with such guests, but you can't cut prices at will.

⑬儿童。儿童也是酒店的客人，服务时既要耐心，又要小心。儿童过分吵闹会影响其他客人，所以必要时应礼貌地提醒他们的父母。前厅服务人员应避免与客人的孩子嬉闹、玩耍，以免影响正常的工作秩序以及引起孩子父母的不满。

⑬ Children. Children are also guests of the hotel, so be patient and careful when serving. Children's excessive noise will affect other guests, so please remind their parents politely if necessary. The front office staff should avoid frolicking and playing with the guests' children, so as not to affect the normal work order and cause dissatisfaction from the children's parents.

酒店大部分客人是友善的，易于合作的。即使有小部分客人比较特殊，这对酒店及员工来说，也是一个挑战的机会。如果酒店的接待服务工作能使客人感到满意，酒店不但会获得可观的经济效益，还会赢得良好的声誉。

Most of the hotel guests are friendly and easy to cooperate with. Even if a small number of guests are special, this is an opportunity for the hotel and employees to meet challenges. If the hotel's reception service can satisfy the guests, the hotel will obtain not only considerable economic benefits, but also a good reputation.

二、掌握与客人沟通的环节
【案例导入】

偶遇贪便宜的顾客

一天上午，酒店大堂结账处有许多客人正在结账，1108房间的刘先生也来到前厅结账，这时结账处接到楼层服务员报告："1108房间少了两个高档衣架。"收银员小陈立即微笑地说："刘先生，您的房间少了两个衣架。"谁知客人好像早已有所准备，立刻否认带走了衣架。收银员小陈马上意识到出了问题，便立即通知了大堂副理，大堂副理在前厅处找到了刘先生。"刘先生您好，麻烦您过来一下好吗？"客人随着大堂副理来到了大厅的僻静处。"刘先生，您没拿衣架，那么有没有可能是您的亲朋好友来拜访您时顺便带走了？"大堂副理婉转地向客人表述酒店要索回高档衣架的态度。

刘先生说："没有，我住店期间根本没有亲友来过。"

"请您再回忆一下，您会不会把衣架顺手放到别的地方了？"大堂副理顺势提醒刘先生，"以前我们也曾发现过一些客人住过的房间衣架、浴巾、浴袍之类的不见了，但他们后来回忆起来或是放在床上，或被被子、毯子遮住，或裹在衣服里带走了，您能否上去再看看，会不会也发生类似情况呢？"大堂副理干脆给了他一个明确的提示。

刘先生："一个破衣架，你们真麻烦，咳，还是我上去看一下吧。"客人觉得越是拖延下去对自己越没有什么好处，便不耐烦地说。

大堂副理："您需要我帮您看管您的箱子吗？"

刘先生："不用，不用，"刘先生忙摇头，一边拒绝一边匆匆地提着箱子上了电梯，大堂副理和收银员会意地相互一望。

不一会儿，刘先生下来了，故作生气状说："你们的服务员也太不仔细了，衣架明明就掉在沙发后面嘛！"大堂副理知道客人已经把衣架拿出来了，就不露声色很有礼貌地说："实在对不起，刘先生，麻烦您了。"为了使客人不感到尴尬，大堂副理还很真诚地对客人说："刘先生，希望您下次来还住我们酒店！我们随时欢迎您的再次光临，再见！"

II　Master the link of communication with guests
【Case Introduction】
Encounter customers seeking free perks

One morning, many guests were checking out at the checkout counter in the hotel lobby, and Mr. Liu from Room 1108 also came to the front hall to check out. At this time, the checkout counter received a report from the floor attendant: "Room 1108 is missing two high-end hangers." Cashier Xiao Chen immediately smiled and said: "Mr. Liu, your room is missing two hangers." The guest seemed to be prepared and immediately denied taking the hangers. The cashier Xiao Chen immediately realized that there was a problem and notified the assistant manager, who found Mr. Liu in the front office. "Hello, Mr. Liu, would you please come over?" The guest followed the assistant manager to the quiet part of the hall. "Mr. Liu, you didn't take the hanger, so is it any possibility that your relatives and friends took it when they came to visit you?" The assistant manager tactfully conveyed the hotel's request to retrieve the high-end hangers.

Mr. Liu said: "No, no, none of my relatives or friends have been here during my stay." "Please recall again, would you put the hanger in another place by mistake?" The assistant manager reminded Mr. Liu. "In the past, we have also found that some of the rooms that guests have stayed in, such as the hangers, bath towels, bathrobes, etc., are missing, but they later recalled that they were either put on the bed, or covered by a quilt or blanket, or wrapped in clothes and taken away. Could you go upstairs and see if something similar has happened?" The assistant manager simply gave him a clear reminder.

Mr. Liu: "A broken clothes hanger, you are really troublesome, umm, let me go upstairs and check it." The guest felt that the longer the wait, the less beneficial it would be for him, so he said impatiently.

The assistant manager said: "Would you like me to keep an eye on your suitcase"

Mr. Liu: "No, no," Mr. Liu shook his head hurriedly, and while talking, he hurriedly carried the luggage to the elevator. The assistant manager and the cashier looked at each other knowingly.

After a while, Mr. Liu came down, pretending to be angry, and said, "Your staff was too careless. The hanger obviously fell behind the sofa!" The assistant manager knew that the guest had already taken out the hangers, so he said politely: "I'm really sorry, Mr. Liu, I'm sorry to trouble you." In order to prevent the guests from embarrassment, the assistant manager also said to the guests sincerely: "Mr. Liu, I hope you will stay at our hotel the next time. We welcome you again at any time, Goodbye!"

【案例问题】

在服务工作中我们时常会遇到爱贪小便宜的顾客，两个衣架本是一件小事，但作为酒店管理人员或服务员应该如何处理呢?

【Case Question】

In service work, we often encounter customers who love seeking free perks. Two hangers are a small thing, but what should be done as the hotel managers or staff?

【案例分析】

我们要善于观察和了解客人的情况，在处理酒店与顾客的矛盾时，要从客人的角度和为酒店争取客源的角度去考虑问题，绝不能当面指责他们，不要让客人难堪，巧妙地维护客人的自尊，这样，既维护了客人的面子，又维护了酒店的形象。这个问题如果处理不好，引起客人恼怒、争吵，便会给酒店带来意想不到的负面影响。

本案例中，当客人感知到自己的行为已被酒店察觉之后，也曾处于一种短暂的心理矛盾中，通过思想斗争，在酒店给予机会的情况下，客人最终还是主动将衣架拿了出来。但我们要知道无论如何，顾客即使做错了事仍然希望得到尊重，当服务人员确定顾客有"不轨"行为后，仍然对其表示"尊重"，并为他设计一个"体面的台阶"，给顾客"尊重"酒店的机会。案例中酒店通过分析顾客心理，在不得罪客人的前提下维护了酒店的财产，这是一种较为常见且明智的做法。

另外，面对客人，服务员没有选择，往往是客人的素质越低，对服务人员的素质要求也越高。有人说："酒店里没有低素质的客人，只有低素质的员工。"所以，酒店服务人员除了努力提高自身的素质，没有别的选择。事实上，如果服务人员自身素质高的话，即使遇到了素质低的客人，也可以处理好宾客关系。

【Case Analysis】

We must be good at observing and understanding the situation of the guests. When dealing with the conflicts between the hotel and the guests, we must consider the problem from the perspective of the guests and the the hotel's goal of attracting customers to the hotel. We must never accuse them face to face, nor should we embarrass the guests, and must cleverly maintain the self-esteem of the guests. In this way, this not only maintains the dignity of the guests but also maintains the image of the hotel. If this problem is not handled well, guests will become angry and quarrel, which will bring unexpected negative effects on the hotel.

In this case, after the guest perceived that his behavior had been detected by the hotel, he experienced temporary ambivalence. After some internal conflict, when the hotel gave the opportunity, the guest finally took the hanger out. But we need to know that in any case, as guests, even if they do something wrong, they still want to be respected. When the service staff determines that the customer has "irregular" behavior, the staff still show "respect" to him and offer him a great way out. This also gives customers the opportunity to "respect" the hotel. In this case, the hotel maintained the property of the hotel without offending the guests by analyzing the psychology of the customers. This is a common and wise approach.

In addition, the staff have no right to choose when they are facing customers. Often the lower the quality of the customers, the higher the quality requirements of the service staff. Some people say, "there are no low-quality guests, only low-quality employees in the hotel." Therefore, hotel service personnel have no choice but to work hard to improve their own quality. In fact, if the service staff themselves are of high quality, even if they encounter low-quality guests, they can handle the guest relationship well.

（一）第一印象

第一印象是持久的印象。大多数客人是从前厅服务人员的对客服务中获得对酒店的第一印象。客人从预订员回复的质量与时间，与话务员、预订员通话时听到的语音、语调，以及从迎宾员、行李员、前台接待员的服务态度和工作效率中所获得的印象，形成了对酒店的第一印象。

为了使客人产生良好的第一印象，服务人员必须注意仪容仪表、个人卫生及保持微笑。前厅服务人员必须注意着装及个人卫生。如果前厅服务人员的工作制服裁剪不合体，肮脏破烂，皱皱巴巴，头发蓬乱，沾满头屑，指甲不净，身有异味，则将给客人留下糟糕的印象。客人从服务人员的着装及个人卫生的状况中，可以想象出酒店的管理水平及服务质量。保持个人卫生与着装的整洁，是对客关系中最基本的要求。由于前厅服务人员接触顾客范围广，他们的穿着打扮必须符合大部分人的审美标准。例如不留胡子，不浓妆艳抹，不滥用香水，不乱佩戴饰物。酒店应明文规定这些方面的具体要求，并把应达到的标准拍成照片，公布在员工过道或员工餐厅内，以便服务人员自觉对照检查。

"微笑"是做好酒店服务工作的一大法宝。前厅服务人员向客人提供服务时，第一个动作应该是微笑。微笑表示欢迎客人的到来，表示愿意为客人提供服务。微笑在对客关系中能起到很大的作用。即使服务人员在工作中出现了一些小差错，客人也会因为与酒店员工之间良好的关系而原谅他们。

（1）First impression

The first impression is a lasting impression. Most guests get their first impression of the hotel from the customer service of the front office staff. The guest's first impression of the hotel is formed from the quality and time of the reservation staff's response, the voice and intonation heard when talking to the operator and the reservation staff, as well as the service attitude and work efficiency of the concierge, bellman, and receptionist.

To ensure guests have a good first impression, service personnel must pay attention to appearance, personal hygiene, and keep smiling. Front office service personnel must pay attention to dress and personal hygiene. If the front office staff's work uniforms are improperly cut, dirty, creased, disheveled hair, hair covered with dandruff, nails are dirty or have peculiar smells, they will leave a bad impression on the guests. Guests can imagine the management level and service quality of the hotel from the dressing and personal hygiene of the service staff. Maintaining personal hygiene and tidy dressing are the most basic requirements in customer relationships. Since the front office staff has a wide range of customers, their dress must meet the aesthetic standards of most people. For example, no beard, no heavy makeup, no excessive use of perfume, and no accessories. The hotel should clearly stipulate the specific requirements in these aspects and take photos of the standards that should be met, and display them in the staff aisle or staff dining room so that the service staff can consciously check themselves against them.

"Smile" is a magic tool to do a good job in hotel services. When the front office staff provides services to guests, the first action should be a smile. A smile expresses welcome to guests and expresses willingness to provide services to guests. Smiles can play a big role in customer relationships. Even if the service staff make some small mistakes in their work, the guests will be able to forgive them because of the good relationship with the hotel staff.

（二）言谈举止

为了使客人对酒店的良好第一印象得以持续下去，前厅服务人员必须注意言谈举止方面的礼貌礼节。

①注意倾听。为了使提供的服务具有针对性，必须注意倾听客人的要求。在倾听过程中注意"视觉接触"，望着客人的眼睛，不能漫不经心地左顾右盼，甚至无礼地

打断客人的谈话。

②使用礼貌语言。客人走近前台，前台服务人员应以亲切悦耳的语音、语调、正确的礼貌用语主动招呼客人。中外来宾都应一视同仁，以礼相待。前厅管理人员应根据操作程序，把对客服务的礼貌用语编成教材。在日常的对客服务中，应不断强化服务人员礼貌用语的意识，这是一项艰巨的工作。另外，前厅服务人员还应注意自己不良的口语习惯，并避免使用酒店的专业用语或当地的方言。

③用姓名称呼客人。用姓名称呼客人与微笑待客一样，是招待服务工作取得成功的又一大法宝。用姓名称呼远离家门的客人，客人的感受是难以用语言来表达的。为了能正确地用姓名称呼客人，前厅服务人员在第一次听到客人名字时要集中注意力记住它，最好把名字记录下来。以便了解客人名字的发音、拼写或字形。可以将客人的姓名与客人长相、职业或其他特征联系起来记忆。了解客人的姓名后，在与客人交谈中应有意识地重复客人姓名，强化记忆。

④仪态。前厅服务人员在客人来往频繁的场所——大厅工作，就像演员在舞台上表演，必须注意自己的仪态。应该做到热情好客，从容镇静，举止大方，风度翩翩，从不表现出懒散笨拙的样子。站立时的姿态应不靠不倚，不背朝客人，不窃听窃语。行走时步子应轻快有力，不垂头丧气、耷拉着脑袋。与客人交谈时，更应注意自己的仪态，因为正确的仪态有助于与客人的沟通。

⑤电话礼节。电话通话时，客人看不到我们，只听到我们的声音，因此服务人员的语音语调要友好热情，发音咬字要清楚，讲话速度要适中，绝不能给对方生硬、冷淡、不耐烦的感觉。

（2）Speech and behavior

In order to make the guests' good first impression of the hotel last, the front office staff must pay attention to the courtesy and manners of speech and behavior.

① Listen carefully. In order to provide targeted services, we must pay attention to listening to the requirements of the guests. Pay attention to "visual contact" in the listening process, look into the eyes of the guests, and cannot look around carelessly, or even interrupt the guests' conversation rudely.

② Use polite language. When guests approach the front desk, the front desk staff should take the initiative to greet the guests with a cordial and pleasant voice, tone, and correct polite language. Both Chinese and foreign guests should be treated equally and treated with courtesy. The front office management personnel should compile the polite language for customer service into teaching materials according to the operating procedures. In daily customer service, the awareness of polite language among service personnel should be continuously strengthened. This is a difficult task. In addition, the front office staff should also pay attention to their bad verbal habits and avoid using the hotel's professional language or local dialects.

③ Address the guests by their names. Addressing guests by name is the same as treating guests with a smile, which is another magic tool for the success of hospitality services. For guests far away from home, the feeling of being called by name is indescribable. In order to correctly address the guest by name, the front office staff must concentrate on remembering the guest's name when the staff hears the guest's name for the first time, and it is best to make a note. In order to understand the pronunciation and spelling of the guest's name, you can associate the guest's name with the guest's appearance, occupation, or other characteristics. After knowing the guest's name, you should consciously repeat the guest's name in the conversation with the guest to strengthen the memory.

④ Deportment. The front hall service staff work in the hall where guests come and go frequently, just like actors on stage, they must pay attention to their deportment. They should be hospitable, calm, decent, and personable, and never appear lazy and clumsy. The posture when standing should not be leaning, nor facing away from guests, and not eavesdropping. When walking, the steps should be brisk and strong, without drooping heads. When talking with guests, you should pay more attention to your deportment, because the correct deportment helps to communicate with guests.

⑤ Telephone etiquette. When talking on the phone, guests cannot see us, but only hear our voices. Therefore, the service staff's voice and intonation must be friendly and enthusiastic, the pronunciation must be clear, and the speech speed must be moderate. Never give the other party a feeling of bluntness, coldness, or impatience.

【拓展阅读】
接打电话时应注意的细节
（一）接电话时应注意的细节

①电话铃声一响，立即用左手拿起听筒。如此时正在与客人交谈，可请客人稍等，先接电话。

②可用愉快的语气根据不同的时间，使用正确的问候语来向客人问好，然后报出部门的名称。绝不能用"喂"称呼对方。在通话过程中，不得提高嗓音，不喊叫。

③如对方未通报姓名，可婉转地说："请问您贵姓？"

④注意倾听对方的谈话内容，并将要点记录下来。电话机旁应放置供记录用的笔、记录本或便条。应用左手拿听筒，右手记录，注意姿态。

⑤通话结束时，应重复重点，以免差错。记录通话日期、时间、对方的姓名。

⑥在接听电话时，如另一个电话的铃声响了，应请对方稍等，然后去接听第二个电话。对第二个电话的处理方法是请对方稍等，或者请对方留下电话号码。应尽快继

续接听第一个电话，第一个电话接听完了，应立即接听那个正在等候的电话。

【Extended Reading】

The details to pay attention to when answering the phone

（1）Details to pay attention to when answering the phone

① When the telephone rings, immediately pick up the receiver with your left hand. At this time, you are talking to the guest, please ask the guest to wait a moment before answering the phone.

② Use the correct greetings to greet the guest in a pleasant tone according to different times, and then report the name of the department. Never use "hello" to address the other party. Do not raise your voice or shout during the call.

③ If the other party did not tell the name, you can say tactfully: May I have your last name?

④ Pay attention to the content of the other party's conversation and record the main points. A pen, notebook, or scrip for recording should be placed next to the telephone. Hold the receiver in your left hand, record with your right hand, and pay attention to your posture.

⑤ At the end of the call, the important points should be repeated to avoid errors. Record the call date, time, and the name of the other party.

⑥ When answering a call, if another phone rings, ask the first caller to hold for a moment before answering the second call. The handling method for the second call is: ask the second caller to wait or ask the second caller to leave the phone number. You should continue to answer the first call as soon as possible. After the first call is answered, you should answer the waiting call immediately.

（二）打电话时应注意的细节

①通话前，做好准备。

②简单问候后，报出单位、部门名称及本人姓名。

③简洁而清楚地讲述事情。

④重复重要的地方。

⑤请其他人通话时，要问清对方姓名。

⑥电话突然中断，应立即再拨打电话。

（2）Details to pay attention to when calling

① Be prepared before the call.

② After a simple greeting, report the name of the company, department, and personal name.

③ Tell things concisely and clearly.

④ Repeat what's important.

⑤ When asking the other person to answer the phone, ask for the person's name.

⑥ If the call is interrupted, you should make another call immediately.

项目二
销售管理

【学习目标】

①掌握前厅客房销售的流程。

②熟练掌握前厅客房销售技巧。

③能准确识别顾客的类型并把握其需求特点。

④能灵活运用客房销售方法实现成功销售。

⑤应用所学的前厅销售知识，正确运用房价的调控方法。

Project 2
Sales Management

【Learning Objectives】

① Master the sales process of the front office of the guest room.

② Be familiar with the sales skills of the front office of the guest room.

③ Be able to accurately identify the types of guests and grasp the characteristics of their needs.

④ Be able to flexibly use guest room sales methods to achieve successful sales.

⑤ Apply the sales knowledge learned in the front office, and correctly use the control methods of room rates.

【案例导入】

春节前期，王先生到三亚亚龙湾红树林酒店前台询问是否还有空房间入住，前台接待人员主动热情并耐心地介绍了酒店的各种房型及特色房型。在交谈中前台接待人员了解到，春节期间客人想带腿脚不方便的儿子来度假养病，对酒店的设施和环境要求非常高。随后前台接待人员向客人推荐了酒店带有厨房的家庭套房和特色的海景套房，并提出可以先带客人参观房间然后再做决定，客人表示同意。

在参观过程中前台人员热情地向客人介绍了酒店的各项设施和特色。在与客人聊天中，客人表示，他对周边的其他酒店都进行了考察，其他酒店的前台员工，都是爱理不理的态度，而红树林酒店的初次服务就给人很亲切的感觉，而且酒店环境空气都很好，这让他很心动。同时客人表示本次海南的旅程主要是想让14岁的儿子来开心养病，孩子因腿脚不方便，需要时刻坐轮椅。

前台员工听后，向客人传达了酒店主打亲子主题的理念，把酒店亲子产品向客人进行了介绍和推荐，在客人看完房间后，对房间的舒适度和空间大小都非常满意，最终预订了两间房，并当场在前台交纳了春节期间的房费。

【任务布置】

①前台接待人员在此次客房销售中，哪些地方做得好？

②通过案例分析酒店前厅销售的流程。

③酒店前厅客房销售需要哪些技巧和方法？

（案例来源：微信公众号 MangroveTreeHR.）

【Case Introduction】

In the early days of the Spring Festival, Mr. Wang went to the front desk of Yalong Bay Mangrove Tree Resort to ask if there were any rooms available. The front desk staff actively and patiently introduced the hotel's various room types and featured room types. During the conversation, the reception staff learned that during the Spring Festival, the guest wanted to bring his son with an injury to his lower limbs to take a vacation to recuperate. He has very high requirements for the hotel's facilities and environment. Then the reception staff recommended the hotel's family suites with kitchens and featured sea-view suites to the guest, and offered to show the guest around the room before making a decision, and the guest agreed.

During the tour, the front desk staff warmly introduced the hotel's various facilities and features to the guest. During the chat with the guest, the guest said that he had inspected other hotels in the surrounding area. The front desk staff of other hotels were all indifferent. But the Mangrove Hotel's first service gave him a very cordial feeling, the air and the environment in the hotel was very good, which made him very excited. At the same time, the guest said that his trip to Hainan was mainly to make his 14-year-old son recuperate happily. The child needs to be in a wheelchair at all times due to lower limbs injuries.

After listening to the guest, the front desk staff conveyed to the guest the concept of the hotel's main parent-child program and introduced the related products to the guest. After the guest saw the room, he was very satisfied with the comfort and size of the room, and finally agreed to make a reservation for two rooms, and paid the room fee for the Spring Festival at the front desk on the spot.

【Assignment of Tasks】

① What did the receptionist do well in this room sale?

② Analyze the sales process of the front desk through this case.

③ What skills and methods are needed to sell hotel rooms at the front desk?

（Case source: WeChat public account MangroveTreeHR.）

【相关知识】

前厅部是客人抵达、离开酒店的必经之地，是酒店对客服务的开始和最终场所，也是客人对酒店形成第一印象和最后印象之处。前厅部是整个酒店服务工作的核心，其首要功能是销售酒店客房及其他产品，并协调酒店各部门，向客人提供满意的服务，使酒店获得理想的经济效益和社会效益。前厅部的每位员工都是销售员，都应利用自身的优势条件，熟悉和掌握工作范围内的销售要求、程序和技巧，适时、成功地进行销售，以实现酒店收益最大化。

【Related Information】

The front office is the only place where guests arrive and leave the hotel. It is the place where the hotel's guest service begins and ends. It is also the place where guests forms their first and last impressions of the hotel. The front office is the core of the entire hotel's service work. The primary function of the front office is to sell hotel rooms and other hotel products and coordinate various departments of the hotel to provide customers with satisfactory services so that the hotel can maximize both economic and social benefits. Every employee in the front office is a salesperson. They should make use of their own advantages to be familiar with and master the sales requirements, procedures, and skills within their scope of work, and carry out sales in a timely and successful manner in order to maximize the hotel's profit.

任务一　客房销售方法与技巧

【案例导入】

某日，某酒店营销经理刘娜接到一位老客户电话，介绍新客户周总预订两个精品花园单间，两天后入住。刘娜查询预订后发现，两天后酒店要接待一个大规模会议团队，精品花园单间已经满房了。

　　刘娜回复周总："感谢您对酒店的信任和认可，我们非常希望能够接待像您这样尊贵的客人。建议您选择入住湖景套房，一间房虽然多了几百元，但是套房临湖，有独立阳台，既可以观赏湖景，也可以品茶聊天，同时，湖景套房还配有免费的鲜花、水果、红酒和洗衣服务，房间面积也很大，装修上档次、有品位，早餐可以在行政楼层用餐，相信您入住后一定会非常满意的。"

　　见周总有些犹豫，刘娜说："我相信您也是非常有品位的，不会单纯地计较房间价格的高低，还会考虑物有所值。请问您是自驾还是乘飞机来呢？如果不是自驾，我们可以派酒店的商务车去机场接您，到店后我亲自陪您和您的朋友参观套房，您到时再决定也不迟。"

　　周总在电话里已经感觉到了刘娜的殷勤好客和专业的职业素养，最终选择了刘娜推荐的湖景套房。

Task 1　Guest Room Sales Methods and Skills

【Case Introduction】

One day, Liu Na, the marketing manager of a hotel, received a reservation from a new customer Mr. Zhou introduced by an old customer and needed to book two boutique garden single rooms, and would check in two days later. Liu Na checked the reservation and found that the hotel was about to receive a large-scale conference team two days later, and the boutique garden single rooms were fully booked.

Liu Na replied to Mr. Zhou: "Thank you for your trust and recognition of the hotel. We very much hope to receive guests like you. We recommended that you choose to stay in a lake-view suite. Although the price of the lake-view suite is a few hundred yuan more, the suite faces the lake. There is a private balcony, where you can watch the lake view, you can also enjoy tea and chat there. At the same time, the lake view suite is also equipped with free flowers, fruits, wine, and laundry services. You can dine on the executive floor. I believe you will be very satisfied after your stay."

Seeing that Mr. Zhou hesitated, Liu Na said: "I believe you have good taste. You will not simply care about the price of the room, but consider the value for money. Will you be coming by car or by plane? If you are not driving yourself, we can send a hotel limousine to the airport to pick you up. After arriving at the hotel, I will personally accompany you and your friends to visit the suite, and it will not be too late for you to decide when you arrive."

Mr. Zhou already felt Liu Na's hospitality and professionalism on the phone, and finally chose the lake-view suite recommended by Liu Na.

【案例分析】

酒店在接待大型会议时，因为会议用房数量大，往往会影响到其他散客的订房需求。

在畅销房型预订满房，而散客又需要预订时，酒店员工一定要做好高价房甚至是"尾房"的合理推销，不要将客人拒之门外。这就要求营销代表熟练掌握业务。比如刘娜对套房的价格、配备、特色、亮点、增值服务等十分熟悉。

营销代表还须热情、主动地为客人想办法，比如刘娜对客人表示感谢的同时，询问客人是否自驾，如果不是自驾，酒店可以派车接客人，而且允诺在客人没有确定预订的前提下派车接并亲自带客人参观酒店等，体现了刘娜的积极、主动与专业，同时也有效地引导客人预订酒店。

刘娜非常懂得顾客心理，在推销的时候先不谈价格，而是重点讲了套房的价值，住套房能够享受哪些服务，让客人感到物有所值、物超所值。

客人是需要尊重的。刘娜在与客人交流时，大赞客人有品位，让客人感受到被尊重，刘娜的建议也非常中肯、合乎情理，在这种情况下达成销售也是情理之中。

【Case Analysis】

When the hotel receives large conferences, the large number of rooms used for the conference often affects the reservation needs of another individual guest.

When the best-selling room type is fully booked but individual guests need to book, the hotel staff must do a good job in the reasonable promotion of high-priced rooms or even "remaining rooms", and do not turn guests away. This requires marketing representatives to master the business proficiently. For example, Liu Na is very familiar with the price, equipment, features, highlights, and value-added services of suites.

The marketing representative must also enthusiastically and proactively think of ways to help the guest. For example, when Liu Na expresses her gratitude to the guests, she asks the guest if they drive by themselves. If they don't drive themselves, the hotel can send a car to pick up the guests, Moreover, this promise is to send a car to pick up and personally take the guests to visit the hotel, etc., under the premise that the guest has not confirmed the reservation, etc., which reflects Liu Na's initiative, and professionalism, and also effectively guides guests to make a reservation.

Liu Na knows the psychology of customers very well. When selling, she didn't talk about the price, but focused on the value of the suite, and the services included, so that guests feel value for money and excellent value for money.

Guests need to be respected. When Liu Na communicated with the guest, she praised the guest for his taste and made him feel respected. Liu Na's suggestions were also very pertinent and reasonable. In this case, it was reasonable to reach a sale.

一、客房销售技巧

前厅部的工作不仅是接受客人预订客房、办理入住登记手续等，还应善于分析客人的特点、消费心理、需求，兼顾客人和酒店双方的利益，运用销售艺术，有效地推销酒店的客房及其他产品。

I　Guest room sales skills

The work of the front office is not only to accept guest reservations, check-in procedures, but also to be good at analyzing the characteristics, consumer psychology, and needs of guests, and to take into account the interests of both the customer and the hotel, and use the art of sales to effectively promote hotel rooms and other products.

（一）做好销售准备

①仪表、仪态端正，表现高雅的风度和姿态。

②前台工作环境要有条理，服务台区域干净整齐，不零乱。

③熟悉酒店各种类型的客房及酒店客人的特点，以便有效地向潜在客人介绍。

（1）Be ready to sell

① Personal appearance must be professional, and the elegant demeanor and posture must be displayed.

② The working environment of the front desk should be organized so that the service desk area is clean, tidy and well-organized.

③ Be familiar with the various types of guest rooms in the hotel and the characteristics of hotel guests in order to effectively introduce them to potential guests.

（二）分析不同客人需求

不同的客人有不同的特点，对酒店也有不同的需求。酒店前厅工作人员要针对客人的不同特点，为客人推荐最适合的房型，这样成功率也会更高。

前厅工作人员在与客人沟通过程中要善于通过客人的衣着打扮、言谈举止、随行人数等方面的信息，充分分析并把握客人的特点（年龄、性别、职业、国籍、旅游动机等），进而根据其需求特点和心理，进行有针对性的销售。

（2）Analyze the needs of different guests

Different guests have different characteristics and needs for hotels. The front office staff should recommend the most suitable room type for the guests according to the different characteristics of the guests so that the success rate will be higher.

The front office staff should be good at analyzing and grasping the characteristics of the guests（age, gender, occupation, nationality, travel motives, and so on.）through the information of the guests' dress, speech and behavior, and the number of people accompanying them in the process of communicating with guests. Then, according to its demand characteristics and psychology, do a good job of targeted sales.

目前酒店面对的客户主要分为以下几种类型。

①商务客人。

商务客人通常是因公出差，对房价不太计较，但对于房间有比较硬性的要求。

a. 安静：周边环境安静，客房隔音效果好。

b. 明亮：光线明亮，有床头灯和书桌台灯。

c. 设备：办公桌宽大，方便处理工作；酒店及房内办公设备齐全，如安装有宽带网或 Wi-Fi 信号强，商务中心配备有传真机、影印机等办公设备。

d. 适用房型：商务房、行政房等。

②休闲度假客人。

休闲度假客人出行主要是为了休闲和放松，所以对于房间品质要求更高。

a. 风景：要求房间窗外景色优美；

b. 设施：对于房间内的设施品质及配备要求更高，浴缸、榻榻米、电影设备等都可以接受；

c. 卫生：房间内要保持绝对的干净卫生，稍有问题都会引起客人的投诉。

d. 适用房型：景观房。

③蜜月情侣客人。

度蜜月的客人是出来感受浪漫的，所以不会希望氛围被打扰。

a. 独立：要求房间有足够的私密性，确保房间独立和安静。

b. 浪漫：房间内可适当增加一些浪漫的氛围，如鲜花布置、酒水赠饮等。

c. 适用房型：大床房、圆床房。

④家庭出行客人。

带小孩的亲子客人及家庭出游的客人集体出游，会偏向于住在一起，所以可尽量推荐套房。

如果同行者中有儿童或者老人，就需要优先按照他们的需求进行推荐房间，如向儿童推荐亲子房，向老人推荐养生房等。

⑤身份特殊客人。

对于社会知名人士，需要安排高档且私密性较好的独立套房。

The guests currently faced by hotels are mainly divided into the following types.

① Business guests.

Business guests usually travel on business and don't care about room prices, but they have more rigid requirements for rooms.

a. Quiet: The surrounding environment is quiet, and the guest room has good sound insulation.

b. Bright: The light is bright, with bedside lamps and desk lamps.

c. Equipment: The desk is large and convenient to handle work; the hotel and the room are equipped with office equipment, such as a broadband network is installed or a strong Wi-Fi signal and the business center is equipped with office equipment such as fax machines and photocopiers.

d. Applicable room types: business rooms, executive rooms, etc..

② Leisure and vacation guests.

Leisure and vacation guests mainly travel for leisure and relaxation, so they have higher requirements for room quality.

a. Scenery: The scenery outside the window of the room is required to be beautiful;

b. Facilities: The requirements for the quality and equipment of the room will be higher, bathtubs, tatami mats, movie equipment, etc. are all acceptable;

c. Hygiene: The room must be absolutely clean and hygienic. The slightest problem can lead to complaints from guests.

d. Applicable room type: senic room.

③ Honeymoon couple guests.

Honeymooners come here to feel romance, so they don't want their atmosphere to be disturbed.

a. Independence: The room is required to have enough privacy to ensure that the room is independent and quiet.

b. Romance: some romantic atmosphere can be appropriately added in the room, such as flower arrangement, free drinks, etc..

c. Applicable room types: queen bedroom, round bedroom.

④ Family guests.

Parent guests with children and guests traveling with families will prefer to live together, so we can recommend suites as much as possible.

If there are children or the elderly in the companions, it is necessary to recommend rooms according to their needs first, such as recommending parent-child rooms to children, recommending health care rooms to the elderly.

⑤ Special guests.

For social celebrities, it is necessary to arrange high-end independent suites with better privacy.

（三）介绍客房时，先价值、后价格

前厅工作人员面对客人时不要总是在价格上与之纠缠，因为价格对于顾客而言永远都是偏高的，他们总是觉得酒店多赚了他们的钱，关键是工作人员要让客人觉得物有所值甚至物超所值。

①先介绍客房的价值。

前厅工作人员在介绍客房时，必须要先对客房做适当的描述，以减弱客房价格的分量，突出客房能够满足客人需要的特点。

②后报客房的价格。

沟通时不能直接报价："客房的价格是××多少，您要不要？"这样非常不礼貌。而是应该在引起客人兴趣后再进行报价，如"有一间温馨浪漫、宽敞的房间"还有"一间舒适、安静、能看到西湖景色的客房""另外一间具有民族特色的、装修豪华的客房"，等等。直到客人表示对某个房间比较感兴趣，再介绍价格。如果客人不满意再推荐其他的产品。

（3）Introduce room value before price

The front office staff should not always be entangled in price when facing customers, because the price is always high for customers. They always feel that the hotel has made more money from them. The key is that the front office staff should let the customers think it's good value for money or even great value for money.

① First introduce the value of the guest room.

When introducing the guest room, the front office staff in the front hall must first describe the guest room properly to reduce the weighting of the guest room price and highlight the characteristics of the guest room that can meet the needs of the guest.

② Introduce the price of the room after.

When communicating with the guests, you cannot directly quote room rates, such as: "The price of this room is ××, would you like it?" This is very rude.

It should be quoted after attracting guests' interest, such as "a warm, romantic, and spacious room" and "a comfortable, quiet room with views of the West Lake" and "another guest room with ethnic characteristics and luxurious decoration" and so on. Until the guests express interest in a certain room, the front office staff would then introduce the price. If the customer is not satisfied, the staff then recommend other products.

（四）有效运用报价技巧

客户报价是酒店为扩大自身产品的销售，运用口头描述技艺，引起宾客的购买欲望，借以扩大销售的一种销售方法。其中包含推销技巧、语言艺术、职业道德等内容，在实际销售工作中，非常讲究报价的针对性，只有适时采取不同的报价方法，才能达到销售的最佳效果。掌握报价方法是做好销售工作的一项基本功，以下是酒店常见的几种报价技巧。

（4）Effective use of quotation techniques

Customer quotation is a sales method in which hotels use verbal description techniques to increase guest's interestin their products, thereby expanding sales. It includes sales skills, language arts, professional ethics, etc. In actual sales work, the specificity of quotation is very important. Only by adopting different quotation methods at the right time can the hotels achieve good sales results. Mastering the quotation method is a basic skill to do a good job in sales. The following are several common quotation techniques in hotels.

①高低趋向报价。

高低趋向报价是针对讲究身份、地位的客人而设计的，以期最大限度地提高客人消费客房的客单价。这种报价技巧是针对客人的情况先向其报出酒店的高价，让客人了解酒店所提供的高房价以及与其相配套的环境和设施，在发现客人对此不感兴趣时再转向销售较低价格的客房。销售人员要善于运用语言技巧说动客人，高价伴随的是精心打造享受，促使客人作出购买决策，需要注意的是报价应相对合理，不宜过高。

① High-low trend quotation.

The high-low trend quotation is designed for guests who pay attention to identity and status, in order to maximize the unit price of guest rooms. This kind of quotation technique is to introduce the high price of the hotel to the guest first, let the guest understand the high price provided by the hotel and the supporting environment and facilities, and then switch to selling lower prices when they find that the guest is not interested in it. Sales staff must be good at using language skills to persuade guests. High-priced houses are accompanied by carefully crafted enjoyment, prompting guests to make purchase decisions. It should be noted that the quotation should be relatively reasonable and should not be too high.

②低高趋向报价。

低高趋向报价是针对那些对价格敏感的客人设计的，既可以减小高价对客人的心理冲击，又符合从低到高的心理接受梯度，同时可以吸引那些对房间价格作过比较的客人，能够为酒店带来广阔的客源市场，有利于发挥酒店的竞争优势。

② Low-high trend quotation.

The low-high trend quotation is designed for those guests who are price-sensitive. It can not only reduce the psychological impact of high prices on guests but also conform to the gradient of psychological acceptance from low to high. At the same time, it can attract those guests who have compared room prices. It can bring a broad source market for hotels, which is conducive to giving play to the competitive advantage of the hotel.

③选择性报价。

选择性报价要求前台销售人员在辨别客人的支付能力基础上，客观地按照客人的兴趣和需要，选择提供适当房价的技巧，一般报价时推荐 2 种或 3 种不同价格的客房让客人自己选择。选择不宜超过 3 种，一方面体现报价的准确性，另一方面避免客人陷入选择困难症。如，"阳面、临街、便于会客的双人套房 350 元""高楼层、安静舒适的双人间 280 元""经济实惠的双人间 210 元"。这样由高到低的顺序报价，客人选择高价位客房的机会更大一些。

③ Selective quotation.

Using selective quotation requires the front desk salesperson to identify the guest's ability to pay, and objectively choose the skills to provide the appropriate price according to the guests' interests and needs. Generally, two or three different price rooms are recommended for guests to choose from when quoting. It is not advisable to choose more than three room types. On the one hand, it reflects the accuracy of the quotation, and on the other hand, it prevents customers from falling into choice difficulties. For example, "350 yuan for a double suite with a sunny side, facing the street, and convenient reception" "280 yuan for a higher-floor, quiet and comfortable double room" and "210 yuan for a budget double room". In this way, the order of quotation from high to low, guests have a greater chance of choosing high-priced rooms.

④利益引导。

利益引导是一种针对已预订客房的客人，采取给予一定附加利益，使他们放弃原预订客房，转向购买高一档次价格的客房的技巧。如"您只需要再多付 20 元，就可享受包价优惠，除房费外，还包括早餐和午餐。"这时客人通常会被眼前利益所吸引转而接受销售人员的建议，其结果是酒店增加了营业收入，同时客人也享受到了更多的实惠。

④ Benefit guidance.

Benefit guidance is a technique to give certain additional benefits to guests who have booked a room so that they abandon the original reservation and switch to booking a room with a higher price. For example, "You only need to pay another 20 yuan and you can enjoy the package price discount, which includes breakfast and lunch in addition to the room rate." At this time, guests are often attracted by immediate benefits and accept the salesperson's suggestions. As a result, the hotel has increased its operating income, and guests also enjoy more benefits.

⑤价格分解。

价格分解是为了降低高价客房对客人的心理冲击，将价格进行分解以隐藏其"昂贵性"的技巧。如，某类型客房的价格是580元，报价时可将80元双早和100元餐费从房价中分解出来，告诉宾客实际房价是400元；假如房费包括洗衣或健身等其他项目，同样应进行价格分解，这样客人心目中高价的压力也会被大大弱化。所以，采用价格分解，更易打动客人，促成交易。

⑤ Price decomposition.

Price decomposition is a technique to reduce the psychological impact of high-priced rooms on guests, and to decompose the price to hide its "expensiveness". For example, the price of a certain type of room is 580 yuan, and 80 yuan for double breakfast and 100 yuan for meals can be decomposed from the price when quoting, telling guests that the actual price is 400 yuan; if the room rate includes other items such as laundry or fitness, the same price decomposition should be carried out, in this way, the pressure of high prices in the minds of customers will also be greatly weakened. Therefore, using price decomposition makes it easier to impress guests and facilitate transactions.

二、客房销售方法

（一）FAB 利益销售法

FAB 利益销售法是销售人员向客人分析本酒店产品带给客人利益的方法。

F 是指属性或功效（Feature 或 Fact），即自己的产品有哪些特点和属性。例如，这间套房临湖，有独立阳台，既可以观赏湖景，也可以品茶聊天。

A 是指优点或优势（Advantage），即自己与竞争对手有何不同。例如，我们的酒店是智慧酒店，您办理入住之后，可以通过微信公众号、刷身份证、密码和人脸识别开门，彻底告别使用房卡的年代，省去找房卡的烦恼。

B 是指客户利益与价值（Benefit），这一优点所带给顾客的利益。例如，湖景套房还配有免费的鲜花、水果、红酒和洗衣服务，房间面积也很大，装修上档次、有品位。

FAB 的意思是在客房的推介中，将客房本身的特点、所具有的优势、能够给客人带来的利益有机地结合起来，按照一定的逻辑顺序加以阐述，形成完整而又完善的销售劝说。

Ⅱ Guest room sales method

（1）FAB benefit sales method

FAB benefit sales method is a method for sales staff to analyze the benefits of the hotel's products to the guests.

F refers to the attribute or function（Feature or Fact）, that is, what are the characteristics and attributes of your product. for example, this suite is facing the lake and has an independent balcony. You can enjoy the lake view or chat with tea.

A refers to the advantage or strong point（Advantage）, that is, the difference between our hotel and competitors. For example, our hotel is a smart hotel, after you checkin, you can open the door through WeChat official account, swipe your ID card, password and face recognition. Say goodbye to the era of using the room card, save the trouble of finding a room card.

B refers to the benefit and value brought to customers（benefit）, the benefit that this advantage brings to the customer. For example, the lake view suite is also equipped with free flowers, fruits, wine, and laundry services, the room is spacious, and the decoration is high-grade with good taste.

FAB means that in the promotion of guest rooms, effectively combine the characteristics of the guest room itself, its advantages, and the benefits that it can bring to guests, and explained in a certain logical sequence to form a complete and perfect sales persuasion.

（二）优惠销售法

优惠销售法是销售人员通过提供优惠的交易条件来实现客房销售的方法。它利用客人在购买产品时希望获得更大利益的心理，实行让利销售，促成交易。例如，"张总，我们酒店最近一段时间有一个促销活动，从即日起至 2021 年 5 月 31 日，IHG 优悦会会员以'春日早鸟优惠'预订，享实'标准价'的基础上再享受 88 折优惠。"

正确地使用优惠销售法，利用顾客的求利心理，可以吸引并招揽客人，有利于创造良好的销售氛围。该方法尤其适用于新会员的吸纳和老会员的复购率提升，也适用于淡季酒店客房的销售，减轻酒店的成本压力，加快客房的周转速度。

使用优惠销售法时要注意两个问题：

①把握好让利的尺度，避免销售成本上升导致销售收益大幅下降。

②保证服务水平不降低，避免让顾客误以为优惠产品是降低质量而不予信任，从而丧失购买的信心，使酒店声誉受损。

（2）Promotional sales method

The promotional sales method is a method for sales staff to achieve room sales by providing favorable trading conditions. It takes advantage of the customer's desire to obtain greater benefits when purchasing products, implement concessional sales and facilitate transactions. For example, "Mr. Zhang, our hotel has a promotion during this period. From now until May 31, 2021, IHG Rewards Club members will book with 'Spring Early Bird Discount' and enjoy a 12% discount off the real-time 'standard price' basis."

The correct use of promotional sales methods and the use of customers' profit-seeking psychology can attract customers, which is conducive to creating a good sales atmosphere. This method is especially suitable for attracting new members and increasing in the repurchase rate of old members. It is also suitable for the sale of hotel rooms in the off-season, reducing the pressure on hotel costs and speeding up the turnover of rooms.

There are two issues to be aware of when using promotional sales method:

① Grasp the scale of profit allocation, and avoid an increase of sales costs leading to a sharp drop in sales revenue.

② Ensure that the service level is not reduced, and avoid making customers mistakenly believe that the promotional product is lowering the quality and not trusting the hotel, thereby losing confidence in buying and damaging the hotel's reputation.

（三）消除异议销售法

前台销售人员在报价后，客人对酒店客房的价格与其他酒店同类产品比较时存在疑问，销售人员可以将酒店该房间的特点与其他同类酒店的客房进行比较，从而使客人了解到该酒店的优势，促使客人购买。比如有客人问，都是四星级酒店标间，为什么旁边的那家价格要便宜一些，而这家要贵一点。销售人员应实事求是地比较所在酒店客房的优势，如房间是智能酒店，超前的服务提高了服务效率，而旁边那家酒店是传统酒店，房间的设施跟不上市场的发展。

消除异议销售法需要前台人员了解并熟知自己所在的酒店和周边同类型酒店的优缺点，从而进行有针对性的介绍。

（3）Elimination of objection sales method

After the sales staff at the front desk makes a quote, the guests have doubts about the price of the hotel room compared to similar products in other hotels. The sales staff can compare the characteristics of the hotel room with other similar hotel rooms so that the guests can understand the advantages of the hotel and make a purchase. For example, the guests questioned that they are all four-star hotel standard rooms, why the price of the one next to it is cheaper, but this one is more expensive. Sales staff should compare the advantages of the hotel rooms realistically. Such as, the room is a in smart hotel, and the advanced service improves service efficiency, while the next hotel is a traditional hotel with room facilities that cannot keep up with the development of the market.

The elimination of objection sales method requires the front desk staff to understand and be familiar with the advantages and disadvantages of their hotel and surrounding hotels of the same type, in order to carry out targeted introduction.

任务二　客房价格管理

酒店客房定价是酒店经营管理的重中之重，进行科学的定价，及时灵活地调控，都有哪些规则及要点呢？

随着经济的快速发展，酒店的数量也在随之增长。在如今各种酒店都在谋求生存和发展的时代，每一个酒店都要加强自身的管理，才能够在竞争中占得一席之地。然而在酒店的管理中，成本管理又是非常重要的一部分。酒店是营利性质的企业，只有控制好成本，才能有所盈利。

Task 2　Room Price Management

Hotel room pricing is the top priority of hotel operation and management. What are the rules and key points for setting scientific prices and implementing timely, flexible price control?

With the rapid economic development, the number of hotels has also increased. Nowadays when all kinds of hotels are seeking survival and development, every hotel must strengthen its own management in order to gain a place in the competition. However, in hotel management, cost management is a very important part. Hotels are profit-driven enterprises, and they can only the costs by controlling be profitable.

一、客房成本费用的构成

在酒店客房中，成本费用是由很多部分共同构成的，主要是客人在入住客房过程中消耗的物资或是责任人所控制的消费，主要包括人工成本、能源成本、餐饮成本、物资成本等。这些都是酒店客房在营业过程中必不可少的。

所谓人工成本，是指酒店工作人员的工资、奖金以及出差费用等。在酒店这一类劳动密集型行业中，人工成本占非常大的比重，所以在人工成本方面也要进行适当的控制，进行一系列的核算，从而降低人工成本。

所谓能源成本，主要是指客人入住客房，客房需要提供给客人的能源所需成本。能源成本主要包括水电费用、供暖费用以及供气费用等。这些能源是客房中必不可少的，是必须提供的，约占总成本的10%。我国当今社会中能源紧缺、供不应求的情况时常出现，所以也必须加强对能源的控制，同时控制能源成本。

所谓餐饮成本，主要是指客人入住酒店在餐饮方面产生的成本费用。这部分费用在酒店的成本中所占比重也是相当大的。所以酒店要着重考虑如何控制餐饮成本从而提升经济效益。

所谓物资成本，主要是指酒店的固定资产，即家具和床等。这些固定资产在客人入住酒店的过程中会折旧，从而产生一部分费用。

I The composition of guest room costs

In a hotel room, the cost is composed of many parts, mainly the materials consumed by the guest during the stay in the room or the consumption controlled by the responsible person. It mainly includes labor costs, energy costs, catering costs, and material costs. These are indispensable in the business process of hotel rooms.

The so-called labor cost refers to the salaries, bonuses, and travel expenses of the hotel staff. In labor-intensive industries such as hotels, labor costs account for a very large proportion. Therefore, labor costs must be appropriately controlled and a series of calculations should be performed to reduce labor costs.

The so-called energy cost mainly refers to the cost of energy required for the guest's stay, which the hotel must provide. Energy costs mainly include water and electricity costs, heating costs, and gas supply costs. These energy sources are essential to the guest rooms and must be provided, accounting for about 10% of the total cost. In our society today, there is a shortage of energy and a situation where energy is often in short supply. Therefore, it is necessary to strengthen energy management and control energy costs at the same time.

The so-called catering cost mainly refers to the cost of catering associated with guests staying in the hotel. This part of the cost of the hotel's expenses is also a considerable proportion. Therefore, the hotel should focus on how to control the cost of catering to improve economic efficiency.

The so-called material cost mainly refers to the hotel's fixed assets, namely furniture, and beds. These fixed assets will be depreciated during the guest's stay in the hotel, resulting in a part of the cost.

二、客房定价的方法

（一）客房定价的基本原理

客房价格一般以供给价格为下限，以需求价格为上限，实际市场成交价格受市场竞争的影响在上限和下限间波动，特殊时期市场成交价格可能会低于产品成本价格，客房产品的价值决定供给价格，客人支付能力决定需求价格，市场竞争决定市场成交价格。

II Guest room pricing method

（1）Basic principles of room pricing

The room price is generally set with the supply price as the lower limit and the demand price as the upper limit. The actual market transaction price fluctuates between the upper limit and lower limit due to market competition. The market transaction price may be lower than the product cost price during the special period. The value of the hotel room determines the supply price, the ability of customers to pay determines the demand price, and market competition determines the market transaction price.

（二）客房定价的基本方法

①成本导向定价法

a. 建筑成本定价法（千分之一法）。

建筑成本定价法又称经验定价法，即以酒店总建造成本除以房间数再除以 1 000 作为每个房间的平均价格。

公式：房价 = 酒店建造成本 /（1 000 × 房间数）

例如，某酒店有 800 间客房，总投资为 18 000 万元人民币，那么每间客房的平均房租为 180 000 000/（1 000 × 800）=225 元。

建筑成本定价方法只考虑了客房的成本因素，而没有考虑会议与餐饮、娱乐等其他各种设施设备投资比例的差异以及供求关系、市场竞争等相关因素，因而缺乏科学性和合理性，只能作为客房定价的参考。

（2）The basic method of room pricing

① Cost-oriented pricing method.

a. Construction cost pricing method（one-per-thousandth method）

The construction cost pricing method is also known as the empirical pricing method, which means the total construction cost of the hotel is divided by the number of rooms, and then divided by 1, 000 as the average price of each room.

Formula: room price = hotel construction cost/（1, 000 × number of rooms）.

For example, a hotel has 800 rooms and a total investment of 180 million yuan, so the average rent per room=180, 000, 000/（1, 000 × 800）=225 yuan.

The construction cost pricing method only considers the cost of the guest room but does not consider the differences in the investment ratio of conferences, catering, entertainment, and other facilities and equipment, as well as supply and demand, market competition, and other related factors. Therefore, it lacks scientific basis and rationality and can only be used as a reference for room pricing.

b. 盈亏平衡定价法（保本点定价）。

盈亏平衡定价法是指在既定的固定成本、变动成本和预计客房销售的条件下，实现销售收入与成本相等时的房价，也就是收支平衡时的客房价格，是一种侧重于保本经营的、在市场不景气时采用的定价方法。

公式：保本点房价 = 全年固定成本总额 / 全年销售客房数 + 单位变动成本。

例如，某酒店有客房 400 间，每间客房分摊固定成本为 150 元，单位变动成本为 40 元，酒店年平均出租率为 70%，那么盈亏平衡点房价 =（400×150+400×70%×40）/400×70%+40=294 元，则高于 294 元的房价方可以盈利。

保本点定价缺点：客房销售数量难以控制，只有达到或超过预期销售量才能取得利润。

b. Break-even pricing method（pricing at the breakeven point）.

The break-even pricing method refers to under the conditions of established fixed costs, variable costs, and expected room sales, the room where sales revenue and cost are equal is the room price at the time of break-even. It is a pricing method that focuses on break-even operations and is used in weak market conditions.

Formula: break-even price = total annual fixed cost / annual number of rooms sold + unit variable cost

For example, if a hotel has 400 rooms, each room has a fixed cost of 150 yuan, a unit variable cost of 40 yuan, and the average annual occupancy rate of the hotel is 70%. Then the breakeven point price =（400×150+400×70%×40）/400×70%+40=294 yuan, a price higher than 294 yuan can be profitable.

Disadvantages of break-even pricing: the number of rooms sold is difficult to control, and profits can only be made when the expected sales volume is met or exceeded.

c. 目标收益定价法（赫伯特公式法）。

目标收益定价法是指以目标投资回收率为定价出发点，在客房成本计算的基础上，在保证实现目标利润的前提下，根据计划的销售量、固定费用和需达到的合理的投资率来决定客房的平均价格。

公式：产品单位售价 =（总成本 + 目标利润）/ 预期销量。

年客房预计销售额 = 酒店总投资额 × 目标投资回收率 + 企业管理费 + 客房经营费用 – 客房以外其他部门经营利润。

公式：计划平均房价 = 年客房预计销售额 /（可供出租客房数 × 预计出租率 × 年天数）。

例如，某酒店有客房 120 间，全年营业费用为 268 万元，税收和保险费为 356 400元，折旧费为 1 484 000 元，合理投资收益额为 2 158 000 元，客房以外其他部门的经营利润为 96 万元，预计年均出租率为 70%。那么年客房预计销售额 =2 158 000+2 680 000+356 400+1 484 000−960 000=5 718 400 元

平均房价 =5 718 400/（120 × 70% × 365）=186.5 元。

c. Target income pricing method（Herbert formula method）.

The target income pricing method refers to the starting point of pricing is based on the target investment recovery rate, based on the calculation of the room cost, and on the premise of ensuring the realization of the target profit. The average price of the room is determined according to the planned sales volume, fixed expenses and reasonable investment rate to be achieved.

Formula: product unit selling price =（total cost + target profit）/expected sales.

Estimated annual guest room sales = total hotel investment × target return on investment + corporate management fee + guest room operating expenses-operating profit of other departments other than guest rooms

Formula: Planned average price = estimated annual rooms sales /（number of rooms available for rent × estimated occupancy rate × number of days per year）.

For example, a hotel has 120 guest rooms, annual operating expenses of 2.68 million yuan, tax and insurance fees of 356,400 yuan, depreciation fees of 1,484,000 yuan, reasonable investment income of 2,158,000 yuan, and operating profits of other departments other than guest rooms are 960,000 yuan. It is estimated that the average annual occupancy rate is 70%. Then the estimated annual sales of guest rooms = 2,158,000+2,680,000+356,400+1,484,000−960,000=5,718,400 yuan.

Average room price=5,718,400/（120 × 70% × 365）=186.5 yuan.

②需求导向定价法

a. 直觉评定法。

直觉评定法是指在分析酒店产品与竞争对手产品的基础上，根据自身的产品特色和可能的服务水平等邀请客人或中间商评价直觉评定价格。

b. 相对评分法。

相对评分法是指通过对周边类似酒店的产品价格进行调查，对不同等级酒店产品进行测评和评分，以获得的分值权重对目标产品进行产品类别的差级定价。

c. 特征法。

特征法要求酒店决策者选取周边不同等级的酒店，请消费者对其产品的可感知度、可靠性、保证性和移情性等特征进行评分，例如，针对酒店产品的服务设施、服务质量、服务效率、地理位置、酒店安全、情感满足等逐一作出评价和评分，求取每个特征的权重，以市场平均价格为基础，乘以每个特征权重，得出酒店的价格。

② Demand-oriented pricing method.

a. Intuitive evaluation method.

The intuitive evaluation method is based on the analysis of hotel products and competitors' products, and guests or intermediaries are invited to evaluate the prices intuitively based on their product features and possible service levels.

b.Relative scoring method.

The relative scoring method is based on through the product price survey of similar hotels in the surrounding area, the hotel products of different grades are evaluated and scored, and the score weights obtained are used to price the target product within its category.

c.Feature method.

The feature method requires hotel decision-makers to select hotels of different levels in the surrounding area, and ask consumers to rate their products and characteristics such as perception, reliability, assurance, and empathy. For example, consumers evaluate and rate hotel products one by one, such as service facilities, service quality, service efficiency, geographic location, hotel safety, emotional satisfaction, etc. and the weight of each feature is calculated. Based on the average market price, the hotel price is multiplied by the weight value of each feature.

③竞争导向定价法

a. 随行就市法。

随行就市法是指以同一地区、同档次竞争对手的客房价格作为定价依据，从而确定酒店的客房价格。

·以同等级别酒店的平均水平作为定价依据。

·追随"领导型酒店"的价格，以减少风险。

以上的定价方法只是基于数学模型和营销理论，还有诸多因素影响客房价格。

b. 主动定价法。

与随行就市定价法相反，主动定价法不是追随竞争者的价格，而是根据酒店客房的实际情况及与竞争对手的客房差异状况来确定价格。定价时首先将市场上竞争对手价格与本酒店估算价格进行比较，分为高、一致及低3个价格层次。其次，将酒店客房的房型、装修、成本、式样等与竞争酒店进行比较，分析造成价格差异的原因。再次，根据以上综合指标确定酒店客房的特色、优势及市场定位，在此基础上，按定价所要达到的目标，确定酒店客房价格。最后，跟踪竞争酒店的价格变化，及时分析原因，相应调整本酒店的价格。

③ Competition-oriented pricing

a. Market-based pricing method.

The market-based pricing method refers to determining the hotel room price based on the room prices of competitors in the same area and at the same level as the pricing basis.

· Take the average room rates of similar hotels as the pricing.

· Follow the prices of "leading hotels" to reduce risks.

The above pricing methods are primarily based on mathematical models and marketing theories, but there are many other factors affect the price of rooms.

b. Active pricing method.

Contrary to the market-based pricing method, the active pricing method does not follow competitors' pricing but determines the price based on the actual situation of the hotel rooms and the difference between the rooms of the hotel and competitors. When setting the price, first compare the prices of competitors in the market with the estimated prices of this hotel, and divide them into three price levels: high, consistent, and low. Secondly, compare the room type, decoration, cost, style, etc. of hotel rooms with competing hotels, and analyze the reasons for the price difference. Third, determine the characteristics, advantages, and market positioning of hotel rooms based on the above comprehensive indicators. On this basis, the hotel room price is determined according to the target to be achieved by the pricing. Finally, monitor the price changes of competing hotels, analyze the reasons promptly, and adjust the hotel's price accordingly.

任务三 信息管理

【学习目标】

①了解什么是信息。

②掌握酒店信息的特点。

③熟悉国内外酒店管理系统。

④熟悉目前酒店常用的 opera 系统的功能。

Task 3 Information Management

【Learning Objectives】

① Know what is information.

② Master the characteristics of hotel information.

③ Be familiar with hotel management systems at home and abroad.

④ Be familiar with the functions of the "opera" system commonly used in hotels.

【案例导入】

喜达屋集团早在 2014 年就开始尝试数据的运用，时任喜达屋集团大中华区总裁钱进曾经表示"喜达屋一直都非常注重数据，集团很多的决定都是以数据作为决策的出发点。喜达屋集团对 SPG 会员俱乐部中重要的会员、客人的数据一直保持持续关注，他们的需求、他们的目的地、他们在入住酒店之后要求我们提供的服务，我们很多的想法和做法都是由此而来。在全球、亚太区、中国区，喜达屋都建立了数据库。酒店是服务性行业，顾客的消费行为和方式的数据对酒店的重要性可见一斑"。

大数据的真正价值不在于它的大，而在于它的全面，全面的大数据是由众多小数据积累起来的，酒店行业从小数据做起，是酒店行业大数据从 0 到 1 的最佳破茧方案，现在绝大多数采用 PMS 处理酒店业务，只要酒店开门经营，数据就无处不在。

【Case Introduction】

Starwood Group began experimenting with the use of data as early as 2014. At the time, Starwood Group Greater China President Qian Jin once said, "Starwood has always paid great attention to data. Many decisions of the group are based on data as the starting point for decision-making. Starwood Group has been consistently monitoring to the data of important members and guests in the SPG membership club. This includes their needs, their destinations, and the services they require us to provide after staying in the hotel. Many of our ideas and practices have come from these. Starwood has established databases in the world, Asia Pacific, and China. The hotel industry is a service industry, and the importance of customer consumption behavior and data to the hotel can be seen".

The real value of big data lies not in its size, but its comprehensiveness. Comprehensive big data is accumulated by a lot of small data points. The hotel industry starts with small data, which is the best solution for big data in the hotel industry from 0 to 1. Now, most hotels use PMS to handle hotel business. As soon as hotels open, data is everywhere.

【思考题】

①什么是数据？什么是信息？

②酒店信息有哪些特点？

③什么是 PMS？目前酒店行业常用的 PMS 有哪些？

【Questions】

① What is data? What is information?

② What are the characteristics of hotel information?

③ What is PMS? What are the PMSs commonly used in the hotel industry?

任务四 酒店信息系统

随着移动互联网技术的进步，中国越来越多的酒店通过使用信息技术来提高自身的管理水平。传统酒店管理与现代信息技术相结合，对酒店做大、做强、管理规范化起到至关重要的作用。同时在信息化的帮助下，酒店行业洗牌加速，单体的单打独斗将日益走衰，集团化与品牌化成为未来的发展趋势。

Task 4 Hotel Information System

With the advancement of mobile internet technology, more and more hotels in China are using information technology to improve their management level. The combination of traditional hotel management and modern information technology plays a vital role in making the hotel bigger, stronger, and more standardized. At the same time, with the help of information technology, the hotel industry has accelerated its transformation, and individual operations will gradually decline, with hotel grouping and branding becoming the future development trend.

一、酒店管理系统概述

（一）信息的含义

数据就是人们通过观察、实验或计算得出的结果，包括数字、文字、图像、声音等。信息就是处理过的某种形式的数据，对信息接收者来说，信息在当前或未来的行动和决策中具有实际的或可参考的价值。在信息时代背景下，通过海量数据的产生、获取、挖掘及整合，逐步实现酒店业务数据、会员收集、非客房服务信息的统一。展现出巨大的商业价值的加工数据后的信息为酒店业态带来的无限可能，信息作为一项宝贵的资源在酒店运营管理中至关重要。

Ⅰ Overview of hotel management system

（1）The meaning of information

Data is the result obtained by people through observation, experiment or calculation including numbers, text, images, sounds, etc. Information is a certain form of processed data. For the information receiver, information has actual or reference value in current or future actions and decisions. In the context of the information age, through the generation, acquisition, mining, and integration of massive data, hotels can gradually realize the unification of hotel business data, member collection, and non-room service information. The information after processing that exhibits huge commercial value brings infinite possibilities for the hotel industry. As a valuable resource, information is crucial in hotel operation and management.

（二）酒店信息的特点

①酒店信息的广泛性。

酒店信息包含的范围极其广泛，既包括酒店内部（如酒店各个部门）的信息，又包括酒店外部（如客户）的信息；既包括酒店经营（如酒店）的信息，又包括酒店员工的信息。内容包罗万象，信息量也非常充沛。

②酒店信息的时效性。

酒店是信息变化极快的场所，随着时间的推移，酒店信息的价值将减少或消失。因此信息的收集、传递和处理要迅速、及时，只有及时地为酒店决策者提供有用的信息，才能提高信息的价值。

③酒店信息的价值性。

酒店管理人员通过大数据管理平台，可收集酒店入住数据、营销数据。在此基础上，对所有数据进行整合分析，从而得到未来营销的预测信息，精准营销，进而满足客人个性化需求，提高客服务的质量；通过酒店内各类信息的感知、及时传送和数据的挖掘分析，帮助酒店达成开源、节流、增效的目的。

④酒店信息的安全性。

在酒店的数据库中有相当翔实的个人信息，比如顾客的姓名、手机号码、身份证、护照、信用卡等。酒店集团掌握的数据库非常庞大，一旦被破解不但会给消费者带来极大的安全隐患，而且还会使酒店陷入极大的信用危机和可能面临的高额经济处罚，所以酒店应该重视信息安全，加强信息安全的投入和维护。

（2）Features of hotel information

① Extensiveness of hotel information.

The range of hotel information is extremely wide, including both information inside the hotel（such as the various departments of the hotel）and information outside the hotel（such as customers）; it includes the information of both hotel operations（such as the hotel）and hotel employees. information. The content covers everything, and the amount of information is also very abundant.

② Timeliness of hotel information.

Hotels are places where information changes extremely fast. As time goes by, the value of hotel information will decrease or disappear. Therefore, the collection, transmission, and processing of information must be rapid and timely. Only by providing useful information to hotel decision-makers promptly can the value of information be increased.

③ Value of hotel information.

Hotel managers can collect hotel occupancy data and marketing data through the big data management platform. On this basis, all data is integrated and analyzed, so as to generate forecasts for future marketing and precise marketing, to meet the personalized needs of guests and improve the quality of customer service; through the perception, timely transmission, data digging, and analysis of all kinds of information in the hotel, help the hotel achieve the purpose of increasing revenue, reducing expenditure and increasing efficiency.

④ Security of hotel information.

There is quite detailed personal information in the hotel's database, such as the customer's name, mobile phone number, ID card, passport, credit card, etc. The database held by the hotel group is very large. Once it is cracked, it will not only bring great security risks to consumers but also cause the hotel to fall into a great credit crisis and may face high financial penalties, so hotels should pay attention to information security, strengthen the investment and maintenance of information security.

二、酒店管理系统

管理信息系统是信息科学的一个分支，是由人和计算机组成的能进行信息的收集、传递、储存、加工、维护和使用的系统。

酒店管理系统是指一种可以提高酒店管理效率的软件或平台，一般包含前台接待、前台收银、客房管家、销售 POS、餐饮管理、娱乐管理、公关销售、财务查询、电话计费、系统维护、经理查询、工程维修等功能模块。

酒店管理软件是指专为酒店（宾馆）提供管理服务的软件系统（Property Management System，PMS），由于酒店前台是酒店业最早实现信息化的部分，所以 PMS 也特指酒店的前台操作系统。

II Hotel management system

The management information system is a branch of information science. It is a system composed of people and computers that can collect, transmit, store, process, maintain, and use information.

A hotel management system refers to a software or platform that can improve the efficiency of hotel management. It generally includes receptionist, cashier, housekeeper, sales POS, catering management, entertainment management, public relations, financial inquiry, telephone billing, system maintenance, manager query, engineering maintenance and other functional modules.

Hotel management software refers to a software system (Property Management System, PMS) that provides management services for hotels (guesthouses). Since the hotel front desk is the first part of the hotel industry to undergo digitalization, PMS also specifically refers to the hotel front desk operating system.

（一）国外 PMS 系统

① EECO 酒店信息系统。

酒店信息系统是美国电子工程公司（Electronic Engineering CO.）于 1969 年开发的。1970 年，在美国夏威夷 WAIKIKI 的 SHERATON HOTEL 装设了全世界第一台 EECO 酒店电脑系统。20 世纪 90 年代在全世界有 600 多家用户，目前已被淘汰。

② HIS 酒店信息系统。

美国酒店业资讯系统有限公司（Hotel Information Systems）于 1977 年成立，全盛期在全世界 80 多个国家拥有 4 000 多家用户，如中国的北京中国大酒店、北京长城饭店、上海锦江饭店等，而香港采用 HIS 系统的高星级酒店最多时占了 75% 左右，目前该系统许多已被更换。

③ Fidelio 酒店信息系统。

1987 年 10 月，Fidelio Software Gmbh 在德国慕尼黑成立。成立四年就成为欧洲领先的酒店软件产品，成立六年跃居世界酒店信息系统供应商之首，后来该公司合并入美国 Micros System Inc.。目前已经在全球 16 000 余家酒店、豪华游艇和休闲别墅使用，在国内四星级以上市场占有 40% 左右的市场份额；在五星级酒店市场，占有超过 70% 的市场份额，而且是目前外资或外方管理的酒店采用最多的软件。1995 年，公司在香港成立了 FidelioSoftware（China）Limited，专门开发中国大陆地区业务。1996 年 8 月在北京注册了办事处，1997 年 7 月在上海成立办事处，1998 年 12 月成立上海分公司。

④ OPERA。

OPERA 系统是美国 Micros 公司在 Micros-Fidelio 系统的基础上开发的新版本，作为企业级软件解决方案包含了 OPERA 前台管理系统（OPERA PMS）、OPERA 销售宴会系统（OPERA S&C）、OPERA 物业业主管理系统（OVOS）、OPERA 工程管理系统，以及 OPERA 中央预订系统、OPERA 中央客户信息管理系统和 OPERA 收益管理系统等，其中 OPERA 前台管理系统是核心部分，简称 OPERA PMS，它可以根据不同酒店之间运营的需求多样性，合理地设置系统以贴合酒店的实际运作 . 并且除单体酒店模式外，还提供多酒店模式，通过一个共享的数据库，为多个酒店进行数据存取甚至相互访问。

除了针对酒店集团和高星级酒店的 OPERA，Micros 公司还开发了精简版 OPERA EXPRESS，缩减了一些高端功能以适合小规模的商业运营，节约使用成本。

（1）Foreign PMS system

① EECO Hotel Information System.

The hotel information system developed by Electronic Engineering CO. in 1969. In 1970, the world's first EECO hotel computer system was installed in SHERATON HOTEL in waikiki, Hawaii, USA. There were more than 600 users all over the world in the 1990s, and they have now been phased out.

② HIS Hotel Information System.

Hotel Information Systems Inc（Hotel Information Systems）was established in 1977. During its heyday, it had more than 4,000 users in more than 80 countries around the world, such as China World Hotel Beijing, Great Wall Hotel Beijing, Shanghai Jinjiang Hotel, etc. The hotels with high-star rating in Hong Kong that use the HIS system account for about 75%. At present, many of the systems have been replaced.

③ Fidelio Hotel Information System.

In October 1987, Fidelio Software Gmbh was established in Munich, Germany. It became Europe's leading hotel software product in its four years of establishment and ranked first among the world's hotel information system suppliers in its six years of establishment. Later, the company was acquired by Micros Systems Inc. of the United States. At present, it has been used in more than 16,000 hotels, luxury yachts, and leisure villas around the world, and has a market share of about 40% in the domestic four-star and above market; in the five-star hotel market, it has a market share of more than 70%, and it is currently the most widely used software in hotels managed or owned by foreign companies. In 1995, the company established FidelioSoftware（China）Limited in Hong Kong to develop business in Mainland China. The company registered an office in Beijing in August 1996, established an office in Shanghai in July 1997, and established a Shanghai branch in December 1998.

④ OPERA.

OPERA system is a new version developed by the American company Micros Systems based on MICROS-Fidelio system. As an enterprise-level software solution, it includes OPERA Front Office Management System（OPERA PMS）, OPERA Sales & Catering（OPERA S&C）, OPERA Property Owner Management System（OVOS）, OPERA Engineering Management System, OPERA Central Reservation System, OPERA Central Customer Information Management System and OPERA Revenue Management System, etc. Among them, the OPERA front desk management system is its core part, referred to as OPERAPMS. It can set up the system reasonably to fit the actual operation of the hotel according to the diversity of operating needs between different hotels. In addition to the single hotel model, it also provides a multi-hotel model. Through a shared database, data access, multiple hotels can access data and share information with each other.

In addition to OPERA for hotel groups and hotels with high stars, Micros has also developed a simplified version of OPERA EXPRESS, which has reduced some high-end functions to suit small-scale commercial operations and save usage costs.

（二）国内主要的 PMS 系统

①西湖软件。

西湖软件始于1988年，连续多年被中国软件行业协会评定为"中国优秀软件产品"，通过国家信息安全评测认证中心认证，被列为国家级火炬计划项目。2006年被石基公司合并，在国内四、五星级酒店市场的占有率超过80%，稳居国内市场占有率第一。作为 Opera 在中国的唯一代理商，可以说一定程度上石基垄断着中国高星级酒店的酒店管理系统。2020年，石基西软践行"云＋移动"战略，全面升级云 XMS 平台，除 PMS 功能以外，云 XMS 还集成了 POS、移动产品、ITF 等模块，广泛适用于单店、集团用户。

②金天鹅。

2003年成立的高科技软件企业金天鹅始终坚持专注酒店管理软件，"北有西软，南有天鹅"。18年的行业积淀，国内首倡的"7×24"小时售后服务体系，功能齐全、操作简单的 PMS 系统，为金天鹅积累了10万＋酒店投资人的口碑。2020年，金天鹅整合 PMS 系统到云平台，自主开发核心产品——2号店长，打造酒店商业数据化服务解决方案，涵盖 IT、供应链和运营三大板块，彻底解决酒店降本增收的难题。

③中软好泰。

中软好泰是携程集团旗下全资子公司，针对不同类型酒店精心打造的 PMS 系列产品，专业版、企业版、国际版的系统划分满足国内外不同类型酒店管理所需，包括传统 C/S 架构产品及基于云技术的慧云酒店管理系统，目前正在为全世界数千家酒店提供管理支持。

④绿云。

绿云创建于2010年7月，是国内专业致力于酒店业信息化平台研发、服务和运行的高科技企业。主要基于云计算技术和 B/S 架构自主研发、运营的 iHotel 酒店信息化平台，已经形成绿云 PMS、Oracle Hospitality（Opera PMS）、数据平台、电商平台四大业务集群，以客史及会员数据为依托，用大数据技术重构线上线下一体化的酒店营销体系。

⑤罗盘。

北京万维罗盘信息技术有限公司成立于2006年，是亚洲领先的基于云计算的酒店系统解决方案提供商。支持48小时断网操作，这个功能可以秒杀一众同行，成功实现了酒管系统—中央预订系统—酒店网站的对接。使用系统时不需要购置服务器、硬件、软件，系统支持永久在线升级，节省系统升级和系统维护人员的成本。

酒店 PMS 在不断变化，根据技术、产品、服务、用户口碑等因素综合形成的 2020 年酒店管理系统的 TOP10，见下表。

2020 年酒店管理系统的 TOP10

排名	品牌名称	品牌指数
1	西湖软件	85.41
2	金天鹅	81.84
3	中软好泰	76.18
4	众芸	73.78
5	绿云	72.69
6	别样红	71.95
7	罗盘	68.29
8	住哲	67.93
9	简单点	65.89
10	云掌柜	53.27

（2）Main domestic PMS system

① West Lake Software.

The west lake software was established in 1988, it has been recognized as "China Excellent Software Product" by the China Software Industry Association for many consecutive years, passed the certification of the National Information Security Evaluation and Certification Center, and is listed as a national torch plan project. In 2006, it was acquired by Shiji Company, with a market share of more than 80% in the domestic four-and five-star hotel market, ranking first in the domestic market. As the sole agent of Opera in China, it can be said that Shiji monopolizes the hotel management system of China's top-tier hotels to a certain extent. In 2020, Shiji Westsoft implemented the "cloud + mobile" strategy and fully upgrade the cloud XMS platform. In addition to the PMS function, the cloud XMS also integrates modules such as POS, mobile products, and ITF, which is widely applicable to single-store and group users.

② Golden Swan.

Golden Swan, a high-tech software company established in 2003, has always insisted on focusing on hotel management software, "Westsoft in the north and Swan in the south".

With 18 years of industry accumulation, the company first advocated the "7×24" hour after-sales service system in China, and the PMS system with complete functions and simple operation has earned the trust of 100,000 hotel investors for Golden Swan. In 2020, Golden Swan integrated the PMS system into the cloud platform, independently developd the core product-the No. 2 store manager, and created a hotel business data service solution, covering the three major sections of IT, supply chain, and operation, and completely helped hotels reduce costs and increase revenue.

③ CSHOTEL.

CSHOTEL is a wholly-owned subsidiary of Ctrip Group. It has wisely developed PMS series products for different types of hotels. The system is divied into professional version, enterprise version, and international version which meets the management needs of different types of hotels at home and abroad, including traditional C/S architecture products and cloud-based Huiyun hotel management system. It is currently providing management support for thousands of hotels around the world.

④ Green Cloud.

Green Cloud was established in July 2010, which is a domestic high-tech enterprise dedicated to the research & development, service & operation of the hotel industry information platform. The iHotel hotel information platform, which is mainly based on cloud computing technology and B/S architecture, is independently developed and operated. It has formed four business clusters: Green Cloud PMS, Oracle Hospitality (Opera PMS) , data platform, and e-commerce platform. Relying on customer history and member data, the platform uses big data technology to reconstruct an integrated online and offline hotel marketing system.

⑤ Luopan.

Beijing Wanwei Luopan Information Technology Co., Ltd. was established in 2006 and is Asia's leading cloud computing-based hotel system solution provider. It supports 48 hours of disconnection operation, which gives it a competitive advantage over peers. It also successfully realized the docking of the management system-the central reservation system-the hotel website. There is no need to purchase servers, hardware, and software when using the system. The system supports permanent online upgrades, saving the cost of system upgrades and maintenance personnel.

Hotel PMS is constantly changing. According to factors such as technology, products, services, user reputation, the TOP10 hotel management system in 2020 is formed. See the table below.

Top 10 hotel management systems in 2020

Rank	Brand Name	Brand Index
1	West Lake Software	85.41
2	Golden Swan	81.84
3	CSHOTEL	76.18
4	Joint Wisdom	73.78
5	Green Cloud	72.69
6	BeyondHost	71.95
7	Luopan	68.29
8	Zhuzher	67.93
9	Jiandandian	65.89
10	Yunzhanggui	53.27

（三）酒店管理 OPERA PMS 的功能介绍

对于单个酒店的运营数据分析来说，PMS 是最主要的数据来源，因为产品、服务和客户的数据全部都在 PMS 当中，可以满足管理者多方位的数据分析需求。当然现在大的酒店有更多的信息化系统，可以作为数据分析的基本来源，比如实时预订系统、网上采购库管系统、酒店收益管理系统、客户关系管理系统、异地虚拟办公系统以及远程教育培训系统等。

OPERA 是美国 Micros 公司针对一系列接待业服务形态开发的软件集合，其中 Opera PMS 是其核心部分，Opera PMS 是目前国际上通用的酒店前台操作系统。它能满足不同规模酒店以及酒店集团的需求，为酒店管理层和员工提供全方位系统工具，以便其快捷、高效地处理客户资料、顾客预订、入住退房、客房分配、房内设施管理以及账户账单管理等日常工作。

（3）Hotel management OPERA PMS function introduction

For the operations data analysis of a single hotel, PMS is the most important data source, because the data for products, services and customers are all in the PMS, which can meet the multi-faceted data analysis needs of managers. Of course, large hotels now have more information systems that can be used as the basic source of data analysis, such as real-time reservation systems, online procurement, and warehouse management systems, hotel revenue management systems, customer relationship management systems, remote virtual office systems, and distance education training systems, etc.

OPERA is a software collection developed by American Micros company for various hospitality services, among which Opera PMS is its core part, and Opera PMS is currently the most widely used hotel front desk operating system in the world. It can meet the needs of hotels of different sizes and hotel groups, and provide hotel management and employees with a full range of system tools to quickly and efficiently handle daily tasks such as customer data, customer reservations, check-in and check-out, room allocation, room facilities management, and account and bill management.

OPERA PMS 系统的主要功能。

①客户资料管理。OPERA PMS 提供客户资料记录功能，全面记录统计包括个人客户、公司、联系人、旅行社、团队、预订源以及零售商等各方面的资料，这些资料是整个 OPERA PMS 工作的基础。可以帮助酒店改善服务质量，提供个性化服务；帮助酒店分析客源市场及利润来源并制订具有竞争力的市场营销策略。

②客房预订功能。OPERA PMS 提供了强大的预订功能，可以进行建立、查询、更新客人预订和团队订房等操作，并提供了确认订房、等候名单、房间分配、押金收取、房间共享、团队客房控制以及批房预留等功能。该功能可以帮助酒店简单快速地制订团队计划；实时监控可用房数并进行房价管理；自动控制预订以达到最佳出租率。

③前台服务功能。前台服务功能是整个酒店运作的焦点，主要用于为预抵店者和住店客人提供服务。该模块功能极其强大，可以处理个人客户、公司、旅行社以及无预订客户的入住服务，还设有房间分配、客户留言、叫醒服务以及部门间内部沟通跟进服务等功能。其应用大大缩短了办理入住的时间，使客人的满意度得到提高，同时便捷的操作也使前台员工感到满意。

④收银服务功能。OPERA PMS 的收银服务功能包括客人账单录入、转账分账、押金管理、费用结算、退房及账单打印等功能。该功能简单、易懂、高效，可以减少账目错误，保证交易安全。

⑤房间管理功能。OPERA PMS 的房间管理功能，能宏观掌握房态的整体情况，有效监督实时房态信息，包括可用房、脏房、住客房、维修房等，这些信息将帮助酒店把房态冲突的可能性降到最低，有效地提高出租率和收入，同时可以有效地安排客房的清洁工作。

此外，OPERA PMS 系统还包括应收账款、佣金管理、报表、后台接口、功能设置等功能。

The main functions of the OPERA PMS system。

① Customer data management. OPERA PMS provides customer data recording function, comprehensively records and provides statistics on individual customers, companies, contacts, travel agencies, groups, sources of bookings and retailers. These data categories form the foundation of Opera PMS operations. It can help hotels improve service quality and provide personalized services; help hotels analyze customer source markets and profit sources and formulate competitive marketing strategies.

② Room reservation function. OPERA PMS provides powerful reservation functions, which can create, inquire, update guest reservations and team reservations, as well as provide confirmation of reservations, waiting lists, room allocation, deposit collection, room sharing, group room control, and batch room reservations, and so on. This function can help hotels make team plans simply and quickly; monitor the number of available rooms in real-time and manage room rates; automatically control reservations to achieve the best rental rate.

③ Front desk service function. The front desk service function is the focus of the entire hotel's operation, mainly used to provide services for pre-arrivals and in-house guests. This module is extremely powerful and can handle check-in services for individuals, companies, travel agencies, and walk-in customers. It also has functions such as room allocation, customer messages, wake-up services, and internal communication and follow-up services between departments. Its application greatly shortens the check-in time, improves guest satisfaction, and at the same time, the convenient operation also makes the front desk staff satisfied.

④ Cashier service function. OPERA PMS's cash register service functions include guest bill entry, transfer account, deposit management, fee settlement, check-out, and bill printing functions. This function is simple, easy to understand, and efficient, which can reduce accounting errors and ensure transaction security.

⑤ Room management function. The room management function in OPERA PMS can offer an overall view of the room, and effectively supervise the real-time room status information, including available rooms, dirty rooms, guest rooms, maintenance rooms, etc. This information will help the hotel minimize the possibility of room conflicts, effectively increase the occupancy rate and income, and arrange the cleaning of guest rooms.

In addition, the OPERA PMS system also includes functions such as accounts receivable, commission management, reports, backstage interfaces, and function settings.

项目三
客史档案管理

【学习目标】

①了解什么是客史档案。

②理解建立客史档案的作用。

③掌握客史档案的内容和建立方法。

④能运用 OPERA 系统建立客户档案。

Project 3
Guest History Records Management

【Learning Objectives】

① Understand what is guest history records.

② Understand the role of establishing guest history records.

③ Master the content and establishment methods of guest history records.

④ Be able to use OPERA system to create customer records.

【案例导入】

一位企业经营者在日本东京投宿某家酒店，由于他习惯使用某一特定品牌的洗发液，于是就请求总台为他更换浴室里洗发液的品牌，这一要求迅速被得到满足。

一个偶然的机会，这位客人到大阪出差。由于上次的体验，他习惯性地来到那家酒店在大阪的连锁酒店住宿。令他惊奇的是，当他来到房间时发现浴室里的洗发液正是上次他要求更换的品牌。这使他由衷地产生一种受尊敬的感激之情。从此以后，他每到外地，首选的住宿酒店就是该酒店的连锁店。

原来，这家酒店将每位曾经住宿过的客人的资料都用计算机存档，把客人的每一个小小要求都记录在客史档案中，并传输给连锁酒店。通过这种方式，这家酒店集团成功地吸引了大批稳定的客源。

【Case Introduction】

A businessman stayed in a hotel in Tokyo, Japan. Because he was accustomed to using a certain brand of shampoo, he asked the front desk to change the brand of shampoo in the bathroom. This request was quickly met.

By chance, this guest went to Osaka on a business trip. Because of his last experience, he habitually came to stay in the chain store of that hotel in Osaka. To his surprise, when he came to the room, he found that the shampoo in the bathroom was the same brand he asked for last time. This made him feel a sincere sense gratitude. From then on, whenever he went to other places, his preferred hotel choice was a branch store of that hotel.

It turns out that this hotel records the information of every guest who has stayed on the computer records every small request of the guest in the guest history record and transmits it to the chain hotel. In this way, the hotel group succeeded in attracting a large number of stable customers.

【思考题】

①什么是客史档案？建立客史档案对酒店有什么作用？

②客史档案包括哪些内容？

【Questions】

① What is the guest history records? What does the guest history do for hotels?

② What content does the guest history records include?

客史档案（Guest History Records）又称为宾客档案，是酒店在对客服务过程中对客人的自然情况、消费行为、信用状况、癖好和期望等做的记录。建立客史档案是现代酒店宾客关系管理的重要一环。

Guest history records, also known as guest record, is a record of the situation, consumption behavior, credit status, hobbies and expectations of the hotel in the process of serving guests. Establishing guest history record is an important part of guest relationship management in modern hotels.

一、建立客史档案的作用

建立客史档案能够使酒店更准确地了解客源结构及客人的需求特点，从而为客人提供有针对性的服务，增强顾客的满意度。建立客史档案对提高酒店服务质量，改善酒店经营管理水平具有重要作用，对于那些力图搞好市场营销，努力使工作卓有成效，并千方百计使自己的一切活动都针对每个客人个性的酒店经理和工作人员来说，客史档案是一个重要的工具。

（一）有利于酒店把握需求趋势推陈出新

通过客史档案的管理和应用，酒店能够及时掌握顾客消费需求的变化，适时调整服务项目，不断推陈出新，确保持续不断地向市场提供有针对性、有吸引力的新产品，满足顾客求新、求奇、求特色的消费需要。

（二）有利于酒店根据用户画像精准营销

酒店可以通过客史档案对客户信息深入分析，全面了解客户的爱好和个性化需要，开发"量身定制"的产品，大大提高客人的满意度；还可以开展个性化服务和一系列"一对一"的情感沟通，使客户对酒店产生信任感，将顾客满意升华为顾客忠诚，使酒店服务的品质得到客户进一步的认同。

（三）有利于酒店根据客户实际科学决策

客史档案为酒店的经营决策和服务提供了扎实的基础材料，使得酒店的经营活动能够有较强的针对性，避免许多不必要的时间、精力、资金的浪费。由于对客户消费情况的熟悉，员工的服务准备更为轻松。良好客户关系的建立，也有助于酒店工作氛围的改善，员工的工作热情、主动精神将得到有效的发挥，酒店整体的工作效率也将极大的提高。

I　The role of establishing guest history records

Establishing guest history records can enable the hotel to more accurately understand the structure of guest sources and the characteristics of guest needs, so as to provide customers with targeted services and enhance customer satisfaction. Establishing guest history records plays an important role in improving the quality of hotel services and improving the level of hotel management. For those hotel managers and staff who try to do a good job in marketing, work hard to make their work fruitful, and do everything possible to make all their activities tailored to each guest's personality, a guest history record is an important tool.

（1）Help the hotel to grasp the demand trend and bring forth the new

Through the management and application of customer history records, the hotel can keep abreast of changes in customer consumption needs, adjust service items in a timely manner, and constantly introduce new ones to ensure that they continue to provide targeted and attractive new products to the market to satisfy the consumer needs for novelty and distinctive features.

（2）Help accurate marketing of hotels based on user preferences

The hotel can analyze customer information in depth through customer history records, fully understand customers' hobbies and personalized needs, develop "tailor-made" products, and greatly improve guest satisfaction; it can also carry out personalized services and a series of "one-to-one" emotional communication, so that customers will have a sense of trust in the hotel, sublimate customer satisfaction to customer loyalty, and the quality of hotel services will be further recognized by customers.

（3）Help the hotel to make scientific decisions based on the actual situation of customers

The guest history records provide solid basic materials for the hotel's business decision-making and services, enabling the hotel's business activities to be more targeted, avoiding unnecessary waste of time, energy, and funds. Due to the familiarity of the customer's consumption situation, the staff's service preparation is easier. The establishment of good customer relations will also help improve the hotel's working atmosphere. The staff's enthusiasm and initiative will be effectively fostered, and the overall work efficiency of the hotel will also be greatly improved.

二、客史档案的内容

（一）客史档案分类

①散客（Individual）。

散客客史档案是指客人在办理预订和入住登记时所留下的第一手资料，主要包括客人姓名、性别、出生年月日、所属单位、常住地、有效身份证件类别、号码、联系方式、到达原因、入住房价、入住时间、付款方式等要素。

②公司（Company）。

公司客史档案主要由双方协议签订时所提供的单位名称、性质、经营内容、地址、负责人姓名、联系人姓名、联系方式、主要消费需求、认定的房价、消费折扣率、付款方式等信息。

③旅行社（Travel Agent）。

旅行社客史档案包括旅行社名称、纳税识别号、地址、邮编以及联系电话，还有旅行社带团来店次数、平均人数、平均留店时间、平均消费水平、具体要求（对用餐、客房、娱乐等方面）、价格优惠等。

④预订源（Reservation Source）。

预订源客史档案包括客人的订房方式、介绍人，订房的季节、月份、日期以及订房的类型等。

⑤团队（Group）。

团队客史档案包括团队的基本情况、组织单位的基本情况和团队组织负责人的基本情况3个方面。其中，团队的基本情况包括团队名称、来店次数、累计人数、平均留店时间、人均消费水平、具体要求（对用餐、客房、娱乐等方面）、优惠价格、是否为协议单位等；组织单位的基本情况包括单位名称、地址、电话号码、单位简介、单位负责人等。

⑥联系人（Contact）。

联系人客史档案一般包括客人的姓名、部门、职位、城市、地址、联系方式等。

Ⅱ　The content of the guest history records

（1）Classification of guest history records

① Individual.

Individual guest history records refer to the first-hand information left by the guest during the booking and check-in, mainly including the guest's name, gender, date of birth, affiliation, permanent residence, type of valid ID, number, contact method, the reason for arrival, room rate, check-in time, payment method and other information.

② Company.

The company's history records mainly include the company name, type business content, address, name of the person in charge, name of the contact person, contact information, main consumer needs, recognized room rates, consumer discount rates, payment methods and other information provided at the time the agreement was signed between the two parties.

③ Travel Agent.

The travel agency history records include the name of the travel agency, tax identification number, address, zip code, and contact number, as well as the number of group visits by the travel agency, average number of guests, average staying time, average consumption level, specific requirements（for meals, rooms, entertainment, etc.）, discount price, etc.

④ Reservation Source.

The reservation source history records include the guest's reservation method, the introducer, the season, month, date of the reservation, and the type of reservation, etc.

⑤ Group.

The group guest history records include three aspects: the basic information of the group, organization's company and the person in charge of the group organization. Among them, the basic information of the group includes group name, number of visits, cumulative number of guests, average staying time, per capita consumption level, specific requirements（for meals, guest rooms, entertainment, etc.）, preferential prices, whether it is a contract company, etc.; the basic information of the organizational company includes the name, address, telephone number, brief introduction of the company, and the person in charge of the company, etc.

⑥ Contact.

The contact history records generally include the guest's name, department, position, city, address, contact information, etc.

（二）客史档案的建立

酒店想要发挥客史档案的最大作用，必须将客史档案纳入到酒店管理系统中。

①传统手工客史档案建立。

a. 收集客户的基本信息，包括客户的名称、地址、电话及个人性格、兴趣、爱好、家庭、学历、年龄、能力、经历背景等，这是建立合格的客户档案的起点。

b. 客户档案的分类整理、更新。

客户信息是不断变化的，客户档案资料也会不断地补充、增加，所以客户档案的整理必须具有管理的动态性。

c. 专人负责。

客户档案至关重要，客户是酒店的命脉，客户档案的泄密，势必影响酒店的发展。因此，客户档案的建立需要谨慎，最好找专人进行负责，以防工作的开展发生推诿、推卸等情况。

（2）The establishment of guest history records

If the hotel wants to play the biggest role of the guest history records, it must incorporate the guest history records into the hotel management system.

① The establishment of traditional handmade guest history records

a. Collect basic customer information.

Collect basic information about customers including their names, addresses, phone numbers, and their personal characteristics, interests, hobbies, family, education, age, ability, experience background, etc., are the starting point for establishing a qualified customer record.

b. Classification and update of the customer record.

Customer information is constantly changing, and customer record data will continue to be supplemented and increased. Therefore, the organization of the customer record must be dynamic in management.

c. Responsible person.

Customer records are very important. Customers are the lifeblood of a hotel. The leakage of customer records will inevitably affect the development of the hotel. Therefore, the establishment of a customer record needs to be cautious, and it is best to find someone to be responsible to prevent prevarication, shirk, etc. in the development of work.

②利用 CRM 系统建立。

CRM 系统是客户关系系统，它能够全面了解并记录客户或合作伙伴的相关资料，跟踪分析客户信息，使企业以更快捷与周到的服务来增加客户的满意度，吸引更多的客户，保留原有客户，增加企业的整体营业额。

a. 移动式建立。

客户来源于五湖四海，只有利用 CRM 系统进行移动式建立，才能确保客户的档案及时得到更新，便于相关领导做出正确的决策。

b. 客户的转接有序。

虽然每个客户都有专人负责，但是中途发生业务员更换也是不可避免的事情。所以，利用 CRM 系统建立客户档案，便于每个业务员了解客户的相关信息，不会导致客户信息跟进的中断，甚至客户流失。

② Use CRM system to establish.

The CRM system is a customer relationship system. It can comprehensively understand and record the relevant information of customers or partners, track and analyze customer information so that enterprises can increase customer satisfaction with faster and more thoughtful services, attract more customers, and retain original customers and increase the company's overall revenue.

a. Mobile establishment.

Customers come from all corners of the world. Only by using the CRM system for mobile establishment can we ensure that the customer's record is updated in time so that relevant leaders can make correct decisions.

b. Orderly transfer of customers.

Although each customer has a dedicated person in charge, the staff will inevitably be replaced in the middle of the journey. Therefore, the use of the CRM system to establish customer records is convenient for each staff to understand customer-related information, and will not lead to interruption of customer information follow-up, or even customer loss.

③利用 OPERA PMS 系统建立。

OPERA PMS 系统有专门的客史档案建立模块 ProRecord，它能通过自动生成和手工生成两种方式全面记录统计，包括个人客户、公司、联系人、旅行社、团队、预订源以及零售商等各方面的资料，这些资料是整个 OPERA PMS 工作的基础。它们可以帮助酒店改善服务质量，提供个性化服务；帮助酒店分析客源市场及利润来源并制订具有竞争力的市场营销策略。

综上所述，建立好的顾客档案，不能束之高阁。而是要积极挖掘，形成严密完整的体系，并对顾客日积月累的消费记录中进行各方面的分析，从而提供有利的决策依据，才能使之成为酒店经营决策的基石。

③ Established with OPERA PMS system.

The OPERA PMS system has a special customer history record building module ProRecord, which can comprehensively record and count including individual customers, companies, contacts, travel agencies, groups, booking sources, retailers, etc. through automatic generation and manual generation. These materials are the basis of the entire OPERA PMS operation. It can help hotels improve service quality and provide personalized services and help hotels analyze customer source markets and profit sources and formulate competitive marketing strategies.

In summary, the establishment of a good customer record cannot be put on the shelf. Instead, we must actively explore, form a rigorous and complete system, and analyze all aspects of the guests' accumulated consumption records, so as to provide a favorable decision-making basis, so that it can become the cornerstone of the hotel's business decision-making.

【具体操作示例】

①登录OPERA后，在OPERA主界面使用以下两种方法之一来调用ProRecords功能：

a. 选择 Reservations 主菜单，在弹出的子菜单中选择 ProRecords；

b. 单击 Reservations 功能区按键，在右面快捷键中单击 ProRecords。

②在 Prorecord Search（资料查询）对话框中单击右下方 New（新建）按钮。

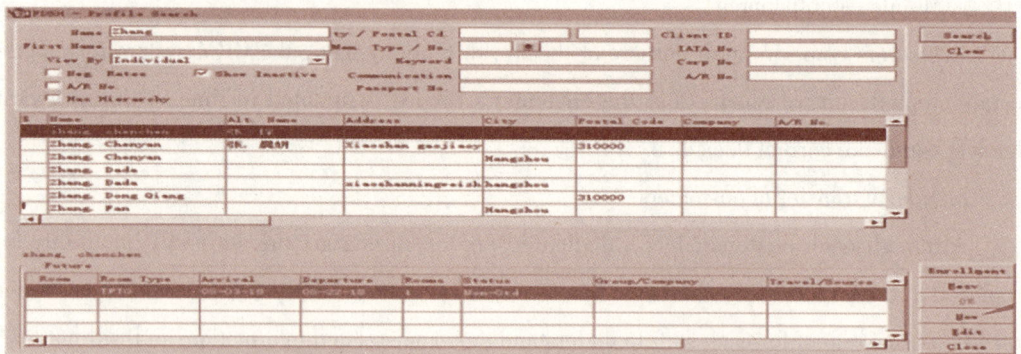

③选择新建档案的类型。

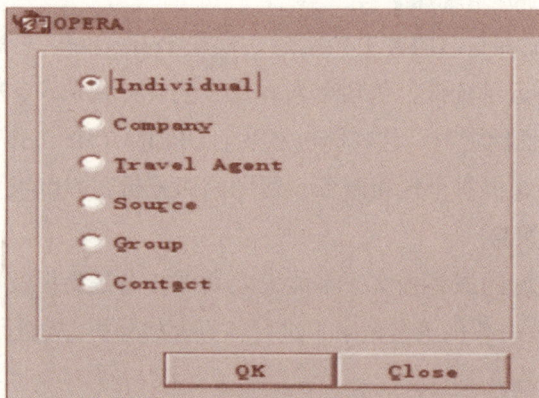

④根据客户类型进行相关信息录入。

【Specific Operation Example】

① After logging in to OPERA, use one of the following two methods on the OPERA main interface to call the Prorecords function:

a. Select the Reservations main menu, and select ProRecords in the pop-up submenu;

b. Click the Reservations function button, and click ProRecords in the shortcut keys on the right.

② In the Prorecord Search dialog box, click the New button at the bottom right.

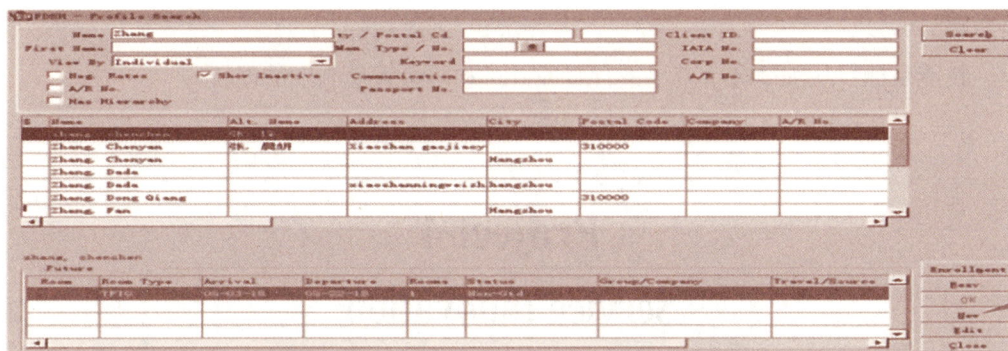

③ Select the type of new file.

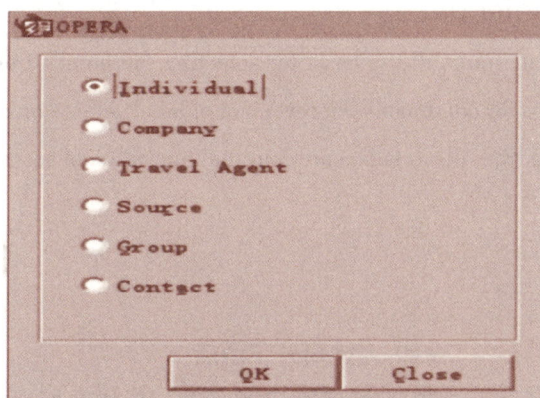

④ Input relevant information according to the customer type.

项目四

服务创新

【学习目标】

知识目标：熟悉酒店前厅服务方式的选择依据；了解酒店服务质量不断改进的四个步骤。

技能目标：从细微环节着手进行服务方式和质量管理制度的创新。

Project 4

Service Innovation

【Learning Objectives】

Knowledge goal: familiar with the basis for selecting the hotel's front office service mode; understand the four steps for continuous improvement of hotel service quality

Skills goal: starting from the details, carry out the innovation of service methods and quality management systems.

【案例导入】

她离开了酒店

A 女士多年来一直是一家中型城市酒店的常客。提供友好轻松的氛围、使客人有种"家外之家"的感觉是这家酒店推销自己时作出的承诺。A 女士很喜欢这种服务，曾经向许多朋友和同事提到这家酒店的个性化服务和轻松的氛围，正是这两点使这家酒店比该城市的豪华酒店所提供的先进产品和服务更吸引她。

A 女士并不知道的是这家酒店最近安装了新的信息系统，正在积极地宣传酒店运用信息技术来"改进已经很出色的顾客服务"的新举措。当 A 女士到达酒店后，她没有被安排入住她常住并且最喜欢的客房，因为其他客人已经入住了她常住的那间客房。不仅如此，当她走进新客房时，她发现该客房还没有打扫过。她来到前台投诉，那天初次上班的前台接待员不知道 A 女士是谁，因此也根本没有意识到她是酒店常住的重要客人。这位前台接待员只知道没有及时打扫房间是客房部的问题。这位接待员告诉 A 女士这个问题会得到解决，但是 A 女士清楚地感觉到接待员认为这是其他人的问题。接待员让 A 女士在酒店的大堂里等候。

在大堂不耐烦地等待时，A 女士看到了酒店的新宣传册，上面写着"提供友好轻松的氛围、使客人有种家外之家的感觉"，还看到了酒店试图运用新的信息技术"改进已经很出色的顾客服务"的新举措。等了一会儿，A 女士又回到前台咨询客房的情况。她看到接待员敲打着键盘，神情越来越沮丧。"这台计算机我怎么也无法使用"接待员抱怨道。A 女士没有理会她的话，她问她的客房收拾得怎么样了。"我正在想办法安排，"接待员回答说，"客房服务员说我要把相关程序输入计算机以后，他们才会去打扫客房。A 女士深深吸了口气，拿起自己的包，转身走出了酒店大门。

【Case Introduction】

She left the hotel

Ms. A has been a frequent guest at a medium-sized city hotel for many years. Providing a friendly and relaxing atmosphere and making guests feel like a "home away from home" is a promise made by this hotel when it sells itself. Ms. A likes this kind of service very much. She has mentioned to many friends and colleagues the personalized service and relaxed atmosphere of this hotel. It is these two points that make this hotel more attractive to her than the advanced products and services provided by luxury hotels in the city.

What Ms. A didn't know was that the hotel had recently installed a new information system and was actively promoting the hotel's new measures to use information technology to "improve the already outstanding customer service." When Ms. A arrived at the hotel, she was not assigned to stay in her usual and favorite room, because other guests had already stayed in the room she used to live in. Not only that, when she walked into the new guest room, she found that the guest room had not been cleaned yet. She came to the front desk to complain. The receptionist who was working for the first time that day did not know who Ms. A was, and therefore did not realize that she was an important guest in the hotel. The receptionist only knew that the failure to clean the room in time was a problem with the housekeeping department. The receptionist told Ms. A that the problem would be resolved, but Ms. A clearly felt that the receptionist thought it was someone else's problem. The receptionist asked Ms. A to wait in the lobby.

While waiting impatiently in the lobby, Ms. A saw the hotel's new brochure, which said "provide a friendly and relaxing atmosphere and make guests feel like a home away from home" and saw the hotel's new measures aimed at using new information technology to "improve the already outstanding customer service." . After waiting for a while, Ms. A went back to the front desk to inquire about the condition of her guest room. She saw the receptionist typing on the keyboard, her expression increasingly frustrated. "I can't use this computer at all," the receptionist complained. Ms. A ignored her and asked how her guest room was cleaned up. "I'm trying to make arrangements," the receptionist replied. The room attendant said that I had to enter the relevant process into the computer before they would clean the room. Ms. A took a deep breath, picked up her bag, turned around, and walked out of the hotel door.

【案例问题】

案例中的 A 女士为什么会离开酒店？

【案例分析】

变革是当今社会不可避免的现实，这是因为我们在持续不断地进行着创新，酒店企业必须利用信息技术加强酒店运营、营销、人力资源等部门的工作效率，但与此同时，更重要的是必须采用统一的技术系统来整合这些职能，以便使服务供应过程更为简单、快捷、高效并更具个性化。技术是辅助工具，高科技永远不能取代高情感。如果企业认识不到这一点，不能将技术或者其他硬件系统转化为服务，更多像 A 女士这样的客人就会流失。创新不只是突破性的巨变，也包括日常的细微变化。酒店服务质量管理的创新也包含这两类。这其中细部的创新是主体，其主角是酒店的员工，而实施大规模变革的推动者是领导层。

【Case Question】

Why did Ms. A in the case leave the hotel?

【Case Analysis】

Change is an inevitable reality in today's society. This is because we are constantly innovating. Hotel companies must use information technology to enhance the efficiency of hotel operations, marketing, human resources, and other departments, but at the same time, more importantly, a unified technical system must be adopted to integrate these functions in order to make the service provision process simpler, faster, more efficient and more personalized. Technology is an auxiliary tool, and high technology can never replace high emotions. If the company does not recognize this and cannot convert technology or other hardware systems into services, more customers like Ms. A will be lost. Innovation is not just a breakthrough change, but also daily subtle changes. The innovation of hotel service quality management also includes these two categories. Among them, detailed innovation is the main key, with hotel staff playing the main rold while leadership acts as the promoter of large-scale changes in the leadership.

任务一　酒店管家服务

　　顾客需求不断变化，酒店的服务方式也在不断创新。这些创新型服务有的来自酒店有意识的安排，有的来自员工的即兴发挥，这些都让客人感受到了酒店对他们的尊重，体会到了酒店的优质服务。

　　上海 R 大酒店以"为所有客人提供 24 小时专业的管理服务"闻名。如果你瞧见哪位服务生身穿白衬衫、红马甲、黑西装外套，毕恭毕敬地向你点头微笑："您好，有什么可以帮您？"没准他就是一位酒店管家，从客人入住的那一刻起，酒店管家会全程陪伴，打点一切。

　　酒店管家首先是一位有心人，接待每一位客人前，酒店管家都必须根据酒店资料了解客人需求，包括客人平时睡的枕头有多高，喜欢鹅绒枕头还是弹性棉的，枕套喜欢用棉布还是丝绸，衣架需要木头的还是塑料的等等。在接待客人的过程中，酒店管家随时用心关注客人，提供完美的细节服务，例如，客人在房间里的冰箱中挑选的是红酒还是可乐？如果是可乐，是百事还是健怡？有的人喝咖啡不放糖，有的只加一滴牛奶，还有人只喝某年生产的酒，并且必定加冰块。有人喜欢用依云水洗澡，有人习惯早起，有人晚上喜欢吃夜宵……这些细节，管家看在眼里，记录在手册上。酒店管家还需要保持专业的仪态和礼节。例如，与客人说话时，距离最好保持在一臂半；敲客人的房门，每次按门铃的间隔，控制在 7s 左右；走路不能东张西望，一旦眼睛余光扫到周围有客人，应立即停下脚步，给客人让路；给客人递笔时，应握住笔的前部，使客人接到的是笔的后部，让他们拿到顺手；送报纸时，将报纸斜靠在手臂上，露出每张报纸的报头，让客人一目了然。管家还必须百般技能样样精通，会熨衣服，会叠西装，能替客人打包行李箱；是个好导游，熟悉当地各种娱乐活动，餐饮地点，能迅速根据客人的喜好，推荐合适的地点，并订餐、订车、订票；如果客人需要，管家还要充当翻译和私人顾问，陪同客人出门游玩；一旦遇到商务客人，还要充当临时秘书，帮助接收和发送电子邮件，复印、打印文件。

Task 1　Hotel Butler Service

Customer needs are constantly changing, and hotel service methods are constantly innovating. Some of these innovative services are carefully planned by the hotel while others come from the improvisation of the staff. All these make the guests feel the hotel's respect for them and experience the hotel's high-quality services.

Shanghai R Hotel is famous for "providing 24-hour professional management services for all guests." If you see a staff member wearing a white shirt, a red vest, and a black suit jacket, he respectfully nods and smiles at you: "Hello, what can I do for you?" Maybe he is a hotel butler. From the moment the guest checks in, the hotel butler will accompany him and take care of everything.

A hotel butler is a caring person. Before receiving each guest, the hotel butler must understand the guests according to the hotel information, including how high the pillows the guests usually sleep, like goose down pillows or elastic cotton, and pillowcases like cotton or silk. Whether the hanger needs to be made of wood or plastic. In the process of receiving guests, the hotel butler always pays attention to the guests and provides perfect detailed services. For example, does the guest prefer wine or coke in the refrigerator in the room? If it is cola, is it Pepsi or Diet? Some people drink coffee without sugar, some only add a drop of milk, and some people only drink wine produced in a certain year, and must add ice cubes. Some people like to take a bath with Evian water, some people are used to getting up early, and some people like to eat late-night slack... These details are in the eyes of the housekeeper and recorded in the manual. Hotel butlers also need to maintain professional manners and courtesy. For example, when talking to a guest, it's best to keep one arm and a half away. When knocking on the guest's door, control the interval between pressing the doorbell at about 7 seconds. Hotel butlers can't look around when you walk. As soon as there are guests around you, you should stop and make way for the guests. When handing the pen to the guests, you should hold the writing end the pen so that the guests receive the no-writing end so that they can get it easily; When delivering newspapers, rest them on your arm, with the headlines facing outward, so that the guests can see at a glance. The butler must also be proficient in all kinds of skills. He can iron clothes, fold suits, and pack suitcases for guests; he is a good tour guide, familiar with various local entertainment activities and dining venues, and can quickly recommend suitable places according to guests' preferences, and book meals, cars, and tickets; If the guest needs, if the butler also acts as a translator and a personal consultant, accompany the guest to go out and play; when meeting business guests, you have to act as a temporary secretary to help receive and send E-mails, copy and print documents.

任务二　首问责任制

首问责任制是指凡是酒店在岗工作的员工，第一个接受客人咨询或要求的人，就是解决这位客人咨询问题和提出要求的责任人。作为一种新的服务理念，首问责任制把管理与创新结合后体现在每一位员工的服务环节中，而管理的技术又使员工素质、服务水平更加优化。酒店是一个出售服务的行业，酒店本身是向客人提供服务的载体，酒店的属性决定了员工必须要为客人提供优质服务，而优质服务单凭热情是远远不够的，需要一种形式来规范服务。首问责任制赋予了优质服务新的内容，进而使酒店对于客人的热情寓于规范服务之中。在这个前提下，把优质服务作为一种特殊商品提供给客人，而酒店则不断创造出更多的商业机会。

按照首问责任制的要求，酒店的岗位员工应该做到以下几点。一是属于本人职责范围内的问题，要立即给客人的询问以满意答复，使客人的要求以妥善解决。二是虽说是员工本人职责范围内的问题，但因客人方面的原因，目前不能马上解决的，一定要耐心细致地向客人解释清楚，只要客人方面的原因不存在了，就应该马上为客人解决问题。三是属于员工本人职责范围之外的问题和要求，首问责任者不得推诿，要积极帮助客人问清楚或帮助客人联系有关部门给予解决，直到客人的问题得到满意答复，要求得到妥善的解决。除此之外，首问责任制还要求员工做好超前服务以及客人离店的延伸服务等。

Task 2　First-inquiry Responsibility System

The first-inquiry responsibility system refers to the first staff member who accept the guest's consultation or request is responsible for solving the guest's consultation problems and making requests for all the employees working in the hotel. As a new service concept, the first-inquiry responsibility system integrates management and innovation into each employee's service process, and the management technology optimizes the quality and service level of employees. The hotel is a kind of industry that sells services. The hotel itself is the provider of guests services. The attributes of the hotel determine that employees must provide quality services to guests, and quality service is not enough just by enthusiasm. It requires a form to regulate services. The first-inquiry responsibility system has given new content to high-quality services, which in turn enables the hotel's enthusiasm for guests by integrating standardized services.

Under this premise, high-quality services are provided to guests as a special commodity, so hotels continue to create more business opportunities.

In accordance with the requirements of the first-question responsibility system, the hotel staff should do the following. First, if is the problem falls within the scope of the staff's responsibility, They must immediately give a satisfactory answer to the guest's inquiries, and give the guest's request a proper solution. The second is that if the problem falls within the scope of the employee's own responsibility, which cannot be resolved immediately due to the guest's reasons. The employee must patiently and meticulously explain to the guest. As long as the guest's cause does not exist, it should be resolved immediately. Third, if the problem and requirements falls outside the scope of the employee's responsibility, the person responsible for the first inquiry shall not shirk, and actively help the guest to ask clearly or help the guest contact the relevant department to solve it until the guest's question is answered satisfactorily and a proper solution is provided. In addition, the first-inquiry responsibility system also requires employers to provide advanced services and follow-up services for guests leaving the hotel.

任务三　客人赏识服务计划

内蒙古 G 酒店为推动酒店服务创新，真正了解客人所需，满足客人多元化需求，推出客人赏识服务计划。客人赏识是对客人的认知过程，就是站在客人角度，通过关注、揣摩客人的喜好来发现对客认知过程，也就是通过每一位员工的用心服务，挖掘客人的内心需求信息，使客人体会到充满人性化、个性化、人情味的服务，给客人物超所值的感受。

Task 3　Guest Recognition Service Plan

In order to promote hotel service innovation, truly understand the needs of guests, and meet the diverse needs of guests, G Hotel in Inner Mongolia has launched a guest recognition service plan. Guest Recognition is the process of cognition of guests. From the perspective of guests, discover the process of cognition of guests by paying attention to the guests and trying to figure out their preferences. That is, through the heartfelt service of each employee, digging out the inner needs of the guests. Ensure that the guests experience a highly personized and human-centered service and give the guests a feeling of value-for-money.

【案例导入】

意外的惊喜

在广州一家外企工作的许小姐，最近由于公司在北京有一业务洽谈，她被派遣到当地工作一个星期。许小姐下飞机后就被安排住进了当地有名的君悦来酒店。这家酒店向来以周到的服务备受好评。入住的这几天里，许小姐也感到非常满意。经过边疆繁忙的会客工作后，许小姐已忙得透不过气来。她把心思全放在了工作的事情上，以至于忘记明天就是自己 25 岁的生日。这天晚上，许小姐在外忙碌了一整天后，拖着疲惫的身体回到酒店。还没来得及用晚餐的她，回到房间后立即打电话到客房部点餐。谁知，早在许小姐入住当天，细心的前台小姐已在入住登记表中发现了她的生日日期，并立刻联系好客房部与餐饮部的同事，分工合作，共同安排为许小姐庆祝生日的有关事情，准备要给许小姐一个意外的惊喜。在接到许小姐的电话点餐后，服务人员马上把早已准备好的礼物和贺卡摆放在布置精美的餐车上，并随同许小姐所要的食物一并送往客房。

没过多久，送餐的服务员前来敲门。许小姐打开门，眼前的情景令她惊喜万分。只见服务员推着一辆铺有美丽淡紫色花布的餐车进门。车上摆放着一束娇艳欲滴的鲜花，还有一个精美的生日蛋糕，蛋糕上的卡通人物非常可爱。生日蜡烛正在燃烧，整个房间都充满了温馨的气氛。这一切都来得十分突然，还没有等许小姐回过神来，服务员已把手中的贺卡递给了她，并微笑着致意："祝您生日快乐！"这时，许小姐才恍然醒悟到今天是自己 25 岁的生日。她激动地对服务员说："真的很感谢你们为我所准备的这一切，我实在太高兴啦！因为工作太忙，我连自己的生日都给忘记了，但是你们却为我安排得这样细心和周到！谢谢！"服务员回答道："知道你喜欢我们为你所做的安排，那实在是太好啦！"许小姐对酒店员工感叹不已的同时，疑惑地向服务员问道："对了，你们怎么会知道今天是我的生日呢？"于是那位服务员向她一一道来……一个星期的繁忙工作终于结束。今天许小姐要返回广州了。在离开酒店的时候，她对前台小姐说："再次感谢酒店给了我一个难忘的生日。以后有机会，我一定会再来的。"前台小姐微笑着回答道："欢迎您再次光临！"

【Case Introduction】

Unexpected surprise

Miss Xu, who works in a foreign company in Guangzhou, has recently been dispatched to work in Beijing for a week because the company has a business negotiation there. After Miss Xu got off the plane, she was arranged to check into the famous local Grand Hyatt Hotel. This hotel has always been praised for its considerate service. During the few days of staying, Miss

Xu was also very satisfied. After the busy intensive meetings, Miss Xu was already too busy to breathe. She was so focused on work, even forgetting that tomorrow would be her 25th birthday. That evening, after a busy day outside, Miss Xu returned to the hotel with her tired body. She had not eaten dinner yet; she immediately called the housekeeping department to order food after she returned to the room. Unexpectedly, as early as the day of Miss Xu's check-in, the attentive receptionist had found her birthday date in the check-in form, and immediately contacted colleagues in the housekeeping department and the catering department, and worked together to arrange a birthday celebration for Miss Xu. They prepared to give Miss Xu a surprise. After receiving Miss Xu's call to order the food, the staff immediately placed the prepared gifts and greeting cards on the beautifully decorated dining trolley and delivered them to the guest room along with the food requested by Miss Xu.

Before long, the staff who delivered the food came and knocked on the door. Miss Xu opened the door, and was surprised by what she saw. She saw the staff pushing a trolley covered with beautiful purple floral cloth into the door. There was a bunch of beautiful flowers and a exquisite birthday cake on the trolley. The cartoon characters on the cake were very cute. Birthday candles were burning, and the whole room was filled with a warm atmosphere. All this happened very suddenly. Before Miss Xu came back to her senses, the staff handed her the greeting card in her hand and greeted her with a smile: "Happy birthday to you!" At this time, Miss Xu suddenly realized that today is her 25th birthday. She excitedly said to the staff: "I really appreciate everything you have prepared for me. I am so happy! I was too busy with work, and I even forgot my birthday, but you arranged for me so carefully and thoughtfully! Thanks!" The staff replied: "It's great to know that you like the arrangements we made for you!" Surprised, Miss Xu asked the staff in confusion: "By the way, how did you know that today is my birthday?" So, the staff slowly explained what happened to her. The busy week is finally over. Today, Miss Xu is going back to Guangzhou. When leaving the hotel, she said to the lady at the front desk: "Thank you again for giving me an unforgettable birthday. I will definitely come again if I have a chance in the future." The lady at the front desk smiled and replied, "You're always welcome back!"

【案例分析】

期望—实际心理是解决这个案例的关键，人们在消费之前对产品和服务有一定的想法和要求，这就是人们的期望值；人们在实际的消费过程得到的真实产品和服务是顾客所感受到的实际值。顾客对期望和实际进行比较后得出了是否满意的结论，即如果期望值大于实际值，顾客就不满意；如果期望值小于或等于实际值，顾客就满意；如果顾客感受到的实际大大超过期望值，顾客就会满意加惊喜。

　　酒店如果提供给顾客意外的服务，会使顾客得到意外的惊喜。这样，顾客得到的实际服务超过他的期望服务，其满意程度就会大大提高。案例中的许小姐得到的实际服务超过了她的期望值，许小姐感受到了这个酒店的服务质量很令她满意。酒店提供给许小姐绝对意外的服务，许小姐得到的实际服务超过她的期望服务，因此许小姐对酒店非常满意。

【Case Analysis】

Expectation-performance psychology is the key to solving this case. People have certain ideas and requirements for products and services before consumption. This is what people expect; the real products and services that people get in the actual consumption process are the actual performance values that customers feel. The customer compares the expectation with the actual performance and draws a conclusion obout his/her satisfaction, that is: if the expected value is greater than the actual performance value, the customer is not satisfied; if the expected value is less than or equal to the actual performance value, the customer is satisfied; if the customer feels the actual performance greatly exceeds the expected value, customers will be satisfied and surprised.

If hotels provide customers with unexpected services, they will be surprised. In this way, the customer's actual service exceeds his expectation, and his degree of satisfaction will be greatly improved. The actual service that Miss Xu received exceeded her expectations. Miss Xu felt that the service quality of this hotel was very satisfactory to her. The hotel provided unexpected service to Miss Xu. The actual service that Miss Xu received exceeded her expectations. Therefore, Miss Xu was very satisfied with the hotel.

任务四　"睡眠管家"服务

　　B 酒店位于纽约商业区曼哈顿，是一家历史悠久的商务旅游酒店，酒店认为服务的卖点不是提供什么高科技产品，而是一晚舒适的睡眠享受。为了保证客人在这座"不夜城"里有充足的睡眠，酒店专门增设了"睡眠管理"这一职位，保证客人在酒店里有优质的睡眠体验。酒店还承诺，如果你在酒店晚上无法入睡，酒店将提供免费的入住服务。酒店为客人准备了 11 种不同类型的枕头，包括填有绒毛的、荞麦粒的、绸缎质地的、防过敏的、充水的、磁疗作用的、柔软的颈枕，防打鼾的，还有瑞典产的"释压记忆"枕头，5 英尺大小，根据人体结构设计的枕头等。除了枕头，酒店特有的床垫是由科技含量高的钢丝弹簧泡沫和高级丝线缝制而成，床上覆盖着床单和羽绒被褥。充满薰衣草芳香的浴宇帮助客人松弛神经，更快地进入梦乡。而酒店的窗户是双层玻璃加上密封窗框，在喧嚣的都市中保证室内的安静。酒店的 SPA 和按摩中心为客人提供舒松筋骨的服务。酒店还提供睡前食用的牛奶和著名曲奇饼干。酒店"睡眠管家"服务的宗旨是"尽力为客人提供优质的睡眠环境，让他们精神饱满地迎接第二天的忙碌工作。"

Task 4　"Sleep Concierge" Service

Hotel B is located in Manhattan, New York's business district. It is a long-established business and tourist hotel. The hotel believes that the selling point of services is not to provide high-tech products, but to enjoy a comfortable night's sleep. To ensure that guests have enough sleep in this "city that never sleeps", the hotel has specially added the position of "Sleep Concierge" to ensure that guests have high-quality sleep in the Hotel. The hotel also promised that if you can't sleep in the hotel at night, the hotel will not charge you for the night. The hotel provides guests with 11 different types of pillows, which are filled with fluff, buckwheat grains, satin texture, hypoallergenic, water-filled, magnetic therapy, soft neck pillows, anti-snoring pillows, and there are "pressure-relieving memory" pillows made in Sweden, five-foot-sized pillows designed according to human body structure, etc. In addition to pillows, the unique mattress of the hotel is made of high-tech steel wire spring foam and high-quality silk threads. The bed is covered with sheets and duvets. The bathroom full of lavender fragrance helps guests relax their nerves and fall asleep faster. The windows of the hotel are double-glazed and sealed with frames to ensure a quiet and peaceful interior in the hustle and bustle of the city. The hotel's SPA and massage center provide guests with relaxing services. The restaurant also provides milk and famous cookies for bedtime. The purpose of the hotel's "Sleep Concierge" service is to try our best to provide guests with a high-quality sleeping environment so they will be full of energy to meet the busy work of the next day.

任务五　创新型服务质量管理制度

肯德基的"神秘顾客"

"神秘顾客"是世界著名的快餐公司"肯德基"首创，成为高效的监督检查系统的一个环节。山姆先生们每月一次或两次不定期地到餐厅用餐，以一般顾客的身份不动声色地进行检查，因此被称为神秘顾客。肯德基来到中国后，也将神秘顾客带到了中国。总公司聘请了国外一家著名的调查公司，由他们派人担任神秘顾客，各分公司经理也不识他们的真面目。神秘顾客的检查在到达餐厅门口时就已经开始，从店面的招贴画到灯光的亮度，从食品的品质、品位到服务是否快捷周到，他们按对各地连锁店的统一要求打分，内容涉及如"收银员是否用目光注视，面带微笑，并向你问候"等各种细节。为保证神秘与适时，神秘顾客评分时须远离餐厅，但离店时间又不能超过 5 min。神秘顾客都不是专业人员，他们完全从普通顾客的角度给餐厅全方位评分。答卷 24 h 内便来到总公司的办公桌上，然后反馈给被评分的公司，由他们根据评分情况调整内部管理。神秘顾客成为肯德基公司内部管理的一种工具，给员工带来压力，员工必须将每位顾客当作神秘顾客服务。

神秘顾客的做法已被我国旅游界所接受，旅游管理部门在星级评定和复核时的暗访，就是采用了神秘顾客的方式。许多酒店在服务质量管理上，也借助了暗访的形式，但大部分酒店并没有像肯德基那样将神秘顾客的管理制度嵌入酒店的经营性管理中。

Task 5　Innovative Service Quality Management System

KFC's "mystery customer"

"Mystery Customer" was created by the world-famous fast-food company "KFC" and became a link in an efficient supervision and inspection system. Mr. Sam visits the restaurant irregularly once or twice a month, and checks quietly, posing as an ordinary customers, so they are called mystery customers. After KFC came to China, it also brought the mystery customer to China. The head office hired a well-known foreign investigation company, and they hired people to act as mystery customers. The managers of the branches did not know them. The inspection of mystery customers begins when they arrive at the entrance of the restaurant. From the posters on the storefront to the brightness of the lights, from the quality and taste of the food to whether the service is quick and thoughtful, they score according to the unified requirements of chain stores across the country, and the content includes "Whether the cashier is watching you with his eyes, smiling, and greets you" and various details. To ensure that the mystery is timely, the "mystery customer" must stay away from the restaurant when scoring, but the time to leave the shop cannot exceed 5minutes. Mystery customers are not professionals. They rate restaurants from the perspective of ordinary customers. The scoring paper came to the desk of the head office within 24 hours and then fed back to the rated company, who adjusted the internal management according to the score. Mystery customer has become a tool of KFC's internal management, which brings pressure to employees, and employees must treat each customer as a mystery customer.

The mystery customer approach has been accepted by the tourism industry in China. The unannounced visits made by the tourism management department during star rating and review use the mystery customer approach. Many restaurants also use unannounced visits in service quality management, but most restaurants do not embed the mystery customer management system into the hotel's operational management as KFC does.